W9-BBK-711

The Ethical Archivist

Elena S. Danielson

SOCIETY OF
American
Archivists

Chicago

Society of American Archivists
www.archivists.org

© 2010 by the Society of American Archivists.
All rights reserved.

Printed in the United States of America.

Graphic design by Sweeney Design, kasween@sbcglobal.net

Library of Congress Cataloging-in-Publication Data
Danielson, Elena S., 1947-
  The ethical archivist / Elena S. Danielson.
    p. cm.
  Includes bibliographical references and index.
  ISBN 978-1-931666-34-2 (alk. paper)
  1. Archivists—Professional ethics. 2. Archives—Moral and ethical aspects. 3. Archivists—United States. 4. Archives—United States. I. Title.
  CD971.D35 2010
  020.92—dc22
                    2010026680

About the cover: The role of archives as institutions of trust is sometimes expressed in beautiful architecture to house venerable library and archives reading rooms. The current challenge is to adapt the time-honored principles of the past into the current era of unpredictable and dizzying change. Ethical principles, while constantly undergoing rethinking and refinement, remain the pillars of a trusted institution. Photograph: Elena S. Danielson. Courtesy of the Morrison Library, University of California, Berkeley.

Table of Contents

Acknowledgments

I AM INDEBTED TO A LONG LIST OF PATIENT COLLEAGUES, WHO HAVE HELPED ME AS I GRAPPLED WITH ARCHIVAL ISSUES AND WHO FILLED IN SOME OF THE GAPS IN MY KNOWLEDGE. A few of these colleagues are listed here: Bradley Bauer, Menzi L. Behrnd-Klodt, Karen Benedict, Linda Bernard, Frank Boles, Teresa Brinati, Karen Butter, Robin L. Chandler, Laura Cosovanu, Richard Cox, Jeffrey J. Crow, David De Lorenzo, Stanton A. Glantz, Mark A. Greene, Patricia Kennedy Grimsted, Kirk Hanson, John E. Haynes, Astrid Hedin, Sara S. Hodson, Polina Ilieva, Tim Ingrim, Laura Uglean Jackson, Petrina Jackson, Randall C. Jimerson, Tara Z. Laver, David McMillen, Lisa A. Mix, Roberta J. Morris, Charles G. Palm, Trudy Huskamp Peterson, Timothy Pyatt, Christopher M. Runkel, Debra Satz, Molly Schwartzburg, Anatol Shmelev, Howard N. Spiegler, Frederick Stratton, Irina Tarsis, Adrian Turner, Anne Van Camp, David Wallace, Tywanna Whorley, Peter Wosh, and Joel Wurl. The staff and publications board of the Society of American Archivists have provided expert advice and professional support. For moral support, I rely heavily on the good company and outstanding communication skills of Gudrun Jones, Marikka Rypa, Ann Watters, and Susan Wyle. In addition, I owe a great deal to the efficiency of the Stanford University Libraries staff. I have incurred an infinite debt to the people I met in the Hoover Institution Archives. There is simply no way to repay this intellectual mortgage except to acknowledge it with sincere gratitude.

In an effort to gain a broader outlook on archival ethics, I have used examples from different cultures and different eras. I am certain that I have not mastered all the details of these examples. The goal is to open up a wider perspective than we normally encounter at our separate desks. If readers find errors of fact or take issue with my conclusions, I would welcome those corrections and amplifications. My own opinions have changed considerably during the course of writing on ethics and will no doubt continue to evolve. While I regret any errors of fact or misinterpretations, if the text stimulates some active thinking on these subjects, I will have accomplished my main goal.

My first lesson in ethics came during the holiday celebrations of my childhood: from my mother, Hilda P. Schafer, who was unable to lie to her children about Santa Claus, and from my father, Louis C. Schafer, a state worker who cheerfully returned expensive presents from industry representatives. Since *his* early childhood, Erik L. Danielson has intuitively supported my career. Most of all, I am grateful to Ron Danielson, who first encouraged me to pursue a demanding career in archives administration, and then enabled me to devote the past four years to private study. He created an ideal workspace at the Santa Clara University Learning Commons, where I do much of my research.

Elena S. Danielson
San Jose, Calif.
July 2010

Professional Ethics for Archivists

The archive is a site of ambiguity.
It is best understood as a contested terrain
for memory construction that in turn
shapes contemporary understanding of society.

—Report, Nelson Mandela Foundation, 2005[1]

LIKE ARCHIVES THEMSELVES, ARCHIVAL ETHICS ARE UNIQUE—UNIQUELY PERPLEXING IN MANY WAYS AND UNIQUELY REWARDING IN OTHER WAYS. Archivists, manuscript curators, and record managers in general contend with ethical dilemmas that are distinct from those of otherwise closely allied professions such as library science or history. Knowingly or unknowingly, archivists encounter ethical issues that are not amenable to easy answers, and they do so on a regular basis. This volume will raise more questions than answers. The theory is that formulating the right questions is more important than a hasty effort at pat solutions. Most chapters conclude with some twenty questions, but there could easily be more. In addition, the text will encourage readers to explore many diverse examples from actual practice, just as business students examine case studies and computer scientists try out simulations. This combination of the Socratic method and case study method is designed to help archivists draw up their own customized policies for decision making in their own specific repositories. This book does not provide legal advice. It does not provide ethics advice on specific examples. Instead, it is intended to present background and perspective.

The ambiguities and contested terrain under discussion may cause some unease. After all, archivists are good at learning rules and applying them consistently. The task here is to learn the range of options, outcomes, and strategies within a flexible framework. The unique problems are ameliorated by the fact that archivists also have unique opportunities to contribute to a more truthful collective memory, a better informed electorate, and a higher awareness of social responsibility. Ethics, then, are not peripheral; rather they are central to archival practice both on a daily basis and in the larger context of social accountability.

Ethics is an intimidating word. There are more definitions of what it is not than what it is. It is not the same as legal or religious precepts, since some laws and religion-based dictates may be deemed unjust, harmful, and thus unethical. The field of ethics covers a major branch of moral philosophy with contributions from some of history's greatest thinkers on the ideal standards for good conduct. This volume is concerned with professional ethics, a specialized occupational context for such standards of good conduct. Because professional ethics may appear to be self-serving for a particular group, some ethicists prefer terms like *practical ethics* or *applied ethics*. Since archivists form a distinct vocation, the term *professional ethics* will be used here, but with the understanding that it is meant to address two levels of concern: How does an archivist make proper choices in accordance with the highest standards of the profession and simultaneously in accordance with certain moral obligations to society? While no one should be discouraged from exploring the thoughts of great philosophers such as Aristotle, Confucius, and Immanuel Kant,[2] the field of applied or professional ethics for archivists exists on a pragmatic level and is fascinating in its own right.

The distinction between ethics as moral philosophy and ethics as an applied practice within an occupational group can be seen in classic dictionary definitions.

Ethic or Ethics

1 plural but sing or plural in constr : the discipline dealing with what is good and bad and with moral duty and obligation

2 a: a set of moral principles: a theory or system of moral values <the present-day materialistic ethic> <an old-fashioned work ethic> —often used in plural but singular or plural in construction <an elaborate ethics> <Christian ethics> b: plural but sing or plural in constr: the principles of conduct governing an individual or a group <professional ethics> c : a guiding philosophy d: a consciousness of moral importance <forge a conservation ethic> 3 plural: a set of moral issues or aspects (as rightness) <debated the ethics of human cloning>[3]

[By permission. From *Merriam-Webster's Collegiate Dictionary* , 11th edition, ©2010 by Merriam-Webster.]

Professional Ethics

Professional ethics is concerned with the values appropriate to certain kinds of occupational activity, such as medicine and law, which have been defined traditionally in terms of a body of knowledge and an ideal of service to the community; and in which individual professionals have a high degree of autonomy in their practice. The class of occupations aiming to achieve recognition as professions has increased to include, for example, nursing, while at the same time social and political developments have led to criticism of and challenge to the concepts of professions and professionalism. Problems in professional ethics include both regulation of the professional-client relationship and the role and status of professions in society. A central question for ethics is whether there are values or virtues specific to particular professions or whether the standards of ordinary morality are applicable.[4]

[By permission. From *Routledge Encyclopedia of Philosophy* .]

Professional ethics evolve out of a shared work experience. Certainly archival ethics have moral foundations. The intellectual task is to incorporate abstract values of fairness, honesty, and integrity into the very tangible craft of the archival vocation. The principles are not cut in stone like the Ten Commandments, or legislated by a parliament like legal codes, or motivated by personally felt religious precepts like a moral code. Instead, archival ethics develop out of the cumulative efforts of many working professionals to solve certain dilemmas that occur on the job from 9 AM to 5 PM. When these experiences are assimilated and shared, the ethical context of the profession improves. The result can be a sense of trust in the integrity of archival institutions.

What should one do, for example, when donors want to control access to their papers? It happens frequently. It was once common for donors to continue to assert the prerogatives of private ownership after transferring their papers to a repository. They sometimes, for example, barred particular ethnic groups from using "their" papers. Periodically, a shared consensus emerges from actual practice. In this case, American archivists now generally agree that even donors cannot impose discriminatory access policies on archives. That kind of consensus is discussed, publicized, and implemented in the work place. It is enshrined in codes of ethics. Over time, the rights of readers have gained ground over arbitrary requests from even the most valued donors. Once the principle of equal access became more universal, basically in the late twentieth century, implementing it became much easier for each practicing archivist.

Other common dilemmas have not yet been reconciled. What happens if a business orders its archivist to destroy company records that may document possible health hazards? Codes of ethics emphasize the archivist's moral obligation to society to ensure the preservation of potentially valuable records. Other provisions emphasize that proprietary information can only be used in ways approved by the company that created it. It is very easy to get caught between obligations to an employer and obligations to society. This is a common experience. As yet, there is no generally accepted formula for managing these cases. Perhaps with more research and with greater autonomy, professionals will find the proper balance between the rights of the employing institution and the rights of society in general.

These two examples are representative of a large number of areas where conflicting rights must be brought into some kind of balance. There is a great need for more work across the entire spectrum of archival ethics.

Codes of Ethics and Professional Autonomy

Writing a code of ethics is a good place to start. Formulating principles of ethical practice certainly benefits both individual archivists and the profession as a whole. It can smooth over some of the rough edges of the work at hand and, over time, can create a public image of integrity and trustworthiness. At other times, "doing the right thing" causes friction with entrenched interests. In those situations, reinforcement from the pooled experience of colleagues is welcome. In the really tough cases, it is reassuring to know that one is not isolated and that the experts are also perplexed. Professional ethics work best as a shared consensus. Trying to follow ethical standards in isolation is rather like being the only honest player at a poker game.

Many occupations have gone through the process of codifying ethical standards. The procedure is seen as an essential step in forming a group identity with boundaries beyond a given employer. The goal is to achieve professional autonomy, sometimes called *ethical autonomy*. This professional identity transcends the demands of a specific office or job. The ethical archivist does not mechanically and mindlessly follow the orders that come from a supervisor. Instead, the process is more of a negotiation. The requirements of the employing institution are harmonized with the principles of the occupation and with its code of ethics. The field of engineering has gone through this evolution. Engineers may need to build a bridge, for example, according to the employer's specifications, but the bridge should not collapse. There are times when engineers need to go back to the boss and explain technical requirements and cost factors in order to construct a bridge that holds up. It is self-evident that both the employer and society benefit from a safe bridge.

Heinz C. Luegenbiehl, an ethicist in the engineering field, explains the function of a code thus: "The adoption of a code is significant for the professionalization of an occupational group, because it is one of the external hallmarks testifying to the claim that the group recognizes an obligation to society that transcends mere economic self-interest." [5] Even without the dangers of collapsing construction, the principle applies to other fields, including archives. There are many similarities. Sometimes a thoughtful archivist examines the official working orders and decides it is necessary to brief the boss on technical requirements and cost factors in order to construct a program that holds up. Over time, both the employer and society will benefit.

Most professions have a working set of principles, either codified or uncodified, that guides members. Usually the guidelines are things one should *not* do: Historians, for example, are admonished against plagiarizing and taking credit for the creative work of others. Ethical librarians do not censor books, or privilege certain patrons over others. They do not violate copyright laws. They do not reveal the books one patron checks out to other patrons. These Mosaic-style principles work well. When there are challenges, such as government officials demanding to see circulation records, or special interests calling for the removal of books from open shelves, a public debate often clarifies the professional norms and expectations.

Despite the many similarities with other professions, archivists and records managers have their own specific circumstances. Of course, many American archivists have the same library school training as librarians. Both professions advocate promoting the maximum use of materials. The similarities are somewhat misleading. Librarians facilitate use of materials that the authors intended to have circulated as widely as possible. Books, whether in paper form or online, are created and published with the unambiguous expectation that they can be freely sold and openly read by the general public. Archivists also facilitate use of materials, but the authors may not have expected their texts to be read by others at all. Archives are inherently different from books in that the ethical space they occupy is fundamentally ambiguous. Archivists promote the use of papers that contain unfiltered information that may be private, libelous, proprietary, or erroneous. Archives are typically the unselfconscious byproduct of clerical work in government offices and read by a small, bureaucratically controlled circle of employees. When the term is used for personal papers, archives are, again, unique, or created in restricted copies, for a limited number of readers, often a trusted group of intimates. Opening these materials to a wide readership creates dilemmas that can be finessed or balanced, but they often cannot be solved definitively. This inherently contradictory nature of archival work is one reason why archival ethics are unique. The basic argument is that the archival profession is faced with ethical dilemmas that are intrinsic to the nature of the work.

As documents are selected and transferred to a repository for the secondary purpose of research, several ethical problems automatically adhere to archiving records and manuscripts: what to acquire, what to discard, how to provide equitable access, how to secure proprietary information, how to protect privacy, how to preserve authenticity, and how to manage displaced archives. On closer examination, it will be apparent that social accountability and social justice are important factors to consider in each of these areas.

Combining Deductive and Inductive Methods in Evaluating Ethical Issues

There are two basic approaches to analyzing these questions. One gateway to archival ethics is deductive in nature, starting from general principles and deducing implications for specific problems. One can take principles from codes of ethics and apply them. Chapter 1 will look at the history of codes of ethics and the different formulations. The Center for the Study of Ethics in the Professions at the Illinois Institute of Technology maintains a website with the text of more than 850 codes of ethics. [6] It includes the code promulgated by the Society of American Archivists, and also various codes formulated by the American Library Association and different history organizations. The deductive approach is similar to the *deontological method*, in that certain principles are recognized as moral obligations regardless of the outcome in real-world situations. On closer examination these codes give conflicting signals and are in some ways inherently self-contradictory. How do you provide open access and still protect third-party privacy rights? How do you preserve the documentary record and still protect an institution's right to dispose of its own property? However beneficial, codes alone do not provide enough guidance to ask the right questions, much less formulate a strategy for accommodating conflicting rights. No one code of ethics on a page "suitable for framing" can encompass the challenges. The process of formulating a code has great value, and such discussions are probably more interesting than the final resulting text of provisions.

Another gateway to understanding archival ethics is more inductive. The abstract codes need to be supplemented with the lessons learned from a broad spectrum of real-world experiences. As in the scientific method, basic facts are assembled first so that patterns emerge inductively. First the problematic areas need to be categorized and compiled in a typology of ethical issues. This volume will examine several such areas. (There are certainly many more than appear here.) Next it is necessary to analyze actual or hypothetical case studies in each area. In natural science the cases are used to extract data. In this study, the cases and examples reveal patterns and pose questions. Reviewing a wealth of examples simulates a long career without the hazards of trial and error. The various components of the archivist's work are separately addressed in seven individual chapters on acquisitions, disposal and deaccessioning, access, proprietary information, privacy, authenticity, and displaced archives. The questions emerge out of real-world situations. Some of the high profile cases are colorful and dramatic, but even the most seemingly mundane collections contain the same fundamental and intriguing issues. Sometimes ethicists link inductive reasoning with the *teleological method*, which focuses on specific examples and analyzes how to achieve the best results. The inductive method, relying heavily on data from many examples, is closer to the scientific method and yields interesting insights that suggest coping strategies when answers are elusive.

A Typology of Ethical Issues

The first issue is selection itself. The volume of paper and online data being produced is vast. Not everything can be saved even if universal preservation were desirable, which it probably is not. When a one-of-a-kind document is discarded as out-of-date, the loss is permanent. The availability of the information in archived documentation depends on the intelligence and foresight used to write retention policies and acquisition strategies. Archivists select something like 1–5 percent of all documents to preserve for their future value to unknown researchers for research topics that have not yet been formulated. Collecting the papers of the power structure is usually well rewarded and follows the path of least resistance. A special effort is required to document marginal and powerless groups, whose contributions are often overlooked. In both situations, donor relations pose challenges. Archivists often reappraise archived materials for deaccessioning, a matter of some controversy. Ethical codes can require certain levels of due diligence. Bar associations mandate clear expectations of performance levels for legal work, and serious lapses trigger penalties for attorneys. How can one mandate creative foresight for archivists to anticipate research trends and topics that will be important to future generations? In chapters 2 and 3, the ethics of acquisitions, disposal, and deaccessioning, which pose endless questions to the profession, are addressed.

Another major problem area, mentioned above, is opening unique and private writings to public scrutiny. Working files contain information intended for specific purposes. Selecting and transferring these files to a repository opens up the number of readers beyond those originally intended, and is thus by definition a violation of privacy. Social security numbers, necessary for filing entitlement claims, may be exposed to readers who might engage in identity theft. It is disingenuous to write ethical guidelines saying that archivists should protect the privacy rights of data subjects. Violation of privacy is part of the process. The real question is how it can be meliorated.[7] Chapters 4, 5, and 6 address access, proprietary information, and privacy.

A large topic fraught with questions is called *authentication* or *diplomatics*. By selecting, transferring, cataloging, and preserving archives, archivists assign significance to documents. How that significance is defined is not always straightforward. Books have title pages with the author, publisher, and date. Most archives do not; most PDF files do not. Someone has to provide that context. This act carries a certain social responsibility with it. How catalogers and processors describe a document will influence how it is perceived within a broader context. Is it an original or a copy? Do digital objects have an "original"? Is a document really what it purports to be? Chapter 7 addresses authenticity, and documents the proliferation of forgeries and misattributions in archives.

The last issue is the displacement of documents. Unlike books, archives are the product of a physical transfer from current working files to a repository for preservation. One could argue that all archives are displaced documents in a sense. They change custody and frequently change legal title. Any move of this kind involves choices. Do the documents go to the Library of Congress or to the National Archives? Will they be placed in a repository that quickly processes the materials or hidden away in a warehouse? Will private papers be sold to the highest bidder or placed in the most accessible venue? Will the documents cross state borders or leave the country of origin? Will they be divided up? Will they be appropriated or outright stolen? Which transfers are appropriate and which are not? Who has the right to make these decisions? Chapter 8 examines displaced and stolen archives.

All of these ethical topics relate directly to the bigger issue of social responsibility in a rapidly changing society. These seven topics are far from exhaustive; there are many other areas that need to be examined. The essays presented here should be seen as part of a larger discussion, with a wide array of issues and case studies. They are intended to provide a foundation for further discussion.

The examples in each of these areas include many cases that are drawn from different cultures and different historical periods. Despite the obvious differences, archival experiences in other times and places point to commonalities and serve to highlight the more enduring and universal values of the profession. There are other reasons for looking further afield. A comparative approach provides a relative basis for evaluating how reasonable certain standards, such as the length of privacy restrictions, actually are. In this rapidly shrinking world, decisions in one country will eventually affect archival policy in others. Privacy safeguards put in place in Europe are affecting records managers in U.S. businesses with an international clientele. In addition, these examples provide a wider perspective. Americans are learning a great deal from a global network of archival ethicists, reaching from Canada to the Netherlands to South Africa and beyond. Often it is easier to discern and analyze unethical behavior in an example taken from a distance, rather than in one too close to home. Yet another reason is that these cases explore the way memory is constructed and how a culture understands itself.

The questions at the end of most chapters suggest a range of responses. Instead of solutions, there is an array of possible strategies. Each professional needs to be aware of these options in order to define the policies that work best in a particular repository. Blanket recommendations seem not to function very well when applied to specific quandaries. It is not far fetched to compare the disposition of an archival collection to a child custody case, in that all factors need to be individually evaluated before finding the best home. Each particular collection has its own personality, background, and requirements. Similarly, each particular repository has its own mission and role. Both novice archivists and experienced ones are engaged in a continuing process of weighing competing interests and balancing conflicting demands. The ongoing decision making is built into the work day. An ethical practice is the sum of many small, carefully considered decisions, based on a combination of deductive and inductive reasoning. By combining principles derived deductively from the codes with patterns obtained inductively from a wide range of specific examples, it is possible to put together a flexible framework for evaluating ethical issues.

Questions for Evaluating Archival Ethics

1. In general, what are the basic categories of ethical issues that occur and can they be discerned in the crush of daily work?

2. When examining a given case, which of these categories are involved?

3. What are the precise facts that are knowable, and which facts are unknown?

4. Is it possible to maintain an open mind and see things from different points of view?

5. How do the facts and issues line up against established ethical standards and codes?

6. How do the issues relate to the ideals of fairness, equity, human rights, openness, honesty, and truthfulness?

7. Are there similar cases that can be examined for perspective and guidance?

8. What are the questions that need to be addressed?

9. Is any damage or harm being done?

10. How urgent is the issue, and how much time is there to make a decision?

11. What values are at stake?

12. Which people are involved and what are their interests?

13. Are there conflicts of interest, especially in financial arrangements?

14. Which colleagues and supervisors should be consulted and informed?

15. Which experts and legal advisors need to be consulted?

16. What are the options and possible strategies?

17. What are the desired outcomes?

18. How do the issues line up against the various options in a decision matrix?

19. How can the desired resolution be harmonized within institutional structures?

20. Has the case been adequately documented for future reference?

This framework may seem too time-consuming. Who can engage in such endless debate? Is this complex evaluation worth the effort? Why enter a profession that has such pitfalls? What *is* at stake is really the collective memory and a truthful historical record. That is no small thing. The results from these myriad ethical decisions contribute to an accurate shared memory and a well-informed citizenry. When it functions properly, such an evaluation is one of the uniquely rewarding aspects of the profession.

Archives and the Construction of Memory

The modern use of archives to verify a truthful account of events owes a great debt to the erudite French Catholic cleric Jean Mabillon (1632–1707),[8] who basically invented the art of diplomatics: originally the close examination and comparison of ancient parchments to determine which documents were authentic and which were forgeries.[9] (Today *diplomatics* is usually used as an umbrella term for authentication of documentation. Only tangentially related to diplomacy, the term *diploma* originally referred simply to a folded document.) Later the German historian Leopold von Ranke (1795–1886) became frustrated by conflicting historical accounts and came up with a methodology for extracting information from eye witness reports and from documents contemporaneous with events. In an effort to stick to knowable facts rather than myth, he promised in his first historical narrative published in 1824 to use "memoirs, diaries, letters, reports from embassies and original narratives of eye witnesses." And, famously, he promised to tell history *as it actually was* (in his words, "wie es eigentlich gewesen"). The phrase he used may have been borrowed from the first sentence of Wilhelm von Humboldt's earlier work "On the Historian's Task" (1821).[10] Ranke's formulation was already something of a topos in the nineteenth century, a part of the intellectual heritage of the early modern age. In previous eras, history had relied heavily on classic mythological models and then the chronicles of miracle-working saints. Ranke himself was a devout, believing Protestant. In recounting events of the past, he put aside the methods of hagiography in favor of ascertaining verifiable facts.[11] Mabillon, Humboldt, and Ranke were motivated by the desire to separate truth from myth and fabrication, or even outright lies parading as history.

Ranke was also reacting against one of his famous colleagues at the University of Berlin, Georg Wilhelm Friedrich Hegel. In essence, Hegel's a priori technique was to posit sweeping historical trends, and then deduce the meaning of events from these higher forces. Karl Marx was famously influenced by the Hegelian philosophy of history. For the school of history influenced by Ranke, factual narratives could only be written inductively on the basis of surviving eye witness accounts, however fragmentary; that is, on the contemporary written record.

Ranke went so far as to assert that there is no history without documents: "We are fortunate where documentary traces remain. At least these can be grasped. But what happens where there are none, for instance in prehistory? I am in favor of excluding this period from history because it contradicts the historical principle, which is documentary research."[12] He decided that prehistory was unknowable. Ranke even decided that early Chinese history lacked enough archives to provide the basis for accurate history since the first emperor of a unified China, Qin Shi Huang, in 213 BCE, destroyed most of the manuscripts of previous eras. Modern historians probably would not dismiss prehistory and ancient China from their purview. The fact remains: the simple acquisition of archives shapes what can be known about events.

That ethical dimension is built into the motivation behind saving and evaluating documents. There is no objective history without documents. Topics that are not documented cannot be studied with accuracy. Already Ranke begs the question: What can one do if a topic is of permanent research interest, and there are no documents? The archivists of his time were passive recipients of government transfers. Archivists over time have answered that question differently: by proactively seeking out and acquiring materials in neglected subject areas. While elite groups throughout history have carved their history in stone, clay, and other permanent materials, non-elite groups need to be purposefully documented. Today we call this *documentation strategy*. With it comes an even heavier responsibility than Ranke would have granted to the guardians of historical records.

Since 1824, Ranke's fame has risen and fallen. He developed a school of historiography, sometimes called *classical historicism*, at the University of Berlin, based on the critical analysis of archives. In 1885 George Bancroft called Ranke the "greatest living historian" on the occasion of Ranke's election as the first honorary member of the American Historical Association.[13] In the mid-twentieth century, brilliant refugee intellectuals such as Ernst Posner and Felix Gilbert brought the best of Ranke's methodology from Berlin to the United States, in places like the relatively new National Archives in Washington. Since then, historical trends have come and gone. Postwar historians were decidedly alienated by Ranke's unsympathetic view of democratic institutions, like constitutions and parliaments. Postmodern writers such as Jacques Derrida, taking a different track, have explored new notions of what is knowable, the uses of historical memory, the limitations of self knowledge, and the chimera of objectivity. They, too, see the collecting of archives as an essential task of society, but one with shifting perspectives on what is "true," a view made famous in Derrida's *Archive Fever*.[14] It is well worth reading what South African archivist Verne Harris has to say about Derrida in connection with his work on preserving the archives of apartheid, in *Archives and Justice*.[15] Because our perception of truth is shaped by what is acquired and saved, acquisitions are by definition highly political and politicized. It is the shadow side of Ranke. He believed that we can only know history that has been documented. It follows, according to Harris's reading of Derrida, that elites only document what they want to have known. In 1998 Harris tried to save the evidence from the South African Truth and Reconciliation Commission, and felt much more could have been acquired for the permanent archives. Harris has also been instrumental in preserving the prison papers of Nelson Mandela. It often takes a single highly motivated individual to rescue the records of the powerless, and to create a verifiable account.

Despite the decline in Ranke's personal fame, his methods have persisted into the current post-World War II and postmodern era in ways that are not always acknowledged or even recognized as his. The historian

Benny Morris has grappled with competing Israeli and Palestinian accounts of the founding of the state of Israel. Morris has revised and refined his interpretation repeatedly since the 1980s as British, American, and Israeli archival sources have become available. As Morris puts it: "I believed, and still believe, that there is such a thing as historical truth; that it exists independently of, and can be detached from, the subjectivities of scholars; that it is the historian's duty to try to reach it."[16] A reviewer explained that "In scholarly argument over what is reliable, Morris is an unbending believer in the value of the paper trail: documents establish fact: interviews with participants are too subjective."[17]

The heart of historical writing is still documentary research. Richard J. Cox and David Wallace have described archives and records as the "scaffolding" of history and social memory.[18] Anyone who has kept a diary over time, and has gone back to read it later, knows well that human memory rearranges and reinterprets events. A diary is written at the time events occur, which is why historians have more trust in diaries than in memoirs. This does not mean that authentic diaries and genuine archives are always accurate. Sworn testimony may not tell the truth about who was where, and when. A laundry receipt may be more accurate on that score. Comparing deliberately produced documents with unselfconsciously produced records is at the core of determining an accurate historical sequence of events. Obviously, dates on documents are not always accurate. One quickly learns to question any date in early January, as the previous year is often given out of habit. In addition to casual errors, bias and subjectivity permeate archives. Truth may not be relative, but the perception of truth is. Despite that fact, even in the post-Derrida and postmodern world, documentary research is the essential tool for determining the correct sequence of events, and even for determining whether a presumed event actually occurred at all. Did the founding fathers gather on July 4, 1776 to sign the Declaration of Independence? No. Did a revolutionary mob in Paris free hordes of political prisoners from the Bastille prison on July 14, 1789? No. These misconceptions, easily corrected by documentary sources, probably serve as harmless shorthand for larger historical movements. Other narratives are more problematic.

Archives, Memory, and Human Rights

One of the most rewarding aspects of archival work is the way it supports core values such as human rights. When it comes to human rights abuses, gaps in the records and falsifications are troubling. Here, the archival process—this search for truth—is a valued ethical standard. Archivists have made immeasurable contributions to an accurate record of the human rights struggle. The following three examples from the Americas, the Soviet Union, and the aftermath of the Nazi regime should serve to demonstrate that there is more to archival ethics than conscientiously following a few rules. There is an integral ethical component to the profession.

The Foundation Narrative of the Americas

The foundation narrative as presented in many American history books is an example of a misrepresentation brought to light by careful archival work. One date that school children are likely to remember is 1492, and they will probably rhyme it with "Columbus sailed the ocean blue." Soon after the American Revolution there was a well-intentioned effort to create appealing stories about the founding of a new nation in the New World, all to instill a sense of pride and patriotism in young students. Christopher Columbus was styled as an inspiring and heroic figure, who discovered that the world was round and not flat, and who discovered America. Generations of students bought into this beautiful interpretation. They often continued to believe the founding myth well into adulthood, even as they learned that since antiquity scholars knew the world was round, and that countless generations had lived in the Americas before Columbus arrived. The Native Americans did not preserve extensive records, but contemporaries of Columbus did, in particular a priest named Bartolomé de Las Casas (1484–1566).

Las Casas also admired Columbus as a heroic spirit who combined bold thinking with physical bravery. That admiration did not cloud his vision, and he was horrified by the enslavement and massacre of the indigenous people under Columbus's control. Las Casas was a natural archivist. His views are well known because he wrote polemical pamphlets denouncing the ongoing brutality, slavery, and massacres. These writings were widely circulated in his lifetime. He deliberately and conscientiously put aside polemics to transcribe every scrap of documentation he could find as accurately as possible, even copying texts he did not understand. He explained his method as different from that of the classical historians of ancient Greece and Rome who loved a good story and lots of mythological anecdotes. In this, Las Casas was a precursor of the Rankean method.

Las Casas combined his own first-hand observations of the Americas with detailed archival work. He transcribed Columbus's extensive travel logs, entry by entry. He read the same volumes Columbus read and painstakingly examined his marginal notes. In the process, Las Casas created a vast, sprawling manuscript, unpublished in his lifetime and preserved in Spain, of the first thirty years of the European experience in the Americas "as it actually was." The manuscript is really a focused archival collection in transcription. Las Casas let the documents speak for themselves, quoting Columbus in full detail. He deliberately avoided mythological treatment of events. The eminent scholar Anthony Grafton used his immense erudition to determine the authenticity and historic value of the accounts.[19] In many ways, Las Casas's long-unpublished documentary history is more chilling than his pamphleteering in that he lets Columbus systematically describe events as they unfold day by day. Columbus took delight in finding peoples that were easy to enslave and brutally work to death in his search for gold and wealth.

Well-educated and well-read modern historians are still shocked to read the archival record and note the discrepancy between their naïve beliefs gleaned from American textbooks and the evidence. The late American historian Howard Zinn opened his history of the United States with quotations from Columbus's journals.[20] Las Casas's diligent archival work preserves our best record of Columbus's own perception of events and gives us our clearest view into a deep human tragedy. The documents Las Casas assembled provide the basis for a truthful history and one that respects the victims of the human rights disaster that occurred. An ethical society is based on a truthful understanding of what actually happened.

Documents from a Parallel Soviet World

Another example of truthful recording of human rights violations comes from the Russian archives. While official propaganda in the Soviet Union painted a positive, almost utopian, picture of modern progress throughout the 1930s to 1950s, armies of Russian archivists preserved the banal official records needed to run a parallel prison economy. These files included reports, budgets, purchasing requisitions, and work orders for operating the extensive political prison camp system. The papers quietly accumulated in closed storerooms. Without access to these official files, novelist Alexander Solzhenitsyn (1918–2008) still found ways to document what he termed the "Gulag Archipelago."[21] An archivist by instinct, he gathered hundreds of eye witness accounts from prison inmates. Families of the Gulag victims hid, at great risk, evidence of the social conditions for political prisoners, sometimes just scraps of paper found in wallets, sketches of conditions in the camps. These private papers were small memorials to family suffering. Solzhenitsyn stitched together what information he could from hundreds of oral histories and informal documents to portray the Gulag as a parallel economy based on slave labor. He termed the work "an experiment in literary investigation" because it required a novelist's imagination to bring life to the bits of evidence he was able to assemble.

The internal working records for this shadow world were never meant to be viewed outside administrative circles and were kept secret. During the unexpected collapse of Soviet communism, Boris Yeltsin's archivist, Rudolf Pikhoia, reportedly armed, protected the files from wholesale destruction during the power struggle in August 1991. In 1992, after the fall of communism, there was enough political will to open up the working files for historical research. Promoting maximum access is one of the great ethical principles in the field. The Gulag documents were microfilmed, and the film sets were marketed to libraries around the world. Hundreds of researchers have scoured these documents. Rosspen, a Russian publisher, issued a seven-volume set of the government documents in paper form with annotations. Dedicated archivists from groups such as Memorial collected and organized personal memoirs and testimonials from victims.

In 2003 the American journalist Anne Applebaum was able to read both the formerly secret official archives and the once hidden private papers. She reconstructed the social history of the Soviet political prisons in her Pulitzer Prize–winning book *Gulag: A History*.[22] Applebaum could confirm Solzhenitsyn's assessment. She wrote movingly in the introduction about benefiting from the tireless work of anonymous archivists, some government employees and some freelance amateurs, without whom the falsified record would stand largely unchallenged.

Today Russian historians are reconceptualizing their historical narrative and rewriting textbooks. Among the nationalists, there is a strong tendency to rehabilitate Stalin as a heroic leader and ignore the depth of human rights violations that he engineered. These historians are operating under a misguided version of patriotism. With the filming and publishing of the documentary heritage, the evidence of the forced labor system is permanently on record. This record honors the victims with a truthful history, and it stands as a warning against Stalinism. That record was made possible by the conscientious work of hundreds of ordinary archivists.

Uncovering a Cover Story from World War II

Every society has myths and cover stories that require a closer examination. A clear example comes from Austria. A popular politician, Kurt Waldheim, lied in his official biography about his role in World War II. He said he spent the war years in law school and claimed that he had no direct knowledge of Nazi atrocities. With this cover story, Waldheim was able to pursue a successful career, serving as secretary general of the United Nations and chancellor of Austria. In Austria, he held a position of high esteem and was strongly supported in democratic elections. An intrepid archival sleuth, American historian Robert Herzstein, located solid evidence of Waldheim's direct involvement in Nazi activities. The most incriminating evidence was on microfilm in the U.S. National Archives, not far from the headquarters of the United Nations, where Waldheim had held forth as an international statesman.[23] Right after World War II, conscientious American and British archivists had made the arrangements for microfilming and preserving the captured German archives prior to returning the originals. They compiled endless volumes of finding aids, and sold both the films and registers to libraries around the world. The work took decades.Without access to these microfilms, there would have been a false understanding of Waldheim's role in history.

Herzstein found other clues in a wide array of archival sources from different countries, some recently opened, others buried in massive amounts of documents. He portrayed Waldheim in a nuanced way, not as a hardened war criminal, but as an active facilitator of the criminal regime. In a democracy, the electorate needs to know the truth about elected officials. Even more so, the international arena needs reliable background information on its leaders.

In all three case studies there were efforts to whitewash history and deny culpability in massive human rights violations. Misguided patriotism and myth-making clouded the public's perception. In all three cases the diligent work of archivists provided a baseline of truth.

Not all archives have such controversial material, yet they do have once-private documentation that corrects assumptions and wishful thinking that could otherwise corrupt the historical narrative and the understanding of events. The Germans, who dealt with the consequences of two tyrannies in one century, have a concept for this process. Actually, they have two words, both nearly unpronounceable to English speakers: *Vergangenheitsbewältigung* and *Geschichtsaufarbeitung*. One refers to mastering the past, the other to working with history. Both terms indicate that the process is a struggle. The balancing act that constitutes archival work provides researchers such as Applebaum and Herzstein with the sources to double check the conventional wisdom. They both found small pieces of the puzzle in widely disparate archives. The Soviet Union and Austria provide dramatic examples of societies that needed to have the official narrative corrected by the archives. Certainly the standardized American historical narrative needs correcting and re-interpretation. In fact *all* countries and *all* communities need this ongoing process of working with history and constructing a realistic, nuanced, and balanced picture of the past, especially the founding narratives of a nation or culture. Access to archives is really nothing less than an essential component of a well functioning democratic society. By memorializing the victims of human rights abuses and revealing the mechanisms of abusive regimes, archives are increasingly recognized for their potential as something of a moral corrective.

Ways to Visualize Archival Ethics

These considerations make it clear, then, that the range of ethical decisions is very wide, much wider than one normally sees during the average workday. The implications of seemingly minor preservation and reading room policies have a ripple effect over time. One way to visualize the ethical landscape for archivists is as a set of concentric circles. In the center are the small daily decisions about acquiring appropriate collections, about avoiding conflicts of interests, about providing equal access to documents, about implementing better indexing tools like EAD, about raising funds to maintain preservation projects; and the list goes on. Beyond the repository level, there is the responsibility to coordinate with colleagues at other institutions to develop standards, to steer collections to the right home, to expose cases of theft and malfeasance. Beyond that is the national level, which includes working with the community of historians for a truthful national narrative, and working with journalists to provide background information on policy debates. The international level is no longer remote, and participation is opening up interesting partnerships to protect our shared cultural property. It is all about accountability and creating the basis for a well functioning democratic society.

Archival work is linked with many complex transactions, such as visualizing the past and providing a baseline for measuring the present state of affairs. Ethical lapses have consequences that hinder these essential societal tasks. Here again, a useful way to envision the different roles is as nested or concentric circles with professionalism in between law and the wider sphere of social obligations.

Law

There is substantial overlap between ethical issues and legal questions. Many of the practical rules for archival acquisitions are designed to accommodate contract law. Acquisitions policies concern property ownership, another major branch of the law. As custodians of intellectual property, many archivists become proficient at interpreting copyright law. Often standard practices codified in archival manuals are defensive maneuvers, intended to prevent lawsuits or create a sense of order that will hold up under scrutiny in litigation. Archivists without legal training need to be aware of basic guidelines, and above all have a good sense of when it is necessary to consult legal counsel, and possibly more than one lawyer. Archivists need to confront the confusion on the books; legal advice is often not consistent from one attorney to another. Judicial decisions are also inconsistent from one location to another, from one decade to another. And laws change. With technical issues such as copyright, the changes can be difficult to implement until they have been clarified in court. Despite these complications, legal compliance forms one of the easier categories to assimilate. An excellent book by an archivist-attorney, Menzi Behrnd-Klodt, provides a range of navigational tools.[24]

Professional Standards

Another category is professionalism. Some practices that are technically legal, such as ruthless competition between repositories for prize collections or denigrating colleagues, damage the profession as a whole. Everyone benefits from minimizing such negative dynamics. Other unprofessional activities may be marginally legal but constitute a conflict of interest that should raise a red flag. Whenever archivists personally collect documents in the same area as their employing institutions, or compete with researchers to publish out of their holdings, or accept personal presents from donors and researchers, there is a breach of professional standards. These issues are often not cut and dried. They may require careful vetting and complex responses. The case studies in Karen Benedict's groundbreaking book on archival ethics supplies a solid introduction to the way skilled professionals think about issues.[25]

Social Accountability

As the keepers of a society's collective memory and identity, archivists hold a role in society that goes beyond the letter of the law or the niceties of professional standards. It is a role that is often not recognized by the society that benefits, or even by the parent institution that shelters the archives and pays the bills. When veteran archivists get together to compare notes, they often reflect on the long-lasting consequences of their seemingly ordinary activities: Which side of a story is documented and preserved; which side gets neglected and discarded? What information gets out to the public in time to affect political decision-making, and what information is locked away until it is too late to make any changes? If archivists new to the profession become familiar with these points early in their careers, it strengthens the integrity of their organizations and facilitates the role of archives as a force for social good. Randall C. Jimerson, Richard J. Cox, David A. Wallace, Verne Harris, and Francis X. Blouin Jr., among others, have worked extensively on the subject of accountability and the role of archivists in society.[26]

In an ideal world, these three categories are neatly nested, the legal principles inside the broader context of professionalism, and the professionalism at the service of society. In reality, conflicts can and do occur. Harmonizing them is one of the challenges of the profession. Fortunately it is an intellectually interesting and culturally fascinating project to bring these factors into alignment.

Advance comments from readers have made it clear that working archivists want a comprehensive set of normative guidelines for systematically deciding ethical questions. Their comments also make it clear that they rather sharply disagree on what those specific guidelines should be. The first chapter, on codes of ethics, reviews the few normative guidelines that have been formulated and agreed upon. The precepts are important to know, but they are by nature very general and difficult to apply. More specific guidelines would be misleading since each archival repository is different. For this reason, there is a serious danger that highly normative solutions could backfire when applied to a particular situation. Giving detailed advice without knowing where it will be implemented or who will apply it is a hazardous enterprise. The topical chapters provide background, but are not a substitute for face-to-face consultation with a knowledgeable lawyer or meetings with department heads. Instead of a cookbook of recipes, this volume relies on the Socratic method and the casebook method to provide background and perspective. Readers should not expect ready-made solutions. The reasons are woven through the text, but for clarity they should be pulled together in one place.

- Archival work has inherently contradictory ethical demands, especially in the areas of acquisitions, access, disposal, proprietary information, privacy, authenticity, and displaced archives.

- There is not, at present, a general consensus on how to find the balance between competing demands in the different problem areas.

- Finding the right balance for a particular repository can be facilitated by examining all the options available and asking the right questions.

- Finding that balance can also be facilitated by knowing what others have confronted and how they dealt with a particular dilemma.

- Each repository, with its unique set of parameters, must calibrate its own balance between competing demands.

- Each archivist needs to take responsibility for decisions based on an assessment of the facts and risks of a particular situation.

The following essays on acquisitions, disposal, access, proprietary information, privacy, authenticity, and displaced documents are intended to tease out some of the dilemmas for the ethical archivist and demonstrate the implications for the wider culture. These essays deploy both deductive and inductive methods of analysis, but there is no attempt to provide easy answers. In some cases only the particular facts suggest particular solutions. At other times, general principles need to be applied. All the case studies and examples used are based on real, not hypothetical, situations. Archivists, like medical professionals, have a duty to keep confidences. In some instances, the details are generalized to protect confidential information. The goal is to involve archivists and curators in a discussion that may in time lead to a broader consensus on ethics than exists today. Our society, of course, is in flux, with a massive loss of confidence in many fundamental institutions. It is all the more important to build trusted archives, both for current policy making, and also as an intellectual life boat for the future. For that reason, one hopes that this discussion eventually also engages historians and the educated public in general, creating an awareness of how our shared memory is constructed. We need cultural bridges that hold up.

CHAPTER 1

Codes of Ethics

The archivist has a moral obligation to society.

—Wayne C. Grover[1]

CODES OF ETHICS ARE LIVING DOCUMENTS, SUBJECT TO FREQUENT REVISIONS AND RETHINKING. The precepts of all ethical codes require frequent discussion and updating. As alluded to in the introduction, the very process of reformulating guidelines and analyzing the implications brings out many important points. Sometimes these lengthy dialogs have more substance than the rules that are eventually frozen into a text. Creating an environment where ethics are directly discussed on a regular basis has a positive effect regardless of the actual code put forward. The Dutch archivist and ethicist Eric Ketelaar compares a code of ethics to a tool that needs to be used and sharpened frequently to keep its edge, by means of ongoing discussions and debates.[2]

There have been many efforts to construct universal principles that apply to government archives, manuscript repositories, and private business as well as religious archives. These codes and statements of principles have not resulted in an iron-clad consensus. It would be a problem if there were no discussion. It is useful to compare the principles articulated in various codes and test their effectiveness in real-world case studies. In the

U.S., these discussions have a history going back more than half a century, and will no doubt continue into the foreseeable future.

In 1955, G. Philip Bauer, assistant to the director of archival management of the National Archives, published a rather stultifyingly factual piece entitled "Recruitment, Training, and Promotion in the National Archives." Bauer delineates the skills and training required for working as an archivist in the National Archives, embedded in the civil service system. In listing the elements of archival knowledge required for the GS-7 level, he supplements the six routine components with a less tangible seventh: "a proper attitude toward archives and archival responsibilities as measured by the standard expressed in the Archivist's Code." The code, widely known as the work of Wayne C. Grover, is simply identified as "Prepared for Use in the National Archives Inservice Training Program."[3] The legendary Grover, a founding member of the Society of American Archivists, served as Archivist of the United States from 1948 to 1965. At this point the word *ethics* is not included anywhere in his text, which Bauer describes as embodying a "proper attitude." Half a century later, after many attempts at defining archival ethics, the goal is still to develop professional judgment and a proper attitude toward archives.

Despite its source in the standardized civil service culture, reflecting its practical emphasis on creating a meritocracy with tests and measurable competence, the 1955 Code is nonetheless a luminous document that deserves to be read carefully by all practitioners, whether in the National Archives, records management, or a private manuscript repository. The opening sentence posits a "moral obligation to preserve evidence on how things actually happened." This precept clearly echoes the famous principle articulated in 1824 by Leopold von Ranke to show history as it actually happened ("wie es eigentlich gewesen") based on primary sources close to the events.

Grover had wide experience in managing military records in World War II and was influenced by the European traditions brought to Washington by another legendary figure, Ernst Posner. Grover credits Posner with providing Americans new to archives management with a broader perspective: "Our newly developing archival profession needed not merely books on archival practices elsewhere, but a man who could talk to us about them in the light of what we ourselves were trying to do. In this sense Ernst Posner has always been to me and to others a walking Office of Education."[4] Posner's training in the Prussian archives was steeped in Ranke's anti-Hegelian inductive reasoning. History was reconstructed from the remaining shards, like ancient pottery. Archives were those shards. In the German context of the nineteenth century, this effort at scientific objectivity was tempered by Ranke's Lutheran moralism. His approach was scientific, but in it he perceived "the hand of God." Prussian archivists were expected to be taciturn keepers of a trust. Such a sense of moralism is also refracted in the postwar American archival environment by Bauer's concept of a "proper attitude" and Grover's "moral obligation to society." The Archivist's Code evolved out of a need for a yard stick to measure this proper attitude and moral obligation.

The genius of Grover's Archivist's Code is that it combines a familiarity with ordinary, often tedious, work routines and an awareness of this larger, moral context. It is worth examining each of the principles. The 1955 text is no longer readily available in print, and the online version has small but important differences from the version published in the *American Archivist* after Bauer's article. The text is quoted below, followed by a few comments. The code itself reads with an almost psalmodic point-counterpoint, balancing the moral and pragmatic demands of the profession.

1.   The archivist has a moral obligation to society to preserve
     evidence on how things actually happened and to take every
     measure for the physical preservation of valuable records. On the
     other hand, he has an obligation not to commit funds to the hous-
     ing and care of records that have no significance or lasting value.

Comments: Preservation of historical evidence in the Rankean sense is the first ethical imperative. Since storage can be expensive, the frugal archivist has to balance such a noble cause with unavoidable economic constraints.

2.   The archivist must realize that in selecting records for reten-
     tion or disposal he acts as the agent of the future in determining

> its heritage from the past. Therefore, insofar as his intellectual
> attainments, experience, and judgment permit, he must be ever
> conscious of the future's needs, making his decisions impartially
> without taint of ideological, political, or personal bias.

Comments: After preservation, selection is the next most crucial and elusive element of the job. This process must be performed with foresight and intuition about emerging fields of research that will require special sources at some future time. Forecasting research trends is an unavoidable requirement for successful selection. Another very different and rather weighty matter is the need to document all sides of an issue, not to preserve just one approach and deaccession competing narratives. Many thoughtful archivists reject the notion of objectivity, viewing it as tacit support for the status quo. Even given that argument, the Archivist's Code is prescient for its time about the need for expanding the concept of collecting in an inclusive way, beyond the boundaries of an individual's personal bias.

This code is intended for employees of the National Archives, which acquires materials through legally mandated transfers from government agencies. For that reason, the entire complex of ethical quandaries surrounding the acquisition of papers by private repositories through purchase or private donation is not addressed.

> 3.   The archivist must be watchful in protecting the integrity of
>   records in his custody. He must guard them against defacement,
>   alteration, or theft; he must protect them against physical damage
>   by fire or excessive exposure to light, damp, and dryness, and he
>   must take care to see that their evidentiary value is not impaired
>   in the normal course of rehabilitation, arrangement, and use.

Comments: This paragraph, expanding on the moral obligation cited in the first paragraph, addresses three rather different threats to a collection: security lapses, lack of conservation treatments, and general carelessness. The papers must be protected against physical damage or loss as a result of use by readers or even by careless staff. Next the archivist is required to enforce environmental safeguards. The third threat occurs during processing and conservation when clues to provenance, such as old labels on file folders and shipping containers, are often obliterated. Archives are evidence, and as such textual authenticity must be protected along with the physical artifact. None of these requirements are cheap. While they sound fairly innocuous and self-evident, these three provisions presuppose a substantial amount of funding, good housing, full staffing, and sophisticated management.

4.   The archivist should endeavor to promote access to records to the fullest extent consistent with the public interest, but he should carefully observe any established policies restricting the use of records. Within the bounds of his budget and opportunities, he should work unremittingly for the increase and diffusion of knowledge, making his documentary holdings freely known to prospective users through published finding aids and personal consultation.

Comments: Here again the ideal confronts reality. As a profession, American archivists and librarians have traditionally promoted free and open access to information as one of the pillars of democratic society. Access is not simply a matter of opening a collection. Potential readers need to know the collection exists and have an idea of the contents to determine what is relevant to their work. This phase of access involves labor-intensive processing, indexing, publication and publicity. These same professionals are charged with enforcing restrictions and limitations on use as mandated by donors, governmental regulation, or the host institution. The 1955 Code does not address the reasons for restrictions such as privacy, protection of intellectual property, lawyer-client privilege, security classifications, etc.

5.   The archivist should respond courteously and with a spirit of service to all proper requests, but he should not waste time responding in detail to frivolous or unreasonable inquiries. He should not place unnecessary obstacles in the way of those who would use the records, but rather should do whatever he can to spare their time and ease their work. Obviously, he should not idly discuss the work and findings of one searcher with another; but where

duplication of research effort is apparent, he may properly inform one searcher of the work of another.

Comments: Again there is point-counterpoint: The reference service should be helpful, but not waste time on frivolous requests. The reference archivists do not gossip about one reader to another one, but they should alert them to parallel research. The question is one of finding the right balance.

6.   The archivist should not profit from any commercial exploitation of the records in his custody, nor should he withhold from others any information he has gained as a result of his archival work in order to carry out private professional research. He should, however, take every legitimate advantage of his favored situation to develop his professional interests in historical or other research.

Comments: This paragraph contains several messages. The civil service ideal is for employees to share their special knowledge freely and live solely on their government salaries. Archivists acquire in the course of their work truly privileged inside information that can be invaluable to the researcher and save enormous time and frustration. Withholding such help or providing it selectively can trigger complaints. There is no explicit prohibition of private collecting, but the wording seems to discourage consulting or other outside pay for the knowledge acquired on the job. It does not directly address the matter of employees who buy and sell manuscripts on the side, a common problem in private repositories. While less prevalent, even government archivists find that insider theft is frequently motivated by private collecting and dealing by employees. A code that covers both private as well as government repositories needs to address this issue more explicitly. As for exploitation of the records for intellectual profit, it has often been seen as a conflict of interest for an archivist to publish based on this inside information in competition with outside researchers, and yet archivists are encouraged to develop their scholarly skills.

7.   The archivist should freely pass on to his professional colleagues the results of his own or his organization's research that add to the body of archival knowledge. Likewise, he should leave to his

successors a true account of the records in his custody and of
their proper organization and arrangement.

Comments: The history of an archival collection is crucial to its significance. Again, this precept requires adequate funding, staffing, well-organized internal recordkeeping, and a system for passing accessible and comprehensible information from one generation of employees to another. In general, it is impossible to comply with any of these provisions without a well-designed organizational infrastructure.

Copies of the Archivist's Code "suitable for framing" were distributed and displayed where employees would benefit. It served, and still serves, as a brief, readable, and insightful guide for professional behavior. Propriety and morality were and are requirements for professionalism.

The 1980 SAA Code of Ethics for Archivists

By the 1970s, the archival profession had expanded. The Society of American Archivists (SAA) had begun to formulate general procedures that created uniform standards for government archivists, records managers, and curators of private manuscript collections. There was a need to modernize the Archivist's Code to include this expanded definition of *archivist* and also to formulate issues in a less moralistic and more pragmatic approach. The SAA Ethics Committee, chaired by David Horn, was tasked with pulling together the text of an expanded, revised, and more up-to-date code, while still retaining that brief format that made for easy reading and wide dissemination. SAA Council approved the mandate for the committee in December 1976, and the final text was approved in January 1980. It was published in the Council minutes with an extensive commentary in the summer 1980 issue of the *American Archivist*. The three-year effort involved examining the codes of ethics for other professions and coordinating with the work of the American Library Association. The practical issues plaguing manuscript curators were added to the mix. The document was revised as a Code of Ethics for Archivists, since the concept of ethics replaced the moralism of the 1955 text.[5]

Suitable to print on a single page, the new code was eleven paragraphs instead of seven. The overflow of ideas appeared in a lengthier commentary. Nearly all the main points of the National Archives text were included. New provisions discouraged competition between archives for the same collection, something important to manuscript repositories. The new text also acknowledged the problems inherent in donor relations: determining whether the donor has full title to the gift or purchase, promoting equal access, and the importance of steering donors away from draconian restrictions. For the first time the issue of privacy was addressed, including third-person privacy rights. The 1980 Code fostered the notion of balancing competing interests and using openness and full disclosure to deflect potential conflicts. So, for instance, under these guidelines archivists were allowed to engage in their own research and publication as long as the employing institution was aware of it, and nothing was withheld from other researchers. This modulated approach is well worth rereading. The concept of ethics as balancing competing interests is now firmly established.

In an article about the rewriting of the code, David Horn stressed that the 1980 Code of Ethics for Archivists was not the end of the process but rather an initiative to open a continuing dialog. In fact, the code has been under constant review since then. Based on this pioneering work, several general principles have emerged. First of all, the code is no longer "a statement of legal or moral imperatives; it is a guide for professional behavior."[6]

Second, Horn emphasized the need for institutions to have a published statement of purpose and clear, written policies. It has become increasingly obvious over time that formalized and well-formulated procedures are the bedrock for ethics in archival practice. Ethical acquisitions and donor relations require written procedures for preparing the warranty of title, deed of gift, or bill of sale. Access is another classic example of the need for procedural guidelines. The 1955 Code emphasized the need to promote access to records. Good will alone will not create open access. It is only possible if large collections that are in demand are cataloged and organized for use. Thus open access presupposes a consistently implemented policy to identify high use collections and queue them for rapid processing. Ethical considerations are too complex to be contained in a simple code, and the overflow is folded into policy guidelines. In fact the archival profession does not work on these issues in isolation. The Society of American Archivists works with sister organizations such as the American Library Association and the International Council on Archives on recommendations. Implementing an ethical archival practice involves a highly complex, well-regulated, and well-networked organization.

One down side to this realization, something not well publicized or widely discussed, is how very difficult compliance is for small or poorly funded archival repositories. The role for amateur collectors and hobby archives shrinks in the face of the responsibilities to history and professional demands.

After considering these factors, another recommendation of David Horn's committee was for SAA to include a book on ethics in its Basic Manual Series, a publishing venture founded in 1977 with the first five volumes. The proposed manual on ethics was not produced. There are several good reasons for this omission. The subject is not amenable to a schematic "how to" manual. Another reason is that ethics, to function properly, require a coherent cultural context, and we are simply not there yet. The different generations of codes are steps in creating that coherence. Such a background for ethical standards does not require uniform thinking; it does require the acceptance of certain core values. How can such values be formulated and promoted? Do they require enforcement?

Rethinking the Code: Normative or Aspirational Guidelines?

The 1980 Code was again revised in 1992. The SAA Committee on Ethics and Professional Conduct was called back into existence as a permanent body reporting to the SAA Council, with a rotating membership. During the decade of the 1990s numerous controversies surrounding archival practice emerged. On the international scene, the fall of communism triggered a reexamination of displaced archives, some dating back to the turbulence of World War II. Regime changes in Africa jeopardized the security of public records. Domestic and international competition between archives for prize collections drove up the price of archival and manuscript collections and began to reduce the availability of freely donated papers. In the background, the digital revolution was gaining force and intensifying all the old problems. In this environment, the Ethics Committee was asked to evaluate certain controversies and issue sanctions. These cases triggered the reevaluation of the code and its relationship to the professional organization. Could individuals or institutions be subjected to investigation to determine if they violated the code? If they had, could they be expelled from membership or somehow reprimanded? Was the model parallel to the Church that can excommunicate members for misdeeds? Or was the model more like the National Geographic Society, where membership is simply a matter of paying subscription dues and receiving a publication?

Several allied organizations do have procedures for punishing violations of their ethics codes. The Manuscript Society, for example, has strict provisions against the sale of stolen manuscripts or forgeries.[7] The membership includes both collectors and dealers. When they pay their dues, they commit themselves to the society's code. Because the Manuscript Society's social events bring together buyers and sellers, the need to promote honest transactions is self-evident. According to its website, the Manuscript Society's board of trustees can investigate violations of the code and expel members if there is a two-thirds majority vote. The threat of expulsion no doubt serves as a deterrent to shoddy business practices. Because the membership reflects the interests of dealers, it has a strong interest in maintaining the rights of private ownership of manuscripts and archives.

Like the Manuscript Society, the Institute of Certified Records Managers (ICRM) also has provisions for decertifying members for code violations.[8] Its members are primarily records managers in industry. The code emphasizes loyalty to the employer, and the position of trust held by records managers. Article 3 reads as follows: "Certified Records Managers shall be prudent in their use of information acquired in the course of their duties.

They shall protect confidential, proprietary and trade secret information obtained from others and use it only for the purposes approved by the party from whom it was obtained or for the benefit of that party, and not for the personal gain of anyone else." Records management is a position of trust. In theory at least, a certified records manager could lose ICRM certification for engaging in "whistleblowing" that reveals company secrets. The International Council on Archives Code of Ethics holds archivists and records managers to a very different standard, separate from that of a given employing institution, as articulated in article 8: "Archivists should not allow people outside the profession to interfere in their practice and obligations."[9] The ICA Code does not have an enforcement mechanism. It is presented as a model that a particular institution could use and could enforce with sanctions if needed.

Archivists and records managers who work for the federal government are required to follow the U.S. Government Ethics Standards. These standards are more general than the old Archivist's Code. They are aimed at eliminating corruption and address general issues such as conflicts of interest, inappropriate gifts, and improper financial transactions. The text includes a warning about enforcement: "Remember, violations may subject you to administrative, civil, or even criminal penalties."[10]

In the museum world, members of the Association of Art Museum Directors found to have broken the code for registrars can be expelled from the organization and their museums could be suspended from borrowing materials or developing joint exhibits with other AAMD member museums.[11]

Do such penalties for violating an ethics code make sense for the Society of American Archivists? The first response to this question was to expand the code in 1992 and add more detail and commentary as guidance. In 1994 SAA formed a permanent Committee on Ethics and Professional Conduct, charged with updating the code as necessary. It was also charged with investigating complaints about violations of the code and recommending sanctions if necessary. Investigations to determine the actual facts of a given case are problematical. Even in a court with subpoena power and testimony under oath, the truth can be elusive. Without those tools SAA could not be sure that the facts were accurate prior to issuing penalties. The committee considered various ways of investigating and mediating or adjudicating disputes. Over time there was a realization of the legal consequences of taking on such a role, and the level of risk involved. The case that forced the issue occurred in 2001. It was a complex case initiated by a complaint from the Communist Party of the United States concerning party records that had been taken surreptitiously to the Soviet Union. A microfilm of these files was eventually acquired by the Library of Congress from the postcommunist Russian archives.[12] An investigation into the facts of the case would require travel, translations, and extensive interviews in Russian and English. It was not clear what the investigation would accomplish. Accusations of unethical conduct could result in litigation, with both SAA and the individual members at risk for punitive damages. The international complexities and legal risks of such a case were clearly beyond the scope of responsibility of the SAA. The threat of deleting a person or organization from the SAA membership rolls does not seem to have much of a deterrent effect, unlike losing ICRM certification.

SAA's consultation with the members of the American Library Association, the Association of College and Research Libraries, and the American Historical Association revealed that these groups had decided against trying to adjudicate their ethics codes. Instead they were treated as persuasive documents and benchmarks. The ALA document is very clear: "These statements provide a framework; they cannot and do not dictate conduct to cover particular situations."[13] The values are very broad: free flow of information, high level of service to all library users, a respect for intellectual property rights, not to advance private interests at the expense of the library or its patrons, objectivity, respect for colleagues, etc. The one concrete issue that the ALA Code addresses is the privacy of the library user. The materials consulted by one user cannot be revealed to others. This provision periodically appears in the press when police agencies try to obtain circulation data with or without a subpoena. Archivists typically follow this provision as well. A journalist, for example, cannot come into the reading room and find out what materials a researcher has requested. One researcher cannot request the names of others who have used a certain collection unless those researchers themselves agree. Other than this privacy provision, the ALA Code of Ethics is very general by intention and does not trigger investigations of ethical lapses or penalties for violations.

Instead of creating the equivalent of reprimands or even disbarment, the SAA Council adopted a more educational approach. When the facts are very clear, and when the issues are clearly within the competence of the archival profession, the SAA Council is free to issue nonbinding opinions based on the principles espoused in the code without invoking sanctions of any kind. The Council currently weighs in on open access to historical records, but would not attempt to take punitive action against repositories or professionals that closed collections. This pragmatic compromise seems to have created the right balance for maintaining ethical oversight without entering into potentially self-destructive legal battles. If such public statements of principle are issued after careful research and worded in a thoughtful manner, they can be very influential. Because a large number of SAA members want stronger ethics enforcement, SAA President Frank Boles explained the logic of using persuasion instead of penalties that probably are not effective in any case.[14]

The American Historical Association has taken a similar approach after determining that investigations and reprimands entail much effort and much legal exposure without necessarily solving any problems. In 2003 the AHA abandoned ethics adjudication after fifteen frustrating years of attempting to directly control behavior.

In 2007 the AHA issued guiding principles for when to take a public stand. The AHA policy should be reviewed by archivists as it emphasizes the importance of equal access to primary sources. It also seeks to prevent commercial ventures or political pressure groups from monopolizing sources. In such cases the AHA feels obligated to take a strong stand. "In particular the AHA should stand ready if political or commercial concerns threaten the professional administration of an archive, historical society or other institution that has custody of sources."[15]

This statement of principles is something that could be adapted for use by archivists. But where does this solution leave the Code of Ethics? The purpose of the code is to provide guiding principles that inspire public confidence and trust.[16] This objective can be achieved with or without penalties. Issuing well crafted statements of principles in response to complaints can be done even without knowing all the facts, by providing professional advice instead. The code serves as a benchmark for those statements, and a public presentation of the basic values at stake. Supplementing the code with some guiding principles would create a useful basis for discussion and debate.

In keeping with this less contentious profile, the Committee on Ethics and Professional Conduct has become a standing body that monitors ethical issues that arise, advises the SAA Council, and recommends revisions to the code. The 1992 Code was drastically reduced and clearly positioned as a standard to aspire to, not as a set of regulations that need to be enforced. The reduced code was approved by the SAA Council on February 5, 2005, and is posted on the SAA website. In 2009 the Committee on Ethics and Professional Conduct decided to revise the text again to reflect the concerns of members and to make the language stronger and more explicit, while still keeping it as an aspirational document. If the profession continues the policy of providing an aspirational code rather than enforcing ethics with penalties, there needs to be a forum for the concerns of archivists who take a different view.

The International Council on Archives Code of Ethics

The timid tone of the 2005 version of the Code of Ethics is openly understood to be a calculated response to the hazards of the American legal system, and an effort to deflect nuisance lawsuits and financial liability. Revisions can strengthen the code, but it remains a document of general guiding principles. The International Council on Archives is not constrained by national legal practice. Its Code of Ethics, adopted by the General Assembly of the ICA at the September 6, 1996 session in Beijing, retains the normative muscle of the 1992 SAA Code. It makes clear that it is not intended to provide specific answers, but rather a framework for the evaluation of questions. Still, the language is quite strong, and unabashedly moralistic. It is structured in ten provisions with an almost biblical "Ten Commandments" feel. It even authorizes the use of sanctions by archival institutions, but leaves the machinery for such punishments unspecified. The code is available on the ICA website.[17] The first, second, and fourth provisions of the code are especially noteworthy.

The first provision of the 1996 ICA Code mandates the preservation of the integrity of archival materials against tampering. From the very outset the code anticipates pressure from "employers, owners, data subjects and users" to manipulate documentation. The authors were cognizant of the inherent temptation to alter the record for political or financial reasons. Such pressure is a fact of archival life. The archival ethical imperative is clear from the start: "The objectivity and impartiality of archivists is the measure of their professionalism." During periods of political turmoil, the selective destruction of records, including deleting electronic records, is a predictable threat to the integrity of the archival record. Such destruction has a long history. Ancient Egyptian pharaohs apparently had the hieroglyphs of predecessors chipped away. In ancient China, incoming emperors would destroy the records of the preceding dynasty to eliminate any potentially compromising comparisons. In the modern age, shredding records was widespread in the former East Germany during the fall of communism in 1989, and in the former Soviet Union in 1991. Systematic destruction of public records occurred during the collapse of apartheid in South Africa. Even in more stable situations, efforts to delete high level email communications in U.S. government offices have come to light. Beyond destroying archives as evidence, there is the danger of archives being "salted" with extraneous documents, an act that can be politically motivated. Archivists face a built-in potential conflict between professional ethics and institutional imperatives in a way that librarians do not.

The second provision of the ICA Code relates to normal archival functions of appraisal, selection, preservation, and maintenance of records. Here again there is a strong professional stance on what archivists should do and should not do, which could easily collide with the motivations of the parent institution. "Archivists should acquire records in accordance with the purposes and resources of their institutions." In other words, new acquisitions should be kept to the recognized "collecting scope" of the institution, and should not exceed the financial resources of that institution to maintain them according to international standards. To make this even more explicit, the ICA Code mandates that archivists "should not seek or accept acquisitions when this would endanger the integrity or security of the records; they should cooperate to ensure the preservation of these records in the most appropriate repository. Archives should cooperate in the repatriation of displaced archives." Basically the second provision prohibits the collecting of "trophy" archives, out-of-scope collecting for purposes of prestige, including national prestige. Few archival employees would have the clout to defy their employer's pressure to acquire image-enhancing collections, such as the official files of a defeated enemy, a common practice throughout history. Napoleon is probably the most famous collector of such archival trophies. The Czechs are still trying to recover documents removed from Prague by the Swedish army in the seventeenth century.[18] The provision is noble, but the chances of a working archivist defying Napoleon or the King of Sweden are remote. As a profession, archivists can and should publicly comment on such violations of archival integrity, even if it is just for the record, even if the chances of restitution are small.

The third ICA provision is straightforward enough; it calls for protecting the authenticity of the collection. The fourth provision again enters difficult territory. "Archivists should be aware that acquiring documents of dubious origin, however interesting, could encourage an illegal commerce. They should cooperate with other archivists and law enforcement agencies engaged in apprehending and prosecuting persons suspected of theft of archival records." Archivists should not accept stolen property; it seems self-evident. As with the trade in paintings, antiquities, and other items of cultural heritage, the sale of archives has become controversial. There is a growing imperative to investigate claims of title, and not accept the seller's first representation at face value.

The remaining provisions are more or less standard: Archivists document the life history of their collections, promote open and equal access while balancing privacy rights, avoid conflicts of interest, update their skills, and cooperate in the preservation and use of the world's documentary heritage.

The ICA has taken a strong stand against destruction of records, the acquisition of trophy archives, and the purchase of dubious collections. It aggressively promotes the protection of archives against manipulation for political reasons, and it promotes the return of displaced archives. These professional standards reinforce the SAA Code of Ethics, but fall short of any method for implementation beyond mobilizing public pressure.

Beyond a Code "Suitable for Framing"

As David Horn stressed, the Code of Ethics for Archivists is an evolving document that reflects emerging standards and changing attitudes toward what is right. There is certainly still a place for a concise summary of principles to guide archivists and to assist with communicating best practices to parent institutions and to donors. There is also an evident need for some kind of apparatus, beyond the confines of a brief Mosaic code suitable for framing, for weighing and evaluating the various dilemmas that confront archivists.

The texts of a sampling of codes of ethics can be found in appendix A at the end of this volume. For current versions, it is always wise to consult the organization's website. If one combs through these various codes, there are dozens of precepts, some highly idealistic, others rather prosaic. Some are controversial and other are plain common sense. The following list of ethical obligations was compiled from the various formulations. It is a snapshot of what professional archivists do:

1. Select archives with respect for provenance and the integrity of collections.
2. Maintain neutrality and minimize injecting personal bias into the workplace.
3. Respect and cooperate with other archives and archivists.
4. Avoid denigrating colleagues.

5. Preserve archives as artifacts from damage and theft.

6. Preserve the authenticity of content and form as evidence.

7. Promote open and equitable access to archives.

8. Promptly publish descriptions of records.

9. Provide helpful reference service.

10. Minimize fees and other obstacles to use.

11. Treat researchers equally.

12. Protect privacy and confidentiality.

13. Protect researchers' privacy by not revealing what materials they use to others.

14. Inform researchers of parallel use only after securing permission from each.

15. Oppose censorship.

16. Respect intellectual property laws.

17. Honor donor contracts and legitimate restrictions.

18. Work with donors to minimize restrictions.

19. Balance open access with protection of privacy.

20. Assist in the repatriation or return of displaced or stolen archives.

21. Decline inappropriate gifts from researchers, donors, and vendors.

22. Avoid conflicts of interest.

23. Avoid personal collecting that competes with one's institution.

24. Avoid outside employment that competes with one's institution.

25. Avoid dealing in archives personally.

26. Avoid making fiscal appraisals for donors to one's own institution.

27. Avoid sequestering archival materials for one's own research in competition with other researchers.

28. Turn down offers of stolen archives or forgeries.

29. Turn down offers of collections that cannot be processed promptly and professionally.

30. Make policies and restrictions public and transparent.

31. Assist policy makers in crafting archival legislation and regulations.

32. Actively participate in continuing education.

33. Obey federal, state, and local laws.

34. Fulfill a moral obligation to society.

Several badly needed safeguards are still lacking in these older codes. Only the 2007 AHA Guiding Principles address the monopolization of the information in archives for commercial profit or political advantage at the expense of research. The challenges of the digital age and globalization have not yet been addressed in formal codes.

The ethical principles under discussion are diverse in range. The emphasis among these thirty or so recurring precepts varies greatly depending on whether the documents are in a government repository, a private manuscript collection, or a private organization. Government archivists are less concerned about cooperative collecting since they have a legally mandated acquisition policy. Manuscript curators need to be very aware of conflicts of interest in negotiating with dealers and vendors. Historical societies need to be sensitive to donor relations. Business and religious archives are less concerned about providing access to outside researchers and more concerned with protecting privileged and proprietary information. In general, however, most of the rules can be applied to all areas.

There are many times when these provisions come into conflict, such as obeying the law and fulfilling an obligation to society. Many informed observers do not feel that complying with the law has any place in a statement on ethics since laws enforce existing power relationships, which may be unfair. The issue of bias is the subtext of precepts regarding acquisition, deaccessioning, access, and authenticity. Many thoughtful observers feel that neutrality is not possible; rather it is, in effect, a default decision to support the status quo. They recommend that archivists maintain objectivity without being neutral. Serving the public may require advocacy on behalf of social justice.

Leading educators such as Randall C. Jimerson have proposed using the codes of ethics or some form of guiding principles to actively promote archival values rather than simply to prevent abuses.[19] This is sometimes called the *teleological approach* to ethics, a way to define the desired results. Former SAA president Mark Greene, in his presidential address in San Francisco, August 2008, advocated promoting ten core archival values which he identified with keywords: Professionalism, Collectivity, Activism, Selection, Preservation, Democracy, Service, Diversity, Use and Access, and History.[20]

Whether or not one agrees with these specific precepts or the list of values, they all have something in common: their goal is to preserve archives as a trusted witness to what really happened. The archives are preserved to be used by independent researchers, examined from all different perspectives. Archivists need to resist the inevitable pressures to repurpose the documentation as a source of financial gain, status, privilege, political advantage, vindication, or retaliation. Archives are to be preserved as a primary source of knowledge, not instrumentalized for other agendas.

CHAPTER 2

The Ethics of Acquisition

Appraisal is the activity whereby archivists identify societal
processes they think are worth remembering and the records
that will foster such remembering.

—Verne Harris[1]

THE FIRST STAGE IN THE LIFE CYCLE OF ARCHIVES IS APPRAISAL AND ACQUISITION. It may involve the selection and transfer of nonactive records to an in-house repository, or it may involve the donation or purchase of manuscripts for research use in a library. Whether through transfers, gifts, loans, or purchases, acquisition decisions directly impact the effectiveness of archival institutions and the profession as a whole. Indirectly, they have intentional (as well as unintended) consequences for research in general and for the shaping of historical memory. These consequences justify the extra time and extra effort needed to comply with ethical requirements, even in a work world filled with competing demands and constrained by limited budgets.

The following example demonstrates how acquisitions procedures can have a drastic impact on the fate of a collection. The Bancroft Library at the University of California acquired the literary papers of the celebrated American author William Saroyan. The collection documented the life and work of a major cultural figure in California. According to press reports, the university assumed it had legal title. The Bancroft's long-term director,

James Hart, had been a close personal friend of the writer. Various portions of the collection had been placed in the Bancroft starting in the 1960s, and continuing into the 1980s. There was no deed of gift. Hart died in 1990. In 1996, the Bancroft unexpectedly received a letter demanding that the rich literary material that constitutes the Saroyan collection be relinquished. This is the letter no archivist wants to receive. The collection was removed by the Saroyan Foundation decades after the initial deposit and re-gifted to the Special Collections Department of Stanford University.[2]

Competition between repositories has been a long-standing problem, often addressed in codes of ethics. Sometimes what is legal may not be ethical. Sometimes good ethics require due diligence about tedious forms and paperwork. Challenges to legal title and ownership are relatively common. It may be a startling case as with the Saroyan papers, or it may simply be the relative of a donor who comes in and asks to retrieve the family treasures. What is best practice and what are the desired results? With consequences such as these, the field of acquisitions deserves serious attention.

A good place to begin the discussion is with some definitions. There are several overlapping terms for the acquisition of archival or manuscript materials, the first step in the archival process. *Appraising* is used in the specialized sense of determining which documents have permanent historical or evidentiary value, not in the more colloquial meaning of setting monetary value. *Solicitation, collection development*, and *documentation strategy* imply proactively seeking appropriate collections. *Loans* and *deposits* are included in the general field of acquisitions. *Accretion, accrual*, and *increment* usually refer to additions to existing collections. *Accession*, either as a noun or a verb, typically combines the roles of acquiring and describing new materials when they are officially added to the archives. *Acquisition* is the most general umbrella term, sometimes used in the singular and sometimes in the plural. The best definition of the process is fairly straightforward. "Acquisition: The process by which archives add to their holdings by accepting material as a transfer, donation, loan or purchase."[3] The definition may seem obvious, but the reality behind it is more complex.

Acquisition procedures take different forms depending on the nature of the repository. Government archives and business archives work with transfer agreements and retention cycles. Private and local archives typically grow through gifts or donations. Many fine manuscript collections depend upon commercial purchases from dealers and auction houses. Often a given repository will rely on a mix of these three main categories, each of which has its own unique complex of issues. The following discussion highlights only the ethical quandaries that come up and does not duplicate or replace the manuals on the subject. This chapter will sketch the terrain in general terms. Each working professional needs to draw up a specific map for navigating around problem areas based on the particulars of an individual acquisitions program. The twenty questions listed at the end of the chapter are intended to help acquisition specialists think through the issues to consider in mapping out a trusted collecting policy. The appendix at the end of the book provides one sample acquisitions policy as a useful model that can be adapted or used as a point of departure for hand crafting an institution-specific suite of policies. Many other samples are available in the literature and online.

A Fundamental Task with an Inherent Dilemma

To start at the beginning, the accumulation of archives and noncurrent government records has roots deep in the ancient world. Ernst Posner's 1972 book on the subject takes the process back to the cuneiform-imprinted clay tablets of Mesopotamia, tablets which often had neat clay labels for identification. Cuneiform documents belong to a continuous tradition that lasted for some three thousand years, far longer than our paper-based practice has been in existence. Posner cites an inscription on an Assyrian building, from the thirteenth century BCE—an inscription that references an even older temple that had been built 580 years prior to the existing monument. He extrapolates that some overworked Mesopotamian clay tablet manager must have been "called upon to furnish information for commemorative inscriptions."[4] It is easy to visualize the powerful ruler asking the custodian of cuneiform records for the date of the earlier building, and the scribe then scrambling among the heavy ceramic documents, fervently hoping that the right chunk of clay had been transferred to the archives centuries before to answer his sovereign's urgent question. Many contemporary archivists have been faced with similar requests: "Do we still have the original blueprints for our building?" In response, the archivist may have to spend hours shifting heavy, oversize boxes, all the while hoping the earlier generation of archivists knew enough to save those fundamental architectural drawings. The ancients knew that collecting archives is important. In fact ancient Babylon's pantheon included one god who presided over archives, Nabu, and also a scribe-goddess, Belet-seri, who kept accurate records. One could make the case that acquiring archives is a fundamental task in any civilized state.

Few archivists are aware at the beginning of their careers just how complex acquisition policies can be. Based on cumulative experience, most practitioners develop, over time, a certain intuition for where the pitfalls are and how to avoid them. The intuition that comes from experience is eventually useful, but it can be painful to acquire. There is a positive side: the very act of selecting materials to save adds value to them. The value is enhanced every time researchers read those materials and bring their own knowledge to bear. The excitement of initiating this scholarly communication with a new acquisition is tempered by the sense of a certain responsibility and trust.

A good acquisitions archivist knows when it is important to collect seemingly unimportant records, even—in some cases— laundry receipts, which can document where a person was on a particular date. No documents, no truth, no history. There are also times when an ethical archivist resolutely turns down attractive donations, as when the papers have an unclear title or when they might pose a financial liability for the archives. In this light, acquiring archives takes on an essential gravity that may not be obvious to the casual observer or the new employee. Here is the essential dilemma: collecting an incomplete record presents a distorted version of events, but a complete set may be too big to search at all. In the last two decades this dilemma has intensified. Electronic records, often vast and unruly, are even more difficult to capture and preserve than traditional paper records.

Collecting archives, then, is a fundamental task of a civilized society, and one that entails some inherent quandaries.

A Map of the Ethical Minefield

What at first glance seems like a simple maneuver, transferring papers from an office or a donated collection from a private home to a formal repository, turns out on closer examination to be surprisingly complex. Ensuring compliance with ethical and procedural requirements at this early stage will prevent a cascade of problems from developing down the road. It is not an accident that the longest section of the groundbreaking SAA manual by Gary M. Peterson and Trudy Huskamp Peterson on archives and the law was devoted to the cluster of issues surrounding acquisitions.[5] In *Navigating Legal Issues in Archives*, Menzi L. Behrnd-Klodt pays extensive attention to three major areas: acquisitions, copyright, and privacy.[6] In the case studies examined in Karen Benedict's pioneering volume on archival ethics, many of the cases stem either directly or indirectly from flawed acquisitions practices. "Procedures for acquisition of collections, especially the lack of signed legal instruments for the donation or deposit of holdings, are a major bane of archives and archivists."[7] Verne Harris has explicated the moral implications of the appraisal process: What does society retain and how does it weave these shreds of history into a narrative? "Appraisal is the telling of a story using records systems and the sites of records creation as the primary raw materials."[8]

Appraising, selecting, and acquiring electronic records involve even greater challenges than those posed by paper records. For example, what does one do with voluminous casual emails, which the writers frequently treat as private conversational communications, yet are crucial to understanding "what really happened," as Leopold von Ranke demanded. Acquiring and preserving email as essential documentation has been an issue since the very beginnings of this technology. During the Iran-Contra investigations of the 1980s, Oliver North assumed that, unlike official memos, email was unofficial communication, easy to delete. The investigators were eventually able to recover the messages as evidence, but it took such a long time that the political impact was blunted.[9] Stated in the simplest terms, democracy works best when there is an understanding of essential records and the motivation to have them archived. Beyond the technical difficulties of appraising and selecting, preserving email and electronic documentation in general is fraught with privacy, authenticity, and copyright issues just as the preservation of paper records is. Most of all, it is the sheer quantity of electronic information that is the biggest obstacle to capturing the record needed in a civilized democracy. Even with massive modern records, completeness is still an issue. Sins of omission are more common than not. A collection assembled without careful thought will typically leave out the essential background story on turning points in history.

In tackling these issues one needs to remember that professional ethics and professionalism cannot be separated. The first essential step is a thorough reading of some fundamental texts such as the classic by T. R. Schellenberg, *The Appraisal of Modern Public Records*[10] and more current work such as Frank Boles's *Selecting and Appraising Archives and Manuscripts,* from SAA's Archival Fundamentals Series II.[11] The index to Boles's volume does not have an entry for *ethics* simply because the topic is interwoven through his entire discussion. The acquisitions literature provides the fundamentals on necessary forms, samples of policies, and the intricacies of donor relations, so there is no need to duplicate that information here.

Shortcuts by undertrained or underfinanced staff are as problematic as they are common. Many repositories, especially those administered by charismatic collectors, have tried an entrepreneurial approach of building acquisitions first and postponing those pesky procedures of appraisal, determining legal ownership, securing title, and negotiating restrictions and access policies until some later time. Whether due to lack of funds or lack of professional staff, or both, collections have frequently begun as growing accumulations of papers, tapes, and drives without systematic donor files or adequate intellectual control. The results are consistent: providing deeds of gift and establishing equitable access policies after taking custody of records will always be more difficult and time consuming than folding them into the acquisitions process from the beginning. As the Saroyan case shows, at times the retrospective work is impossible or too late. The same dynamic can occur with underfunded repositories in which dedicated professionals are simply unable to keep all the bases covered.

In some of the most egregious cases, well-intentioned archival programs simply unravel. The sad history of the venerable New-York Historical Society demonstrates the perils: A careful study by Kevin M. Guthrie determined that the "Society's history provides a dramatic illustration of what can happen when the relationship between an institution's mission and its collections is not carefully managed. The uncritical accumulation of materials for many, many years played a major role in creating financial obligations that far exceed the Society's present capacity to meet them."[12] This case will be examined in detail in chapter 3. More than one important repository has been cavalier about paperwork while aggressively collecting: some valuable collections that are acquired without deeds of gift are eventually reclaimed by previous owners, and other messy acquisitions become tied up in litigation and controversy over access and ownership. The waste of effort and money can be monumental, and most of all the loss to research can be tragic in such situations. One should, by all means, take advantage of the dynamic leader to attract donors, as long as that charisma is tempered by someone who knows the nuts and bolts of ethical acquisitions.

Mission Statements and Collaborative Collecting

While it may sound self-evident, a mission statement is essential and needs to be spelled out with some attention to detail. Acquisitions programs are strengthened and many potential conflicts are automatically averted when the repository's administration has a clearly articulated sense of mission and purpose. The 2005 SAA Code of Ethics explicitly advocates the advantages of a collaborative "guild" approach to collecting policy in section 2: "Archivists cooperate, collaborate, and respect each institution and its mission and collecting policy." In order to respect the mission and collecting policy, they first have to exist, be drafted, approved, periodically updated, posted on the website and distributed. Samples of mission statements and collecting policies can be found in various publications of the Society of American Archivists. One model worth emulating is the set of clear collecting policies posted by the American Heritage Center of the University of Wyoming, available on its website, and found in appendix B.[13]

Once the senior staff formulates a focused mission statement—stakes out its territory, in a sense—the repository can then coordinate with other archives in a rationalized network that divides collecting responsibilities into logical groupings. The vexed task of assembling a complete yet accessible archival record is distributed among a variety of institutions according to areas of expertise. This somewhat utopian vision would diminish wasteful competition, and maintain the integrity of collections by keeping them together as a coherent whole rather than splitting them up among various locations. And related collections would be housed together for the benefit of researchers.

Formalized collection coordination, such as the library world's Farmington Plan[14] or the former Conspectus program of the Research Libraries Group in the 1970s and 1980s, provides an idealized model for collaborative collection development. Compliance is always voluntary and based on good will. Certainly some competition and overlapping collecting can be healthy. Duplicate collecting has the advantage of maximizing long-term preservation and safety from natural disaster, the principle sometimes called "lots of copies keep stuff safe." And a limited number of competing research centers, if they are geographically dispersed around the country, will facilitate research by shortening travel time for local scholars. While respecting these qualifications and exceptions, collaborative collecting as a general principle no doubt maximizes what each repository can accomplish with its budget and staff. It maximizes the research value for scholars. Informal referral networks based on collegial relationships have proven themselves as more effective than formal agreements in steering collections in the right direction and avoiding the dismemberment of documents and collections.

Sharing collecting responsibilities is as much a necessity as a courtesy. No repository, however large, can be comprehensive. Even the vast U.S. National Archives and Records Administration specializes in preserving selected official American government records. It would not make sense for NARA to enter the field of international literary manuscripts, for example. Likewise it would be foolish for a literary repository to collect records generated by a U.S. government office. Increasingly this latter point is a matter of law: government-generated records should be recognized as government property. It is also a matter of ethics: government records are best maintained together with related materials by experts trained in the intricacies of the bureaucracy. And it makes good sense.

Surprisingly, then, large quantities of government records have escaped into private repositories, including documents with security classified markings, such as "Top Secret." The keeping of official government archives has a highly inconsistent history in the United States, with lapses that verge on the irresponsible. Unlike European officials, their American counterparts, especially in earlier eras, often treated correspondence and memoranda as personal property in a way that would be unthinkable in most countries. Government workers who would never consider stealing a statue in the hallway walked off with packing boxes full of government documents when they left office. These documents can show up in donations from private individuals.

Even U.S. presidential papers were considered the president's personal property until the 1978 Presidential Records Act which did not go into effect until 1981, astonishingly late. The fifty states did not consistently assert ownership of gubernatorial papers until recently. Sometimes they did not have adequate housing, as was the case in California for most of the twentieth century until the construction in 1995 of a new archives facility in Sacramento. Legislation formalized the state's ownership only after much California history disappeared into private hands.

The dislocations created by this situation in past decades is unlikely to be rectified retroactively as retrieving stray government records involves prohibitive expense and unpleasant disputes. Transferring government documents out of private hands into official archives may never happen on a systematic scale. Prevention is perhaps the only cure. It is important to remember that this historically casual approach to government records in the United States is no longer acceptable. Past practice is not considered best practice. Without some very persuasive justification, the ethical archivist in a private repository will turn down the offer of papers that are government property and refer the donor to the appropriate official in the local, state, or the national archives.

Thus, the ethical archivist makes objective recommendations on the best home for collections. Sometimes this means turning away a valuable collection that is out of scope and finding a more suitable archival home for it. An acquisitions archivist's loyalty to broad professional standards will ultimately profit the home institution. If all acquisitions curators did this in a symmetrical way, the mutual benefit would be enormous. If some follow these guidelines, while others "poach" on other specialties or troll for inappropriate trophy collections, the disposition of materials becomes distorted. Worse, there is an impact on the marketplace for manuscripts, and prices can be driven up artificially. Moreover, out-of-scope collecting complicates the work of research which flourishes when related materials are held together in the same place.

Split Collections and Dismembered Documents

Financial exigency, divorce, arguments, emigration, war, travel, and legal disputes all have a way of splitting up collections even as they are formed. Often such vandalism is technically legal, but with care the damage can be prevented or at least minimized. When experienced curators are offered a new collection, they know to investigate whether there are dispersed components at other locations. Ethical collectors advise donors and sellers on the advantages of retaining the integrity of a collection, even if it means resisting financial gain. When the division of a collection is unavoidable, the next step is to share finding aids, descriptions, and even copies if possible.

While very few collections are what could be called totally "complete," the venerable archival principle of *respect de l'intégrité des fonds* is still the prevailing ideal.

The Martin Luther King Jr. papers are a classic example of a split collection.[15] (This example will be examined in greater detail as a case study at the end of the chapter.) There are three competing institutions with King papers, much to the distress of researchers. By coordinating efforts repositories can help maintain the integrity of collections and facilitate scholarship. Both the Society of American Archivist's 2005 Code of Ethics, section 5, and the International Council on Archives Code of Ethics, section 2, promote the efforts to keep collections intact. One can approach the issue either inductively using examples, such as the Martin Luther King Jr. papers, or deductively using general principles. The conclusion is the same: treating archives as trophies or as a source of windfall profit often results in divided collections and reduces their research value. Researchers and the general public benefit from preserving collections as an organic whole rather than splintering them.

The author is familiar with one case in which a film collector offered his vast set of historic footage to a private repository, and he demanded an equally vast price, well beyond the archives' budget. After the collector's death, his heirs sold the collection to the same repository for a much-reduced sum. Thrilled and self-congratulatory with the benefits of waiting out the issue, the acquisitions archivist was unaware that the heirs had split the collection and sold half of it to an individual private collector thousands of miles away. This action was perfectly legal, and it made good financial sense. The film collection was their private property, but dividing it violated the integrity of the collection. Greed is not the only motive. Some donors try to please several constituencies by providing gifts of papers to the archives of several favorite organizations. Archivists simply need to be alert to this possibility and provide the donors and their families with guidance. It is much better to learn this lesson from case studies than from actual experience.

Throughout history, split collections and divided manuscripts have obstructed research. Biblical scholarship, for example, has been complicated by the dispersal of source manuscripts. About half of the fourth century Codex Sinaiticus, considered one of the oldest and most complete Greek manuscripts of the Christian Bible, has survived. These remaining pages have been separated with unequal portions located in four disparate locations. After a detour to Leningrad, the largest portion is now in the British Library. Orphaned pages and fragments are also located in St. Catherine's Monastery near Mount Sinai in Egypt, at the University of Leipzig in Germany, and in the Russian National Library in St. Petersburg. While the monks of St. Catherine's Monastery consider the dispersed pages stolen property, none of these other sites would willingly surrender such a cultural treasure. The leaves have been dispersed for more than a century and a half.

In 2009 a digital version finally reunited the remaining text of the Codex Sinaiticus for the benefit of scholarship and also for the appreciation of the manuscript as an aesthetic, historical, and venerated object.[16] While a virtually reunited document is a great boon to scholars, it does not exonerate theft in any way. On a practical level, virtual documents are never as valuable without the intact original as the basis for authentication. And certainly the digital surrogate image does not retain the tangible aura of the real thing.

The Codex Sinaiticus was dismembered by overly zealous nineteenth-century scholars. Dealers frequently commit intentional damage. Old manuscripts, especially illuminated ones, are often torn apart so that each leaf can be sold separately for a higher total price, and thus the intellectual and aesthetic coherence of the original work is compromised. If pages disappear into various private hands, it may become impossible to reassemble even a digital facsimile of the whole from the separated parts. If the heirs of the purchasers do not understand the value of the individual sheet of paper, the chances of loss are very great. The cultural damage done by the practice of dividing manuscript pages has been enormous.

Looting and dismemberment of manuscripts seem to go together. An exhibition at the Morgan Library in 2009 highlighted the career of an Italian abbot named Luigi Celotti who acquired choir books that the French had looted from the Sistine Chapel. He cut out the miniatures and borders and reassembled them for sale in London at Christie's in 1825.[17]

Another classical example of this reprehensible practice was the work of the unscrupulous Parisian dealer Georges Demotte (1877–1923) who tore apart the pages of priceless illuminated seventeenth-century Mughal dynasty manuscripts from India, even splitting the individual folio pages to sell each side, recto and verso, separately to maximize profit. It is the archival equivalent of melting down fine jewelry for the value of the gold metal alone. Demotte was responsible for the loss of context about the refined culture that produced extraordinary manuscripts and miniature paintings—the same culture that created architectural marvels such as the Taj Mahal.[18] One of these Mughal treasures, the "Late Shah Jahan Album," was produced ca. 1650–1658. It was looted during the sack of Delhi in 1739 during Nadir Shah's invasion of India. In the late nineteenth century it was taken to Russia and eventually landed in the hands of an Armenian dealer who took it to Paris in 1909, where it was sold to the notorious Georges Demotte. He mutilated the manuscripts to maximize sales: among other things he cut and pasted miniatures over calligraphy. The one hundred known surviving leaves of this particular album are scattered in eighteen different collections in seven different countries. Many leaves are assumed to be hidden in private collections. For scholars, "trying to examine all of these firsthand is almost impossible."[19] As a result the works are difficult to date, and much text has been obliterated.

One would like to think that these nineteenth- and early twentieth-century cases are relics of the past. Unfortunately the practice of separating the leaves of codices continues. Purchasing such separated leaves encourages a business practice that literally dismembers cultural heritage. There is evidence that this destructive practice has been accelerating in recent years to take advantage of loosely controlled online auction websites such as eBay. The accelerating commodification of cultural property is becoming a danger to the integrity of the historical record.

Not just dealers are at fault. Likewise, in the case of institutional records or literary manuscripts, private owners often are tempted to remove and sell off individual pieces, separate items with notable autographs, for example.

The owners may be oblivious of the damage to the intellectual coherence of the collection as they introduce gaps into the record. Individual manuscripts and archival collections are frequently split up by the estate or even the creator of the records for a large variety of reasons. Sometimes simple financial distress motivates the owners of valuable papers to sell off separate lots of papers over the years to the highest bidder as needed.

As professionals sensitive to these issues, archivists can counsel the owners about preserving the integrity of their documents. Recommendations can be made as to the most appropriate home for the materials. There are ways to compensate for perceived financial disadvantages of retaining the integrity of a collection. When such donations are eligible for tax breaks, the archivist can provide a list of experienced appraisers, so that the donor may select one to help with tax deductions. At times, tax deductions for gifts can be as advantageous as a sale. Ascertaining the eligibility of a donation for a tax break requires some research. The archivist must be careful not to give tax advice, but rather remind the donor to explore the possibilities with a qualified tax advisor.

Generally speaking donors are flattered to learn of the greater value of an intact collection, and can be influenced to follow ethical guidelines. Good publicity and a well-designed exhibition of a new collection are often worth more to the donors or sellers than maximizing the cash payout. An ethical acquisitions negotiation requires extensive discussion. It is necessary to offer the owners of cultural legacy all the appropriate options.

In certain circumstances it can require fortitude on the part of an acquisitions archivist to turn down the offer of a partial collection or fragmentary document and to encourage its reunification with the rest of the original material. There may be pressures from the parent institution to accept it as a matter of prestige or to accommodate the interests of financial supporters. If the mission statement and collecting policy are in place in advance of such offers, and if they are well written, the justification will be much clearer to higher management, and pressures will be easier to resist.

There may be exceptional situations in which it is simply best for the materials if the curator decides to acquire separated and orphaned documentation to preserve it, especially if the current owner is unlikely to reunite it with the rest of the collection or unable to protect it from damage. Such decisions require a certain finesse, extensive knowledge of the field, good communications with colleagues in the field, and above all the ability to place the integrity of the historical legacy above immediate advantages. The long-term welfare of the archives and its parent institution should be taken into account and weighed in the balance. Such decisions should be carefully documented with the reasons for making an exception to the rule of preserving the integrity of the fond or collection.

It is widely acknowledged that carefully coordinated specialization is mutually beneficial and maximizes the financial reach of each institution, large and small. A coherent archival collection almost invariably has in its history an administrator who was able to turn down a collection as inappropriate. Knowing what not to collect is just as important as knowing what to acquire. That is why the mission statement is the key to keeping the collection focused and consistent with ethical collaborative practices.

Diplomatic skills are of great use in maintaining an ethical practice. With practiced tact, influence can be applied both to donors and to the parent institution. Due to the technical requirements of the collecting process, the mission statement must be written with significant input from practicing archivists.

The Authority to Collect

Well-publicized mission statements facilitate collaborative collection development, a basic ethical principle that promotes the integrity of collections in a mutually beneficial manner. Closely related to the mission statement is the authority to collect. Collecting policies and guidelines expand on these two basic documents, and define how the mission will be implemented in concrete terms. Traditional archives have been governmental offices of sovereign states. The mandate to collect has been built into the legal structure for the government to manage its own property. The transfer is from one internal department to another. In these cases the mandate is fairly self-evident, but the work benefits when the authorization is spelled out on two levels. The exact legislation authorizing the archives should be clear and simple. Then it is supplemented by procedural regulations that can be easily modified as the situation changes. What are the obligations of the departments to preserve and turn over noncurrent records? What are the retention and disposal cycles? Who is responsible for selection?

Transfers of Government Records

The way in which government agencies transfer noncurrent records to the archives is a technical subject in its own right. What the ethical archivist needs to be aware of is how the custody of archival records is in some sense a map of power relationships and a test of sovereignty. After the fall of communism in the Soviet Union in 1991, President Yeltsin issued a presidential decree for the preservation of government archives. The decree mandated the transfer of obsolete records from the Soviet Foreign Ministry to the newly reorganized State Archives of the Russian Federation. Yeltsin claimed the records as property of the state. Decree or no decree, the transfer never took place. The ministry insisted on guarding its own history and had the power to do so. Likewise, transfer of the Soviet KGB files to the new Russian Archives Service was ordered, and ignored. In apartheid-era South Africa the security services simply destroyed documents rather than turn them over to the national archives, which was perceived as hostile once it was run by the new democratic regime.[20] Implementing seemingly self-evident principles will not infrequently trigger power struggles with unpredictable outcomes.

Government archives belong as property to the government, which in general terms has the legal power to keep or destroy or restrict them at will. Ethical issues begin to apply as a government recognizes the right of the public in a democracy to accurate information about its leaders, the rights of one branch of government to know what is going on in another branch, and the rights of historians to primary sources in the great tradition of Leopold von Ranke. Here again access is a map of power. Technical legal requirements can be manipulated and changed by those with authority. As described above, government archives generally have two types of authorization documents: a legislative mandate to follow, and then as a separate document a more detailed acquisitions policy that is easy to update as needed. One issue that has been debated extensively is just who is responsible for selection of the records to be retained. Traditionalists such as Jenkinson place the responsibility with the office that generated the papers in the first place on the assumption that it knows best what is important.[21] In practice government offices are focused on current operations, and not primarily concerned with their own history. For that reason the trend has been for subject specialists within the archives to take on the responsibility for selection, a task with weighty implications.[22] In an ideal world the originating agency begins the appraisal process. The archives oversees implementation of retention cycles and completes the appraisal after taking custody.

The importance of ethics comes into play on both collective and individual levels. Two generally accepted principles should inform legislation governing the retention of documents by official agencies: (1) Archivists need to have the authority to ensure that documents are preserved long enough to be evaluated for enduring value and not destroyed until that determination has been made, and (2) a democratic society makes the information in its documents accessible to the greatest extent possible, consistent with protection of state security and the privacy of its citizens. The next level of ethics confronts individual government employees. If, for example, a supervisor orders that certain internal emails be deleted and there is a mandate to preserve records for evaluation by the archives, the employee has some difficult decisions to make. Destruction of legal evidence is, after all, a criminal offense. Here the value of a written mandate becomes clear.

Transfers of Business Records

In a mechanism analogous to governmental archives, private organizations and commercial ventures retain certain files of permanent interest that they generate themselves in the course of doing business. Again, it is private property that they produced and they own. The organization or business needs to draft some kind of mandate for the preservation of essential records. The mandate should assign responsibility to one office. Sometimes business archives begin as a subsidiary of the information technology (IT) department or as part of the legal office. It is not a bad idea to have a lawyer-archivist oversee essential records. Business recordkeeping generally starts with the retention of files for legal, tax, and audit purposes, and then often expands into organizational history, documentation for annual reports, and public relations. As with government archives, organizational and business archives benefit from both a clear mandate stating authority to collect (citing the date of a resolution at a board of trustees meeting, for example) and a fuller acquisitions plan that clarifies points such as whether to collect from outside the organization to supplement internal files, access policies, etc.

The mandate should clarify lines of responsibility for selecting, transferring, and establishing retention schedules. Without clear authorization, there will be duplication of effort and inconsistent preservation habits. That all sounds well and good, but implementing systematic cross-departmental recordkeeping is never simple. Lateral attempts at coordination will usually run afoul of the territorial instincts of managers. Leadership and directives need to come from the top of the hierarchy.

As with government records, private business records are increasingly understood as a cultural legacy belonging to society as a whole with the ethical dimensions that entails. Ethical business archivists are very alert to both official and unstated boundaries between proprietary information for internal use only and public information. A careful access policy defining that boundary prevents conflicts over time as both internal and outside researchers request to see documents. Even in a private business archives, archivists occupy a position of public trust. They balance transparency while protecting confidential information, knowing that sensitive material that is not carefully restricted is likely to be destroyed.

Ernst Posner explained the traditional belief that the best archivists were by nature private people not given to gossip. The archivist "must not be talkative, but must have his tongue in his heart and not his heart upon his tongue. He should have adequate fundaments and should in general talk very little lest he blab out the secrets of his registry."[23] While the protection of state and trade secrets remains important, Posner did not anticipate the role of archives in public relations—a role which requires archivists to publicly advertise and interpret their holdings. (Wells Fargo Bank, for example, used its corporate archives to good advantage to strengthen its corporate identity going back to the era of stage coaches.) Balancing open communication with the public and guarding privileged information will remain a challenge for business archivists.

Private and Nonprofit Collections

The United States enjoys a rich tradition of private and nonprofit archives. Most of them build their collections through donations. Private collectors can be individuals, historical societies, special interest clubs, or research institutions in the full range of sizes and resources from impoverished to heavily financed. University archives are often especially distinguished. Acquisition archivists at these institutions develop sometimes elaborate programs of donor relations to build up a network of supporters and contributors, usually centered around a common interest in local history or a particular historical subject. While gifts have been the norm, in our free market society it is easy for these private collectors and independent institutions to purchase archival materials as normal property. Often there are hybrid situations, such as a business archives that purchases private papers that supplement institutional history, or a university archives that expands into collecting related materials from alumni bequests or auctions either related to university history or the interests of faculty.

When the ownership and title to papers change hands, unlike the simple departmental transfers in government or business archives, the ethical and legal problems are complex. Privately run, self-appointed archives should draft a mandate or founding document authorizing collecting, just as government archives do. Legal counsel is absolutely necessary to establish the appropriate standing to accept donations as tax deductible gifts. The lawyers are responsible for getting the paperwork filed properly. The ethical archivist is required to involve lawyers at the right times, especially when a collection is founded or reorganized, and to call in counsel for periodic review of procedures.

These organizations have a greater need for a detailed and coherent collection policy than government archives do. The ethical archivist knows to keep his own repository's collecting policy up to date and to implement the policy in a focused way. Collecting policies, discussed below, help keep donor relations professional and straightforward. The desired outcome, from an ethics point of view, is to create a rich collection without encumbering the institution with unrealistic financial obligations for storage, maintenance, and use.

Many individual collectors, obviously, have no mandate or authorization to collect beyond the funds to purchase at auction, and lack the networking skills to garner donated materials. Such collectors are much less likely to have any written collecting policies beyond personal interest. They actually need those tools as much as government or business offices. Such collectors should be just as fastidious about contracts.

Deeds of gift and warranty of title are just as essential for acquisition of archival documents as for the acquisition of a car or piece of real estate. While rare, private collections assembled by wealthy individuals famously form the basis of a number of great libraries and archives. Private collections of rare books and manuscripts are more feasible than private collections of archival collections. Digital collections may start modestly as a history teacher's syllabus and then expand in importance beyond the classroom. Founding a private archival collection is not easy to do well. The author knows a number of distinguished individuals who attempted to create scholarly archival collections on particular topics without institutional support, professional staff, and a clear mandate. They were rapidly disillusioned.

Harmonizing Policies with a Parent Organization

Few archives are able to exist independently. Most are embedded in a larger organization that provides funding, manages personnel, and hosts the archives in its facilities. This support also creates dependency on the good will and understanding of the host organization and its own network of sponsors. And it sets the stage for various conflict of interest scenarios. While building archives without a parent institution is almost impossible, building them within a parent institution creates two sets of missions. These separate agendas at times collide. The issues tend to arise from the complexity of maintaining professionalism within a larger institution with different priorities.

Several of the ethics case studies examined in Karen Benedict's book involve this relationship between the archives and the parent institution, starting with case 1.[24] In this example, a long-term member of the host institution has a sense of entitlement to an informal appraisal of his donations, even though it is considered a conflict of interest for the receiving institution to assign monetary value for a donor's tax deduction. The correct answer is to provide the donor with an acknowledgment letter that describes the gift, and states that no items of value were given to the donor in exchange. This letter would be enough to substantiate a small tax deduction, and to provide documentation for a professional appraisal that would justify a larger deduction. The subtext of case 1 is fear of alienating the host institution's supporters. This apprehension is based on the real possibility of serious negative repercussions: loss of standing with the parent institution, possible reduction in support and funding. The best protection is a reputation for solid professionalism backed up by written and widely distributed policies.

The Society of American Archivists has provided a genuine service by publishing brochures on the process of setting up a collection and the principles that apply. This is objective professional advice and can help the working archivist demonstrate that the ethical guidelines are generally accepted and not his or her own invention. These can be found on the SAA website under "Publications, Brochures."[25]

In case 32 of Benedict's book, a major financial donor demands the destruction of a letter in a collection that defames a deceased relative.[26] The suggested solution involves temporary restriction rather than destroying the document or imposing a long-term restriction. The solution preserves the document for future research and simultaneously addresses the privacy concerns of the family. Again, as in case 1, the subtext is the implicit threat that the donor will withhold future funds if his demands are not met. Harmonizing professional standards with donor requirements is one of the daily tasks of the ethical archivist. It can be difficult or even impossible to implement best practice without prior good will. Good relations with donors, typically generated by frequent tours and presentations, create a sense of professional authority that is like money in the bank when the time comes to negotiate.

For private institutions, the issue is harmonizing professional standards with the demands of the parent institution and its financial donors, who typically receive a tax benefit for their gifts. Financial donors can readily find a different beneficiary for their largess. Their personalities and interests will shape the collecting opportunities available to the archives, and influence the style and image of the archives.

For governmental institutions, the issue is harmonizing professional standards of a civil service with the demands of appointed chiefs, who typically represent the interests of a political party. For entry-level archivists the exposure is minimal, though there may be pressure to suppress compromising information.

Just as legal requirements for nonprofit organizations are different from profit-centered corporations, the ethical requirements can be different as well. While corporate archivists are charged by law with preserving documentation required for tax and audit purposes, they also protect proprietary information and keep company trade secrets. Restricting the information in archives is more acceptable in a corporate archives than in a nonprofit one. There are exceptions. Corporate archivists also open records to assist in managing the company's public image by participating in public relations work, by using photographs and company history to create good will. They need to be able to locate materials during litigation. Anticipating this function in acquisitions work, they need to clarify which records must be restricted and which can be made public. The parent organization funds the archives in part out of the requirements for risk management, and the archivists as a result need to be protective of the company's reputation unless there is a higher issue at stake, such as public safety. Since papers can pile up quickly, they need to have a retention and disposal cycle in place even before the documents are transmitted to the archives from offices. Instead of a deed of gift they need transfer documents that record retention and confidentiality requirements.

Establishing Guidelines and Collection Policies

One way to avoid some of these acquisition quandaries is through appraisal guidelines and collection development policies. Guidelines can be very simple in outlining what types of materials are sought, what topics and subject areas are of interest. Both focus and flexibility in collecting scope are important. Focus provides the archives with a demonstrable area of expertise that will be a magnet for other materials of that type. It can deflect pressure to collect superfluous, out-of-scope collections. Flexibility is essential in making strategic exceptions to the collection scope. Accepting an occasional "vanity collection" is not unethical. As Frank Boles points out: "To argue against a ten-foot, out-of-scope acquisition that is associated with a $10 million gift is both a losing proposition and a foolish one."[27] The ethical archivist needs to balance focus and flexibility, harmonize the mission of archives with the mission of the parent institution.

In addition to subject areas, the guidelines should deal with the context of the materials. New acquisitions should have a detailed and verifiable provenance; the donor or seller should be able to demonstrate a clear warranty of title. Guidelines should also define what types of materials are not sought. It could be very helpful, for instance, if the guidelines exclude collections that consist of newspaper clippings from newspapers that have already been digitized and indexed in major databases. A donor may treasure a clipping album assembled by a beloved relative and assume that the archives shares the emotional connection. With prior written instructions, it is somewhat easier to maintain professional objectivity in the face of pressure.

There are other factors that may be usefully included in the guidelines. There may be limits to the size of collections that can honestly be assimilated by the repository given its storage capacity and staffing levels. It is unethical to acquire a collection that cannot be properly managed within the resources of the institution.

The written policies should also explicitly state that the repository cannot supply an estimate of the financial value of a donation for tax purposes, as that is normally considered a conflict of interest. The obligation of the repository is to provide a full acknowledgment of the gift and a description of its size and content. It is possible to provide a list of several professional appraisers without recommending any one in particular. Then the repository is obligated to assist the outside appraiser in making the financial evaluation, which must be based on actually examining the collection in person. With this policy in place in writing, it is much easier to resist pressure from a donor to "just tell us what it's worth; you know better than anyone." Sometimes that donor is technically correct. As required by ethics, the author provided a donor with a list of professional appraisers, without making a particular recommendation. The donor-selected financial appraiser was challenged by the IRS for too generous a valuation. The author spent a great deal of time and research providing the appraiser with the necessary background information and text to defend the valuation rather than let the donor pay unnecessary penalties. It would have been much simpler for the archivist to do the financial appraisal in the first place with the proper explanations and citations, but it would have constituted a conflict of interest.

According to Frank Boles, serious attention needs to be paid to "a deed of gift, one of the most important legal documents the archivist will ever sign."[28] The Saroyan and King examples alone are enough to serve as a warning. Firm documentation of title is the backbone of protecting one's holdings. If the deed covers the key provisions, a host of problems will be prevented. Ownership—clear title to the physical papers—is just one component. Intellectual property needs to be clarified. Who owns the copyright and how is it to be administered? Do other family members or business partners have an interest in the donated papers, or think they do?

Are there competing claims to the materials? It is better to simply ask the donor about competing claims early in the negotiations, than to contend with an irate relative after paperwork has been signed.

In recent years standards on warranty of title have tightened up. A dealer's own claims of clear title, especially to Native American artifacts or materials of foreign provenance, are no longer sufficient without some kind of objective documentation of provenance. One eminent curator, Marion True of the J. Paul Getty Museum in Los Angeles, was prosecuted in Italian courts for years over purchases made through well-known dealers—a once perfectly acceptable practice that assumed the dealer would be held accountable for any dispute over ownership. This is no longer a safe assumption. In 2009, the Italian judge presiding over the case joked that he hoped it would come to a conclusion prior to his retirement in three years.[29]

The United States signed the 1970 UNESCO Convention on the Means of Prohibiting and Preventing the Illicit Import, Export and Transfer of Ownership of Cultural Property. Generally speaking, this states that foreign documents that left the country of origin after 1970 require documentation that they were legally removed and that title is valid. In 2008 the United States finally signed the 1954 Hague Convention on the Protection of Cultural Property in the Event of Armed Conflict. Many museum and archival acquisitions practices, once considered normal, are now subject to more stringent standards. As with acquiring partial collections and fragments of manuscripts, if there is a determination that the acquisition of a collection of dubious provenance will protect it from damage or loss, this should be documented as a particular exception to standard procedures to verify title. There should be provisions for return to the legal owner if conditions for preservation improve. All acquisitions archivists need to be familiar with the UNESCO Convention and the Protocols for Native American Archival Materials, discussed in greater detail in chapter 8.

The acquisitions policy should also require clarification of restrictions. Are there sensitive documents that need to be restricted to prevent invasion of privacy? Can the restrictions be kept to a minimum? Do the restrictions have an end date? Does the donor or seller understand the principle of equal access? One donor was very anxious for his father's papers to be made available for research to vindicate a controversial career. The donor was quite clear in a telephone conversation about lifting the restrictions. When one of his father's political enemies cited the papers in a negative article, the donor was incensed. He had wanted the papers shown to friendly researchers, but not to unfriendly ones. To him this was patently obvious. Equal access was not a concept for him. It is common for donors to treat the archives as their own personal property after transferring ownership. Many donors will call and say that a certain friend should have access to a closed collection. Most archives will show restricted materials to family members if the donor agrees. Another exception that proves the rule may be permitting an authorized biographer privileged access. Access must be negotiated during the acquisition process and formally stated in writing in the deed of gift itself.

Loans and deposits are a very difficult area, and need to have a sunset clause. The loan or deposit agreement should from the outset have a "vesting period" at which time the collection becomes the property of the repository unless the depositor contacts the archives prior to that cut-off date. It is fiscally irresponsible to devote institutional funds for long periods to materials that can be reclaimed by the original owner. Restrictions and access policies for loans should be as clearly delineated as those for gifts or purchases.

The repository may also need to reveal what would be expected if it experiences a sudden financial reversal. Will the repository have the authority to sell or transfer the collection in the future? To dispose of duplicate or out-of-scope materials? There are sample forms widely available that can be used for transfer of documents and title, but the wording needs to be vetted periodically by the in-house legal counsel, if possible, to bring them up to date, and to cover any problems specific to the repository.

Financial Transactions

It is the financial side of acquisitions that can be the most difficult to manage. Determining a fair price for a collection is particularly difficult with unique items—the very definition of an archival collection. There is no consistent, objective "value forum" for pricing documents. Competitive auctions are the main means of determining value in the commercial arena. Most manuscripts are sold quietly without auction competition, based on a "gentlemen's agreement" negotiated between the seller and buyer. One can and should research the selling price of similar materials whenever the data is available. Each offer creates demand, and potentially drives up the price for the next purchase. Because of the effect of gossip on price, it is best to insist on a nondisclosure clause in any bill of sale, and emphasize to the seller the seriousness of keeping the price confidential to prevent artificial booms. When the national press asserted that Stanford University had paid a high fee for the Allen Ginsberg papers, in the million dollar range, other holders of archival collections reevaluated their demands upward.[30] Competition between archives creates bad feelings and also drives up the seller's sense of entitlement. One should be alert to feigned competition and pressure tactics. Efforts to keep prices down can backfire, as happened with the film collection mentioned above. Negotiating the price should begin with a very clear description of the collection, its contents, extent, and any particularly rare or valuable items. Keeping records correlating the types of collections and the prices paid can provide parameters. The seller or donor should be aware of the huge financial investment each acquisition, even gifts, entails in storage space, staff time, and materials.

The archivist needs to be alert to a number of issues involving money and gifts. Consider the following scenarios, all of which happen with some frequency, sometimes innocently, sometimes not.

- What if the seller is a personal friend of the archives' administration? What is the appropriate response if a supervisor instructs the acquisitions archivist to purchase a collection at a level above normal market value?

- It happens that many of the best professional collectors also have their own private collecting interests: is that a conflict of interest? Is it permissible to collect privately in the same area as one collects for an employer? Should an archivist privately purchase books or manuscripts from a dealer that sells to his employer? What if the area of collecting is similar but not identical? Most codes of ethics flatly prohibit employees from collecting in the same area as their institution. The conflict of interest and the temptation to use the institution for personal gain are self-evident. And the opportunities for insider theft are dangerous.

- What if a friendly donor transfers a collection to the archives and then generously tells the acquisitions archivist to take one of the more appealing items as a Christmas present for himself? It sounds sinister, but in fact some very honorable people have been known to do just that. When is a gift a bribe for special treatment?

- What if a donor makes an unusually generous donation of rare manuscripts and then starts to make demands on the staff for special attention, perhaps favored access to restricted collections?

- What if a financial contribution is tied to acquiring certain out-of-scope materials?

- What if a financial contribution to acquire archives is diverted to nonarchival functions?

The subject of gifts is usually addressed in government archives with clear written policies, such as the federal government's Standards of Conduct. Private archives are usually less well regulated. With the very best intentions, the author has politely turned down gifts—and instructed staff to do the same—erroneously thinking the donor would be pleased with the high ethical standards in play. The generous donors often felt very insulted, especially those donors who come from cultures where gift-giving is an essential social grace. And the staff members deprived of mementos of the transaction also felt cheated. One especially thoughtful donor simply presented a gift directly to the staff member. Like government agencies, private archives should consider a similar blanket gift prohibition in a written policy. The fact is that any archivist with a substantial acquisitions budget will have many dear friends.

Purchasing archives and even acquiring them as donations will always be an inexact science. Reviewing the twenty questions at the end of this chapter, consulting with colleagues and the archives' administration, taking the time to work through each issue, and always being willing to walk away from an inappropriate situation, should provide a basis for ethical dealings. Ethical acquisition procedures are certainly a worthy goal in and of themselves. In addition, maintaining these standards will hopefully prevent a chain reaction of problems, many of which have a way of lingering for decades and longer.

The stakes are higher for nongovernmental repositories and the temptations for unethical transactions are also higher. Government archives struggle to provide a smooth working relationship between departments and the archives, but the transactions do not involve cash payments. Private archives are able to purchase materials on the market. How does one determine the fair market value of materials that are unique, one of a kind? Auctions determine value by competing bids, and artificial competition can drive the prices up to artificial levels for unethical purposes. It is worth considering an ethical acquisitions model that balances interests without opening up opportunities for abuse.

Arbitrary financial transactions are often at the heart of ethical lapses in the acquisitions process. Determining the monetary value of documents is not an exact science; there is no inerrant invisible hand of the marketplace. Donors feel cheated after gifting papers if another person signs a hefty bill of sale to transfer his treasured documents to the archives. If one seller thinks he has received less than another, the acrimony can affect donor relations.

Donations and Purchases

Over the years the commodification of archives has driven up the auction value to an extent that acquisitions budgets are seriously strained. The very purpose of archives becomes threatened by this escalating market mechanism because the most appropriate repository may not be the best funded. There is a great need for an initiative to counter this trend by making gifts or donations the default mode of archival acquisitions for most private repositories. In this scenario, purchases would be an exception that requires justification. For elite, rare manuscript libraries, which function rather like art museums, purchases will no doubt remain the main mode of building the collection. For the vast majority of private and academic archives, donations remain the only satisfactory method. If there is a general consensus to avoid bidding wars, everyone will benefit and resources will go into preservation and access rather than acquisition.

Instead of starting the acquisition process by haggling over the price of a collection, perhaps it is a useful exercise to think through what a repository pays in services for each collection it accepts. What are the elements that go into the archives' expenses? **Size** is the first consideration. Larger collections require larger storage space, more housing materials such as files and boxes, and more staff time for cataloging even at the collection level. **Research value** is an essential component of the cost to the archives. Documents with unpublished information need more detailed indexing to provide access for researchers to these new resources. Conscientious archives will process collections with high research value in greater detail than more mundane ones, and the staff costs will be correspondingly higher. **Artifactual value** plays a significant role in the cost of preservation. One need only think about the cost of housing the Declaration of Independence in the National Archives. A rare, irreplaceable document might require special high-tech security and higher than normal environmental controls.

When archival policy is properly implemented, the higher the auction value of the papers, the more expensive they are to maintain. In many cases the correlation is very close, close enough to warrant an equivalency. The auction value of a manuscript collection based on its size, research value, and artifactual value is relatively equivalent to the cost to the repository for properly processing and preserving it. The higher the monetary value, the higher the necessary institutional investment.

Bearing this in mind, one could generalize that a collection worth fifty thousand dollars, based on size, research value, and artifactual value, would over time cost the archives at least that much just to store, catalog, process, preserve, and access. If the archives promises the owner of the materials to conduct these functions in a responsible manner in keeping with the value of the collection, the archives is providing the equivalent of an honest sale price, but without the exchange of cash.

There should be a fundamental understanding that merely accepting a collection as worthy of preservation inherently covers the fair price and possibly more. Some repositories maintain that the preservation costs are higher than the auction price, and this is no doubt true in many cases. Accepting a gift is taking on a financial responsibility in perpetuity. In that sense an acquisition is not an asset, rather in business terms it is a liability. The higher the appraised value of a collection, the more expensive it is to maintain.

For purposes of maintaining an ethical practice, it would be useful to have a generally accepted acquisitions model with certain basic elements. First it should be understood that the purpose of the archives' existence is the preservation of cultural heritage. Secondly, archives cooperate in carefully assessing the nature of collections in order to place materials in the most appropriate archival setting. Third, before accepting materials, the archives must be capable of responsibly storing, processing, and preserving them. Fourth, the many layered commitments of the archives in accepting a collection typically more than cover the auction value in general terms, making gifts the most ethical and appropriate means of placing documents in archives for the long-term preservation of their cultural value. This exchange of documents for long-term curatorship is a special relationship meant to save valuable cultural heritage and should not prevent the donor from recovering the monetary auction value, at least in part, from tax deductions as prescribed in the legislation current at the time of the gift. Obviously such tax deductions would be based on independent appraisals. If private repositories were able to make the donation the primary model, much unethical practice, especially involving manuscript dealers and agents, would be circumvented.

Admittedly, this model for ethical acquisitions, resisting commodification and substituting justified donations for market purchases, is somewhat utopian. The marketplace in material culture is unlikely to go away. But using this model as a baseline helps shift values away from market considerations, such as the current auction value of an autograph, to cultural values, such as the resource value for scholarship. One of the moral foundations of archival ethics is an appreciation of the profound cultural value of archives, separate from the market value. The profession as a whole needs to create an atmosphere where this distinction is understood. A consensus on this point would help curators reinforce each other's resolve to refocus emphasis on the proper care of archival materials and our joint heritage. The deleterious effects of the commodification of archives can be seen in the history of the Martin Luther King Jr. papers.

Acquisitions Case Study: The Martin Luther King Jr. Papers

The Martin Luther King Jr. papers are a priceless American treasure. King is an icon in American history, so it is fitting that the disposition of his archival legacy is the subject of intense public and professional concern. Many countries would consider the papers of such a towering and influential national figure a matter of cultural heritage and intervene to ensure the integrity and preservation of the collection. Instead the papers have been repeatedly jeopardized by competition and commodification. The main body of King's work is divided among three different repositories: the Howard Gotlieb Archival Research Center at Boston University, the King Center in Atlanta (also known under its previous name, the Martin Luther King Jr. Center for Nonviolent Social Change), and Morehouse College's

Robert W. Woodruff Library of the Atlanta University Center. As a result of archives competing with each other over several decades, access to the originals has been difficult and unpredictable. To compound the problem, a grounded understanding of his writings and legacy has been hampered by the idea that invaluable cultural heritage, like decorative antiques, can be divided up and converted into large sums of cash.

What do the ethical codes say about competing archives and divided collections, and how can those standards be applied?

The Society of American Archivists Code of Ethics, in its various versions, makes an effort to minimize competition between archives. Section 2 of the 2005 Code stipulates: "Archivists cooperate, collaborate, and respect each institution and its mission and collecting policy."[31]

The 1996 ICA Code has a more explicit injunction in sections 2 and 10:

> Archivists should acquire records in accordance with the purposes and resources of their institutions. They should not seek or accept acquisitions when this would endanger the integrity or security of records; they should cooperate to ensure the preservation of these records in the most appropriate repository. Archivists should cooperate in the repatriation of displaced archives.
>
> Archivists should promote the preservation and use of the world's documentary heritage, through working co-operatively with the members of their own and other professions.
>
> Archivists should seek to enhance cooperation and avoid conflict with their professional colleagues and to resolve difficulties by encouraging adherence to archival standards and ethics. Archivists should cooperate with members of related professions on the basis of mutual respect and understanding.[32]

The history of the King papers deserves detailed treatment, partly as a cautionary tale. It illustrates the chain of problems that occur when fundamentals are neglected in the beginning. Selecting the most appropriate repository, signing a deed of gift, clarifying access policies from the outset, providing for additions to the collection over time, retaining the integrity of the collection, making a commitment to professional standards of care, and promoting maximum use of the materials are essential to a good foundation of an acquisitions process.

Selecting the Most Appropriate Repository

King himself transferred a substantial set of papers to Boston University starting in 1964, around the time he received the Nobel Prize. It was a hectic period in a tumultuous career. Considering the threats to his life, the safety of his papers may have been a major consideration. King had spent most of his life in Atlanta, where his family had deep roots. One would have expected a southern institution to house the papers of a Nobel Prize winner from that region. The South was also the scene of his challenges to segregation and home to his most dangerous enemies. Removing papers from their native territory can be justified when they are in jeopardy, which may have been the case. King received his PhD at Boston University and met his wife in Boston, but otherwise had little contact with the institution. The special collections program is famous for collecting the papers of actors and Hollywood figures. Even today King shares the Boston University website with images of entertainment stars. The university has never specialized in the civil rights movement. The university, at least initially, did not devote a great deal of attention to the collection, where it languished with minimal processing for decades. Collecting archives and papers on the civil rights movement was simply not a focus of the mission statement or collecting policy.[33]

Signing a Deed of Gift

The transfer of papers to Boston University was accomplished by means of an exchange of letters, a once-common practice. The original paperwork for the Martin Luther King Jr. papers at Boston University indicate that King intended to make a loan or deposit that would convert to a gift to the university over time. The terms were never finalized in a formal contract. Access policies, increments, and the commitment to professional care were left to chance. Political figures, especially those embroiled in ongoing struggles, simply cannot be expected to think through the technical details. The archives staff has an obligation to manage the paperwork and guide the donor.

Providing for Additions to the Collection

After King's assassination in 1968, the family retained papers from his office and his home. The family established the Martin Luther King Jr. Center for Nonviolent Social Change (now the King Center), located in Atlanta, Georgia. Most pre-1961 papers have remained in Boston and most post-1961 papers have remained in Atlanta. Much material, especially the notes for sermons, stayed in the family home until the death of Coretta Scott King.[34] Other fragmentary materials are found in hundreds of locations, some in private hands. Harry Belafonte received several major King documents, which he tried to sell at public auction in 2008, but withdrew after public protests.[35]

Retaining the Integrity of the Collection

Several efforts were made to reunite the papers. In 1985 Coretta Scott King invited Stanford University historian Clayborne Carson to edit Dr. King's papers for publication. The multivolume publication brings together the widely scattered texts for the benefit of research. In 1987 she began an effort to retrieve the original materials in Boston to unite them with the papers in Atlanta. Boston University was unwilling to surrender such a treasure, and the effort led to a lawsuit, which went to trial in 1993, just as the publication program was gaining momentum. The first volume came out in 1992, and the second in 1994. James O'Toole, an expert archives witness in the 1993 lawsuit over the collection, originally favored uniting the collection in Atlanta. He testified that the university had not provided appropriate levels of professional care. He found evidence that at least one item was lost. The university's commitment to the subject area was notably weak. He based his judgment on the code of ethics that emphasizes the need for preserving the integrity of collections and the importance of minimizing the competition between archives. He did have reservations about criticizing Boston University, since denigrating colleagues is also against the code of ethics.

In the end, despite O'Toole's criticism, and even in the absence of a deed of gift, the court in this case decided in favor of the university. The decision was narrowly based on property law that treated archives as objects, no different from a dispute over the ownership of furniture. There was no consideration of the special historical significance of the papers as a unified whole. The collection remained divided with little cooperation between the two repositories. The case demonstrates how accommodations that are technically legal may not be sound from a professional and ethical point of view.

Making a Commitment to Professional Standards

While in 1993 O'Toole believed that King's papers would be better managed in his home town, at the King Center in Atlanta, over time, O'Toole began to doubt the center's commitment to the professional management of its historical legacy. Processing was slow, preservation was inadequate, and access was difficult. Maybe the court made the right decision to let Boston University retain the King papers. After the death of Coretta Scott King in 2006, the situation became even more acute, as the estate put a large collection of King papers up for auction at Sotheby's, with the expectation of realizing many millions of dollars in the sale. The commodification of the King legacy directly threatened its integrity. The public outcry helped galvanize supporters who raised promises of $32 million to keep the papers in Atlanta, and housed them at Morehouse College, King's undergraduate alma mater. The King Library and Archives at the King Center in Atlanta holds significant King papers, as well as the archives of the Southern Christian Leadership Conference and other major civil rights organizations. Today the King papers are separated in three locations—Boston University, the King Center, and Morehouse College—while Stanford University houses a collection of copies drawn from hundreds of sources, assembled during the publication of the King papers.

Promoting Maximum Use

Fortunately, there is a mostly happy ending to this tale. To a large extent, King's extraordinary writings have finally become accessible. This was first accomplished through the published works, edited by Clayborne Carson.[36] In 1985 Carson turned the limited funding that was initially available into an advantage by hiring an army of student research assistants. These young scholars received hands-on training in the King legacy and learned how to use the papers to understand his thinking. Now technology has been used to reunite the collection with high-quality scanned images.[37] The copies assembled by Carson have been converted into a virtual archive of King papers in addition to his series of weighty published volumes. In this collection, students can find the image of a memo written to J. Edgar Hoover by an FBI special agent on January 4, 1956. This now-declassified and still heavily redacted letter documents the FBI's efforts to find "derogatory information" about King.[38] Morehouse College and Boston University have also prepared and contributed components for the virtual archives, called the MLK Jr. Archival Collaborative and funded by the Andrew W. Mellon Foundation. After decades of divisive competition, threats of auctions, and obstructed access, curators in Boston and Atlanta are cooperating, as envisioned by the archival code of ethics. If the program proceeds according to this vision, the results could be remarkable. This kind of documentation gets to the core of history as it actually happened. However, a virtually reunited collection is still something of a consolation prize. There is no substitute for an intact collection of original materials under a single protective umbrella.

In fact, a great deal of solid research has been accomplished on King's legacy and the civil rights movement, despite the obstacles posed by the poorly coordinated management of the archives over the decades. The scars remain. Unusually stringent intellectual property controls hamper the use of copies. One wonders how much more scholarship on King would have been possible, and sooner, if the cultural legacy had been maintained as a coherent whole, as ethics require. Even more importantly, how much more of this history could have been presented to Americans growing up after his tragic assassination in 1968. One can make the argument that competing archives have seriously impeded the education of a generation of Americans in their own history.

The King papers case raises a number of questions that illuminate the underlying principles of archival work. Establishing a good foundation from the very start of the acquisitions process is key to preventing disputes and lawsuits down the road. To some extent, such procedures as securing a valid deed of gift are management issues. But the ethical component is linked to the recognition of the value of archives beyond monetary gain, beyond the marketplace, and beyond institutional trophies. When papers preserve the shared remembrance of society, they become a shared cultural heritage. In these cases the traditional archival concept of respect for the integrity of the collection is something more than a professional technicality. Remembering is a core value.

Questions for Evaluating Acquisitions

To avoid some of the pitfalls in the examples above, and to achieve a fair and productive acquisitions program, it is useful to have a checklist to work from. Information professionals such as librarians, archivists, and IT specialists as a group are proficient at following rules. If there were a tablet of Ten Commandments for ethical acquisitions, archivists would implement them with a high level of consistency. No such commandments exist. Here are twenty questions to ponder that will bring a greater degree of clarity, specific to each institution and to each contemplated acquisition. Before placing a call to a potential donor or seller, or contacting an office about a transfer of records, know how to discuss the following twenty questions. Every working curator should expand this list with questions that are specific to the given repository, its mission, authority to collect, and acquisitions guidelines.

1. What is the mission of the organization?
2. Is the authority or mandate to collect archives governmental, institutional, or private?

3. What is the legal relationship between the archives and parent organization and the relationship between their missions? Is the organization for profit or nonprofit?

4. What are the collection development policies and appraisal guidelines, written and/or published?

5. Is the collecting scope flexible or exact?

6. How does one coordinate acquisition policies and overall mission?

7. How does one coordinate acquisitions practice with staffing and storage capabilities?

8. Are there guidelines to prohibit curators from personally collecting in the same area as the repository and to prohibit the acceptance of gifts from donors?

9. What is the primary clientele: government, corporate, or private?

10. What is the secondary clientele: open to the public or restricted?

11. Who are the donors: affiliated offices or private individuals or both?

12. What are the tools to determine provenance and warranty of title? Are there other claims to the material?

13. What are the legal tools to transfer records: deed of gift, bill of sale, deposit or loan agreement?

14. What are donor guidelines regarding restrictions, retention schedules, and deaccessioning?

15. What are the donor guidelines regarding financial appraisals and tax deductions?

16. What are the guidelines regarding copyright and intellectual property?

17. Are there clear guidelines to prevent conflicts of interest between the acquisitions archivist and the donor?

18. Are other repositories competing for this material, or are other portions of the collection already held by other archives? Are there claims from family, governments, or ethnic groups?

19. In the case of a purchase, how is a fair price determined? Is the acquisition linked to a financial donation or organizational support? Are collateral gifts or exchanges involved?

20. Are there types of materials or essential topics that have been traditionally excluded and need to be proactively sought out as a matter of social justice?

CHAPTER 3

The Ethics of Disposal

The truth is, archivists select a few records for inclusion in the archives and consign the vast majority of documents to the dumpster.

—Frank Boles[1]

ACQUISITION IS ONE SIDE OF THE COIN, THE OTHER SIDE IS ELIMINATING SUPERFLUOUS, FRIVOLOUS, OBSOLETE, ILLEGIBLE, DAMAGED, AND OUT-OF-SCOPE MATERIALS THAT OCCUPY EXPENSIVE SPACE AND REQUIRE EXPENSIVE MAINTENANCE. Appraisal selects items for retention, reappraisal selects items for disposal.

As Boles points out, disposal is a normal occurrence in archives. It can take place at any point in the life cycle of records. Documents may be purposefully or inadvertently destroyed in the originating agency and never transferred to the archives. During a transfer, inappropriate items are routinely removed. Once in the archives storage rooms, collections may pile up unexamined and unaccessioned for some time. In these cases the delayed sorting prior to accessioning will remove extraneous items. After a collection is officially accessioned, retention cycles may dictate when to destroy documentation that has exceeded its shelf life. Other times, cataloged collections are reassessed for their appropriateness to the institution's mission statement and the reappraisal may well target items for return, transfer, sale, or destruction.

The standard definition of *weeding* from the SAA Glossary is broad in nature: "The process of identifying and removing unwanted materials from a larger body of materials." The definition for *deaccessioning* is more specific: "The process by which an archives, museum, or library permanently removes accessioned materials from its holdings."[2]

This discussion will address the disposal of unaccessioned materials as well as fully cataloged collections. Both types of disposal will be discussed. The main reason is that the general public does not make a distinction between accessioned and unaccessioned archives when they respond to reports that documents have been destroyed. In addressing the implications of removing archival materials, it is necessary to consider public perceptions and reactions. Whether fair or not, the public often judges document disposal by archivists and librarians as an ethical failure. Sometimes the public is right, and sometimes the public is confused. Either way, public perception matters if the archives are to function as a trusted institution.

Disposal is one of several areas of archival practice with an inherent contradiction that needs to be managed and balanced. It is a "hot button" topic that is known to raise blood pressure even before the facts of a given case have been determined. This chapter will review the two main opposing views in the archival community that periodically erupt into controversy. This overview is followed by a casebook with seven examples of disposal and deaccessioning. An analysis of the last case, from New York, suggests a way of balancing the two approaches over time. The case also demonstrates the need for more research and discussion of this topic. Armed with an understanding of the debate in the profession and with a survey of actual cases, it should be easier to distinguish between irrational rants that frequently erupt and the genuine alarms that call for the preservation of endangered archives. It should also be easier to formulate well-tailored policies that take the best from the different schools of thought on the subject.

There is a running debate in the archival profession on disposal, and it parallels a similar debate in the museum world. The argument against systematic disposal runs like this: Once a unique archival item is destroyed, that piece of history is gone forever. Once archival material has been selected for retention and accessioned into the holdings with accession numbers and cataloging descriptions, it acquires a special protected status. The more seriously the staff takes its work, the more seriously it reviews any decision to rescind that protected status, however necessary. Retention is the default mode, and disposal requires extensive justification. The manner in which this is done reveals the fundamental principles of an organization.

The argument for aggressive weeding and deaccessioning is also persuasive: all well managed archives, in fact, need to have periodic cleanups. The cleanup may range from the trivial to the substantial. It may involve removing or deleting extraneous materials that inadvertently were included in an archival collection, such as runs of ordinary magazines. It may involve removing an entire collection that is useful for research but out of scope, such as displaced government papers that are best reunited with similar materials in the originating agency's official archives. Disposal is the default mode, and retention requires extensive justification. Such winnowing, weeding, and pruning may be time consuming in the short term, but can significantly improve the quality of the organization's holdings in the long term.

This discussion, then, addresses one of the fundamental dilemmas of archival work: the inherent tension between the mandate to preserve cultural heritage in perpetuity, and the practical need to dispose of out-of-scope materials. In this, as in other quandaries, there are more questions than answers. The issue of the sale of selected holdings will be treated separately.

The emphasis in this chapter is on the more philosophical concerns surrounding the disposal of documents; it is not a "how to" guide. (Reference to such guides can be found in the endnotes and the appendix.) Of the different types of disposal, deaccessioning from an established and cataloged collection is the most complex. One can summarize the deaccessioning process in four separate steps: reappraisal, review, removal, and disposal. The following summary is not meant to be exhaustive, but merely an outline of the usual procedures, as a point of reference for discussing the ethical implications.

First, a policy on reappraisal needs to be in place prior to targeting collections for removal.[3] For most archives it may be wise to post this policy on the institution's website, rather than making decisions in secret. The policy should delineate the factors in decision making: redundancy, low research value, out-of-scope content, obsolescence, illegibility, damaged condition, etc. Selection needs to be supervised by professionals with in-depth knowledge of the collections and their histories. Next, governing documents need to be carefully reviewed as to who has the authority to deaccession and under what circumstances. In a government repository, one needs to determine the officially sanctioned retention schedule; in a private collection, one needs to examine the deed of gift for permission to deaccession. Once the legal issues are clarified, the next step is to determine the best disposition of the deaccessioned materials. The staff needs to explore options such as returning unneeded materials to the original source, finding a more suitable repository for a transfer, merging the papers with related collections in other archives, or disposing of materials. Destruction is the last resort. If papers are to be destroyed or electronic text deleted, sampling should be considered to ensure a good sense of what was removed. Each stage of the process needs to be documented, and any major decisions should be made in consultation with more than one experienced staff member. Deaccessioning should be accompanied by a plan to more tightly focus appraisal and selection in the first place to prevent the need for reappraisal in the future. The Society of American Archivists Acquisition and Appraisal Section reviews best practice and should be consulted for the latest recommendations.

When written up in an official policy, even in a summary such as this one, the process does not sound threatening. To the general public, removing a collection and disposing of it is far from neutral. If accessioning confers a form of protection, then deaccessioning strikes people as akin to removing a species from the endangered list and exposing it to predations. The word carries a negative connotation with many curators and archives supporters. While it is a normal archival function in the retention cycles of business and governmental archives, in manuscript repositories and private archives it is typically less routine and even more fraught with controversy. A manager's rational "weeding" program may appear to be barbaric, irreversible cultural destruction when written up for newspaper or magazine readers. The frightening image of a history-filled dumpster seems to hang over the subject, but analysis and planning can tame these anxieties. There are two major reasons for removing archives from an existing collection:

- **Deaccessoning to maintain a collecting policy:**   One reason is to refocus a collecting area to permit the acquisition of more appropriate materials and improve the overall quality of core collections. This process is a predictable part of management, and should be accounted for in the policy guidelines of all archives.

- **Deaccessioning to raise funds:**   Another reason is to realize cash during times of financial stress by selling high value items such as autographs or paintings. This strategy is unpredictable and treacherous from a public relations standpoint, and while hopefully infrequent, such an eventuality should be thought through prior to a crisis.

These two motives need to be analyzed separately, and illustrated with examples. There are sometimes links between the two. The last case study—the New-York Historical Society—provides an example of this. The lesson from this case is that undisciplined collecting and failure to deaccession to refocus a collection can lead to financial liabilities that require the sale of treasured materials. As in other chapters, there are more questions than answers presented here. The casebook is followed by a checklist of questions to pose in the more difficult situations. In the long term, if done transparently and appropriately, disposal and deaccessioning strengthen the collection.

Maintaining a Collecting Policy: The Pragmatists vs. the Idealists

While deaccessioning is an acknowledged collection management tool, there is an ongoing debate over the best way to use it. Basically the controversy is between the pragmatists and the idealists, and this professional argument has been fought out in the professional literature for decades. The pragmatic school of thought sees the need for systematic discipline in paring down holdings before they spiral out of control, which in large repositories is a real threat. The idealists, on the other hand, view the collections as a shared legacy held in trust for society and for the future, not something the current custodians themselves own. The pragmatists try to return out-of-scope materials prior to accessioning, and they combine that strategy with reappraisal of older accessions to eliminate bulk and redundancy. They often use techniques such as sampling for low value items (such as routine reports) and microfilming or scanning for high volume materials (such as constituent mail). Then the originals are frequently shredded or pulped. Done conscientiously, weeding can require a great deal of time and planning.

The idealists see deaccessioning as an exception to normal procedures, something that occurs rarely and is decided on a case-by-case basis. Perhaps there is a curatorial decision to transfer orphan materials to a more appropriate repository, or return displaced archives to the original home, but in this view such steps require lengthy evaluation. The time idealists spend on evaluating transfers and on preserving and processing unweeded collections is balanced by the time saved in reappraisal efforts. In terms of effort on a daily basis, it is hard to say which school has it easier or which has greater benefits. The idealists treasure the unexpected evidence revealed in unsanitized archives and the rewards of what might be termed benign neglect, one of the virtues of traditional old world archives. Unweeded collections are more likely to preserve the lock of hair that can now reveal valuable DNA evidence, the laundry list that proves when a person was in residence, the old trunk that the papers were shipped in, the uncensored early draft with a politically incorrect viewpoint, the envelope with a handwritten note or wax seal, or the instructions to servants whose contributions are otherwise lost. The difference in orientation between the pragmatic and idealistic schools can be thought of as the distinction between good housekeepers and temple guardians. They each have a role.

Both sides can justify deaccessioning to maintain a collection, just with different opinions as to the level of weeding that is required.

Managers of large collections almost always ascribe to the pragmatic view on deaccessioning to preserve the focus of a collection and to keep its size literally manageable. Their statements on the subject evoke negative reactions from others who may not have faced the direct challenge of floods of incoming materials, some of questionable value. In 1981, a famous debate on the topic erupted in response to an article by Leonard Rapport. He reversed the normal procedure by which archivists are required to justify deaccessions. Rapport's thesis was that the archivist must make the case for retention of materials, not the case for disposal. If one cannot fully justify keeping a set of papers, they should not be occupying valuable space.[4] The burden of proof is reversed. This thesis was reinforced by an adjacent article by Frank Boles advocating sampling as a tool for retaining the sense or essence of a collection without the clutter of a complete series. Boles cited the earlier work of an American Historical Association committee that he says "legitimized the wastebasket as an archival tool," and in fact a tool that was not used enough.[5] The discussion has continued in the pages of the *American Archivist*, especially the Winter 1984 issue, and at well-attended conference sessions ever since.

The idealists typically work in rare manuscript collections, where the volume of materials is normally smaller, and by definition rarer, with more of a museum character. These advocates include writers such as Karen Benedict, who defended retention in perpetuity as the default assumption, with deaccessioning as an exception, to be determined on a case-by-case basis.[6] She decoupled the value of archives from the frequency of use. A great deal of material on the lives of early nineteenth-century women and slaves has been disposed of as too trivial for use in historical research. Today, of course, we wish we had that documentation. The author has witnessed the removal and disposal of some valuable materials by inexperienced staff; it would be naive not to concede that this does happen, but hopefully only as a rare exception. The debate continues. In a 1995 thesis, Mary Ledwell also opposed using deaccessioning routinely as a management tool.[7] Both advise caution. Both advise against evaluating collections according to how much they are used. They have a valid point. The disposal decisions should not be based solely on the level of actual use, but on the potential for research value.

The museum community has addressed the issue as well, and it typically comes out on the side of the idealists. The American Association of Museums Code of Ethics is somewhat vague on the subject of disposal, but the tone is one of limiting it rather than using it as a systematic management practice. The code's emphasis is on the museum's mission to preserve rather than discard:

- acquisition, disposal, and loan activities are conducted in a manner that respects the protection and preservation of natural and cultural resources and discourages illicit trade in such materials
- acquisition, disposal, and loan activities conform to its mission and public trust responsibilities[8]

Maintaining public trust is part of the mission, and that mission maps over from museums to archives. In general, public opinion is also on the side of the idealists as the case studies will demonstrate. Even private organizations that legally own their holdings are seen as a public trust. When the press reports cases of deaccessioning, the underlying assumption is that it is a violation of that trust.

The defense of deaccessioning was revived in 1996 by Kevin M. Guthrie, an information management executive with a background in engineering and business. Following a study of the repeated financial crises that temporarily closed the New-York Historical Society in 1993, he assessed the financial structure of the library and archives with the eye of a businessman. From this perspective, any gifts should benefit the institution, not the donor. The donor, he decided, should endow any gifts of manuscripts to pay for the ongoing maintenance, and the institution should protect its right to sell any of its property. He deplored the "uncompromising theology" opposed to such sales of cultural property, and asserted the importance of "destigmatizing deaccessioning."[9] Guthrie's analysis of the

New-York Historical Society case will be explored in greater detail at the end of the chapter. Despite Guthrie's impassioned argument, deaccessioning continued to be controversial another decade later.[10]

In 2006, Mark A. Greene would ironically describe his experience in an article with the title "I've Deaccessioned and Lived to Tell about It: Confessions of an Unrepentant Reappraiser."[11] He described his experience reorienting the collection of the American Heritage Center at the University of Wyoming. First he determined that the holdings were bloated with materials of low research value. Then he secured institutional approval to write a new collection policy and found funding for a complete reappraisal of the existing collection. Over a period of five years, the American Heritage Center deaccessioned hundreds of collections, more than nine thousand cubic feet of papers. He transferred some collections to more appropriate repositories and returned others to the donors. About 9 percent of the deaccessioned material was destroyed. While Greene did not need to monetize collections out of financial necessity, and did not in fact sell collections, his deaccessioning guidelines provide for sales in some cases, but with important restrictions. Under his guidelines, sales would not be permitted to university employees or their families, for example.

While archival managers over the centuries have resorted to surreptitious and discreet discarding, Greene was completely open about the process from the outset and promulgated his institution's selection and disposal policies on the website for the American Heritage Center. He clearly believes in openness on principle, but he also was able to deploy transparency as a preemptive strategy to deflect criticism. His experience grew out of simultaneous efforts to build and to prune collections on the American West. He was not attempting to sell pricey items to fill a gap in the operating budget. Instead he established a methodology for maintaining collections with high research value and manageable size. Deaccessioning was the tool to achieve these two objectives with a certain synergy. The resulting policies are very detailed, which makes them easy for the staff to implement. This kind of above-board procedure can work well as an approach to deaccessioning.

In the dispute between the pragmatists and the idealists, one can make the case that both sides of this controversy have valid arguments. Instead of framing the question as an either/or debate, there may be various ways of combining the best principles of each side. The idealists have an important point: archives are held in trust for the public and for future generations, even archives owned by private institutions. The pragmatists also have a point: how many container loads of requisition files, trip reports, laundry lists, computer printouts, and floppy disks can a repository accept before the collection becomes unusable?

Canadian archivist Terry Cook eloquently expressed the dilemma: "Destroy the wrong records and you jeopardize the rights of citizens to redress, the need of government to consult records on a recurring basis, the demands of all manner of researchers to unravel the past and the cravings of a nation to understand itself. Keep too many records and you create a paper haystack in which few needles can ever be found, involving enormous storage, administrative and indexing costs that governments and society have shown no great willingness to bear."[12] While old-fashioned microfilm and newer scanning techniques can solve some storage problems, they pose enormous difficulties in funding, cataloging, and the periodic migrating of digital data. The loss of digital images from the early years of space exploration has taught us a hard lesson. The newer technologies also require expensive maintenance: the periodic migrating of data to new formats as old techniques become obsolete. Even with microform and scanned copies, one needs to do something with the originals, which are often consigned to the dumpster or shredder. For these reasons, appraisal and reappraisal require great care by highly trained professionals, and this same care needs to be exercised in discarding the dross that impedes access to valuable materials.

Both librarians and archives managers not infrequently have difficulty with collateral damage from misdirected good intentions in this area. When the public becomes aware of the destruction of archives and library materials, there is often a protest. These protests can be well informed and timely warnings against the eradication of invaluable historical sources. Other times they are misinformed and hinder the effort they intend to support. Righteous indignation has its role in correcting malfeasance. It can also get the wrong person fired. Deaccessioning is a topic best thought through in advance of a confrontation. One needs some awareness of the dynamics to avert the kind of emotional outburst that in the end does more harm than good.

Social historians, for example, are often dismayed when archives discard ephemera.[13] Archivists collect records of permanent value, but the very act of collecting adds value of its own in the form of context. Baseball cards and comic books may look like a child's temporary amusement to an archivist struggling to document high politics and diplomacy. To a social historian, baseball cards and comic books are sacred relics of the American way of life. Many people are quite passionate about antiquarian collectibles. A systematic collection of baseball cards will have both research and artifactual value—and be very popular with a certain clientele. An archivist who has experience clearing out attics, however, knows that not all childhood mementos can be saved, or should be saved. A repository that specializes in social history will preserve those baseball cards in a consciously constructed context with other, similar iconic items. Another repository might return them to the donor, or donate them to a library that specializes in them—and document the process.

The debate really opens a window on one of several intrinsic ethical dilemmas of the archival profession. One could argue that there is not a correct side and a wrong side to reappraisal if the purpose is to refocus the holdings according to a sound collecting policy. The problem is to find the right balance and that balance will be different for different repositories depending on their collecting strategy, clientele, available space, staff expertise, organizational history, and many other factors. A sound written policy is based on a complex algorithm of competing factors and underlying values.

Selling Deaccessioned Cultural Materials

Deaccessioning to manage a collection is one thing. Selling off holdings to raise cash is a separate issue, and a vexed one. An undisciplined collecting program can eventually lead to financial exigency and panic sales of treasures.

There are some basic rules that can be generally agreed upon. The first rule is that any such effort to raise cash should target the sale of out-of-scope or duplicate materials, not the core collection. A second principle, borrowed from the museum world, is that funds realized from sales of holdings should only be used to purchase acquisitions that are more appropriate. Ideally such a sale should be conducted within the curatorial goals of a well-focused collection development policy. Members of the organization and their relatives should not be allowed to bid on the sale. The money that is realized from the sale needs to be tightly sequestered, placed in a form of internal escrow, until it is used for other acquisitions. Money is fungible, and the temptation to launder it and recycle it for other uses, such as an executive bonus, is often great.

From the perspective of museum ethics, a duplicate print or out-of-scope painting can ethically be deaccessioned and sold to realize funding for purchasing artworks that are a better fit with the mission of the organization. Selling items to support operating expenses is considered unethical except in cases of dire financial emergency. It is a form of cultural cannibalism. If the financial problems are recurring issues due to structural weaknesses within the organization, sales merely prolong the agony before implementing an essential reorganization. On rare occasions, then, it may indeed be appropriate to sell a highly valued piece to underwrite the acquisition of more appropriate materials. Otherwise sales are only to be used as a last resort, to ward off financial instability. The Code of Ethics for Museums formulates this concept as follows:

- Disposal of collections through sale, trade, or research activities is solely for the advancement of the museum's mission.

- Proceeds from the sale of nonliving collections are to be used consistent with the established standards of the museum's discipline, but in no event shall they be used for anything other than acquisition or direct care of collections.[14]

The art market is a highly developed, international network, with a long history. As cultural property, archives are similar to art, but there are also significant differences. An old master oil painting may have a history of numerous owners who bought and sold it over the centuries. In contrast, buying and selling archives is an exceptional act, not a common transaction. There is an assumption that an archival collection is donated or sold just once, to a permanent home that will maintain it for all time. There is another difference: most archivists care not only about removing out-of-scope items, and replacing them with more appropriate materials, they also care about the fate of what is deaccessioned. Archivists will typically retain inappropriate items until a good home is found.

The provisions for sale in the deaccessioning guidelines at the University of Wyoming allow for a discounted sale if it is to a particularly suitable repository. It might be preferable to sell the item for a lower price to a public institution that makes it available than for a higher price to a private collector, who may not provide access. This provision is especially interesting. Here the principle of access trumps maximizing profit for the selling institution.

The important point is that these measures need to be taken thoughtfully, calibrating the ethical context, and not done in a rush as a panic response to a budget problem. The pressures may be great. During the economic crisis of 2008, the author received an unsolicited and unwelcome email from an auction house offering its services to sell manuscripts to raise funds. This auction house was obviously positioning itself to benefit from the financial crisis in an opportunistic manner.

Auctions and trades are, of course, technically legal if the institution owns title to the property in a legal instrument such as a deed of gift or bill of sale. Sometimes the sales of deaccessioned materials are done secretly in an attempt to evade controversy. Secrets have a way of becoming public and raising suspicions that the process is illegal or unethical, even if it is not. Sometimes an auction is conducted with full publicity in the hopes of attracting a financial angel to come to the rescue. That is also a risky strategy. As seen in the previous chapter, the proposed auction of Martin Luther King Jr. papers triggered a national outcry.

The general consensus among museum directors is that cultural artifacts should not be capitalized or used as collateral for loans to cover normal operating expenses such as meeting payroll or building endowment. The two exceptions are sales to fund the acquisition of more appropriate materials, and to strengthen the permanent retention and care of the core collection. This is a useful guideline for archives as well, although most archivists would prefer that even in the case of a sale, the archives should be transferred to the best home where they will be accessible for use, not to the highest bidder.

A recent search for "Abraham Lincoln" on eBay resulted in half a dozen purported Lincoln autographs for sale. While not as common as in the art world, the fact remains that archivists do both buy and sell at auction, sometimes with enthusiasm, and eBay is increasingly one of the venues.[15] Archivists may want to think through whether the museum world's restrictions on such sales make sense for their particular circumstances.

The museum consensus was tested by financial reality in New York State in 2008–2009 when several major cultural institutions attempted to avert financial shortfalls by selling artifacts and paintings. The public was outraged. The response was a bill introduced into the state legislature to prevent the capitalization of museum collections.[16]

Well-intentioned regulations to block the selling of cultural artifacts, such as legislation proposed in New York in 2009, could have unintended negative consequences. Governing boards need people with experience steering businesses through financial ups and downs. Responsible trustees need to know that they have the freedom to protect the institution in question from bankruptcy. With restraints on deaccessioning, some executives would decline an opportunity to serve as an archives or museum trustee. They would see it as a conflict with a trustee's responsibility to ensure that the institution is financially sound, especially if the choice should come down to whether the board or the bankruptcy court decides what to sell.[17]

The other side of the argument was well expressed by James C. Dawson, chairman of the cultural education committee for the New York State Education Department, Board of Regents: "Cultural institutions hold artifacts in trust for the public, and deacquisition should only take place under very narrowly prescribed circumstances. And selling collections for operating funds or for capital improvements is not in the public interest."[18] In other words, a museum cannot sell a Chagall painting in order to fix the air conditioning, even though the painting may be damaged by lack of air conditioning. A museum may sell a Chagall in order to purchase a more appropriate work. One hopes that the better focused collection that results appeals to the ticket-buying public and indirectly raises revenue for the air conditioning.

This rule is a safeguard against hasty decisions to monetize cultural property to pay operating expenses. It also recognizes the principle that cultural property has values beyond a given market price. In the example above, if an oil painting were used to pay for an air conditioner, that equipment would wear out within a few years. A masterpiece of a painting, like a rare manuscript, continues to provide aesthetic pleasure that does not wear out and has no price tag.

Weeding, disposal, and deaccessioning can be done in an ethical manner as an integrated collection management strategy, and in fact need to be done to prevent bloated, unfocused, and ultimately unusable collections. In sum, it can only be done in an ethical manner if there is a clear mission statement and transparent procedures in place. It requires collaboration with other archives for transferring materials to the most appropriate home and reuniting separated collections. Sales of archives need to be scrutinized carefully to avoid conflicts of interest. As with art work in a museum, the archives might possibly be sold to refocus a collection, but should not be monetized to pay operating expenses like the electrical bill. In addition, archivists should consider the best home for anything that is weeded or deaccessioned. Destruction of archival materials should require a complete justification, based on established policy. Processors need clear guidelines to distinguish what they can discard using their own judgment (duplicates, ordinary magazines, shopping lists, sandwich wrappers, worthless envelopes) and items that require consultation prior to disposal (unread floppy disks and back-of-the-envelope notations might be in this category). Since the guidelines need to be handcrafted specifically for the repository and the nature of materials collected, blanket recommendations are misleading. For collections of outdated case files, for example, the guidelines may mandate that destruction be combined with sampling. For classified documents, authorized personnel with clearance need to prepare a destruction certificate and log in the actions taken. With well thought out provisions, the archives can maintain high standards that inspire credibility.

Bearing in mind that an ethical program can be put in place, a trusted archival program needs to communicate those standards to its constituencies. Communication is part of due diligence. The following cases triggered great concern that improper destruction of records took place. Sometimes deliberate destruction of historical evidence occurred, and sometimes there was simply the misguided perception of wrongdoing. These are rather traumatic cautionary tales. Some professionals were publicly criticized in the press; some lost their jobs. Case studies are meant to provide the lessons of real-life experiences without the real-life aggravations. The message is not that one must be timid and fearful of deaccessioning and disposal; rather the message is to learn the signs of potential conflict in time to avoid it. Perhaps this is merely damage control. In the real world, professionals who care about their institution's reputation need to pay attention to public relations. Again, it is professional due diligence. Credibility is the goal.

Destruction of Records: A Casebook of Examples

Thinking through real-life examples, then, is a useful tool to illustrate the dynamics at work, a painless substitute for real-life experience. The following casebook of seven examples is not meant to cause alarm. Instead it is intended to provide low-risk exposure to the types of incidents that occur so they can be assessed calmly in theory before the practitioner has to deal with such things in the workplace. They help sort out the different categories in play: minor weeding versus the removal of treasured artifacts, authorized destruction versus unauthorized, the disposal that occurs in originating agencies versus disposal under the supervision of a trained archivist, rare archives that function like museum artifacts, and more routine office files that require bulk processing and "bulk" disposition decisions. Each practicing archivist needs to evaluate the mix in the given workplace and determine which principles best apply.

The first three examples involve government records. Two recent cases from national archives, in Canada and South Africa, demonstrate how in one situation the righteous indignation triggered by document destruction was misdirected and in another it was necessary in the struggle to preserve evidence of human rights abuses. A third example shows how casually American government agencies can discard records prior to appraisal in disregard of normal regulations. These first three examples come from the highly instructive book of case studies edited by Richard Cox and David Wallace.[19]

Case One: False Alarm Over the Destruction of Immigration Records in Canada

Terry Cook relates a situation where accessioned government records were destroyed in the normal course of business. He was implementing routine Canadian Archives retention cycle policies when the news services heard about the destruction of immigration records. Coincidentally, the justice department had begun to look for Nazi war criminals who had illegally sought refuge in Canada. Reporters assumed that the destroyed immigration records contained information on these suspects, and that the files were destroyed deliberately to eliminate evidence. Provocative headlines screeched that "Key documents have disappeared from the vaults of the National Archives," and that the archivists were guilty of "dereliction of responsibility." [20] Fortunately, Cook had followed procedures faithfully, documented the process, and saved samples of the types of materials destroyed. In the end, after considerable investigation into the issues,

Cook was vindicated by the official report.[21] The immigration records did not contain evidence of criminal activity. The Canadian National Archives was not guilty of dereliction of duty. The reporters overreacted to what had been a possibility of loss of evidence. In this case suspicion was misplaced, but the possibility always haunts the process of disposal. While vindication is sweet, Cook would clearly have preferred to avoid the battle in the first place.

This is a success story. By following good policy and by patiently working with critics, Terry Cook's implementation of normal deaccessioning procedure was exonerated in the end. There is no substitute for good policy. It is unlikely that Cook could have avoided the initial bad publicity because of the politics involved. He did the right things in managing the retention and destruction cycles of the records in his custody. He defended his policy intelligently and eventually turned the tide of disapproval. While not always possible, it sometimes helps to "look around the corner," and see the political context. When there are unusual political factors at work, it makes sense to take some extra measures—perhaps getting a second opinion, postponing, or documenting the disposal with more extensive justification—to prevent unnecessary grief. Sometimes a monitored blog can keep interested parties posted on what is actually happening and at the same time provide the archivists with feedback and a sense of public opinion.

Doing the right thing does not always avert problems. Depending on the political climate, ethical decisions may trigger difficulties, particularly if the actions go against conventional wisdom or go against the power structure. Bad publicity can leave lingering doubts about the probity of the archives. Since professional ethics are based in a group's shared values, it is often counterproductive to go it alone. Efforts need to be made to communicate those values to a wider audience, and Cook was able to do this despite initially hostile reactions.

Case Two: The Purposeful Destruction of Evidence of Human Rights Abuse in South Africa

Verne Harris documented the loss of official South African government records, not yet accessioned into the State Archives Services. During the transition to democracy and the transfer of power in 1990–1994, the apartheid government "routinely destroyed public records in order to keep certain processes secret," he charged. The materials were not in the custody of the State Archives Services, but were still located in the originating government agencies. As could be expected, the various security and police services were highly motivated to destroy the records used to enforce apartheid and obstruct the African National Congress. The destruction, on a massive scale, was purposeful and coordinated: "large-scale sanitization of its memory resources, a sanitization designed to keep certain information out of the hands of a future democratic government."[22] Destroying evidence, whether accessioned or not, is both illegal and unethical. At the same time, blowing the whistle on that game is a risky decision, not to be taken lightly. Harris, an archives employee at the time, was unable to activate the archives leadership into opposing the destruction. After exhausting official channels, he turned to unofficial ones and leaked information to the press, the African National Congress and other anti-apartheid groups. After the fall of apartheid, the South African Truth and Reconciliation Commission valued Harris's courageous and independent actions and determined that the official State Archives Services had been negligent in failing to prevent the destruction of the documentary record. Harris was vindicated for going to the press with insider information in an effort to protect evidence of human rights abuses.

This case demonstrates the dynamics of operating ethically during a transition as the rules are in flux. Harris, like Cook, did the right thing. Harris rescued much history. But working in isolation, he had limited means to halt the destruction completely and substantial incriminating evidence disappeared. The destruction of accessioned materials within archives can occur during times of political stress, as we know from the collapse of communist regimes in 1989 and 1991. Unappraised papers stored in the originating agencies are, almost by definition, far more vulnerable to destruction prior to accessioning into a repository. In times of rapid political change, both accessioned and unappraised records are vulnerable and extra care needs to be taken. There are times when alarms need to be sounded and whistles blown.

Case Three: Purposeful Destruction of American Records

The destruction of evidence can also occur in democratic societies. Shelley Davis worked for eight years as a historian in the U.S. Internal Revenue Service. Her work was hampered by the lack of primary sources. After some inquiries she discovered a situation of institutionalized "massive document destruction."[23] Again these were official government records that were destroyed prior to accessioning in the archives. As Davis interpreted the Federal Records Act, she believed that it was illegal for a federal employee not to take action to save valuable records. Her well-intentioned efforts to secure the records resulted in her losing a position as historian of the IRS.

Both the South African case and the IRS case show how easy it is for government agencies to evade laws and regulations mandating the preservation and transfer of official government documents. This is not just a problem in underdeveloped countries. This is a problem in the U.S. as well. National archives typically do not have the clout to stand up to entrenched government agencies. The security services in all countries have privileges that few archivists can successfully challenge. In the United States, the IRS has a powerful, self-protective bureaucratic culture that is difficult to challenge for different reasons. Verne Harris was able to blow the whistle on malfeasance and still thrive as a professional archivist. Shelley Davis followed the rules and lost her job. Lawyers for government employees in whistleblowing cases agree that Davis's fate is more typical. This is a fact of life. In these three situations, vital government records were destroyed. In the Canadian case the destruction was justified. In the South African case the destruction served a political agenda. In the IRS case both politics and self-protective bureaucratic behavior were involved.

The Shelley Davis case might have had a different outcome in a different culture. In countries that follow British traditions, such as Canada, retention requirements are quite strict for government offices and even government-funded institutions such as museums. In one interesting case, a personnel dispute in a Canadian museum got to court, and it was determined that the relevant memos were emails that had been deleted. The director was let go, and the new director joked that his first order of business was to regularize the handling of email communications. The essence of the joke was that this was something trivial, but in fact it is only trivial when there is not a dispute.[24] Americans can learn from these other systems and adapt what works to conditions in the U.S. The profession as a whole needs to learn how to influence the way legislation is written.

To be successful, professional ethics require political clout more often than not. To protect government records, one needs both clout and well crafted policies. One good example comes from the concise language in the California State Archives website. It makes the chain of authority very clear when it comes to records disposal. Two separate authorities must authorize the destruction of any state records:

> It is imperative to remember that "no record shall be destroyed or otherwise disposed of by any agency of the state, unless it is determined by the director [of General Services] that the record has no further administrative, legal or fiscal value *and* the Secretary of State has determined that the record is inappropriate for preservation in the State Archives" (Government Code 14755a). If records are being destroyed without the prior approval of DGS and the Secretary of State, the agency is violating the State Records Management Act.[25]

As Shelley Davis learned, mandating retention is one thing, implementing it is another, and trying to prevent destruction of records can lead to the loss of a job. The higher the level of government, the higher the political stakes. It is no accident that the most controversial cases of record destruction occur in Washington. Since the advent of electronic communication, the White House has been asked to supply emails to document events under investigation, from the Iran-Contra scandal in the Reagan administration to the Valerie Plame Wilson investigation over two decades later. These disputes over government email will no doubt recur on a regular basis until sound procedures are in place. Meanwhile, the problem of deleted email will not go away.[26] When the electronic files cannot be found, the responsible parties typically say they were deleted. Trust in the executive branch is badly compromised as a result. The Presidential Records Act, which came out of the Watergate scandal, continues to be a political football between the executive branch and Congress on one hand and historians on the other. Retention and disposal are not just technical issues. They are ethical and moral ones.

Like government records, the disposal of privately held manuscripts and cultural property can set off false alarms. The next two cases deal with the perception of misconduct by a member of the public and by a donor.[27]

Case Four: Misunderstood Disposal in a Private Repository

A distinguished member of the university community was walking behind the archives building and past the dumpster where trash is collected for pick-up. A brisk wind blew several photographs of historic personalities from the dumpster into his path. He recognized the historic nature of the images, became very upset that they had been discarded, and confronted the archives administration in righteous indignation. As it turns out, the photos were defective, nonarchival copies. The originals were safely stored in the stacks, and better quality copies had already been produced for exhibition purposes. The complainant had been allowed to express such anger that he could not back down without losing face. Even after the facts emerged, he continued to believe that the archives had callously and unethically discarded valuable historic photographs. At this point no amount of reasoning could change his mind. Such seemingly trivial incidents can easily escalate into full confrontations. One cannot help but sympathize with the academic who valiantly defended the preservation of history. And yet he was misguided, causing unnecessary consternation and raising unfounded suspicions of the archives in the university community.

The most damaging aspect of the case is that his false alarm may have desensitized the scholarly community to future complaints about genuine losses of documentation. It is wise to take complaints seriously from the beginning, even if they are not well-founded, lest they get overblown and develop into unnecessary controversy.

Case Five: Disposal and Donor Relations

In another case a donor in a tropical area shipped a large packing case to the archives, a private academic repository. Upon its arrival and inspection, staff discovered that the contents did not correspond to the description of what was to be sent. Instead of original documents, the crate contained readily available newspapers and magazines. It appeared as though some office storage closets had been emptied of old subscriptions that had piled up over the years. Worse, there were unexpected and unwelcome guests in the form of a swarm of termites. The staff had to act quickly to verify that there were no unique materials involved, inform the donor of the situation, verify legal title, acquire approval for rapid destruction, and document the disposal, all before the vermin could contaminate the building and the rest of the collection. In this particular situation the destruction occurred prior to accessioning. The donor seemed initially in agreement with the plan of action, but the destruction was still heavily documented in memos that could be easily located. The staff thought the action was well justified and easily understood, case closed. Unexpectedly, several years later, the donor returned and alleged with considerable vehemence that rare historical documentation had been callously destroyed. He actually believed that the materials had great research value, and he had no remorse about the danger his shipment had posed to the entire archives. Fortunately the documentation was sufficient to justify the archivists' actions, and the administration was not persuaded by the donor's allegations. The lesson here is the importance of documenting the approvals and justifications for disposal even if the reasons appear to be self-evident.

Case Six: Cultural Property Crusades

A scandal with more serious repercussions comes from the library world in the work of the well-known novelist Nicholson Baker. This is a classic case in which the disposal of cultural property raised a great controversy and resulted in the termination of a hard-working library director. While the items in question here—catalog cards, books, and newspapers—are not specifically archival, the problem of disposing of cultural heritage is much the same. Archivists responded to the case at the time with well-reasoned arguments. One needs to be familiar with the arguments on both sides and how they were sorted out in the end.

In a series of articles for the *New Yorker*, then in a book entitled *Double Fold*, Baker examined in fastidious detail, and with stylistic panache, the destruction of major American cultural assets.[28] The first article gave an account of the scrapping of traditional library card catalogs as online catalogs began to take over; Baker lamented the loss of the lovely cream-colored 3 x 5 inch cards that have a small hole punched on the lower edge for a retractable rod that holds the cards by the hundreds in long narrow drawers. He described in exquisite language the way generations of librarians annotated the more important holdings on these cards, and the well-thumbed ones that obviously attracted a greater readership than the pristine cards. It is a sentimental article with high literary merit. Readers at the time were shocked and alarmed, but today, after more than a decade of digital progress, the piece appears very quaint. Few productive scholars could afford to go back to the charming old catalog cards, when so much more information, including online annotations, can be found quickly in public access online catalogs even from remote locations. Contemporary scholars are happy to find what they need from their laptops in such online sources as JSTOR and Google Books. At the time of his writing, however, Baker provided a real service in pointing out flaws in the online catalogs. Most of these drawbacks have been addressed over the years with neat solutions as the cost of computer technology has come down, and its flexibility has increased. Several libraries have saved and repurposed the handsome wooden card catalog cabinets as antiques or used them for donor walls and other nostalgic displays. Over time the manual accession records in older archives turn slowly into antiques, some with artifactual value.

In 1996, Baker's next *New Yorker* article on the destruction of cultural property had graver consequences. San Francisco had passed a proposition to fund a new municipal public library in 1988. By 1996 a completely new, palatial, high tech library opened at the Civic Center close to the location of its former home, an outmoded but gorgeous stone Beaux Arts building. The city librarian, Kenneth E. Dowlin, poured money into information technology, which he rightly saw as the inevitable new wave. The construction of the new library was an opportunity to facilitate the shift in emphasis from print to digital information. When the new building opened, Baker charged that "more than half the library's collection now resides in closed unbrowsable stacks" and that Dowlin "sent more than two hundred thousand books to landfill—many of them old, hard to find, out of print, and valuable."[29] Dowlin was forced to resign. Both the reality and even the perception of the cavalier disposal of books and archives can have consequences.

A few years later, Baker took on the results of massive microfilming projects in the mid-twentieth century, in particular the common practice of disposing of original newspapers after they have been microfilmed. Some of these practices were so clearly sensible that there was no controversy. For example, congressmen would have unsolicited constituent mail microfilmed and then dispose of the voluminous originals. Baker rightly saw some materials, especially newspapers, in a different category as cultural artifacts: "If you call Hammacher Schlemmer, say, or Potpourri, or the Miles-Kimball catalogue, to order an 'original keepsake newspaper' for the day a loved one was born, you're buying something that was once part of a library collection."[30] The process of discarding cultural materials— library materials in this case, but with even more emotional implications for unique archival materials—is seen as desecrating the temple. The best rebuttal is probably by Richard Cox.[31] Cox's defense has been vindicated by time. In this case the loss of newspapers in paper form has been compensated for by online archives such as NewspaperARCHIVE.com, the NYT Archives, the TimesMachine, and the Electronic Edition of the

New York Times. The original problem has mostly been solved with technical means, but the technical solutions have their own access problems, which will be addressed in the chapter on access.

Both Baker and Cox are still worth reading as fundamental background on the idealist vs. pragmatist controversy. Baker is one of the most articulate representatives of the idealist school. Cox brings a healthy dose of pragmatism to the argument. What lesson can one learn from this and the other examples? First of all, extreme care needs to be exercised in any disposal or deaccessioning process. Tossing out paper text and deleting electronic records will always be vulnerable to criticism. That fact alone should motivate professionals to select with great care and to prune prudently once materials are in the door. Regardless of whether the particular repository adopts a pragmatic or idealistic approach, or a mix of both, good policies are the essential first step. There is no substitute for well-trained and supervised staff. Preventive measures to anticipate and avoid even the appearance of discarding archives in a careless manner will save time and aggravation in the long run. It is simply worth the effort.

Sometimes pulping, shredding, or deleting is the best method for disposal of duplicate and nonarchival materials. The process must be documented to avoid any suspicion. Sampling is a good practice so one can demonstrate the nature of the discarded materials, as Terry Cook did. Other times, what might be called "open preemption" is the best strategy. If the archives needs to sell a beloved but out-of-scope treasure to raise money in tough times, going public from the beginning might deflect the kind of scandal that thrives on secrets. It may also motivate a financial gift to rescue the collection. For institutional archives, such as business archivists managing internal records, the normal course of operations can include well-defined retention and destruction cycles. If the records are shredded according to a predictable schedule, potentially embarrassing materials about internal disputes are eliminated in an accepted routine. The courts apparently will accept this. No business, even an honest one, wants to see its internal records on the Internet as happened with the cigarette papers, which will be discussed in detail in a separate chapter. [32] Once there is a legal challenge, no relevant records can be deleted or destroyed because the act would constitute destroying legal evidence.

As seen in cases four and five, the vehemence of a dispute is often in inverse relationship to the validity of the complaint. It is best to view such incidents not as annoying distractions by the misinformed, but as a wake-up call—an opportunity to review procedures and refresh the staff's knowledge of ethical norms and best practice. Often managers identify so closely with their organizations that the first reaction is self-defense. The general public, including reporters, tend to view defensiveness as a sign of guilt. A wise and ethical manager will cultivate a circle of advisors who can provide perspective and objectivity in confidence. As in so many cases of archival ethics, transparency, well-considered procedures, and well-trained staff members can prevent serious lapses. A repository that has good inventories that make it clear which items are most valuable and most relevant to the collecting mission facilitates the identification of duplicates, out-of-scope materials, or documents with low research value. Justifying the removal, transfer, sale, or destruction of such materials becomes a matter of routine maintenance. The goals are clear: to refocus the collection, to underwrite more relevant acquisitions, or to provide for the preservation of the core collection.

Once suspicion has been aroused, and when it gets to the point of righteous indignation, as it did in the San Francisco library community, it is difficult to mollify. One cannot expect the general public to understand the relationship of originals and use copies the way a working archivist does. Arguing is not an effective strategy. Prevention is the best cure. A website with clearly articulated policies averts much controversy, as Mark Greene has demonstrated. An institutional tradition of generous outreach programs and well-designed public relations builds confidence. A longstanding good reputation in the community will buffer the righteous indignation in situations where the decision to deaccession causes public concern. A longstanding program of well-managed exhibitions should be part of any archives program, and really proves its worth by establishing public trust in the commitment to preservation. The objects themselves should communicate care and dedication much better than words do.

The final case study has already been touched upon, but it deserves a more detailed look. The New-York Historical Society case reinforces the lessons learned from other examples.

Case Seven: Selling Private Assets

The New-York Historical Society, which was founded in 1804, owns art, artifacts, archives, and books worth more than a billion dollars. On February 3, 1993, the society's board voted to shut the doors of this venerable institution, at least temporarily. Despite the huge monetary value of its assets, it only generated one million dollars in annual revenue, not enough to run an organization of its size and meet a payroll. Its annual offsite storage cost alone was half a million dollars. The board intended to deaccession and sell off twenty million dollars in assets to cover operating expenses. This attempt to monetize some of its assets by selling a portion of its holdings precipitated a storm of protest. Headlines accused the society of "plundering the past," "abdication of responsibility," "rattling toward disintegration," and "raiding endowment to pay for growth."[33]

No leader wants to preside over such a debacle. This case, as mentioned above, deserves a closer examination because it entails many elements that are common to different branches of the cultural heritage field, including archives. The Andrew Mellon Foundation, which had been assisting the organization, commissioned Kevin M. Guthrie to write an analysis of what went wrong. It is not an exposé of incompetence by a particular director; the society had a series of hard-working, well-meaning directors. Guthrie came to the conclusion that the problems were not personal but structural. He also concluded that retention and disposal practices from many years earlier cast a long shadow over the decades of decline.

The New-York Historical Society is one of the oldest and most prestigious in the nation. The society, for example, owns 435 original watercolor paintings for John J. Audubon's *Birds of America*. This one collection is worth many millions of dollars. From the beginning its mission was too broad and its funding too uncertain. The misalignment triggered a succession of financial crises. The first brush with bankruptcy occurred as early as 1825. "The Society had a long history of accepting anything and everything that was given to it with little regard for the quality of the gift, the institution's capacity to absorb it, or the relevance of the gift to the Society's mission."[34] There were other crises—in 1899, 1917, 1945, 1971, 1974, 1984, 1988—and the moment of truth in 1993. The misalignment was certainly chronic and structural.

Guthrie identified a number of structural weaknesses in addition to the oldest problem of an undisciplined accumulation of materials without a clear collecting focus. The mission was vague: just to collect. It succeeded too well. The society did not use professional norms to catalog and inventory its burgeoning collections, many of which deteriorated unknown and unused in storage. It cut itself off from the library and museum communities that were forming in the nineteenth century. It cut itself off from the changing demographics of New York, as the city became a mecca for immigrants from around the world. With its preoccupation with the genealogy of the early New York families, it developed a reputation of being elitist but not interested in serious historical research. It stopped requesting municipal funds in the mid-nineteenth century, and waited over a century before applying officially for funding from New York's cultural budget. All the while, the Metropolitan Museum was receiving generous municipal support. A small number of large bequests postponed the pressure for more careful management, for a well defined mission, and for securing continuous revenue. Whenever the pressure did hit—when the stock market declined, or the bequests were exhausted—there was no mechanism to bring the budget into balance. The temptation at these times was always to monetize cultural assets. This is where the issue of deaccessioning came in.

As early as the 1930s, a rare set of Egyptian artifacts and mummies were sold off. Clearly, ancient Egypt is not the most appropriate collecting area for the New-York Historical Society. It should not have accepted the items in the first place. Many of the acquisitions came with restrictions. The society had promised certain donors to preserve materials in perpetuity. During one crisis in 1970–1971, financial ruin was averted by selling paintings. First the society had to secure court permission, known as *cy pres*, to circumvent the terms of the original gift. There were more sales in the 1980s. In 1987 one of the most energetic board members, Barbara Debs, resigned over the attempt to raise money through deaccessioning, although she did eventually return. These one-time sales did not correct the structural problems, and were simply temporary, stop-gap measures. In that sense the sales were ultimately futile, because they only served to postpone the final reckoning.

This case illustrates why museum codes prohibit the use of sales revenue to pay operating expenses. The New-York Historical Society apparently did not sell archives, which are more difficult to market than paintings and artifacts. As a general rule, rare documents with auction value should be treated both as museum items and as archives. Some archives have been tempted to cannibalize their holdings by selling valuable autographs and historical documents with name recognition value to help bridge an ordinary budget gap. It would be wise for archivists to follow the museum community in clearly acknowledging the unethical and counterproductive nature of such a transaction.

The press reports accused the society of unethical deaccessioning and plundering the past. Guthrie concluded that the society did not err by deaccessioning too much, but erred by not deaccessioning enough throughout its history. The society should have pruned the collections all along to keep them in scope and in scale—in other words, to maintain a coherent collection policy. If they had done so, it would not have been necessary to target their treasures for sale to pay operating expenses. A more pragmatic management would have supported greater idealism in the end. Guthrie went on to ponder a better understanding of the subject of cultural property: "In the final analysis, the decision about whether an item should be deaccessioned depends on many factors. The nonprofit community would benefit greatly from a thorough and objective investigation of the complexities. As part of such an assessment, one useful framework for identifying both when deaccessioning is appropriate and what should be done with the proceeds might be to focus on the source of the cultural component of a nonprofit asset's value, that is, its relevance and importance to the mission of the nonprofit entity."[35] In other words, we need to do more research on the subject of deaccessioning.

All seven cases demonstrate that there is a role for the pragmatists as well as for the idealists. The tension between the two roles is inherent in archival work and cannot be resolved in a simplistic manner, but it can be balanced. It is time to reframe the issue, and remove the Manichaean "either/or" nature of the debate. In a sense the argument has been based on a false dichotomy. The task is to combine the role of the "keeper of the flame" and the role of the "efficient manager." Temple guardians can learn to be good housekeepers, and efficient managers have been known to rescue rare and vulnerable items from cleanup operations. The best analogy might be a classic Japanese gardener, the kind that prunes extensively but with great care for both the health and aesthetics of the trees.

There is also a public relations role for keeping the public engaged and informed. First of all, it helps prevent misdirected righteous indignation and wasted efforts. And second, there are times when it may be important and necessary to harness protests against the destruction of documents for legitimate causes, such as the preservation of the records of apartheid in South Africa or, closer to home, the records of the Internal Revenue Service and White House emails.

Crafting a weeding and deaccessioning policy specific to the given institution's requirements, training the staff in that policy, cultivating a good working relationship with other agencies, maintaining good public relations—all of these traditional assignments help bring the disposal problem under control and avoid the kind of lapses discussed in several of the examples. The concluding twenty questions are not intended to replace the solid guidance provided in the SAA series of manuals, but rather to help sort through the ethical issues, particularly in the more sensitive cases. Armed with an awareness of the issues, each institution needs to find its own balance between pragmatism and idealism. While there are as many formulas for this as there are repositories, credibility should be the common desired result.

Questions for Evaluating Disposal Decisions

Several recent books provide good checklists for deaccessioning and disposal.[36] There is no need to duplicate that guidance here. The following questions are intended to start the evaluations particularly in two situations: when a repository is drafting its policies or when it is considering a particularly sensitive deaccessioning or disposal quandary. The sample policy from the American Heritage Center addresses nearly all of these issues. In exceptional cases there may be a need to take extra care, but normally, once sound policies are in place, the evaluation process is built into procedures and becomes routine and less time consuming.

1. What process is used to identify materials for disposal and deaccessioning, and is it done in an objective and careful manner?

2. Is a clear distinction made between accessioned and nonaccessioned materials?

3. Is a clear distinction made between procedures to screen extraneous inappropriate materials from a collection that is a "keeper," and to dispose of a collection in its entirety, the latter being far more serious?

4. Have the archives' governing documents been examined for the authority to dispose of materials and the process to do so?

5. Is the authorization in a particular case in writing, confirmed by more than one person, and properly filed for future reference?

6. Has the staff double checked who owns legal title to the collection and any instructions in the deed of gift or donor correspondence?

7. In the case of government archives, are the instructions in the retention cycles clear and unambiguous?

8. Does the documentation include an analysis of the value of the collection as a historical source, and was the value, or lack of value, determined by the cognizant curators in the relevant field?

9. Does the documentation address the pertinence of the collection to the mission of the institution and the collecting policy of the archives?

10. If the physical condition of the archives is a factor, has the preservation officer been consulted on issues of reformatting or rehousing?

11. Is there public sentiment about the targeted materials, and will their destruction cause more damage than good?

12. Has the staff explored the option of returning the deaccessioned materials to the original owners or their heirs?

13. Has the staff explored the option of transferring the deaccessioned materials to a more appropriate repository?

14. Is there an intention to sell the materials for fundraising, and if so how would this be interpreted by the press or by donors?

15. If physical destruction is indicated, has the material been sampled for future reference and is the method of destruction appropriate?

16. Have all stages of decision making been documented, including a standardized form that captures the relevant information in the case?

17. Have all of the stakeholders in the collection been consulted with tact and diplomacy?

18. Have the curators reviewed the collection development policy to prevent the acquisition of inappropriate materials in the future?

19. Has legal counsel reviewed the transfer contract to ensure the authority to dispose of any unwanted property in the future?

20. Is the director of the institution prepared to defend the decision if it is challenged?

CHAPTER 4

Equitable Access

Everyone has the right ... to seek, receive and impart information and ideas through any media and regardless of frontiers.

—*The Universal Declaration of Human Rights*
Article 19, the United Nations, December 10, 1948[1]

WHEN JOHN HOPE FRANKLIN (1915–2009) WAS A HARVARD GRADUATE STUDENT CONDUCTING RESEARCH FOR HIS DISSERTATION, HE WAS DENIED ACCESS TO SEVERAL ARCHIVES' READING ROOMS BECAUSE OF HIS RACE. Clearly both a personable and patient scholar, he was able to negotiate with the archives' directors to set up special arrangements and work around the restrictions. Franklin went on to write seventeen books and to receive many honors over the course of his long career.[2] While Franklin ultimately prevailed, undoubtedly many other people in his situation were simply discouraged and never managed to get around the barrier of inequality. Quite a few important collections in the United States were originally closed to specified categories of users—such as women, Roman Catholics, Jews, or even just the donor's nephew—restrictions that have since been lifted by more enlightened management.[3]

Hopefully, such arbitrary discrimination is now a thing of the past, but as some barriers come down others arise. Market forces and globalized technology are building other types of barriers in the form of gated communities of data. Some barriers result from restricting sensitive content:

the professional literature justifies restricting over a dozen different categories of papers, as discussed below. Achieving open and equal access is an ongoing struggle.

The freedom to "receive and impart information and ideas through any media and regardless of frontiers," as enshrined in article 19 of the Universal Declaration of Human Rights, is now a major tenet of American practice. Information professionals are committed to provide open and equal access to books, archives, records, and digital media, to the extent consistent with legal provisions for security and privacy, by balancing these conflicting rights. Most versions of the codes of ethics for archivists advocate unhampered use of archives, including article 6 in the 2005 SAA Code of Ethics for Archivists:

> Archivists strive to promote open and equitable access to their services and the records in their care without discrimination or preferential treatment, and in accordance with legal requirements, cultural sensitivities, and institutional policies. Archivists recognize their responsibility to promote the use of records as a fundamental purpose of the keeping of archives. Archives may place restrictions on access for the protection of privacy or confidentiality of information in the records.[4]

Equal access without discrimination or preferential treatment is a hard-won principle. Its value has not always been self-evident, either in the centuries-old archives of Europe or in American institutions.

The major thesis of this chapter will be developed in the context of "ground truth" and real-life examples: achieving open and equitable access is the result of complex ongoing transactions. There is an inherent tension between the legitimate right to information and legitimate restriction of proprietary data. For this reason, access policies must be drawn up and periodically revised with great care by experienced archival professionals. The seemingly boring policies have serious consequences, some intended and some unforeseen. The examples will show that professional archival ethics are linked to both moral values (even saving lives, as in the case of tobacco research files) as well as democratic values, such as preserving accurate information for the voting public, as in the case of access to White House email traffic secured by the National Security Archive.

In this discussion, the term *access* covers a range of meanings, from purely physical access in the reading room, to user-friendly websites, to privileges for use, to intellectual access through finding aids and databases. Intellectual access is provided by technical staff. Hands-on access is provided by the reference staff. All of the different functions are intertwined and need to operate together smoothly. The finest, most detailed finding aids will not reach the right scholars without a coordinated interpretive program from reference staff. In fact, occasionally the technically best-crafted finding aids are incomprehensible to the most knowledgeable historians, who may be less adept with online tools than younger novices. From the standpoint of the researcher, the one thing that matters is getting to the relevant documents.

Sometimes the term *equitable* is substituted for *equal*, to suggest that there are situations when it is reasonable and appropriate to provide one researcher with more in-depth help than another. Common sense dictates that both a widely published scholar and a first-year student may require more time from reference staff than the average reader. The point is that all researchers should receive the type of help they need. Traditionally this service has been provided in a physical reading room, although increasingly access assistance takes place via email, links, and texting in a virtual arena.

Reading Room Fundamentals

Access services are key to the reputation of the archives. The reading room is the public face of the archives. In this space, readers judge the staff and the institution as a whole. For detailed guidance, archives staff should keep close at hand Mary Jo Pugh's access manual *Providing Reference Services for Archives and Manuscripts.*[5] The book has an extensive bibliographical essay which obviates the need to duplicate the fundamental references here. There are certain basic ethical standards for access services that have

developed over the years. These standards can be summarized fairly suc-
cinctly in a single paragraph:

> The reference archivists are required to be courteous and helpful to
> all readers without playing favorites. They are expected to project
> an image of trust and integrity. While maximizing access, they are
> expected to be discreet and not reveal privileged information.
> Without a subpoena, they are not supposed to reveal to others what
> items a particular researcher has requested. At the same time, if they
> see parallel research projects, they are expected to ask permission of
> each researcher separately, and then, with permission, inform each
> one separately of the possible duplication of effort. They are primarily
> supposed to help others with research, but they are encouraged
> to conduct research of their own either with permission of their
> supervisors or on their own time. In doing their own research, they
> are not allowed to sequester or restrict interesting files so that they
> can publish first. They may privately collect manuscripts only as
> long as it is not in the area of their employer. Privately collecting
> manuscripts in the same subject area as the repository at which they
> are employed would constitute a conflict of interest. Most obviously,
> they are not supposed to indulge in any "insider trading," that is,
> using the privileged information that they acquire in the course
> of their work for unfair gain. They are not supposed to accept any
> inappropriate gifts that could look like a bribe. They are charged with
> protecting the archives from misuse and theft. They are charged with
> applying the reading room regulations fairly and answering reference
> questions promptly. Most of all, they provide open and equal access
> to primary sources.

Of all of these seemingly common-sense provisions, the most difficult
to implement is that of open and equitable access.

A good argument can be made that the three areas of archival work
with the most difficult legal issues and ethical dilemmas are acquisitions
(addressed in a previous chapter), access, and copyright. Providing access—
physical, administrative, and intellectual access—is at the heart of reference
services. Copyright, which can be interpreted as an access issue, is also a

component of the ethics of reference. There is a definite tension between the twin roles of controlling access and promoting use. The dynamics in this balance have shifted dramatically several times in modern history. Each shift has left traces in the access policies of repositories, which are sometimes only comprehensible from a historical perspective. One can broadly define the changing role of the archivist as a shift from gatekeeper to facilitator, mediator, and advocate. Just as a consensus was formed about open and equitable access, the online environment intensified the struggle between proprietary control and free use of information. A new layer is being added to the intrinsic dilemma of providing fair access.

The Archivist as Gatekeeper vs. the Archivist as Facilitator

Who gets in through the archives' door? Writing in 1956 in the *American Archivist*, Howard Peckham wrote of the model repository: "If it should open its doors to competent scholars, then it should close them to those who are not competent."[6] Today it seems presumptuous that a reference archivist would vet a researcher's competence. Peckham's view was not uncommon at the time and was linked to older customs, some of which have left lingering traces in access policies.

Archives have a far longer history in Europe than in the United States. For centuries in the European tradition, archives were treated as secret state papers, a tool for designated representatives of a sovereign state, not accessible to the common people or to foreigners. In Prussia the state archives were named the Geheimes Staatesarchiv, using the word for secret or privy, *geheim,* in the very title. Access by trusted historians depended on privilege and connections. In nineteenth-century Russia, the great poet Alexander Pushkin had to petition the Tsar himself for "the permission to occupy myself with historical research in our state archives." The Tsar personally granted the famous author's request. That kind of access was reserved for a few very privileged intellectuals of the higher aristocracy.[7]

Traditionally reference archivists have played a gatekeeper role. A service oriented staff was not the norm. They enforced rules on who was permitted into the archives reading room, and then determined who was allowed to see what. First the applicants for using the archives were screened for their qualifications, then the documents were screened for restrictions. While access in state archives was the privilege of highly placed government officials for performing their duties, a few historians were allowed into these hallowed halls as an exception. In these traditional archives the staff would turn away the unworthy, and hold back materials often at their own discretion. These modes of access evolved out of the ancient customs found in European government repositories, ecclesiastical manuscript collections, and the private collections of wealthy aristocrats. The papers were the absolute property of the state, the church, or elite families, who had historic entitlements—and often historic reasons for secrecy.

The first cracks in this fortress opened up in the Enlightenment of the eighteenth century. Open access to public records in Swedish archives can be traced back at least to 1766.[8] By that time, what we might today call transparency was already a strong element of Scandinavian culture, rather typically stronger there than in other European countries. In a small, predemocratic monarchy such as Sweden at the time, open records functioned both to enforce conformity to social norms among the lower classes and at the same time to reduce the potential for serious abuses of power by the elites. In larger countries such as France, violent clashes between different classes forced open the public records, at least in part. It is the populist orientation of the French Revolution that is generally credited with launching the public archives tradition. To remind Americans of this principle, Ernst Posner cited article 37 of the Messidor decree issued in 1794 following the French Revolution: "Every citizen is entitled to ask in every depository…for the production of the documents it contains."[9] In the nineteenth century, access to government records in European countries was still generally tightly controlled by entrenched political and religious elites, while in the United States official archives were not systematically collected at all.

Over two centuries the trend toward open access has been gradually strengthened. The Council of Europe has come out in favor of open and free access in principle, within certain constraints. Archival experts have made recommendations for implementing a modern European policy on access to archives. The section on ethics is worth summarizing.[10] The general policy is the now-familiar one of open and equal access. The first principle is that "Access to public archives is a right." This derives from the ideals that emerged in the French Revolution. The corollary is that the right to have access to archives should apply to all users. The European Council has been working on the complex project of harmonizing access policies across Europe. All restrictions, in this view, should have an expiration date, and restrictions should apply equally to all users. This sounds very familiar. However, the authors go on to recognize the normal European practice of closing all governmental files transferred to the archives uniformly for thirty years, and closing all files with personal information for 100 to 120 years after the birth year of the "data subject." Despite a sincere commitment to open access, in practice records are routinely closed for decades. And scholars' credentials are still vetted.

First, there are problems when records are closed for lengthy restrictions. Open and equal access does not seem very helpful if records are closed for decades, basically until the people most directly interested in them are dead. Here is the crux of the ethical dilemma posed by access questions, only magnified by European practices of lengthy and automatic blanket restrictions. From the American perspective, government archives need to be made available promptly, barring some security issue. The most compelling reason is the need to know what government is doing in order to vote intelligently and to formulate responsible public policy. Timeliness counts. A second reason is that historians are increasingly interested in current events—the history of the present—an area once thought to be the purview of journalism rather than historiography. History now begins with yesterday. A third reason is to let individuals know what documentation has been saved concerning their lives, the right of access by so-called data subjects during their lifetimes. For all the lip service to transparency, governments find ways to close archives. In the European tradition blanket closure is used to restrict access; in the American tradition there is heavy reliance on classifying large swaths of archival documentation.

In addition to restrictions on the documents, archivists screen researchers and their projects to determine who gets access to records. As to vetting researchers' qualifications, most Americans, especially those denied access, would consider this historic archival custom to be excessively stringent and capricious and simply unacceptable. Increasingly most democratic countries have achieved a public consensus that open information benefits society as a whole. The notion that the archivist could rule on a researcher's competence to use the material is generally deemed elitist and undemocratic—in a word, unethical. It was once the norm, and still remains surprisingly common. And it is sometimes justified.

Where is the line between protective policies and obstructive ones? Europeans and Americans usually draw that line in different places. For a traveling archivist it is always an interesting exercise to request access at different institutions in different cultures.[11] Most try to balance the modern sense of a universal right to information with older provisions to preserve the prerogatives of sovereignty and privilege. There are continuing preferences for national academic users and discrimination against foreigners and outsiders. In 2000 the author asked about access to the Hungarian security police files in Budapest. The archives director politely explained that an American would not be able to see the files of the communist-era secret police, but that Europeans would be able to gain access because European and Hungarian laws were compatible, but American laws were not. While Americans react negatively to this explanation, in conflict with the right to information regardless of frontiers, many Europeans tend to agree with the principle involved.

For the most part, American reading rooms permit access to anyone willing to show identification and abide by the rules for safe handling of materials. Letters of recommendation or advance notification of publication plans are usually not a factor in gaining admission. Several examples of more restrictive access policies, from Britain, California, Germany, and Russia, illustrate the lingering access restrictions from an earlier era that have persisted into modern times, particularly in older, more traditional institutions. In government archives the restrictions seem to stem from a desire to preserve the prerogatives of sovereignty. In elite manuscript collections the restrictions are driven by two kinds of concerns. The first is the physical preservation of delicate and often ancient documents. The second is the prevalence of sensitive information in manuscript collections. This protective attitude is at odds with current, use-oriented American practice, but it can be well justified. Just as with deaccessioning, discussed in the previous chapter, there is an inherent conflict between protectionism and pragmatism. The question is not which side is right, but rather what balance is right for a particular institution.

Tradition in a British Library

Since Shakespearian times, the archivists of the University of Oxford's Bodleian Library Special Collections have been very protective of their materials. This gatekeeper mentality has had a positive effect. This respect for the archives has helped to preserve and protect them from loss and wear. In 1654, the Bodleian archivists purportedly turned down a request from Oliver Cromwell himself to borrow a manuscript. When a researcher visits the Bodleian to conduct research, there is a detailed application and screening process. In 1998 the author complied with these procedures and then was photographed. Then the archivists administered an archaic oath that had to be repeated out loud. Researchers promise not, among other potential transgressions, to bring kindling into the reading room as it constitutes a fire hazard. The admission process dates from Sir Thomas Bodley's own statutes, which he issued in the early 1600s. It has an undeniable antiquarian charm. Today independent researchers still need to establish their credentials, demonstrate the seriousness of their work, prove that they cannot conduct this research from published nonarchival sources, and produce references to vouch for them.[12] For independent researchers there is a modest use fee that can be waived in hardship cases.

Those scholars permitted into the facilities at the Bodleian must adhere to time-honored restrictions. For instance they may only read personal documents if the authors are already safely dead. In one famous case,

Kingsley Amis, the inconveniently living author of certain archived letters, gave written permission for the researcher to see those letters, but the
Bodleian still denied the request as a violation of privacy. Amis requested
copies of his own letters for himself, which was allowed, and then forwarded the copies to the researcher.[13] Independent scholars who clear these
hurdles and abide by the ancient rules may encounter a new restriction.
The Bodleian cannot guarantee them access to all online resources, since
they are governed by restrictive licensing agreements.

Tradition in an American Library

While the pattern of screening researchers and vetting their topics has never
been common in the United States, there are a few exceptions. Following
venerable European traditions, the reference archivists at a prestigious
American rare book and manuscript library, the Huntington Library in
California, require independent scholars to submit justification for their
research topics, explain their qualifications, supply two letters of recommendation, and wait three weeks for an answer. The process and its justification are very similar to that of the Bodleian Library at Oxford. Applicants
are scrutinized carefully to determine whether they are sufficiently scholarly
to use the manuscripts. Preference is given to those with a book contract.
Reading rare manuscripts inevitably subjects them to wear, and this process
ensures that use is targeted for those scholars most likely to publish and
advance knowledge of the materials. In contrast, the Bentley Historical
Library at the University of Michigan, for example, does not vet researchers.[14] Each repository has found its own access formula in keeping with its
history and collections. Would it make sense for the Huntington Library to
let just anyone handle the Gutenberg Bible? Probably not. The Huntington's
restrictive access to rare and fragile manuscripts is ameliorated by generous
outreach and exhibition programs for the public. This program opens up
the collections for the public's appreciation without subjecting them to
heavy use. Each institution has to find its own balance between protectionism and pragmatism, between gatekeeping and facilitating access.

European Archives

Governmental archives have additional layers of control to negotiate in providing access to the public without impeding the ability of a sovereign state to protect its citizenry. Though also historically linked to ancient European traditions, the modern German State Archives, or Bundesarchiv, has become increasingly open to research, and supports the notion of freedom of information as one of the pillars of democracy. There is a user-friendly website with clear information, and extensive online finding aids. German archivists have found a way to balance democratic traditions of transparency with respect for governmental requirements for confidentiality. In some regards the Germans are more restrictive than the American archivists, and in some regards they are more open. A well-funded and well-organized system, the Bundesarchiv serves as a model for many other countries, and is a useful example.

As mentioned above, the Germans use a standard blanket restriction on government documents of thirty years after transfer to the archives. This makes the archivist's job much easier as individual documents of recent history do not need to be individually vetted. As to screening researchers, in principle, everyone is eligible to use state papers that are over thirty years old. Historians are encouraged to use the German archives, but they must submit both the topic of research as well as the intended purpose for approval. Access is limited to materials on the topic as formulated in advance. Information gathered for one approved publication or project cannot be reconceptualized and reused for a different topic later without going back to the archives for permission.[15]

In this model, use of information from state archives in unapproved ways is an affront to sovereignty. This prior control strikes many American-trained researchers as an affront to freedom of information, a kind of prior censorship. And then there is a certain follow-up control. The archives, also by long tradition, request copies or at least citations of all publications that reference their collections. One cannot help but wonder whether a publication critical of the state would affect access to the archives at a later point. The gatekeeper function is retained but tempered with an extremely welcoming and helpful reference service and powerful online finding aids.

An instructive exception to this general thirty-year restriction was formulated specifically for the East German secret police files, known as the Stasi archives. Special legislation made the files available under controlled conditions soon after the fall of communism. Victims of surveillance could see the files kept on them immediately.[16] In the initial phase, millions of ordinary citizens saw their own files, but were barred from viewing the files of others out of privacy concerns. Also under controlled conditions, the policy promoted scholarly research and use by journalists. German archivists well into the twenty-first century considered this exception for the Stasi archives regrettable.[17] There was a strong preference in the German archival profession to treat the Stasi files consistently under the same laws as the West German archives. Instead, the German parliament approved a detailed and lengthy policy, which balances privacy and state security concerns with access. The many pages of provisions screen various categories of papers and different categories of applicants. The complicated procedure provides the most open access policies in the world for political police archives, more open than the files of the FBI and CIA in the United States. A huge staff with a large budget implements the German Stasi archives program. As a result, the German public has an unusually accurate and nuanced image of recent history, as it actually happened.

From an American perspective, the German access policies appear to be a very complex balancing act. Ancient prerogatives of sovereignty and privilege continue to be protected under the thirty-year restriction, while elaborate provisions and exceptions accommodate modern demands for rapid and equal access in a democratic society, especially to topics of intense interest. There probably is no simple solution to the inherent dilemma of access. Complex access policies may be the future of archives.

Russian Archives

Like the Germans, the Russians have seen a revolution in their archives. In the Soviet era Russian archives were famously secret, restricted, and nationalistic. There was a simple system for ensuring that Russian scholars had privileged access to Russian archives. Orlando Figes vividly described the experience prior to 1986.[18] Foreigners had no access to finding aids, but they needed to request materials by citation. They only knew that documents existed once they were cited by Russian scholars. It was a tidy way to favor "native" scholars. Then requests for documents would be evaluated by a representative from the dreaded secret police, the KGB—a chilling effect, to say the least. When they were granted access, foreign scholars had to work in a separate reading room, isolated from the Russian historians. To further inhibit fraternization, they were not allowed access to the canteen. Figes found a loophole in the system: in the men's room, he would offer cigarettes to chain-smoking Soviet colleagues in exchange for archival file numbers. Every restriction seems to serve as a challenge to evade it.

The fall of Soviet communism in 1991 provided an unprecedented opportunity to open up the largest remaining cache of secret files on the cold war. The severe restrictions of the Soviet era were loosened up dramatically during the Yeltsin revolution and the fall of communism in 1991–1992, when freedom of information took on anarchic forms. Old habits die hard, and the new post-Soviet parliament, or Duma, acted quickly to reassert sovereign privilege over access to state papers in a series of legislation from 1993 to 1995.[19] Letters of recommendation have always played an important role in the application process. Some readers received privileged access and others were turned down, in a manner puzzling to Western researchers. The same scholar could see a document on one visit, but be denied access on a later research trip. Documents were declassified and then some were reclassified. Still, it was possible to talk about a door opening to the Soviet archives.[20]

The rules stabilized in the late 1990s. Regulations from 1998 specify that "all users have equal rights of access to documents in the archives" (article I-4), yet letters of recommendation are still required. There is also a certain tension between the theory of free access and the detailed tracking of each researcher's plans for publication. Similar to the German system of oversight of the intended use of the archives, scholars in the Russian archives are required to "Furnish the required reference to the source for any archival information received that may be cited or published,…in accordance with the Law of the Russian Federation" (ch. 12, sec. 2). And they are required to provide either a "bibliographic reference or a copy of any publication prepared on the basis of documents in the archive."[21] In both the German and Russian policies, many traditional access restrictions have been lifted and replaced by monitoring a researcher's publication plans.

In the Russian law on archives, there are very detailed provisions for protecting privacy, sufficiently restrictive to squelch almost any research project on a contemporary topic. These laws are not always enforced, but they remain on the books. Such provisions are something of a sleeping giant.

As exemplified in the access policy of the Bentley Historical Library, most American manuscript collections are open to all researchers who are willing to supply identification and sign an agreement to abide by the rules for the safe handling of materials. It is rare to require letters of recommendation, or to monitor publication plans in advance. Usually the only demand is for a researcher to credit the repository when something is cited in print. Copies or even notification are not required. American governmental archives, such as the Library of Congress and National Archives, have liberal policies for access to special materials in this tradition.[22] According to the NARA website: "Anyone can use the National Archives. You do not need to be an American citizen or to present credentials or a letter of recommendation." Does this mean that anyone can handle the Declaration of Independence? Or see recent CIA documents? Certainly not. There are many constraints on free access to information regardless of media or frontiers.

Perhaps the most common residual obstacle to access both in the United States and abroad is not the formal requirements or procedures, but rather a gatekeeper mentality that can turn away researchers more effectively than any rules. For instance, if a researcher is left waiting for an hour to receive a reader's card, all the rules on open and equal access are moot. Uncommunicative staff will simply have a chilling effect. Various codes of ethics have actually tried to require a welcoming environment. It is the duty of the archives management to develop a service orientation that colors all phases of the operation, from the construction of finding aids, to the website, to negotiation on deeds of gift, to the front door, to turnaround time on answering email, and to the staffing of the reference desk.

As sketched above, over the centuries a profound shift in the attitude toward openness has taken place, and it has transformed the role of the reference archivist. There are residual traces of protectionism, and often they can be justified. In general, most reference archivists take pride in creating a user-friendly environment and encouraging use. The sense of the public's entitlement to information has been growing at an accelerating pace. Traditionally restrictive repositories in Europe and the United States have increasingly liberalized their policies and compensated for residual restrictions with various outreach programs. Open access is not altogether new, of course. Its basis can be found in the eighteenth-century Enlightenment in France, and also in Sweden where openness has long been a valued part of the culture. Americans, in particular, can take pride in having established some of the most welcoming reading rooms in the world. It is part of our legacy. Certainly the founding fathers were persuasive advocates of freedom of information, especially in the form of freedom of the press. The great public library expansion of the nineteenth century is definitely part of this movement toward making more information available to the general public, regardless of an individual's formal qualifications.

The American Library Association Code of Ethics places helpful and welcoming service prominently as its first article: "We provide the highest level of service to all library users through appropriate and usefully organized resources; equitable service policies; equitable access; and accurate, unbiased, and courteous responses to all requests."[23] The ideal of a taciturn unsociable archivist as described by the European archivist Ernst Posner never fit well in the American information landscape.[24]

Since the late twentieth century, the public has tested this commitment by demanding more and faster access to documents that illuminate both current events and historical ones. These demands have found expression in the Freedom of Information Act and various "sunshine laws." American archivists, with their strong ties to the American public library tradition, have worked hard to keep up with the new demands. They have embraced this openness as a self-understood function of a healthy democratic society. The charge to maximize open and equal access is articulated in the joint ALA-SAA statement on access. The first article of the 1994 version reads as follows:

> A repository preserves collections for use by researchers. It is the responsibility of a repository to make available original research materials in its possession on equal terms of access. Access should be provided in accordance with statutory authority, institutional mandate, the Code of Ethics for Archivists, the Standards for Ethical Conduct for Rare Book, Manuscript, and Special Collections Librarians, and this Joint Statement. A repository should not deny access to materials to any researcher, nor grant privileged or exclusive use of materials to any researcher, nor conceal the existence of any body of material from any researcher, unless required to do so by statutory authority, institutional mandate, or donor or purchase stipulation.[25]

Archivists in the U.S. not only went along with the paradigm shift from screening out researchers to actively promoting use, they probably initiated it. The archival reference service now functions as a mediating or facilitating role, opening up access to the maximum level allowed within legal and institutional constraints. The reference archivist is a guide through the bewildering forests of finding aids and databases to locate relevant information, as defined by the researcher, not the archivist. The reference archivist still has to enforce restrictions that protect privacy, trade secrets, or security-classified information. This gatekeeper role underwent a profound transition during the past decades and has been greatly reduced to a secondary task. Instead, archivists began to encourage wider use even by nontraditional scholars: younger students were made welcome; genealogists were provided with assistance, even those without book contracts.

The reference archivists typically put effort into minimizing restrictions and eliminating ones that are no longer necessary. They have become skilled in interviewing researchers to maximize the relevant materials they can locate for them. They place calls to sister institutions for more materials, and even help with finding accommodations and transportation. Most of all they have become experts at interpreting the confusing array of finding aids, registers, and indexes that vex research for the uninitiated, and negotiating through tangles of descriptions to find the "smoking-gun" document. Then the researcher publishes the results. In this shift from gatekeeping to mediation, the self-effacing reference archivists function like anonymous Sherpa guides taking mountain climbers up the slopes of the Himalayan mountains, and then letting the foreigners in the land take the credit and glory for reaching the goal.

In her manual on reference service, Mary Jo Pugh has described this fundamental transformation: "In general, the archival profession has moved from a custodial role, in which the archivist's primary duty was to protect repository collections by limiting use, to a more activist role promoting the wider use of archives."[26] Despite the residual gatekeeping duties, she concludes: "Equality of access is now the governing principle for use of records in most repositories. Information to be protected is identified and segregated during acquisition and processing. Access policies are therefore administered, but not determined, at the reference desk." She supplies a helpful checklist for keeping procedures in line with this goal.

American professionals have confronted the inherent illogic of advocating transparency on the one hand and then on the other hand imposing privacy and other restrictions. These conundrums have received extensive treatment at SAA conferences and in the literature.[27] But they cannot be neatly resolved.

Constraints on Open Access

The principle of open access, then, is tempered by a surprisingly large number of privileged categories of information. Since Behrnd-Klodt and Pugh provide great detail on these conditions,[28] they will simply be summarized here:

- *Security-classified documents,* such as those with the U.S. government "top secret" designation, fall under the most serious restriction; the intent is to protect national security secrets. Complex laws and rules govern the handling of such materials. These laws frequently change. Given the serious consequences of mishandling classified information, a surprisingly large amount of classified documentation has found its way into private hands and into private collections. Any documents, even seemingly innocuous ones, with such top secret markings or stamps should be sequestered until qualified, cleared professionals can examine them and determine their status. The best resource is the Information Security Oversight Office (ISOO) of the National Archives.[29] ISOO experts know the complicated regulations for handling classified materials. They can help identify which documents are candidates for declassification so that they can eventually be returned to normal storage. Not just anyone with a clearance can see any classified documents. There has to be a "need to know." Americans respect the classification of documents from allied governments. Declassification of documents held by a government agency may be requested through the Freedom of Information Act or FOIA. Until the FOIA procedure is successfully completed, only cleared personnel should handle classified documents, even obviously innocuous ones.

- *Donor imposed restrictions* need to be carefully negotiated at the time of acquisition to ensure that they are provided with a reasonable end date and that the restrictions are applied equitably. Exceptions such as privileged access for an authorized biographer should also be considered very carefully. Inappropriate or discriminatory restrictions on older acquisitions should be renegotiated with the donor or heirs according to current practice.

- *Privacy* may need to be protected for some period of time. Privacy protection generally expires when the person dies. There are exceptions in cases of celebrity. The family members may require privacy protection even after the death of the person in question. Just what information is considered private or sensitive varies widely. One donor was perfectly agreeable to releasing information about her father's extramarital affairs, but did not want to release a letter she wrote fifty years ago mildly criticizing her sister-in-law. There is general agreement on the need to conceal such things as social security numbers and private bank account numbers to prevent identity theft and electronic pilfering. As such information may be sprinkled throughout the collections, it is not an easy rule to implement. An effort should be made to redact out such private data by deleting from the online use record, but with a clear indication of what has been removed. With paper records the practice has been to photocopy the document, black out the information, and then re-photocopy the redacted text for the use copy. (See chapter 6.)

- *Trade secrets* are typically jealously guarded by business archivists. Industrial espionage is a big business and guarding against it requires constant vigilance on the part of commercial enterprises. (See the discussion of the cigarette papers case in chapter 5.) While business archives are the property of the corporation that generated them, there is a growing sense that the right to information extends to historical records in private corporate archives. Such archives contain a great deal of social history and economic history that belong to the larger culture that made the company possible. At issue is the time at which these records should be released from the proprietary claims (ten years? twenty years?) and be made available to the public.

- *Personnel records* are typically privileged during the lifetime of the subjects. Information on promotions and reprimands is especially sensitive. Papers relating to university tenure decisions are prone to litigation and should be guarded from casual eyes. Objectivity can be difficult. One donor was adamant about opening foreign military personnel files in his collection because he felt strongly that they had historical significance. When asked if he would want his own U.S. Army personnel file available for anyone to read, he was just as adamantly opposed. Data subjects should have access to the information in their own files, but third parties should not.

- *The attorney-client privilege* has a long history. It also has a long history of abuse as a shield for protecting incriminating materials from the legal process of discovery.

- *The priest-parishioner relationship* has typically been protected to preserve the confidential relationship in confessional conversations.

- *The husband-wife relationship* has certain privileges of privacy.

- *Medical records* have come under very strict legal restrictions. Every archivist managing medical files needs to be conversant with the latest regulations in this area, typically referred to by the acronym as HIPAA since the Health Insurance Portability and Accountability Act has a privacy rule.

- *Student records,* such as grades, are also considered privileged, sometimes even restricted from parents of adult students. This category is usually referred to as FERPA, from the Family Educational Rights and Privacy Act.

- *Journalists' sources* have traditionally been shielded. Collections from reporters should be examined with this in mind and discussed with the donors.

- *Library and archives circulation and use records* have traditionally been privileged. If a journalist phones the archives and asks whether a certain person has used a certain collection, normally that information is not divulged without a subpoena.

- *Internal financial records* of the host institution will be saved in many institutional archives, and these are typically not revealed except to high-level executives. Any archivist in charge of such materials needs to have a clear understanding of who has access rights and carefully document each use and the required permission.

- *Exceptionally rare and fragile records* may be restricted for preservation purposes. In these cases a surrogate use copy should be prepared as quickly as possible in some form. Microfilm, photocopy, and digital copies have all been used successfully as stand-ins for fragile originals.

- *Unprocessed collections* may be restricted until there is intellectual control. This constraint has several justifications. Without a register, it would be difficult to verify a theft from the collection. Without a register, it would be difficult to determine if the collection contained privileged information. The sheer volume of modern records and the mandate for increased access is eroding this constraint. An argument put forth by archivists Mark Greene and Dennis Meissner, that time spent on detailed processing delays research, is gaining national support.[30] Increasingly, unprocessed materials are being opened for use with minimal processing (either collection-level descriptions or preliminary inventories). The responsibility for compliance with constraints on revealing privileged information is shifted from the archives to the researcher. Given the size of modern collections this is the pragmatic solution. It is not clear whether court decisions will always support this practical approach.

- *Copyrighted materials* are sometimes restricted as the only sure method of preventing copyright violation. One repository was threatened with a lawsuit over the unapproved publication of a document even though the publisher had received a letter from the archives specifically prohibiting him from publishing the copies he had made. Every archivist needs to bookmark the section on copyright in Pugh's SAA manual on reference and update it as needed. Just knowing to provide a link to a digital text rather than the text itself can prevent legal difficulties. It is a good practice for libraries and archives to maintain online copyright reminders based on legal counsel and updated regularly for advice on such things as electronic coursepacks and podcasting.[31]

- *Licensing contracts for databases* comprise another restriction that is becoming controversial as more people find that the documents they need are online and available only to subscribers to a commercial service that may cost thousands of dollars or more a year.

- *Authorized biographers* sometimes restrict materials for their exclusive use. This is a controversial restriction. Often donors or heirs will select a biographer and then reserve the papers until the biography is published. For the safety of the papers, it is best if they are in the archives while the biographer works and not in the writer's own home or office. Such discriminatory access may be justified for a limited time if it protects the papers from damage, dispersal, or loss during the writing of such a book. Stanford law professor Gerald Gunther retained exclusive access to the papers of Judge Learned Hand for decades while composing the great jurist's biography. One reviewer estimates that Gunther spent thirty-seven years writing the biography. Many scholars chaffed at the loss of easy access to the Hand papers, but the resulting biography has been acclaimed as a magnificent contribution to legal history.[32] Does a superb biography justify unequal access to cultural patrimony? One can argue both sides.

One restriction that is *not* acceptable is for archivists to withhold materials from reading room use while they themselves prepare documents for publication. The Loewenheim case of 1970 established this principle.[33] The American Historical Association (AHA) looked into Professor Francis Loewenheim's charges that staff at the Franklin D. Roosevelt Presidential Library had improperly withheld documents from a researcher in order to publish the information first themselves. The AHA absolved the archivists of wrongdoing, but emphasized that withholding documents would have been unethical if it had actually happened.

The list of restricted categories is long. These accepted restrictions do not all carry the same weight, and there are many significant exceptions. The ethical implications become interesting when such standard restrictions collide with the right to know. Then the ethical archivist has a challenge in negotiating the best balance of rights. Open access may trump restrictions in cases where the topic is sufficiently important to the public welfare. Accelerated access to relevant information is required when public policy is being formulated. No archivist, however good at mediation, can navigate these obstacles in isolation. And often the correct procedures can be very complex, and sometimes expensive to implement. The importance of coordinating with legal counsel and the higher administration is made clear in the case of the cigarette papers, described in detail in chapter 5.

In almost every restricted category there is a famous exception that proves the rule. In the case of security-classified documents, the first and most serious constraint on access, proper maintenance and storage can be time-consuming and expensive to enforce correctly. Any archivist in charge of such papers first needs to attend special workshops and then needs to educate the archives' parent institution about the proper procedures. Only in the gravest situations has the release of classified information been condoned. The primary example is the Pentagon Papers, top secret documents that were illegally released to the press in 1971 by Daniel Ellsberg. The papers revealed details of secret decision making in the Vietnam War, important information that had been withheld from the American public. After a hard-fought battle, both in the courts and in the arena of public opinion, influential policy makers sided with freedom of information: the country simply had a need to know the facts.[34] Using similar logic the courts decided in favor of open access to the cigarette papers, even though these papers were originally thought to be covered by the attorney-client privilege and definitely contained proprietary trade secrets. The Diane Middlebrook biography of poet Anne Sexton used medical therapy tapes that many psychiatrists considered privileged (see chapter 6). Archivists need to be very familiar with these restricted categories, but also with the history of exceptions in order to provide higher administration with seasoned advice when necessary.

The archival community in the United States and the American public have reached a consensus on the value of open and equal access. On rare occasions open and equal access even trumps security classification, proprietary trade secrets, and privacy, but only if the issue is sufficiently important. Since the eighteenth century, restrictive archives both in the United States and in Europe have modified their procedures in the name of democratic openness. The tension between openness and privilege appeared to be in equilibrium. Then the information technology revolution led to an entirely new set of issues that soon pervaded the archival and information business. The large-scale digital library brings with it another set of access dilemmas. And information technology is combining with several other seemingly unstoppable forces—and transforming the ethics of archives. Mapping hard-won and long-cherished values over into the digital environment is the new challenge.

Proprietary Control vs. Free Access in the Digital Environment

For half a millenium, since the Gutenberg revolution in the fifteenth century, there has been a clear distinction between a published book and a manuscript. The book allows multiple identical copies to be distributed among many readers in many locations. Manuscripts since antiquity have been less stable objects: unique originals have been laboriously copied with many alterations and variants. The manuscripts that serve as the basis of books typically undergo numerous drafts and changes prior to freezing into the more fixed print version. Where do cumulative online texts fit into this schema? Take for example the articles in Wikipedia that are subject to constant revision. It is no accident that information technology (IT) professionals call these unstable texts *documents* and have turned the word *archive* into a verb describing ways to save text in all its variants. This digital format shares many attributes with archives and is increasingly a subject for the archival profession. Is digital text a publication or a document?

American courts have interpreted digitized documents as publications. There is logic to this viewpoint. In the case of the cigarette papers, this interpretation of digitized text as a publication, one that is protected by the First Amendment, saved the archives from surrendering pirated copies. Microfilm versions of archives have long been called *publications*.

Both online and microform versions of archives allow the text to be distributed among many readers in many locations—the very definition of a publication.

Digital texts, unlike books and microfilm, are subject to many revisions and changes, even tampering and hostile vandalism. Migration from one platform to another can introduce both intended and unintended alterations in format and text. These digital objects typically exist in many versions with deletions and additions—much like a manuscript.

To establish an authoritative version of a literary masterpiece, an editor must determine the correct chronological sequence of manuscript drafts, and then study related documentation to determine the author's final intent. It is recognized as a complex editorial job to establish a "critical edition." With digital texts, it can also be a challenge to find, analyze, and properly sequence the variants. In a way, digital texts, because of their extraordinary mutability and wide distribution, are even more challenging. One can even conceptualize digital texts as "permanently variable" manuscript drafts. Certainly the articles in Wikipedia are intended to be constantly in flux, constantly debated, corrected, and expanded over time. With Wikipedia, these changes are consciously tracked in a detailed and transparent way as the text is constantly corrected and theoretically improved.[35] (It should be noted that erroneous information extracted from these texts can be embedded in other documents that remain uncorrected as the source article is updated.) For most web pages, tracing earlier versions is a hit and miss operation, depending on such things as the "Wayback Machine" of the San Francisco-based Internet Archives and cached pages on Google. These efforts at fixing ephemeral and mutating texts are remarkable for what they can do, but in the end they cannot capture deep web structures, password-protected sites, or subscription based web pages.

The version of text you see today may not be the one your colleague told you about yesterday. Authentication is again a major preoccupation, as it was in the pre-Gutenberg era. As online text increasingly supplements and replaces paper-based text, even in the newspaper field, digital objects will have more in common with manuscripts and archives than with print publications. Abby Smith reached a similar conclusion. She observed that many digital sites are "collections of archival materials that, in the analog realm, would go to a special collections library without being published."[36] It is interesting to see how much of traditional archival practice translates over to digital formats. It is also interesting to see how many longstanding archival ethical concerns also have pertinence in the digital realm. Authenticity is a major one, as are issues concerning privacy, piracy, and—especially—equal access. In fact, in each of these areas, including access, the digital format seems to amplify the scope of the traditional analog problem.

The question needs to be asked: should archivists concern themselves with databases and digital objects? Once archival material has been scanned and entered into this format, it is now a different genre in worldwide distribution, no longer contained by the traditional archives reading room. Should these tools be left in the hands of IT experts who know so much about the highly convoluted coding that is involved? The question is answering itself. Archivists have readily accepted computerized versions of finding aids, and then watched as these tools are filled out with full text online, as is happening with the evolving Online Archive of California. Archivists are required to facilitate the reformatting of materials to digital form and help with the search functions. Archivists must be prepared to appraise born-digital documentation in the originating offices, and confront it increasingly in new acquisitions. In these roles, archivists are already participating as advocates for open information in a rapidly evolving digital world.

The answer to the question, then, is *yes*; archivists need to be actively involved in the management of digital primary sources. They need to advise on the architecture of databases to preserve the two simple principles of open and equal access. Both the technical and the commercial sides of this complex of issues need to be confronted directly. There is good news and bad news on this front. The story starts with the latter, but it ends with some very promising developments.

With this digital revolution, the ground under archivists is shifting. It is not entirely clear how things will unfold, but very powerful societal forces are at work. They are irrevocably changing the information environment.

The forces behind this transformation are linked to the rapid development of computer technology since the introduction of the World Wide Web in 1993–1994. The networked global environment is impacting the flow of information—the way information is recorded, stored, accessed, and restricted. There are both financial and political consequences. The globalized marketplace impacts archival practice. This effect is easy to visualize. The growth of commercial packaging of archives has led to the commodification of the archives as products for licensing as commercial databases. Another effect that is basically political and more difficult to manage is the way real and perceived security threats impact the flow of information. Unpredictable and unfamiliar forms of terrorism and globalized gangsterism have emerged in the twenty-first century. Throughout history, security threats and political challenges have created the dual danger of intrusive monitoring of private information and aggressive censorship of public information: in effect, controlling access to information. In response to the 9/11 tragedy, the U.S. government decided it needed to monitor communications more extensively and intrusively. In response to political challenges, China has experimented with limiting access to certain sites on the Internet in order to squelch opposition. These factors are all interconnected with the advances in information technology. As information brokers, archivists are at the center of the IT storm.

The digital environment impacts responsible access in unpredictable ways. There is more information available, but less reliability and more efforts at controlling it. These forces are likely to continue impacting access, even as a huge influx of digital documentation is transferred to archives. The fragility of digital archives is a pressing concern. The ultimate restriction on access is the permanent loss of documentation. Digital preservation is a highly technical subject, certainly beyond the scope of a book on ethics. What is relevant to archival ethics is the urgent need to protect cultural heritage that is in digital form from major threats: technical, commercial, and political. Digital data is heavily mediated by a technical interface. To be read that interface needs to be maintained, and maintenance is expensive. One can visualize the issue as the need to repurchase ballooning digital archives every four or five years. Both the cost and the volume of digital documents are threats to access.

New archival acquisitions are arriving in repositories as electronic databases—each with its own quirks, each with masses of unsorted data. Some times these electronic formats are scans of data gleaned from paper sources, other times they are born digital. Such databases contain too much material to simply print out, and the printouts would not preserve the interaction function for conducting searches with combinations of keywords. The shift from paper reference to digital is unavoidable. And it is unavoidably complex, which complicates the implementation of the seemingly simple imperative for open and equal access.

The computer industry is driven by the profit motive, which created a tsunami of commercial innovations. Archives are valuable assets. It was only a matter of time for companies that specialize in marketing microform sets and online journals to begin absorbing out-of-print books, and then archival resources.

Commodification of Information and the Ethics of Access

Database technology is presenting a dilemma for advocates of open and equal access during the transition from paper-based to online research modes. There are unprecedented opportunities for open access to data never before accessible. There are countervailing trends that are preventing large segments of the population from seeing information that they may need. Some obstacles are the result of the commodification of data, others come from the technical complexity inherent in these tools. Archival materials are being swept up into a bewildering array of database formats just as newspapers, journals, and books have been.

Tomas A. Lipinski has done groundbreaking work on the growing commercial threat to the right to information as codified in the Universal Declaration of Human Rights. Access to information is a critical need in a democratic society and should be guaranteed to every citizen. The trend toward a proprietary ownership of data and the right to information are clashing. Lipinski perceives that the former has the advantage: "Commercialization of information is gaining 'juristic and ideological ascendancy.'"[37]

One cannot blame an industry for exploiting a marketing niche that provides tempting profits at the expense of the values of a profession. It is up to that profession to structure the negotiations with commercial vendors in a more appropriate way. But how? Commodification of archival materials presents a special problem that needs to be carefully considered. Commercial vendors that provide online access to journal articles, newspapers, and books charge heavy subscription fees that only large libraries can afford, and negotiate restrictive licensing agreements that limit the people eligible to use them. A large university library, such as the one at Stanford University, may have subscriptions to over seven hundred licensed electronic databases for locating journal articles and other research information. These are package deals with overlapping coverage: some materials are duplicated, other runs of periodicals have large gaps. For many journals, comprehensive access to the entire run requires using a patchwork of print editions plus microfilm, microfiche, and digital surrogates. Different titles require piecing together the complete run differently. The expense limits access to members permitted under the licensing agreement, thus hampering the ideal of egalitarian availability of information. The ad hoc free market history of these services means that they are incomplete, incompatible, and often awkward to use, thus hampering intellectual access.

The market forces are hard to resist. Some research libraries are spending more acquisitions dollars on databases than on print materials; sometimes the electronic version of a journal is priced higher than the print version. Several large companies have been marketing digital archives. Industry giant Google, famous for digitizing books, has looked into large-scale scanning of primary source materials. As these companies assimilate archival sources, the same issues emerge.

In commodifying print materials, database vendors do not have an absolute monopoly. In most cases, widely distributed print versions of the articles are available at public libraries or through interlibrary loan agreements. The main advantage provided by the commercial vendor is speed and ease of use. When a vendor acquires exclusive rights to archival materials that are unique and one of a kind, the public does not have a readily accessible alternative source. When the commercial licensing model is used for archives, even the purchaser does not have the materials in any permanent form: the data goes away as a result of a lapsed payment, shifting company ownership, or changing company policy. Some vendors of online journals have been known to remove articles from the database. During economic downturns, libraries are forced to cut back on subscriptions. With print there are back issues on the shelf. With online products there is the definite risk of having nothing to show for previous payments unless the contract was carefully negotiated with that eventuality in mind.

Archivists interested in preserving equal access to primary sources in the digital environment need to consider what has happened as academic journals went from print to digital format. Database vendors charge what the market will bear. For some of them, the price is negotiable and they do not want one institution to know what another is paying. Information on pricing is typically not available on company websites. One outstanding source for journal articles is JSTOR, which started as a grant-funded database and is now a not-for-profit venture. The subscription cost for the nonprofit JSTOR database is still too high for many libraries. Other for-profit vendors charge even more. For quality products, subscriptions costing twenty thousand dollars per year are normal; some subscription costs can reach one hundred thousand dollars per year. In ten years, such a subscription becomes a million dollar acquisition—and the library does not even own it, but is essentially leasing it on a yearly basis. Often there is a cost for the back file as a one-time payment, then an additional yearly cost. Few middle-tier institutions can afford annual subscriptions in this range. Even if one hundred students accessed the database yearly, the cost per actual use could be in the thousands of dollars. Many research libraries are reaching a tipping point in that more than half of their acquisitions budget is spent on digital sources. Digitized sets of archives are among them.

Increasingly, the text of laws, legal decisions, and building codes are only available from commercial vendors for a hefty fee. This model is not inevitable. The European Union uses EUR-Lex, which provides direct and free access to all European Union law. There are some grassroots efforts to provide American laws in an "open source" mode, but so far the progress has been slow. Commercial interests have been allowed to monopolize the market. With archives, there has already been some loss of control over microfilm and digital surrogates, but since the process is at an earlier stage, there may be time to reestablish a better balance of interests.

This pricing of information has created three tiers of libraries: the haves and have nots, and those struggling in between with minimal resources. Even within a well-funded university, certain high-end legal databases are made available only to law faculty and law students. Humanities students, paying hefty tuition for the privilege of attending the school, may want to conduct research on a legal topic and be denied access. Members of the general public and unaffiliated scholars are completely excluded from the information club. Independent scholars who gain access to the rare original documents at the Bodleian may not be able to use the online databases because of the licensing restrictions. The promise that digital tools would expand access to archives is threatened by the profitable marketing models from the world of academic journals.

The business models for these information providers are constantly evolving. The companies are bought, merged, and sold on a regular basis, jeopardizing the continuity of their product. These businesses have provided valuable services, but it is up to the customers to keep them customer-oriented. That requires constant monitoring and quality control. One resourceful online company repackaged the chapters of out-of-copyright books as new articles and was able to market this bogus online resource to a large number of university libraries that were purchasing by blanket order without much oversight. Price gouging began with new marketing strategies for scholarly journals in the 1980s. Academics researched and wrote articles to win tenure, and typically were supported by their university salaries while they did so. They were delighted to see their research in print. (It is a rare academic who gets paid for a journal article.) Then the publishers print and distribute the journals, selling them back to the very institutions that provided the free intellectual labor. Over a period of about a quarter of a century, the price structure for journals exceeded inflation by a wide margin, and journals became a bigger cost than books in acquisitions budgets. The same marketing strategy can be applied to the scanning and distribution of digital copies of archival materials. Vendors and corporate support play a key role in the research community, but it is a matter of defining the right role and managing the right balance.

And the digital sources sometimes inexplicably disappear from the Internet. One example is the case of the "Paper of Record," a digital archive of early newspapers including rare Mexican newspapers. It was being used avidly by historians, happy to avoid a long-distance trek to sort through crumbling newsprint. Even briefly using documents printed or written on brittle old newsprint paper can result in a distressing scene: a library table and floor covered with the crumbs of history. The digital version was a welcome improvement for both access and preservation. Then it just disappeared. It was quietly purchased by Google and taken offline. There were plans for it to reappear, but at any time the company can impose a high price for this now monopolized and commodified resource.[38] In another case, the Research Libraries Group (RLG) created the Cultural Materials Initiative, a subscription database of digital surrogates of manuscripts and other cultural objects from dozens of institutions. In 2007 the database was cancelled when RLG merged with the Online Computer Library System (OCLC). These cases demonstrate the fragility of the digital archive and the implications for access.

Increasingly, information has become commodified and assigned a price in the marketplace. Even nonprofit providers may charge hefty fees and make decisions based on financial rather than cultural values. The government-provided database PACER, which provides access to legal documents from the courts, requires a credit card to cover access fees that may be higher than the cost of providing the service. The main obstacle is no longer a gatekeeper physically restricting access, but a high price tag that ensures that only the wealthiest institutions get a license.

Large corporations have contracted for exclusive rights to market surrogate copies of archival collections. Microfilm sets of archives are already prohibitively expensive, not just for individuals but also for many institutions. The author is familiar with one microfilm project where the product was so expensive, in the half million dollar range, that fewer than ten libraries around the world could afford a complete set. In theory a competing company could rescan the documents and sell them competitively at a lower price. Realistically, no archival administrator would want to subject a collection to the stress of scanning more than once.

Google has famously experimented with digitizing both book and archival formats on such a huge scale that some observers worry about the monopolization of digitized materials. Google's management seems on the whole to be very enlightened, and interested in broad access. We know from the experience with digital journals that once a monopoly on digital assets has been established, the temptation for price gouging will be difficult to resist. There are many companies trying to get a foot in the door. It can be very tempting to allow a commercial venture to do the scanning in exchange for a digital preservation copy. When that arrangement creates an exclusive and pricey product, it may be worth rethinking the most ethical access strategies for a nation's cultural property that should belong to its citizens.

With paper archives, faculty can visit the institution that holds them and work there. It requires time and travel funds. With commercial document databases, the information may be as close as a reading room with WiFi, but access may require affiliation with the possibly elite institution that bought a restrictive licensing agreement. Instead of the secrecy and restrictions of traditional archives, the obstacles to access come from the commodification of data, including the information derived from archival formats. The open and equal access needed for a healthy democracy is impeded just as successfully by these financial obstacles as by any physical barriers.

As technology evolves, access requires knowing how to reformat databases for accessibility, and also knowing how to navigate legacy databases. Migrating data is a well-known problem. The rapidly changing software and hardware platforms, a form of planned obsolescence, ensure that sales are robust, but the result is much lost data as systems crash and are replaced by new models. Even the technical wizards at NASA discovered in 1999 that they could not read digital files from the 1975 Viking space probe because of obsolescence. For very valuable digital objects, such as early photographs of outer space, it may be cost effective to retroactively invent drives to read the obsolete formats, a digital preservation process called "emulation." But normally the cost is prohibitive. Outmoded formats have long been an issue: just try to find a Dictaphone to play a recording belt from the 1960s. Increasingly the problem will escalate until a common ground for compatibility standards is established.

One unsung hero is retired NASA archivist Nancy Evans. Her first contribution came in 1986 when she recommended the preservation of images from the 1966–1967 Lunar Orbiter in climate controlled storage. This was the era when a great deal of the fragile digital imagery from space was being lost through neglect as images degraded over time and equipment for reading them was discarded as obsolete. Evans knew that the preserved, but obsolete, two-inch Lunar Orbiter magnetic tapes would be unreadable without the specialized tape drives, most of which were being destroyed. Evans had the foresight to rescue four of the devices, each of which weighs half a ton and is the size of a refrigerator. She simply stored them at her home. Now they are being refurbished to bring back images from the moon landings.[39] Certainly nothing in the code of ethics would require an archivist to store large pieces of obsolete equipment at home for two decades. The formal rules did not help; only the deeper ethical values of the profession provided the context for her decisions.

One point needs to be clearly recognized: attempts by industry to protect products from competition by creating artificial incompatibility have played a major role in obstructing free use of information in all media and across all frontiers. Computer products come in a bewildering array of formats that effectively diminishes equal or equitable access. One savvy researcher will work from his office Internet connection and get full text documents immediately with a few clicks. Another will waste a day's valuable time trying to get past passwords and incomprehensible instructions.

At present we are stuck in a kind of technological Darwinism; it is the research survival of the technologically fittest. Those researchers who catch on, get to the text; those who are more focused on content than on database architecture are left on hold listening to classical music while they wait for tech support to answer the telephone. And to take the Darwinism example a bit further, no one researcher, however brilliant, can possibly learn all the quirks of all databases. It takes start-up time even for the computer adept, so researchers learn some strategies and formats and not others, something like the evolutionary specialization that Darwin found in the Galapagos Islands.

Interdisciplinary research is heavily hit by this process of specialization and compartmentalization. Frequently even a single database will have more information than a typical researcher has the savvy to unlock. Some historians can use some functions and others rely on different aspects. The widely differing interfaces can be very confusing even to the most skillful scholars, who can be expected to master a few of them but certainly not all. This is sometimes referred to as "feature shock"—too many features to master. Researchers should not be expected to spend their valuable sabbatical time learning new interfaces as the familiar ones become unusable due to planned obsolescence.

As the situation stands, digital databases, including archival ones, are plagued by five serious flaws:

- exclusive licenses
- incompatible technical architecture
- rapidly changing software
- impermanence
- high cost

All five characteristics probably enhance profits, but they are incompatible with ideals of open and equal access. There is certainly an important role for commercial vendors, but these corporations need to serve the information community, not the other way around. Can there be an alternative that recaptures the old nineteenth-century ideal of a noncommercial, free learning commons?

Can Archives Be "Open Source"?

The Internet is fundamentally an access tool. Reference archivists, often erroneously regarded as rather stodgy, immediately began to pay close attention to the potential of the web, as attested to by the topics that began to show up at SAA conferences starting in the 1980s. They saw the connection between instant access to government records and transparency in a democratic society. Archivists and librarians have long espoused a lofty faith in the power of knowledge to support a just and well-functioning society. The goals continue to be open and equal access to the information and evidence contained in archival materials. Archival theorists, including Margaret Hedstrom, Paul Conway, David Bearman, and many others recognized the ephemeral quality of digital documents very early.[40] It is worth looking at their list of publications and papers to see how much serious attention has been given to the issue even as sources are being transformed faster than anyone can fathom or control them.

Then and now, the major complaint from archivists has been the lack of infrastructure and standards. The technology marketplace has been either reluctant or unable to construct simple standards for compatibility and interoperability. The archival profession is dependent on commercially developed products. In the short term, incompatible components provide companies with a competitive advantage. In the long run, it hampers the development of a coherent information policy.

Daniel V. Pitti, who pioneered the Encoded Archival Description standards, is fond of quoting Charles C. Jewett's 1853 report on constructing library catalogues: "Now, even if the one adopted were that of the worst of our catalogues, if it were strictly followed in all alike, their uniformity would render catalogues, thus made, far more useful than the present chaos of irregularities."[41] The situation in the twenty-first century can once again be described as "the present chaos of irregularities."

The 1920s were probably the golden age of standardization as the Department of Commerce worked with industry to produce voluntary uniform sizing for manufactured products from bricks to bedsprings. It was in the 1920s that the Bureau of Standards worked with the U.S. printing industry to establish 8 ½ x 11 inches as the standard letterhead size.[42] This simple, freely adopted standard created a wave of increased access to information in ways the original Committee on the Simplification of Paper Sizes in 1921 could not have imagined in their wildest flights of futuristic fantasy: typewriters with a uniform width for the carriage, compatible fax machines at distant locations, and computer printers that print 8 ½ x 11 inch pages. In the archives, this simple standard, which originally had something to do with the size of Dutch paper molds of the seventeenth century, enabled the use of manuscript boxes in mostly uniform sizes filled with uniform folders. In the digital realm, such consistency to eliminate waste and facilitate accessibility remains elusive, despite many determined attempts.

The proliferating archival databases have evolved in an unregulated free market environment without the kind of uniformity that was still possible in 1921 when paper size was standardized. Archivists have certainly attempted to rationalize access to online information with standards. Already in the 1980s RLG and a group called the National Information Systems Task Force (NISTF) launched the uniform standards for collection-level description called AMC, based on the Machine Readable Cataloging (MARC) format. The MARC AMC format worked well for the collection-level description, but it could not be expanded to accommodate finding aids, which average twenty to thirty pages, and can run to thousands. And MARC AMC was "flat," unable to track the nested hierarchical relationships in archival registers.

IT professionals collaborated with archivists to create EAD, Encoded Archival Description, an invaluable tool for creating compatible registers with online file-level descriptions, as developed by the Berkeley Finding Aid Project. Daniel V. Pitti, recognizing the need for an access tool independent of software and hardware, took advantage of the newly available Extensible Markup Language (XML), a simplified version of the

Standardized General Markup Language (SGML). The alpha version of EAD was released in February 1996 and rapidly became a national standard with international participation. It soon became possible to search through thousands of finding aids at hundreds of institutions. In 1998 the Online Archive of California (OAC) encompassed 2,697 EAD finding aids. At that point there were no discrete text objects, but already 168 finding aids contained embedded digital images. By 2009 some 150 separate institutions had contributed 11,840 EAD finding aids to the OAC; these finding aids included 179,209 discrete image objects and 10,846 discrete text objects.[43] One relatively simple break-through idea opened up a universe of access through compatible finding aids. It was a stunning success.

What began as an online set of local finding aids turned into a state-wide union catalog with links to digital surrogates. From the beginning in 1994, Daniel Pitti envisioned the finding aids as gateways to digital objects, either as full text or images. It was to be an expandable access tool, one that would both increase use and save wear on the original. The goal was enhanced preservation linked to enhanced access: "by making surrogates of the most used portions of our collections available, we can simultaneously increase access and limit physical access to endangered collections."[44] Fifteen years and hundreds of thousands of searches and "hits" later, that goal is being realized. It will be interesting to see how much full text is eventually made available for unmediated use and how much material will only be cataloged and still require a visit to the archives reading room. Researchers, of course, much prefer the unmediated direct access. The obstacles are both legal (copyright and privacy concerns) and technical (coping with the complex and expensive scanning, coding, and metadata requirements that are often beyond the means of the contributing archives). Each contributing repository decides on its level of involvement. The rate of growth will vary depending on economics, but the direction is clear. Researchers are closer to their dream of sitting in their offices and accessing unique archives from scores of geographically dispersed locations.

The integration of finding aids with full text digital documents as available on the Online Archive of California constitutes a union catalog in the fullest sense. All twelve thousand finding aids from 150 different archives use the same interface; anyone, anywhere in the world, can access these digital primary sources. There are no user application forms, no letters of reference, no reader cards, no user fees, no subscriptions, no exclusive licenses, no passwords, no oath. And it works. But it is expensive and vulnerable in times of economic stress. It is not clear whether or for how long the system will remain free of charge.

Initial funding for development came from University of California internal grants. The grant money enabled the pilot project to provide mark-up services for repositories that did not have the technical knowledge to do it themselves. As grant money was exhausted, the technical side had already become easier with the use of templates and boilerplates. As funding permitted, smaller repositories outsourced the scanning and mark-up chores—a proper use of commercial services—and the repositories still retained control over the archival sources. Using the same principles, many other regional union catalogs have formed both in the U.S. and Europe. EAD, METS, PREMIS, DACS, Dublin Core, and the Archivists' Toolkit are all highly useful initiatives in creating interoperability. Both the Library of Congress and the National Archives have invested heavily in the search for solutions.

Some of the pioneers in providing online access to archival finding aids in a fee-free environment include the Online Archive of New Mexico, Texas Archival Sources Online, Kentuckiana Digital Library, North Carolina Encoded Archival Description, Northwest Digital Archives, Virginia Heritage, and Rocky Mountain Online Archive. The British have developed A2A (Access to Archives). MALVINE covers Manuscripts and Letters Via Integrated Networks in Europe. There is also the Archives Hub. It is an impressive accomplishment in less than two decades.

The Library of Congress has more than nine million digital manuscripts and other multimedia objects on its American Memory Website. The National Archives has created two systems, one for finding aids (Access to Archival Databases), and one for digital documents (Archival Research Catalog). Keeping track of all the websites is a formidable task, which requires a free subscription to a website evaluation site such as the Librarians Internet Index or the Public History Resource Center or sites such as ResearchBuzz.[45] There are simply not enough cross connections between online primary sources. And there is a disconnect between the digital scanned paper item and the description and identification of that item. The good news is that integration is feasible. It does take political will and the ability to negotiate the right relationships among commercial, nonprofit, and public institutions.

We do have a workable open-source model to compete with the commodification of information. The ongoing challenge is to work individually and as a profession to integrate commercial and not-for-profit initiatives in a way that takes advantage of the strengths of each for the purpose of better utilization of data. It is a moving target. As these access tools grow, they become very expensive to maintain.

The fact remains: these well-crafted and well-funded efforts have not tamed the proliferating and sometimes deliberately confusing array of access tools, inconsistent coverage of archival sources, and confusing vendor-provided interfaces that serve commercial purposes more than the principle of access. The vigor of the professional databases is periodically threatened by the unpredictable economic crises that hit nonprofits and universities particularly hard. It makes an archivist nostalgic for the days when the weighty red books known as LCSH, issued by the Library of Congress with uniform subject heading lists, organized knowledge for the nation. Their reassuring presence in the reading room guaranteed that any researcher could find the keys to the kingdom. No more.

No reference staff can solve these technical access problems directly. Instead of confronting traditional restrictions imposed on paper documents by a protective donor or institution, we confront the practical restrictions imposed by a complexity that simply takes too much time or money to master. Must we delete article 6 of the SAA Code of Ethics?

There are two fronts in this war. One consists of small meliorations on a case-by-case basis by enlightened staff. The other is a united advocacy role by the profession as a whole to recommend better industry practice for the benefit of research. No one knows the researchers' problems better than the reference archivist and no one is better able to aggregate the experience in a way the individuals themselves cannot. Reference archivists are reinventing their traditional role as mediators in this space between chaotic data and the information seeker. From personal experience, the author senses that the motivation for taking on such a huge task is highly idealistic, and tied to the ethics and core values of the profession.

What are archivists doing to maintain equal and open access in the online environment?

- Archivists are essential in identifying aging digital data at risk and recommending preservation reformatting. The reference archivist knows what collections are in demand. While ideally all electronic data would be scheduled for migration to current formats, it is not a bad fallback position to prioritize those databases most in demand. Researchers will find problem areas that are not obvious from the finding aids. Reformatting researcher-identified obsolescent formats is a pragmatic way to ensure that the materials most in demand are the ones that receive funding for treatment first. Reference archivists supply a valuable service by assisting in this area to ensure that needed information is not lost. These are small ameliorations that add up. But more global strategies are also required.

- On a larger stage, there is a responsibility for creating a trustworthy infrastructure of reliable standards. Ethical reference archivists find themselves working as the advocates for researchers. The foremost task in the current era is the construction of technical tools for integrating digital documents in a user-friendly format available free on the Internet—systems with an emphasis on accessibility and authenticity. The UCSF Tobacco Control Archives form a model for topic-focused full text collections, also available free of charge. The Online Archive of California serves as a model for open, equal, and free access to finding aids.

- The venerable values of public service, long practiced in archives reading rooms, will need to be expanded and redefined for the virtual reading room. If researchers are finding archives on the Internet in their offices, reference service needs to find its way into offices as well. The Tobacco Control Archives placed millions of pages of full-text documents online. In 1995 about two thousand users accessed the equivalent of four million pages from the cigarette papers. "Internet reference use has been enormous, and it would have been impossible to successfully meet the demand in a traditional, supervised reading room environment where staffing is minimal."[46] Distributed information demands a virtual reading room with assistance provided by email, text messaging, and blogs. If reference services do not make this transition, the functioning of the information society will be distorted.

- Championing the old public library model of open access to information free of charge will continue to be a major challenge in the foreseeable future. There is an opening for steering new development away from fee-based licensing of information. Commercial ventures are sensitive to public opinion and can be influenced to provide free access to basic information, or to keep use fees within a reasonable range. One example is the opening to the public of OCLC's catalog utility World Cat on the Internet in 2006. World Cat has expanded its entries to include books, articles, archives, manuscripts, and multimedia.[47]

A highly useful volume on the subject, *Archives and the Digital Library*, edited by William E. Landis and Robin L. Chandler, is peppered with the usual alphabet soup of acronyms typical of any writing on technical subjects: On one page alone the reader encounters MODS, MARC, METS, CDL, ICT, JARDA, MOAC, XSLT, URL, HTML; on the next page CSS, CMS, XTF, DLF, CMIG, DLXS, EAD, ARKS, GenDB, OAC, MOA2, etc.[48] In the midst of the tech speak in this volume are words like trust, authenticity, disclosure, reliability, stability, fidelity, integrity—words with ethical content. What is a trusted repository? What is object integrity? Old-fashioned Sunday School virtues are suddenly emerging in the midst of highly technical discussions of digitization: "for the digital repository, trust involves scholarship, authenticity, reliability, and persistence over time and has little relationship to immediate financial rewards."[49] These are moral and ethical concepts in the development of archival databases.

With the concept of the trusted digital repository, the ethical ideals have reached a new level and a new challenge. Historically the first phase in archival practice was veiled in secrecy and privilege. The trusted medieval archivist protected his patron's secrets from prying eyes. He kept Cromwell from removing a manuscript from the Bodleian Library. The Enlightenment-era archivist ensured the authenticity of the public record for the greater good. Then, gradually, the democratic principles of open and equal access began to take hold and slowly became established in theory and practice both in the U.S. and Europe. Archivists were at the forefront of the movement to provide direct and free access to information. Library and archives codes and access policies were adamant on the subject. Late twentieth-century archivists worked toward a model of transparency and equality. The postmodern archivist has a more complex challenge: preserving a sense of trust in the face of massive change. Business plans to monetize the data in archives offered both great opportunities for improved access and at the same time the threat of expensive and exclusive "gated communities" of information. The digital revolution provided huge profit incentives for commercializing journals, then books and archives. The information profession failed to bring the vendors' skills and resources "under the tent," to utilize the business models in ways that would support free research. The open source movement is countering that development, but as yet there is no equilibrium. New ethical codes need to address this issue. The profession as a whole needs to formulate a twenty-first-century version of the successful public library movement that began in the nineteenth century and flourished in the twentieth. The charge is to make large quantities of data open, available, and usable. Commercial tools need to be rationally structured in the service of open and equitable access to all media, across all frontiers. Just as the equal and open access policies of the of the recent past fueled creativity and innovation, freeing digital archives of excessive financial obstructions and licensing restrictions will undoubtedly open up entire new fields of inquiry, and take learning and scholarship in new directions.

Questions for Evaluating Access Policies

1. Does the repository have a well-worded policy mandating open and equitable access for use of the collections?
2. Is the staff trained to provide courteous and appropriate reference help to all readers without "playing favorites"?
3. Does the reference staff coordinate with the technical services staff to improve intellectual access?
4. Are obstacles such as photocopy fees kept to a minimum?
5. Do readers receive training as appropriate in using both manual and online finding aids?
6. Does the repository have a welcoming and helpful website?
7. Is there clarity about restrictions so that no one makes an unnecessary research trip?
8. Is there an outreach program to ensure that those who need the information in the archives know it is there?
9. Are staff trained not to sequester materials so that they can publish first?
10. Are staff trained not to accept inappropriate gifts?
11. Are staff trained not to gossip about researchers?
12. Does the staff keep circulation records and the researchers' collection requests confidential?
13. Are staff trained to request permission from each reader first, then only with permission to notify them of parallel research?
14. Does the administration work to maintain policies that foster the maximum use of the collections?
15. Does the administration coordinate with other archives on interoperable access tools?
16. Do staff members know not to collect personally in the area of their employer so as to avoid any conflict of interest?
17. Does the higher administration provide adequate legal support for access decisions?
18. Does the higher administration provide accounting and financial support to ensure proper financial transactions?
19. Does the archives staff project the core values of openness and integrity?

CHAPTER 5

Case Study:
The Cigarette Papers

I would not have continued the fight if I didn't feel strongly about freedom of information.

—Karen Butter[1]

THIS CHAPTER ANALYZES A SINGLE CASE STUDY, ONE THAT HAS BEEN REFERRED TO SEVERAL TIMES IN THIS TEXT BECAUSE OF ITS IMPORTANCE. The case is primarily about open and equal access to once-privileged proprietary, internal business archives. In addition, the study cuts across many other fundamental ethical topics: respect for property rights, the acquisition of stolen papers, the authentication of a gift without reliable provenance background, third-party privacy in massive amounts of data, privileged circulation and use records, attorney-client privilege, freedom of information, and the right of citizens to be informed about important public health issues that affect their welfare. The case diagnoses what happens when different ethical imperatives come into conflict and how the professional archivist negotiates these conflicting interests. It demonstrates the way digital technology can be used to great strategic advantage in the process. With its David and Goliath dynamics, it shows how librarians and archivists evaluated risk in the face of a potentially long and expensive lawsuit.

The conflict between tightly restricted, proprietary records and the public's right to vital information exploded in the 1990s during the fiercely fought "tobacco wars." The competing demands of private corporations and public health advocates were no longer just abstract ethical dilemmas. Archivists were confronted with controversial issues from the entire range of fundamental archival problems. It would be difficult to formulate a hypothetical case study that more effectively demonstrates the values at stake than the "cigarette papers," as the case is known. The tobacco wars were most fundamentally about two charged issues: serious health hazards and access to records about them. Fortunately, a series of court decisions around the country, as well as the Multistate Master Settlement Agreement of 1998, delivered to the public massive amounts of research and medical and corporate documentation.[2] Several books and numerous articles summarize and analyze these mountains of paper.[3] The cigarette papers case is emblematic of a host of existing conflicts between privileged information in private business archives and the public interest. Archivists will no doubt continue to find such documentation, often unexpectedly, in the course of their work. Thinking through the issues in advance provides a framework for making rational decisions under pressure.

Archivists played a crucial role in the tobacco controversy at a pivotal moment in 1995. The management of access to documents was a key element in the drama: who gets to see what, and how quickly? The archivists involved were working in an impassioned environment as the press, congressmen, judges, product liability lawyers, defense attorneys, and business executives were vying for advantage in a war with numerous fronts around the country and some billions of dollars at stake. All the players wanted rapid access to information; some wanted exclusive access.

The following narrative provides an overview of the different factors at play in this drama. It leads to a discussion of whether this case can be used as a model, and, if so, under what circumstances.

In 1994, an anonymous whistleblower, who called himself Mr. Butts after a well-known cartoon character, leaked thousands of copies of highly confidential, internal documents from the Brown and Williamson Tobacco Corporation (B&W), the third largest tobacco company in the United States. Various sets of copies were circulated to the media, to Congress, and to academics over the course of several months. The copies were passed around in a surreptitious manner due to fear of retaliation from B&W—well-justified fear, as it turns out. Eventually, proprietary and privileged information from the previously secret papers, some ostensibly covered by the attorney-client privilege, rapidly became public in three different arenas. On May 7, 1994, journalist Philip J. Hilts published an article in the *New York Times* entitled "Tobacco Company Was Silent on Hazards." In June 1994, Congressman Henry Waxman opened congressional hearings before the Subcommittee on Health and the Environment, which subpoenaed documents and sworn testimony from B&W executives. As to academia and archives, on May 12, 1994, a box containing about four thousand pages of B&W internal records arrived at the office of Professor Stanton A. Glantz at the University of California medical school in San Francisco (UCSF), where he had been researching the health dangers of smoking. This was apparently a larger set of papers than Hilts had acquired. It is not clear exactly how the copies got from "Mr. Butts" to Professor Glantz, or how many hands they passed through, but word was out.

Glantz had already heard about the papers. After looking through them, he immediately determined that they were authentic, partly because there were several chillingly accurate references to Glantz himself in them. B&W soon confirmed the authenticity of the papers when they demanded their return as stolen property. Upon reading the copies, Glantz recognized trouble. In an interview fifteen years later he recalled thinking about the implications: "This is litigation, and I'm not a litigation guy."[4] At the same time, for a public health researcher interested in the medical effects of tobacco, reading the papers was like "an archeologist finding King Tut's Tomb." The data filled gaps in his research. Glantz analyzed the "smoking gun" documents for a series of articles on tobacco industry research into the health dangers of their products. While he did not advertise the existence of the materials, word got around fast. A stream of people contacted him about reading the cigarette papers. Glantz was concerned about the dual task of preserving the hotly contested data and providing other researchers with access in an orderly fashion.

In the summer of 1994 he placed the documents as an unrestricted collection in the UCSF library where there was a new archival collecting focus relating to tobacco use and public health—an initiative called the Tobacco Control Archives. Glantz already had a collection in the UCSF archives. While it is normal procedure for faculty to preserve their research sources in this manner, the transfer was not a simple transaction in this case. Often sensitive materials are held back from the archives, but Glantz had come to respect the librarians' commitment to freedom of information a decade earlier.

In the 1980s, Glantz acquired a pirated copy of an antitobacco film, *Death in the West*. As a result of a tobacco company lawsuit, a court in Britain had ordered the destruction of all copies and out-takes of the footage. Glantz asked his legal counsel at the university how to protect this rare surviving print. This occurred back in the era before copies could be made easily from European audio-visual formats. The attorney suggested placing the video in the library, where it would be both preserved and made accessible. Legal counsel advised that courts are very reluctant to remove materials from libraries. Such decisions could be seen to violate First Amendment protections. "This was my first engagement," said Glantz in the same interview, "with libraries as subversive places." By subversive, he referred to a profession capable of doing "the right thing" in the face of well-financed opposition.

Ten years later, in 1994, as researchers learned about the purloined papers by word of mouth, Glantz was again faced with the same issues he confronted with the pirated film: how both to preserve the materials and provide access. The library and archives again seemed like the most logical place to manage the documentation that arrived anonymously. By then he had supplemented the leaked copies with additional materials that were being released by the tobacco companies in an attempt to defend themselves. When read together with the purloined papers, the voluminous documents produced by the companies fit like jigsaw pieces into the larger picture and were ultimately self-incriminating.

Karen Butter, the director of the UCSF library and archives, accepted the transfer of the cigarette papers to the archives with the usual record transfer forms, but she knew this would be an unusual case and understood the scope of the problem immediately. "We knew we were in for a battle from the beginning, but I (and Robin Chandler as well) felt this was the right thing to do."[5] Her first step was to line up legal support, not just for Glantz, who as a faculty member had a privileged position, but also to protect the ordinary library and archives staff, who might be more vulnerable in a legal battle. "We had many meetings with both the UCSF and UC legal counsel in the process of accepting and making the gifts available," she explained. Butter, not a contentious person by nature, was very familiar with the American Library Association's work on freedom of information, and knew the territory. She felt a strong obligation to make the information available. If UCSF did not open this public health information, she believed that it was unlikely anyone else would. At the same time, she opened the collection in a neutral way, without unusual publicity and without any official interpretation from the staff, whatever their personal opinions might be.

The UCSF archivists quickly organized the papers and opened them for public use—a completely normal procedure when donors do not impose restrictions. Given the controversial subject matter, however, opening these papers was a courageous act certain to draw a strong response from B&W. It would inevitably embroil the library and its parent institution in a battle with a powerful adversary—something that risk-averse archivists tend not to do under normal circumstances. Glantz and the archivists were taking on an enemy capable of aggressive tactics, including personal retaliation.[6] Glantz acknowledges that he feared that the university attorneys might make him "walk the plank"—withdrawing support for access to the cigarette papers.[7] But the University of California, with its long history of defending academic freedom, was supportive of both Glantz's research and the unrestricted availability of his sources in the archives. The university took a stand in favor of open and equal access.

B&W executives believed that the papers had been illegally pirated and were essentially stolen property. Under ordinary circumstances, one could easily understand this perspective. In their view, internal corporate records covered by the attorney-client privilege and by trade secret protections had been unlawfully released. Predictably, B&W filed suit against the university to demand the return of the documents. B&W also sent private investigators into the UCSF reading room to monitor and photo-graph use of the collection. They demanded access to circulation records to determine who actually used the papers. In the U.S., the American Library Association and the Society of American Archivists have a long tradition of protecting user information. Their advocacy of the free flow of information has not extended to their own circulation records. For the staffers, these intrusions must have been a serious test of their resolve. On May 25, 1995, the California Superior Court for the City and County of San Francisco denied the company's request. B&W also failed in efforts to block the release of documents by Congress and in several court cases around the country. Various courts came to parallel conclusions in favor of the freedom of information. The archivists could continue to provide access to the cigarette papers.

And the demand for this information was huge, certainly beyond the capacity of the UCSF archives reading room. A solution was on the horizon. Scanners were becoming commercially available and the World Wide Web became easily accessible with the emergence of user-friendly, graphical browser technology. The UCSF staff immediately saw the util-ity of digitizing the cigarette papers and took advantage of the new tool. CDs were made, which helped ensure that the documents' content could not be "returned" to the company. At midnight of June 30–July 1, 1995, within a few months of the favorable court decision, UCSF placed thou-sands of scanned, indexed, and searchable documents on the Internet for immediate use, free of charge. Glantz and his colleagues published a set of related articles in a dedicated issue of the *Journal of the American Medical Association* (JAMA), which also appeared in July 1995. Like the opening of the archival collection, the publication by JAMA was considered by many to be a courageous act at the time. Conveniently for the users, the documents referenced by Glantz in the articles could be called up in their entirety on the UCSF website for verification and independent interpretation.

Controversial political decisions are typically made in a charged atmo-sphere at moments of mobilized public opinion, at a time when speed and ease of access to information are vital. In such an environment information that requires a cross-country trip is not "open" even if there is no formal restriction on use. In this case the website was accessed within minutes of the release. During the first year it was available, researchers from forty-four thousand different addresses viewed approximately half a million pages of documents. The CD-ROM version of the documents was produced for sale at $250. It sold well, despite the existence of the online version. There must have been some concern that the online version might be dismantled at some point, making a more permanent version desirable. At the same time, the distribution of CD versions made moot any efforts at dismantling the website. The site remained stable and growing. A new chapter in free and equal access opened up.

Karen Butter had to contend with the consequences. This stand for principles came with a price tag. "The legal challenge was very, very time consuming—both in working with our legal counsel, responding to requests from Brown and Williamson and in giving depositions. I would not have continued the fight if I didn't feel strongly about freedom of information."

As stated above, Glantz and his collaborators were attacked by the tobacco industry; there were numerous attempts to undermine their careers. They accepted the rough, personal nature of the fight and persevered. Because of the controversy, they had difficulty attracting a commercial book publisher to issue their findings; their book, *The Cigarette Papers*, was published in 1996 by the University of California Press. Archivists ensured that all the documents cited in the book, as well as the text itself, were available online, initially by subscription and later completely open and free of charge.[8]

The cigarette papers contained two levels of documents, one embedded in the other. One level consisted of proprietary scientific research funded and conducted by the cigarette industry into the role of tobacco and its pharmacologically active ingredients. The second level of information consisted of corporate strategies for concealing their own findings. What did the contents of the papers reveal?

According to Glantz's analysis, the documents reveal an expensively funded campaign to disseminate a false interpretation of medical data. Some would interpret this as a conspiracy to commit fraud. Glantz

cataloged these discrepancies between internal research findings and public corporate statements.[9] In addition to concealing industry-sponsored
scientific research that documented the medical dangers of their product,
the company leaders formulated strategies for obfuscating similar reliable
evidence emerging from independent research and actively denying the
harmful effects of tobacco.

One especially grave allegation concerns the recruitment and subsidy
of respected medical experts to support the company's public interpretation of medical evidence. Glantz provides a list of medical consultants,
some from prestigious institutions, and the funding they received from
B&W—totaling some twenty million dollars from 1972 to 1991.[10] The
documents indicated that some of the funding was diverted through third-
party organizations to conceal the source. In essence, Glantz accused the
tobacco industry of corrupting the search for knowledge.

B&W paid particular attention to refuting evidence of the addictive
nature of nicotine in order to defend smoking as a voluntary choice and
shift any blame for adverse effects to the victim. For the same reason huge
resources were expended to refute the medical evidence that passively
inhaling "second hand" environmental smoke can cause fatal disease,
even though industry-funded scientists confirmed independent research
determining the effect.[11]

The papers themselves appear to show an awareness of the sensitivity
of these materials. Information was deliberately routed through law offices
apparently in an effort to protect them from discovery with the shield
of the attorney-client privilege.[12] There were instructions for destroying
documents.[13] There may have even been attempts to ship particularly
incriminating papers out of the country, beyond the reach of American legal
jurisdiction.[14] As to the validity of Glantz's interpretations, readers are free
to evaluate these conclusions by referring to the documents themselves.

Did open and equal access to the cigarette papers have an impact? The
documents were used, at least as background, in a series of product liability
suits and lawsuits by states to recover medical expenses to treat preventable
diseases caused by tobacco products. In his foreword to the 1996 volume of
Glantz's book, C. Everett Koop, who served as surgeon general from 1981

to 1989, states that the documents revealed a level of scientific information that was not available to him at the time he was charged with protecting the nation's health. Based on these documents, he regretted not taking more decisive actions: "I have often wondered how many people died as a result of the fact that the medical and public health professions were misled by the tobacco industry."[15]

The tobacco wars reached the highest levels of government. In 1996, under the Clinton administration, the evidence that nicotine was as addictive as heroin was sufficiently strong to place cigarettes under the jurisdiction of the Food and Drug Administration. In 2000 the Supreme Court withdrew FDA control, only to have the issue revive during the Obama administration in 2009. As the battles continue, the documents are in a stable form, instantly available and searchable. The information has become better understood and widely disseminated. It resulted in local ordinances to restrict smoking in bars, restaurants, and offices. A grass roots movement took shape, first in small communities such as Lodi, California, and then spreading throughout the country. Gradually, smoking tobacco, which had recently been considered socially acceptable and even stylishly attractive, came to be considered offensive and unhealthy and was banned from public spaces. The culture changed. If the papers had remained in Glantz's San Francisco office, results may have been different.

The UCSF archivists have taken the project to the next level, continuing to add materials from a variety of sources as they become available. The Legacy Tobacco Documents Library comprises some ten million documents for a total in the range of fifty million pages. In addition, there is a growing library of videos, including television advertising over the decades. It is quite easy to compare what the industry knew about the health hazards at a given time with the presentation to the public during prime time. The Legacy Tobacco Documents Library remains a heavily used resource years later, and its impact is far reaching. In 2009 Kirsten Gillibrand was appointed senator from New York to replace Hilary Clinton. It became known that Gillibrand had worked as an attorney for the tobacco industry, and a key word search using her former name, Kirsten Rutnik, revealed numerous references in memos that clarified the level of work she was doing for the tobacco industry.[16]

By opening access, the UCSF archivists ensured that hard data has been available during these national debates. Was it legal? In case after case the courts consistently placed freedom of information about a dangerous health hazard above legal technicalities. Important factors weighed in the decisions included (1) the life-and-death nature of the information and the primacy of the public welfare; (2) the availability of a digitized version that constituted a publication protected by the First Amendment; (3) the misuse of attorney-client privilege by the tobacco companies, which drew particular ire from the judges; and (4) the finding that the original documents were not stolen, only copies, so the corporation still had its property.[17] Basically the public's right to know information about its health trumped the corporation's claim to proprietary information. Anything less, according to one judge, would be an "inversion of values."[18] The cover-up of medical research data was judged to be fraud perpetrated by a conspiracy. The judicial branch made the release of the cigarette papers legal, at least ex post facto.

Opening the cigarette papers, it is now established, was legal—but was it ethical? After the announcement of online access to the papers in July 1995, the archivists' Internet discussion group (Archives and Archivists Listserv) buzzed with arguments and counterarguments.

The final chapter has not yet been written, but the basic issues can be seen, at least in outline. On the negative side of the balance sheet are many serious concerns that would normally prompt restrictions: Provenance is the cornerstone of archival theory, and the provenance of the material was murky at best when it was first made public. The document copies were clearly pirated by a disgruntled internal employee. They were selectively chosen by someone hostile to the company, exposing the collection to accusations of selection bias. There was no attempt to balance the documentation with materials favorable to the tobacco industry, creating the impression of political advocacy. The information opened by UCSF was clearly proprietary and highly confidential even if it was recorded on copies. A well-known consequence of prematurely opening sensitive material is that the owners of such potentially controversial documents will take preventive measures such as sanitizing and destroying archives rather than chance exposure. No one denies that the attorney-client privilege was violated. No one denies that the privacy of the named individuals was violated. Copyright and trade secrets were also involved. The UCSF staff is highly trained and very aware of all of these issues. They knew all along that releasing such documentation was not to be done lightly. Factored into their decision was a highly persuasive countervailing argument.

On the positive side of the balance sheet is the gravity of the subject. The American public has a right to know, and in a timely fashion, as policy is being formulated. Freedom of speech is a fundamental condition for a successful democratic process. It is essential to emphasize that the role of the archives is to open for free review information that is needed as the basis of a national discussion. The archivists themselves presented the documents in context but also in a neutral way, free of commentary, editorializing, or advocacy. Even in articles reporting the history of the cigarette papers, the staff remained professional and reported on the access process, leaving the content to the readers to evaluate. This restraint is key to the credibility of their work. It provides the ethical bedrock for access decisions. Access was taken to a new level. The online availability of the papers resembles a publication. Blocking access to the Internet site would be similar to prior restraint in traditional paper publication.

The cigarette papers, now far more than the original set that arrived anonymously in 1994, contain a great deal of data on individuals. UCSF deals with privacy issues on a case-by-case basis. If, for instance, there is a complaint that private data, such as social security numbers, appear online, measures are taken to redact out the personal information as long as it does not compromise the document's integrity.

While the unique aspects of the case are groundbreaking and fascinating in themselves, it is important to remember the mundane details. As innovative as the UCSF staffers were in dealing with the cigarette papers, they adhered to certain basics of archival practice. To begin with, the papers were precisely within the collecting scope and mission of the archives and its parent institution. The research papers are directly related to the scientific mission of the medical school; the corporate records are useful for the public university's role in promoting good health as a public service. The original deposit was donated by a UCSF faculty member, and collecting faculty papers is a core assignment. Beyond adhering to institutional goals, the staff exercised a high level of professionalism. They correctly appraised the nature of the documents sent anonymously to Glantz. They correctly determined that the content was authentic, even though the provenance was not known until much later. The content was of great importance for the public welfare even though the papers were fragmentary, disorganized, and initially from just one individual company. The staff also appraised the political context of the documents accurately: Congress and the press were already discussing these materials; they had to be made widely available as quickly as possible to support this discussion. The staff was prepared to use newly emerging technical tools to facilitate the process. They firmly believed that the benefits of open access outweighed the costs, but it took strength of character to stay the course. The archivists created a highly innovative access model within a traditional archival framework.

Should this case serve as a precedent and model in similar situations? When egregious practices cross a certain line, the civility of formal ethical standards need not and should not be misused to cover up malfeasance and fraud. Situations arise where the benefit of open access overrides considerations such as attorney-client privilege. Here is where the archival profession needs to do some work with legal experts and ethicists to determine just where to draw the line. The cigarette papers case demonstrates that there are circumstances where open and equal access is the prime consideration. One participant in the Internet discussion group phrased it this way: "archivists should avoid political advocacy as a profession, but we cannot shun the responsibility to promote the public's right to know."[19] The UCSF professionals made an ethical choice that required an awareness of the larger social context of the documents in question and went beyond routine procedures. The decision made a difference in public perception of a social issue at a crucial moment.

The UCSF archivists were able to defend the choice against formidable opposition because of legal and logistical support from their parent institution. It would be naïve to ignore the fact that unswerving support from the University of California legal department was absolutely essential to success. Much as one would like to think that truth always prevails in the end, and that good decisions are always recognized at least eventually, effective ethical choices often also require substantial resources.

Are the tobacco companies the only industry that has systematically covered up vital public health data? Probably not. Archivists and records managers are likely to encounter similar controversial materials. Returning to the central question: should the lessons from the cigarette papers provide a model to evaluate the risks and benefits of freedom of information? In most cases, companies have been able to assert their right to keep internal records private. How grave does the danger have to be to justify opening privileged documents? Usually whistleblowers do not succeed, and often they suffer career setbacks. How certain must the manager be of all the facts before making a decision to go public? How does one guard against false either/or dilemmas? The choices usually fall along a broad spectrum. Making ethical choices requires the ability to see both detail and the big picture, with both a microscope and a telescope. It is not easy to remain objective and find the threshold where the public interest outweighs the company's rights. Several factors came together to make the cigarette papers a major case in support of the free flow of information. Courts decide on very specific cases, and often with inconsistent results. In the conflict between proprietary information and the rights of the public, decisions are also made on a case-by-case basis, and the decisions are heavily dependent on the exact details. Even so, it would help to have more research and discussion on how to achieve a balance of proprietary and public rights to information.

While better parameters would be welcome, in the end, an individual makes a decision, and no textbook can dictate the correct answers. Asked if she would do it again, Karen Butter was unequivocal: yes, of course. Even knowing the consequences, she would do the same thing again.[20]

Blowing the Whistle

The cigarette papers case began with an employee surreptitiously copying privileged documents from business records and leaking them to the press and other outlets of public information. This case is highly unusual. However, all types of archives have the potential for a collision between the interests of the organization and greater social values. The scenarios sketched below come from seven different types of private and government archives: manuscript, state, foundation, national, corporate, religious, and university archives. Should archivists "blow the whistle" if they are in these situations, and more importantly, how should they cope with the conflict of interests involved?

Attorneys familiar with whistleblower cases stress that successful outcomes are extremely rare. However noble, most employees who accuse their institutions of wrongdoing damage their own careers without remedying the problem they identified. Individual employees facing an ethical quandary have limited access to the full story, and in most cases they do not know the full factual background of the circumstances that trouble them. The lack of complete knowledge makes it easy to attack the credibility of the accuser, no matter how just the cause. In such circumstances it is easy to become emotional about perceived malfeasance or injustice, but that emotion can cloud one's judgment. Organizations are self-protective of their reputations, and most do not tolerate employees who go to the press with allegations. The legal protections for whistleblowers are an incomplete patchwork of inadequate provisions and typically are not very effective. Some films and fictional accounts have romanticized whistleblowing as a brave and dashing thing to do. The reality is usually far from romantic. For archivists, who have a position of trust and access to proprietary and restricted information, revealing those secrets can be seen as a violation of professional ethics.

On the other hand, a good citizen cannot ignore blatant wrongdoing. Experienced attorneys advise taking the time to learn as many facts of the case as possible in a calm and deliberate manner. They suggest going through channels in the organization if needed, speaking in confidence, maintaining trust with colleagues, and exploring a variety of remedies. If the situation becomes emotional, one's objectivity can be compromised. Once an employee becomes isolated and perceived as a troublemaker, the career consequences are severe, even if the whistleblower tries to change jobs. The sacrifice may be in vain. Revealing or protesting against an ethical lapse is thus a very serious matter, not to be done on a whim. It is potentially libelous and can have serious consequences. One should not encourage anyone to serve as a whistleblower without a realistic assessment of the situation. To take that step is a very personal decision, one that should be discussed well in advance with family and with legal counsel.

Seven Scenarios

The following case studies, while generalized, are based on actual incidents, typical of the profession, in various types of archival repositories. A code of ethics is helpful, but in addition archivists need to develop coping skills to navigate situations such as these. These cases are meant to provide food for thought, not to provide answers or solutions.

1. Manuscript collection: A manuscript dealer has befriended lonely elderly people, stayed in their homes, and walked off with manuscripts to sell later to others, such as your repository. Can you buy the papers? Do you have an obligation to call the police? Is it theft? Elder abuse? Or none of your business? What if the elderly are not concerned about the missing papers?

2. State archives: You are processing financial records and suspect that a secretary had embezzled funds from the agency that transferred the papers to the state archives. It happened four years ago. Are you obligated to report your suspicions, and to whom? What if it happened ten

years ago? Does the timing matter? Does the amount of money involved matter?

3. Foundation archives: While processing personal papers from a wealthy donor you find evidence of a large financial contribution, tax deductible, to your repository, on the condition that the money be used for acquiring archival materials relating to China. The check was cashed years ago, and no Chinese manuscripts have been purchased. You bring this to your supervisor's attention, and he is unconcerned. Has your ethical obligation been fulfilled by reporting through the chain of command? Do you go over his head? Do you go to the press?

4. National archives: Your supervisor tells you to shred some "duplicate" documents. You suspect they contain evidence of improper use of power to fire a government employee for partisan reasons. Is it best to shred without reading, so it is not your problem? Do you refuse? Are you required to report? What if you are not entirely sure what happened, but are assuming it was improper?

5. Corporate archives: You are a business archivist transferring records that show your company deliberately withheld product liability information from injured consumers. What do you do?

6. Religious archives: Letters in the archives accuse priests of improper and illegal behavior with minors. Do you have an obligation to report to the police?

7. University archives: Your repository has received a large collection without an inventory from an alumnus. In the boxes you find envelopes containing a white powder. What do you do? Just return them? Have them tested? Report to your supervisor? Report to police?

CHAPTER 6

Archives and Privacy

No one shall be subjected to arbitrary interference with his privacy, family, home or correspondence, nor to attacks upon his honor and reputation.

—Universal Declaration of Human Rights, article 12 (December 10, 1948)

You already have zero privacy. Get over it.

—Scott McNealy, CEO, Sun Microsystems (2007)

There is no more privacy. Get over it.

—Vinton Cerf, "Father of the Internet" and vice president of Google (March 5, 2009)[1]

THE BASIC CODES OF ETHICS FOR ARCHIVES AND MANUSCRIPTS ALL MANDATE THE PROTECTION OF PERSONAL DATA FOUND IN DOCUMENTS. Privacy protection is one of at least eighteen recognized constraints on open access, but this rapidly changing concept is sufficiently fundamental to deserve a separate discussion. Is a respected zone of privacy a universal human right as solemnly pronounced by the United Nations in 1948? Or is it an antiquated relic of a vanished era like the rotary telephone, as leading technology leaders have emphatically declared? How do archivists navigate between these two views? Private information in open archives is a problem that will not go away and does not have easy solutions. What follows here is the pragmatic perspective of a hands-on archivist and emphatically does not constitute legal advice. European examples are included because they provide a foil for seeing our own system. In addition, there are interesting innovations emerging from Europe that may be useful and adaptable to the American context. Of particular interest are efforts to combine more protection of private data with increased use of the same data using certain safeguards, as will be seen in the example at the end of the chapter.

American archivists exposed to European archival practices have analyzed how sensitivity to private data in archives varies with culture, era, and context. Trudy Huskamp Peterson, for many years a high-level archivist with the National Archives, has detailed the extra privacy precautions she encountered while assigned to appraise records from the FBI for transfer. Mixed in with the papers to be evaluated were private income tax returns. She was barred from even briefly glancing at the tax returns, which were physically covered up with brown paper. They were private, and even her confidential role as archivist did not permit her temporary access. Research into American practice reveals that in 1924 and again in 1934, the U.S. Congress tried to make income tax data open to the public. Both times the law was rapidly repealed, and since then an American citizen's tax returns are strictly controlled. With certain specific exceptions, personal income is private information, shared only as part of the obligation to pay taxes to the state. The obvious conclusion is that income information and tax data found in archives need to be restricted.

Given that experience, Peterson was surprised to learn that in Sweden personal income tax information is considered public, and is systematically made available by the government.[2] Government records have been remarkably transparent in Sweden since the mid-eighteenth century, slightly before the French Revolution that led to the public records tradition in France. A Swedish tax calendar publicly posts the taxable income and capital gains of both individuals and companies. It is a centuries-old Swedish institution. Such calendars can be easily found in public libraries. Today there is a user-friendly government website where the latest tax listings can be ordered for a reasonable fee.[3] A cheerful cartoon figure on the website suggests that a user can look up his boss's income, what colleagues and friends earned in the previous year, and the solvency of any Swedish company. Such openness would probably not be accepted by most Americans.

This openness is surprising in view of the fact that Sweden passed the first ever national data protection laws in 1973. But there is a distinction: in Sweden, openness is not perceived as a problem, but control is. Once computer-assisted data manipulation became technically feasible, Sweden began passing legislation to control the way information is matched and repurposed. Today, Swedes may lodge complaints about targeted marketing from companies identifying and aggregating personal preferences (a common practice in the U.S.), but the level of one's taxable income is public information. The issue here is who controls the information, and how it is manipulated.

The violation of privacy is an intrinsic and unavoidable part of archival work because it involves the secondary use of documents, which were originally created for another, so-called primary, purpose. The U.S. Department of Health, Education and Welfare in 1973 attempted to preserve privacy by prohibiting the secondary use of personal information without the permission of the data subject: "There must be a way for an individual to prevent information about him that was obtained for one purpose from being used or made available for other purposes without his consent."[4] This prohibition on repurposing data has rarely been successfully implemented in the United States. Privacy legislation in Europe typically incorporates a similar principle prohibiting secondary use of data; these laws—at least in theory—are enforceable.

To reiterate the basic thesis: records, archives, and manuscripts are transferred from a private zone to a public arena. They are created in offices within a narrow and defined context, and then relocated to the archives for secondary purposes, such as research by unknown persons for unpredictable uses. Information that was recorded in private is exposed to new, judgmental eyes. Incoming correspondence and emails from third parties are generally included in the transfer, even when the letter writers have no way of knowing that their private thoughts are in an unrestricted collection. Both those who wrote and those who received the letters lose control of the way the information is used. While the author of a personal diary may give permission to open the contents for research, the third parties mentioned in such a diary probably have no idea their names and reputations have been exposed in this way. Traditionally, archivists have attempted to ameliorate the most egregious violations with blanket restrictions on access. Balancing privacy and open access has always been one of several ethical quandaries that are inherent in archival work. Given the acceleration of technology, maintaining control over personal data is now an even more pervasive problem. Information technology forces a choice: develop new, more modulated strategies to protect privacy or abdicate responsibility for it altogether.

Just defining privacy can be problematic. What is clear is that privacy is not the same as secrecy. Privacy is the ability to control personal data—how it circulates in society, in archives, in publications, and on the Internet. In its June 1995 report, the Information Infrastructure Task Force defined privacy as "an individual's claim to control the terms under which personal information—information identifiable to an individual—is acquired, disclosed, and used."[5] That control, or lack of it, casts a long shadow beyond individual lives and influences our perception of history in general and social history in particular.

This discussion will first analyze the personal side of privacy based on the lives of four remarkable cultural figures, whose documents have survived to varying degrees in historical, literary, and academic archives. By examining the details of their lives, it is clear that each of these figures had much to hide, but also something worth preserving. The examples demonstrate how the survival of cultural heritage depends on trusted archives and well-crafted donor agreements. Then the focus will shift to a historical sketch of approaches used in different countries and different eras, and a survey of fundamental charters, codes, tort law, and statutes that control access to private data. The summary will propose four basic approaches to applying privacy principles to archival practice and look at the obstacles to implementation posed by technology and globalization. In conclusion, it will attempt to make the case for preserving privacy despite the intrusive nature of modern technology. As always, there are more questions than answers.

Four Lives

Protecting individuality or selfhood is at the heart of privacy. For this reason the first examples are biographies. The biographers in these examples used documents to uncover the private lives of an American founding father and an unacknowledged founding mother, a Nobel Prize–winning German novelist, and a Pulitzer Prize–winning American poet. Three of these subjects were powerful writers, who drew on their unconventional personal experience. One voice in this quartet, and probably the most interesting, was regrettably lost. All of them had to find a way to protect themselves from excessive exposure during their lifetimes. They violated the taboos of their times. As a result, their families experienced difficulties long after the subjects died. How were the documents managed? In the first case the surviving documentation is frustratingly scant, as though much has been sanitized. As to the German novelist, we know some papers were rescued and others deliberately destroyed. In the last case, privileged documentation was given exclusively to the biographer, and then after serious controversy, was locked up tight.

Thomas Jefferson and Sally Hemings

During his presidency Thomas Jefferson made some alterations to his famous Monticello home in Virginia. He added venetian porches to the outside of his living quarters. Louvered blinds allowed him to look out from his porches, but others on the outside could not look in. The additions distorted the perfect proportions of his architectural masterpiece, but they allowed for privacy even as his fame attracted more and more attention. Keeping a barrier between the public arena and the private sphere was essential to maintaining his dignity and supporting his legacy as the most eloquent proponent of liberty among the founding fathers. After his death, his acknowledged family polished the legend.

Stories about Thomas Jefferson's private relationship with his slaves, and allegations of an unacknowledged, de facto marriage with one of them, Sally Hemings, had been circulated by his political enemies since his nomination to the presidency. Some of Hemings's descendents preserved a shared family memory that corroborated the rumors. Only recently have DNA results added supporting evidence to the allegations. The closer examination of his private life has drastically revised the perception of his character. Some facts will always be unknowable. It remains: the man most closely associated with the American concept of personal freedom had a private life inextricably linked with enslavement, with multiple ironies and tragedies.[6] Jefferson and Hemings never spoke publicly about their relationship. After his death Hemings retained a few mementos, such as his inkwell and glasses that she gave to her son—mute testimony. In the absence of letters and diaries, we will never know how Sally Hemings emotionally navigated her situation, or how the brilliant Thomas Jefferson reconciled his Enlightenment ideals with his Byzantine reality. One wishes that the veil of privacy had allowed for some traces to be kept in secret until a later and freer time. Their private lives remain an enigma.

Sally Hemings's biographer, Annette Gordon-Reed, opens her book with a meditation on one revealing private document that did survive, the famous Jefferson "Farm Book," which she saw at the archives of the Massachusetts Historical Society.[7] Gordon-Reed looks at Jefferson's account book from two perspectives. To his official family, it must have been an innocent document that bore witness to Jefferson's diligence as a manager, something they could preserve and take pride in. He recorded in great detail the names of his slaves, the distribution of clothes, fish rations, blankets, and shoes. He also listed which slaves were leased out and which were retained. Sally Hemings, the woman who shared his life in his screened private quarters, and her children, appear in such account books as property, like livestock. All the while recognizing Jefferson's greatness as a leader, Gordon-Reed also sees the "Farm Book" from a less innocent perspective: "it was wrenching to hold the original and to know that Jefferson's actual hand had dipped into the inkwell and touched these pages to create what was to me a record of human oppression."[8]

Even the sketchy evidence from the private sphere at Monticello tells volumes about the complex American experience and has implications beyond Jefferson's venetian porches. Jefferson read his countrymen correctly. However common the practice, interracial sex was prohibited by a powerful taboo, enforced by law, custom, and social pressure. He knew that if the rumors about his private life had been confirmed, his role in history as a founding father would have been badly tarnished. Two centuries later, as evidence accumulated, the emerging story was still perceived as shocking by many. Household accounts date when Jefferson began to buy Hemings fine clothing in Paris. The bare facts from the ledgers in the archives date Jefferson and Hemings's propinquity over many years, and the timing of the birth of her seven children. While possible, it is unlikely that there was not an intimate relationship between them. Although there is not enough archival evidence to reconstruct the full story, the naïve image of Jefferson, as perpetuated in generations of high school history books, is no longer tenable. The most plausible narrative, stripped of dishonest discretion, dismantles one polished founding myth, but it makes way for a more meaningful one, although one that is necessarily incomplete. Jefferson knew about liberty and oppression from direct personal experience.

The intuitively felt right to know the truth about the founding of the country is hampered by lack of documentation. The closest mention in Jefferson's writing is an oblique reference: admiration for a painting of Abraham, Sarah, and Hagar, a biblical tale that broadly parallels his own. There is no Hemings diary. It is a huge loss to American history. A distrust of public opinion and a lack of means to secure the story from political enemies until the death of the participants contributed to a gap in history. It is the very facts that might seem most private and embarrassing that can be essential information for understanding social history—in this case the history of race in America.

It is the role of archives to negotiate that private space and allow potentially embarrassing facts that have a wider historical significance to survive until they can be properly evaluated. The nature of taboo varies widely from one culture to another as does the perception of what is private. Certain elements are constant, and one is the need to preserve evidence from the private sphere. The second example concerns a very different biography from a different society and different century. It also illustrates the same point, but from a more modern perspective.

Thomas Mann

In 1933, friends warned Thomas Mann not to return to Germany from a European lecture tour. The extraordinarily gifted German novelist, who won the Nobel Prize in 1929 for a work he had written decades earlier at age twenty-five, was stranded in Switzerland. He was unable to return home to Munich because his political candor had aroused the ire of the Nazi authorities. As his trip abroad turned into involuntary exile, he became very agitated. He instructed his son Golo to return to their Munich house and remove the contents of the locked safe in his study, giving strict instructions not to read them. Golo, young at the time, casually entrusted the materials to the family chauffeur to ship to his father. The chauffeur stole the papers and turned them over to the Nazi authorities. Mann became distraught, fearing that the contents would be read and used as propaganda to discredit him, both in Germany and abroad where now he had to make a new career. "My fears are mainly and almost exclusively focused on this attack on the secrets of my life. Terrible things, fatal things can happen."[9] He lived in terror until the diaries were safely back in his possession. He engaged a savvy lawyer who successfully retrieved the files, the contents kept secret from everyone including his wife and closest associates. According to his family, he was enormously relieved, a weight lifted from his heart. Soon his estate in Germany would be confiscated by the Nazis, and later much was destroyed in World War II.

During World War II Thomas Mann lived as an exile in the palm tree–fringed paradise of Pacific Palisades, California, but there was trouble in paradise. Despite his firm and repeated denunciation of totalitarianism of all kinds, Mann was accused of communist sympathies by certain uninformed critics during the red scare at the end of the war. The FBI kept a file on him, detailing his opinions. In 1945, Mann burned most of the diaries, which had been retrieved under such dangerous circumstances in 1933, in an incinerator in his backyard. He decided to save just five thousand pages, which he wrapped and sealed. He disingenuously labeled them "without any literary value," with instructions to keep them sealed for twenty years after his death. After World War II, Mann and his wife relocated again to Switzerland, bringing the secret diaries with them. After his death in 1955, his family contemplated the proper disposition of his papers. Some thought was given to selling his literary manuscripts and diaries to a library in the United States for a substantial amount of money. However, the family was so grateful for the refuge they had found in Switzerland, first when the Nazis threatened them in Germany and then a second time after the war, that in the end they decided to entrust his surviving papers, including the sealed packages, to the archives of the Swiss Federal Institute of Technology Zürich (Die Eidgenössische Technische Hochschule Zürich, known by the initials ETH), where the twenty-year restriction on the diaries was strictly observed. No doubt the Swiss reputation for discretion was a contributing factor to the decision.[10]

What *was* it in those private journals that could have been so dangerous? Mann was a dignified presence, the embodiment of political and personal rectitude. A staunch supporter of the American effort in World War II, he was untainted by Nazi sympathies. Accusations of communist leanings were far-fetched. Unlike many of the other, more bohemian, exiled writers and artists, Mann enjoyed a long and harmonious marriage. He and his wife, Katia Mann, produced a large family of six talented children. In the photographs, it is clear how he doted on his bright grandchildren. Whether in Munich, Princeton, California, or Switzerland, Katia created the ideal home atmosphere. In his hushed study, the staid author, in a stiff white collar, wrote a sustained series of brilliant novels and stories, brimming with colorful characters. Intense philosophical disputes alternate with irony and slapstick: a cracked reflection of the tragedies he had witnessed in the twentieth century. In 1975 Peter de Mendelssohn published a biography celebrating Mann as a brilliant but conventional author.[11] The biography was timed to coincide with the centennial of his birth. It was to be the last naïve biography of Thomas Mann. His diaries were unsealed that very year.

When the diaries were opened and published, the first volumes, edited by Mendelssohn himself, totally revised the image of the stodgy patrician.[12] The diary entries were written by a man who was consumed his entire life by suppressed homoeroticism. Today the revelations from the private diaries are considered essential background for understanding his greatest works. For modern critics, it would be dishonest to try to write about Mann's work without acknowledging the central fact of his homosexuality. In retrospect, any alert reader should have noticed Mann's emotional orientation even without the diaries; only convention blocked the awareness. When Mann was growing up, homosexual behavior, while common enough, was illegal in Germany, as it was in Britain and the United States. During the Nazi period homosexuals were actively persecuted and sent to death camps. If the hostile German authorities had exploited the diaries in 1933, they could have destroyed his livelihood and his hard-earned reputation in the United States.

By the time Anthony Heilbut's biography of Mann appeared in 1996, the world had changed.[13] Ignoring Mann's propensities would have incurred ridicule. Had Mann or his family destroyed all of the diaries out of prudery or fear, the depth of his life and work would have remained an enigma. The compulsively written diaries, unlike his novels, are unflinchingly honest snapshots of each day. Like his novels, they reflect his keen powers of observation. If he had had the confidence to save all of them, the literary world would undoubtedly be a richer place. It is possible that an important human document, with value beyond the literary world, went up in smoke in a backyard in California. At least the five thousand surviving pages were protected. One must admire Mann's wife and children for respecting his instructions to preserve them in the first instance, and to keep them under seal for twenty years after his death. His family, apparently intuitively, understood the reasons for the restriction. The trust they had in the ETH Zürich archives was well placed.

In different centuries and different cultures, Thomas Jefferson and Thomas Mann were both public figures, celebrities who protected their privacy, and with good reason. Both took pains to protect their personal secrets beyond the grave. Certainly rumors about the two famous men were largely suppressed during their lifetimes, and credible revelations came into the public domain long after the death of the subjects. Had the general public known more about their violation of fundamental taboos, their ability to achieve what they did would have been seriously undermined. When the truth did come out, the revelations were considered shocking, even though knowledge of their life stories should have rendered the news unsurprising.

Anne Sexton

The next biography confronts the taboos of mental illness, errant behavior, and incest. It is an established principle that the medical details of the mentally ill are private and restricted from the public eye. As an individual with impaired judgment, the vulnerable victim may not be capable of informed consent. Should someone with known mental illness be allowed to release sensitive personal data? The public and professional prohibition against releasing privileged medical files was tested in 1991. The Anne Sexton case is a bellwether for the loosening of restrictions when there is a strong case for furthering research. Diane Wood Middlebrook researched the life of the Pulitzer Prize–winning American confessional poet, Anne Sexton, who had suffered from debilitating mental illness and used poetry to stave off suicide for as long as she could.[14] During extensive psychotherapy sessions, her psychiatrist, Martin Orne, taped her conversations with her knowledge as a tool to help her remember what she said. From the taped conversations, one could conclude that she was a victim of incest in her youth and a perpetrator of misconduct as a mother. There is no question that her family life was frequently thrown into turmoil because of her erratic behavior and excesses. Dr. Orne encouraged her writing as a means of fending off depression. His moral support and encouragement contributed to her literary success. After Sexton's suicide in 1974, Stanford English professor Diane Middlebrook was able to persuade Orne to release the tapes for her use. She says that the materials confirmed much that she had already learned, but also forced her to rewrite the book and reassess Sexton with fresh insights from the tapes. The book unleashed a storm of controversy over the ethics of revealing private medical information.

Many factors counteract the privacy argument and the confidentiality of medical records. First of all, Sexton was proud to be a published poet, and apparently happy to reveal in her writings personal facts that most middle class American women would go to some lengths to conceal. Public figures and celebrities do not enjoy the same level of privacy as those who do not seek the limelight. By the time Middlebrook began her biography, Sexton had already died, and privacy is generally believed to end at death. Her daughter and literary executor approved opening the tapes for Middlebrook's use. Most compelling was the fact that Middlebrook was engaged in writing a groundbreaking biography that substantially contributed to a better understanding of Sexton in particular and poetry by women in general. Who could, in good conscience, hamper such an enterprise?

The negative side has sound arguments as well. While not exactly universally famous, Sexton was in fact a public figure. She was deceased, but her husband and other family members who had suffered from her destructive behavior were not. They are discussed in the tapes as third-party, involuntary subjects. Not all family members welcomed the revelations. For one thing, it is difficult to interpret therapy tapes. Only a naïve biographer would assume that restricted tapes are somehow more honest than other evidence. Conversations with a therapist are not necessarily straightforward or accurate. Sexton herself was aware that she presented herself as a different persona to different people.

Another factor is Middlebrook's charisma. She was a woman of great beauty and enormous charm. Would a less attractive biographer have been as persuasive and successful in securing access? Was an exception made because of the biographer's famous panache? Diane Middlebrook herself seemed to take an intellectual interest in the controversy, although her opinion was very clearly on the side of sacrificing privacy for scholarship.[15] Many other psychiatrists worried that this well-known breach of the ethical code would erode the carefully constructed privacy walls around their less famous and very vulnerable patients.

The questions remain: What if Sexton had not been a recognized poet? What if Middlebrook had not been an inspired biographer? The results could have been a shabby, tabloid-style expose. In that case, the emotional cost to family members would not have been balanced by a contribution to scholarship. Is quality research a valid defense? Beyond this issue of quality, does the tightening of federal law on medical files in 1996 change the nature of the argument? (See the description of HIPAA legislation later in this chapter.) In 1991 use of the tapes was decidedly unethical but not illegal. Now it may also be illegal without prior approval from the data subject or from an institutional review board. The book in and of itself makes a strong case that exceptions should be permitted to advance knowledge. It is not clear what would happen today if the doctor, author, and publisher chose to ignore HIPAA.

Background materials should be made available in biographical research to corroborate the author's interpretation. In the case of therapy tapes, is equal access a good idea? Virtually all of Sexton's papers are housed in the Harry Ransom Center of the University of Texas, Austin. One over-size box containing Middlebrook's transcripts of the therapy tapes and Sexton's diaries is closed until after the death of Alfred Muller Sexton, Anne Sexton's husband, or with explicit permission for use by the Sexton family. Middlebrook, as the authorized biographer, received privileged access to the closed portion of the collection.

These lives demonstrate the intricate interplay between private and public domains in the face of strong societal taboos. In Hemings's case, the diary was probably never created in the first place. Her reticence was not merely an artifact of an earlier age. Hillary Clinton famously explained that she could not in good conscience keep a diary as first lady for fear that it would be subpoenaed and made prematurely public.[16] In the Thomas Mann case the diaries were written, although most, but not all, were destroyed.

Confidence in the discretion of the archives and in the enforcement of restrictions demonstrably contributes to the creation and preservation of important documentation. The Anne Sexton therapy tapes were preserved in great numbers, some three hundred. The resulting biography landed on the *New York Times* bestseller list, a rare feat for the biography of an honored but still somewhat obscure poet. In this case the materials were released in an unorthodox manner that drew strong criticism from the psychiatric profession and great appreciation from the general public. They are now restricted.

While very different personalities, these remarkable people needed to protect a zone of privacy even as they drew on their private experiences in their creative work and thinking. Without privacy, much of the creativity might have been squelched or eviscerated. Their families also sought that protection by destroying or restricting documentary evidence. The evidence that has survived provides important insights into history and human nature.

The main lesson for archivists is that calibrating privacy restrictions can be important. Often, of course, donors impose frivolous, capricious, and unnecessarily lengthy restrictions on their papers, sometimes motivated by an inflated sense of self importance. These stories bring back the impelling logic of providing a safe haven to preserve private data as it ages into historical and cultural evidence. Because the time that process requires can be lengthy, institutional continuity is essential. It seems most likely that personal evidence about Jefferson and Hemings was destroyed for lack of trusted archives. The fragments inadvertently embedded in account books are all the more precious. Thomas Mann and his family did not trust either the United States or Germany to keep faith with his need to protect his deepest secrets and most private thoughts. Fortunately they found a third option in Switzerland, where Mann's stature as a writer was admired and his privacy as a person was respected. Both literary and social history owe a great debt to the archives in Zürich for quietly abiding by the reasonable provisions of the donor agreement. Anne Sexton's private thoughts became public soon after her death, in a way that is considered unethical by most psychiatrists and psychologists, and probably by many archivists as well. Middlebrook's biography of Sexton ensured that her place in American literature was secure, but at the price of her husband's own privacy and peace of mind.

What does an archivist take away from these contrasting stories? One can perhaps place the issue in the "Goldilocks" framework of three categories: too little, too much, or just right. Any Jefferson-Hemings documentation was no doubt too sensitive and too restricted, to the point that it mostly perished. The Anne Sexton documentation was released too early, and possibly harmed innocent third parties, then withdrawn from use for literary scholarship. One can make the case that the restriction on Thomas Mann's private papers was "just right." The papers were not released prematurely; the restriction period was reasonable; and once the papers were opened, they have remained open to everyone. The relationship of trust between the donor's family and the institution is the key element to success. That relationship makes it possible to tailor restrictions and provision to just the right fit. Well-crafted privacy protections in donor agreements create a buffer that in the end enables more private information to be preserved.

A Survey of Privacy Safeguards

These brief glimpses into the lives of some remarkable people demonstrate the importance of preserving a private sphere for a reasonable period of time. Archivists play a crucial role by managing the opening of private information. In these cases, individual donor agreements regulated the process. There are other fundamental privacy safeguards in the form of charters, codes, tort law, and statutes. One expert in the field, Robert Ellis Smith, has compiled a listing of some seven hundred U.S. state and federal privacy laws.[17] It is a bewildering thicket of legislation. Americans have an inconsistent view of what should be kept private and what can be made public. That confusion is reflected in legislation that careens back and forth between transparency and protectionism over time. We have not yet found the balance that is "just right." European and American archivists are both grappling with these same issues, and both sides of the Atlantic have much to learn from each other.

The best survey of American law and practice can be found in the privacy reader edited by Menzi L. Behrnd-Klodt and Peter J. Wosh: *Privacy and Confidentiality Perspectives: Archivists and Archival Records,* and in Behrnd-Klodt's *Navigating Legal Issues in Archives,* two essential works.[18] There is no need to duplicate this work in detail, but the following brief overview will provide a comparison with other models.

While a sense of privacy is embedded in customary practices going back to antiquity, its appearance in American law was scant until the modern era. The protection of private information in personal papers is alluded to in the Fourth Amendment to the Bill of Rights: "the right of the people to be secure in their persons, houses, papers and effects."[19] We know that both Thomas Jefferson and Benjamin Franklin were concerned with privacy. Jefferson, who encrypted his letters, did not trust the integrity of the postal employees. Franklin, who was in charge of the colonial mail service, issued a regulation forbidding postal employees from opening mail. From this we know that privacy was a concern. It was not articulated in tort law until the famous article by Samuel D. Warren and Louis D. Brandeis in 1890, and the equally famous commentary by the preeminent scholar of tort law, William L. Prosser, in 1960. Brandeis was motivated by the intrusions made possible by then-new technology such as cameras and high speed newspaper printing presses, something we can relate to today.

European archivists have traditionally used lengthy restrictions on personal data to ensure that private information does not emerge until after the death of the subject. And these restrictions, from an American viewpoint, seem too long—as long as the life of the subject, and often longer than the interest in the topic. Russian law restricts private data for seventy-five years. In France some restrictions can extend to 120 years. In Germany government records are not released until thirty years after transfer to the archives. If records contain personal data, they are not released until ten years after the data subject's death. Well-defined exceptions are built in to allow people to see the data collected on themselves, and there are provisions for research.[20] In other countries the privacy requirements are often spelled out at the highest level, in national constitutions. While only tangentially protected by the Fourth Amendment to the U.S. Constitution, the inviolability of epistolary correspondence and private papers is explicitly protected by the constitutions of Argentina, Bolivia, Yugoslavia, Egypt, Iraq, Lebanon, Belgium, Denmark and Luxembourg.[21]

The European Union has been gradually harmonizing its privacy laws. The right to privacy is clearly delineated in the 1948 United Nations Universal Declaration of Human Rights, written in response to the dehumanization that occurred during World War II. The Europeans adapted the U.N. statements in the European Convention on Human Rights in 1950. With European integration, more explicit directives have been promulgated that are generating more consistent national legislation. Of course, the U.N. Declaration of Human Rights is not a binding document. As European integration continues, the European Convention increasingly does have the force of law in more and more countries. Article 8 of the convention has been the driving force behind data protection legislation in various EU members. The first data protection legislation was passed in the German state of Hesse in 1970. In 1973, Sweden passed the first national data protection laws, as mentioned above. By 1980 the Organization for Economic Cooperation and Development, a European agency, created nonbinding recommendations for protection of personal information. Then, in 1995, a formal directive began to shape national legislation: EU Directive 95/46/EC on the protection of personal data. Already, the sweeping European law on data protection is affecting American business practices in the international marketplace as well as the transfer of information about global crime. The laws target large databases. Progress has been made in Canada and Europe to encourage open access without abandoning privacy as a protected human value. As yet, however, there is no harmonized European law on archives specifically.[22]

Over the years the U.S. Congress has passed a series of statutes that regulate private information. Those archivists in charge of security, educational, or medical files will need to become familiar with the relevant provisions in special workshops and in greater detail than provided here. All archivists need to have an awareness of how they function; fortunately, accessible guides have been published by the Society of American Archivists.[23] Of these statutes, the ones of greatest concern to archivists are known by the acronyms FOIA, FERPA, HIPAA, and the USA PATRIOT Act. A brief chronological summary shows how they developed over the past few decades.

In a victory for openness, Congress approved the Freedom of Information Act in 1966. FOIA created a process for citizens to gain access to restricted government information. The difficulty is to release government records and at the same time block any embedded private data or security-classified information. These categories of data are frequently blacked out (redacted) and the sanitized copies released. At times entire pages are redacted out, and the process becomes a charade. While the process is slow and cumbersome, and the materials are sometimes unduly redacted, over time a flood of previously restricted archival material has been released.

Eight years later the pendulum began to swing in the other direction. While FOIA was opening up information, pressure was building to limit access to personal data. The result was the Privacy Act of 1974 that protects certain categories of personal information and also attempts to regulate data matching, the aggregation of dispersed facts into a profile. The act covers federal agencies only, not state agencies or organizations in the private sector. It covers American citizens, but it does not cover non-U.S. citizens, including immigrants, in this country without legal authorization.

That same year, 1974, saw the passage of the Family Educational Rights and Privacy Act (FERPA), frequently referred to as the Buckley Amendment, which contains numerous provisions. Among them are rules to protect data collected by universities on students. Students and their parents are given access, but the materials cannot be released for research during the given student's lifetime. The law is ambiguous as to the actual definition of which educational records are protected, and for how long. There is no provision for an institutional review board to approve research projects that aggregate data and conceal personal names. As a result, the legislation meant to protect students' privacy has had a chilling effect on institutional research that would benefit students. University archivists have been constrained by this legislation just as sunshine laws were freeing up other institutional information. One hopes that in any future revisions of the legislation, university archivists, who have to implement educational records laws, will be involved in drafting the exact wording to prevent such ambiguity and confusion.[24]

In 1996, the Health Insurance Portability and Accountability Act addressed access to personal medical information. HIPAA has been amended several times since. A niche protection like FERPA, HIPAA follows the trend to tighten up private information, even as FOIA works to improve access to government information. Even before HIPAA, medical records were considered confidential. In particular, psychiatric records that contain the type of confessions most likely to cause embarrassment have been under special protection. Research hospitals such as Johns Hopkins have long used an institutional review board to approve research using such medical and psychiatric archives while protecting privacy and confidentiality. A research application needs to be made to a board of experts, which then determines whether the scholar can see the archival record, and what level of detail can be revealed. Many consider these records restricted in perpetuity, which in the modern age seems increasingly untenable. The Johns Hopkins solution seems to be a reasonable compromise, but a very cumbersome one that in itself slows down access to private information. It is also inherently unequal and elitist access, as only high quality research survives the scrutiny of the board. Just as FERPA has inhibited research on university students, HIPAA has had a chilling effect on the analysis of health information that is needed to support sound public health legislation.

The fear of terrorism unleashed by the tragic events of 9/11 triggered a series of intrusive laws. The USA PATRIOT Act was passed immediately following the Al Qaeda attacks of September 11, 2001. It eased the access of law enforcement agencies to private data contained in emails, telephone communications, and other records. While primarily targeting foreign communications, the law enabled the government to access the private communications of untold numbers of citizens without using the normal search warrant. This legislation marked a reversal of the trend to protect private information while opening up public records. The 2002 Homeland

Security Act reinforces the provisions of the USA PATRIOT Act in establishing an agency to gather intelligence information using sophisticated data mining techniques. The act also contains a utopian provision that this aggressive aggregating of personal data shall be conducted in compliance with the Privacy Act. Managing the government records affected by the USA PATRIOT Act and the Homeland Security Act will create archival headaches for generations to come.

Over the past few decades, privacy concerns have made it harder to conduct serious research on universities and public health topics, but security concerns have made it easier for the government to intrude on the private lives of its citizens. It is unlikely that this contradiction will be resolved any time soon. It is imperative that archivists weigh in on information management legislation to make it consistent and meaningful in practice rather than an exercise in responding to the latest complaint or crisis.

For both Europe and the United States, the basic issues are transparency, data protection, and control. It is not unusual for archivists to encounter correspondence, including love letters, in personal papers, as well as evidence of unconventional behavior. As mentioned above, the European approach is to use blanket restrictions to prevent private data from becoming public during the subject's lifetime. Few American historians would tolerate such restrictions that defer the examination of events for nearly a century. The inherent violation of privacy that occurs in secondary use of papers has not resulted in large scale lawsuits against archives, at least not as of this writing.

According to Menzi L. Behrnd-Klodt: "Many archivists fear that a professional misstep may result in an invasion of privacy lawsuit. In fact, few, if any, such suits have been successfully litigated against archives."[25] The legal liability has been minimal, although that could always change. Even in the absence of lawsuits, the ethical liability remains: no truly professional archivist wants to be responsible for causing pain and distress.

One can make four broad generalizations, although there are exceptions to nearly all of them.

1. In general, privacy is thought to end with the death of the person concerned. Individuals do not always agree with this principle. Certainly Thomas Jefferson wanted his privacy to extend in perpetuity. Thomas Mann wanted it to extend until twenty years after his death.

2. In general, celebrities are judged to have voluntarily surrendered much of their privacy rights by deciding to live in the public eye. They are judged differently from people who deliberately shun exposure and demonstrate that they seek privacy. While public figures have fewer privacy rights, they may have a "brand" or "trademark" that they can claim against use by others. In the case of iconic figures such as Elvis Presley or Marilyn Monroe, ownership of their image and "brand" may be inherited by family members after the celebrity's death. Certainly families of public figures have a vested interested in retaining privacy rights as long as possible. On rare occasions, celebrities are able to win violation of privacy lawsuits. Jacqueline Kennedy Onassis succeeded in obtaining a judgment against an intrusive freelance photographer. Ralph Nader won a large cash settlement from General Motors, which had subjected him to eavesdropping, wiretapping, stalking, and spying.[26]

3. In general, American historians and archivists see a connection between open access and a healthy democracy. For this reason, in conflicts between access and privacy, strategies are put in place to attempt to open as much data as legally possible.

4. In general, both conservative and liberal Americans are more suspicious of governmental intrusions into privacy than market or research-driven intrusions. Currently corporations are aggregating huge quantities of data on consumer behavior without much oversight on how that

information is used. Academic work is often allowed the benefit of the doubt: high quality scholarly research that reveals private information is frequently felt to justify the means, as in the case of Anne Sexton's psychiatric tapes. The American experience has led to a long series of specific federal laws to protect defined areas of privacy in limited ways. Some of these are listed in the appendix. The European experience has led to very complex, comprehensive, but increasingly uniform data protection legislation. American business is already encountering difficulties complying with European data protection standards. And in the global marketplace the compliance problem will no doubt grow over time.

As we have seen, privacy varies from one culture to another. To make the task even more challenging, the sense of personal entitlement to privacy evolves and changes a great deal over time. Seen from a longer perspective, it is not a static concept, but essentially a moving target. And some knowledgeable experts believe the era of protecting private lives is already over.

Has the Battle for Privacy Already Been Lost?

Archivists worry a great deal about their role in protecting privacy. They work diligently to comply with the regulations set forth by FOIA, FERPA, and HIPAA. Historically the greatest privacy protection has been obscurity: the information is open and available, but hidden in heaps of dusty files, difficult and time consuming to access. Technology, as we all know, has changed and challenged this protection. Vast amounts of personal data once considered private can be easily gleaned in a few minutes. A number of the scientists most closely involved with the development of the Internet boldly state that privacy is gone. Are they right?

Highly detailed basic information is available in various public access forms, some for free and some for a modest charge. The search and match features of the program rapidly compile what would have taken years of manual searching. Enter a name, and one can instantly find a phone number, address, and map showing the location of a person's home and directions to that location. Social security numbers are also for sale on the Internet. The ease and speed with which personal information becomes available and distributed is the essence of the invasion of privacy. It is probably safe to say that with the current trends in technology, there will be a tug of war between the technological forces that break down private walls and the efforts of companies, governments, and individuals trying to preserve some zone of privacy.

Many people feel that privacy is basically gone in the modern world, and see little point in fighting back, as governments and companies automatically collect data and powerful programs can match up private information. This premise is addressed by Reginald Whitaker in his book entitled *The End of Privacy*.[27] Others are taking extra measures to counter automated intrusions. Some efforts have been made for voluntary data protection; some advocate strong legislation such as the data protection laws in Europe and Canada. There is a constant struggle between efforts to open archives, especially public records, and efforts to protect the personal data of individuals, which may be embedded in public records. Ethical archivists need to periodically review their procedures to see if they continue to comply with changing laws and changing national standards.

With the combination of new technology and a free market spirit of "anything goes," the issue of privacy, then, is becoming more acute. A feature of Google Maps called "Street View" is created by cameras loaded on vans that systematically drive through neighborhood streets. It provides images of people's homes linked to their street addresses. In the United States that intrusion has been passively accepted. After all, anyone can drive by, take a photo on the street, and post it online. If the photography had been government sponsored, perhaps there might have been a protest. Individual complaints of invasion of privacy have been dealt with by the company on a case-by-case basis, by blurring car license plates or people's faces. That means that people unaware of the photos, or unequipped to effectively file a complaint, do not have any blanket protections. Should an archivist take pains to conceal private data, such as home addresses and car license numbers, when the same information can be accessed by anyone in the world with a few clicks on Google?

In Germany, Google Street View ran into stronger resistance than in the United States. Germans have had to grapple with a complicated and tragic history of human rights abuses, and issues like privacy are taken very seriously. German authorities were not happy with the American-style solution of blurring the offending image on the public version of Street View; they wanted the source data deleted in a way that it could not be used ever by anyone. Google's web page rather disingenuously provides a libertarian argument that streets are public spaces and hence street level photography is not a privacy issue. Publishing random photography of public street scenes cannot be prevented without violating the First Amendment, but the systematic display and distribution of detailed images and information about private homes, using powerful technology, takes this exposure to a different level, one where privacy is definitely diminished.

Background search websites use powerful matching technology to compile information on individuals from a large array of public databases. Initial findings are typically free of charge, while a schedule of fees enables one to gather more detailed personal data, such as criminal records. Even the low-level free search provides information that many people would wish to keep private, such as age, "unlisted" home addresses, etc. This is the kind of information that archivists have traditionally tried to protect with various strategies. In using case files, researchers are sometimes asked to sign an agreement not to publish personal data. Archivists have spent much staff time double photocopying documents with such information as personal addresses redacted out with swaths of heavy black ink. The painstakingly redacted information is now, likely as not, readily available online.

For every privacy protecting strategy, there is a "work around strategy." In the 1970s the Census Bureau decided to sell some of its data to commercial firms to raise funds. It devised a strategy to protect the privacy of the data subjects, the American people, by deleting personal names. Within five years the marketing firms were able to match the Census Bureau data with information from other sources, such as phone books, to reconstruct the complete record. One of these firms, Donnelly Marketing Information Services, claims to keep track of 125 million people. Since then targeted marketing has become a huge industry. As one commentator said: "Our every click will be watched."[28]

Efforts to shut down revealing websites have been overturned on appeal as a violation of the First Amendment. One website encourages violence against abortion providers. It publicly reveals private information about doctors who perform abortions, information about where to find them, their homes, cars, and families. In cases like these, the First Amendment has been used to defend the public exposure of private information.

In rapid succession, social networking sites such as MySpace (2003), Facebook (2004), and Twitter (2006) encouraged millions of participants to voluntarily share private information in the name of forging online communities of "friends." University students, whose grades are sacrosanct under FERPA legislation, post embarrassing photographs of unscholarly behavior for all to see, including prospective employers. After decades of efforts by archivists to protect the rights of individuals, people are surrendering their privacy of their own accord. What would Louis Brandeis say about freely surrendering the honor and reputation he so highly valued? There is, however, a positive side to this erosion of boundaries: opening personal communications has a way of undermining official secrecy. In the 2009 Iranian elections, Facebook and Twitter were used to circumvent Iran's official restrictions and allow information to flow among dissidents and to reach the outside world.

Privacy provisions are often used as a subterfuge to block access to archives. There are many cases in which privacy protection is used as a false pretext for maintaining unnecessary secrecy. The National Security Archive (NSA) encounters this problem on a regular basis and provides public exposure in many cases. This organization was founded in 1985 by a group of researchers to bring together declassified U.S. documents at George Washington University. Despite the official sounding name, it is a private institution, largely funded by grants. Its goal is to simplify access to material released through FOIA requests. As FOIA requests have opened up vast quantities of archival materials, the redacted documents are released to the individuals making the request. As a result, the materials, while unrestricted, have been scattershot as to topic, location of declassified copies, and their ownership. The NSA aggregates declassified documents and digitizes the results for open access. Their website has assembled and indexed about five hundred thousand pages of declassified documents, largely acquired through FOIA requests. The NSA has systematized the released information according to topics, enabling full access to the scans and facilitating searchability. The potential of FOIA-based research has been increased exponentially as a result.

Not surprisingly, the NSA often runs up against objections to opening archives. In response to this resistance, the organization has established an annual "award" for the most creative dodges from government agencies wishing to avoid revealing information from FOIA requests. The award is called the "Rosemary" in honor of Richard Nixon's secretary Rose Mary Woods, who famously claimed during the Watergate scandal to have accidentally deleted eighteen and a half minutes of incriminating taped conversations from the private talks. In 2009, the Rosemary was awarded to the FBI. According to the NSA the FBI initially refused a request to declassify documents relating to the murder of journalist Daniel Pearl in Pakistan. The FBI requires a signed privacy waiver for documents relating to living individuals. In this case they required a signed privacy waiver from captured 9/11 planner Khalid Sheikh Mohammed. It was not forthcoming, and neither were the documents, at least until the foolishness of the privacy waiver was publicized. The NSA claims that the FBI turns down 66 percent of FOIA requests. And privacy is deliberately used as a tool in blocking compliance.[29]

Easy access to private information online has made an end run around legitimate efforts at protecting privacy in archives. Once-normal safeguards, such as requirements for privacy waivers, have been subjected to inappropriate abuse. The entire effort to devise privacy-saving strategies now seems entirely obsolete, basically moot. Or is it?

The Case for Privacy Protection

One of the most eloquent defenses of privacy was articulated by Heather MacNeil, a Canadian archivist who is in some ways closer to the European tradition, in her well-received volume published in 1992, *Without Consent: The Ethics of Disclosing Personal Information in Public Archives.*[30] The very next year the Internet began to unleash a tsunami of personal data, instantly available worldwide. In 2004 MacNeil published an update that acknowledged the inevitable damage to civil liberty posed by online data: "The vast quantities of ostensibly innocuous information on citizens, combined with the technological capacity to link information from a variety of sources, will result in a less spontaneous and, ultimately, less free society."[31] Her argument is based in part on the rights of the vulnerable members of society to avoid embarrassment and harassment.

Privacy has been valued in many societies and cultures over the centuries. Excessive scrutiny is often believed to exert a deleterious influence on the healthy development of children. American presidents have tried, usually with limited success, to shield their offspring from the questions of reporters, intrusive cameras, and exposure in the press.[32] Should archives protect the private data in their custody on children, who are among the most vulnerable members of society?

In many contexts, being seen or discussed in public has been considered damaging to a woman's modesty. Until quite recently, a respectable American woman's name was only to appear in the press at birth, marriage, and death. Both traditional Islamic architecture as well as Japanese palaces provided windows with special screens so women could look out and see the street without being seen themselves. In nineteenth-century America, porches were often provided with one-way shades. Screens similar to those on the venetian porch designed for Monticello by Jefferson could be purchased for ordinary homes. An advertisement for one American company proclaimed "She can look out, but you can't look in."[33] Traditional modesty has become a battleground as electronic imaging invades women's lives. There are competing pressures to pander to the demand for images, on the one hand, and to cover women up, quite literally with veils and burkas, on the other. In some countries, both trends seem to be expanding as the middle ground shrinks. As digital photography begins to filter into archives, should there be some cultural awareness and consideration of the dignity of female subjects?

Even for men, family life has been seen as more felicitous and secure if it is screened from view. Many cultures try to create a wall between the public and private spheres. Artists who go on retreats often do so in the belief that privacy enhances creative abilities. Likewise, religious practices are held to be more sincere if they are conducted away from public view. Privacy provides protection from self-consciousness and the fear of criticism. Efforts at protecting privacy are particularly pronounced in defense of weaker members of society. The privileged nature of many types of communication—medical records, religious confessions, legal consultations—derives from an effort to protect the vulnerable. Even powerful figures such as Thomas Jefferson needed that private zone. What is lost when those barriers come down?

As discussed in this chapter, the American defense of privacy seems to be motivated largely by a distrust of government intrusion. This motivation is best illustrated by the insurmountable political resistance to any form of national identity card. National identity cards are considered practical, useful, and normal in most industrialized countries, and have not led to oppressive government practices. American public opinion would not tolerate the imposition of such an ID card in the United States, where it is seen as dangerous trespassing on private space. Instead there is a default patchwork of fifty different drivers' licenses, many of them easily forged, which are used for national identification purposes. Social security numbers were not originally intended for any purpose other than assisting in distribution of benefits, and they are very easy to steal or misappropriate.[34] As a whole, Americans would rather depend on easily forged drivers' licenses and easily stolen social security numbers than submit to the invasion of privacy that a national identification card system would require. The American public, however numb from the technology revolution, still wants some kind of privacy barriers.

The larger threat to privacy is from the marketplace, beginning with targeted marketing and the recombination of data on individual purchasing habits that intrude into the personal sphere with information on the purchase of medications and beverages. At present this information is accumulating in databases, offices, and the business archives of various commercial firms and marketing services. This data is something of a sleeping giant. The potential exists that this information, once aggregated and sorted, bought and sold, can be used in unexpected ways, including public disgrace, secret extortion, or political manipulation. Has it gone too far to stop? Is there any reason to do so?

A case can be made that these threats only strengthen the argument for protecting privacy more forcefully. One can argue for the need to continue the established archival practices that treat privacy as a fundamental human right and a treasured value in any civilized society. The old techniques should not be discarded, but they are inadequate for the new challenges. The profession needs to explore the emerging information landscape and find new protections that can be integrated with the goals of openness and transparency.

Four Approaches to Reconciling Privacy and Access

There are charters about privacy. Codes of ethics address the issue. Tort law and federal statutes complete the array of formal and customary regulations. How does the working archivist follow legal and ethical guidelines and reconcile the competing demands of privacy and access in the new online environment? There are three main approaches to preventing violation of privacy, and an emerging fourth default mode. One approach is to shift the responsibility to others. This can encompass a dual strategy of deferring exclusively to the donors' judgment on what to restrict and then insisting on self-policing from researchers. A second approach is for the archives staff to take responsibility for restricting sensitive information by proactively screening collections. A third approach involves controlling how the information is used by researchers, normally with institutional review boards. The emerging default mode is to respond to complaints on a case-by-case basis, thus shifting responsibility to the data subject.

Shifting the Responsibility to the Donor or Researcher

By far the most common American approach for private repositories is to restrict private information only at the specific request of the donor, and then for a limited time. This means that donors must identify privacy concerns in the collections they transfer to the archives. They are responsible for any consequences if sensitive information is exposed. In government archives the responsibility can be placed on the originating agency, in accordance with traditional archival theory. This approach has certain practical advantages. The archivist is not put in the position of policing what researchers see and of censoring the morals of the people represented in the papers. If there is no proactive effort by the archivists to screen out private materials, then lapses are the fault of the donor, not a failure of the archives policy or procedure. Whatever information surfaces for researchers is used at their discretion, and the researcher bears any blame for publishing private data. Privacy protection is an unseen transaction between the donor and the researcher. In theory, at least, the archivist is off the hook. Thus much slips into public view in the reading room or online without any prior screening, especially if the donor does not bring it to anyone's attention, or if the originating agency does not have the time for prescreening. Given the volume of modern archives and papers, this is a convenient strategy; screening collections of one hundred boxes or more, not atypical, would be a hardship in terms of staff time required.

While this policy may seem to evade time-consuming responsibilities, it is not a panacea. Donors who feel that the family's honor has been damaged probably do not care about such things as staff time or censorship. They may not care that the burden of screening and restricting sensitive materials was considered the donor family's responsibility. They may not appreciate the refined strategy of holding the researcher responsible for revealing secrets. If harm is done to a person's reputation, the archivists do bear responsibility to some degree despite the best efforts to shift the burden. Frequently the family members want the papers open for research to enhance their reputation, but then will object strenuously if damaging private information is published. They know, emphatically, that they did not intend that to happen. And there have been embarrassing denunciations of archivists in prestigious publications as a result.

Prior Screening of Collections by the Archives Staff

Sara S. Hodson at the Huntington Library described a case in which the family of a deceased writer was so adamant that their famous relative's private life not be revealed that they considered burning the papers. To them, ordinary restrictions seemed too unreliable.[35] The family's honor was too important to take any chances. Most manuscript curators have encountered similar cases. Because of this well-known aspect of donor psychology, most manuscript repositories will perform at least some screening of collections. The director will discreetly contact a donor if there appears to be embarrassing material, and politely double check with the donor about access prior to opening a collection for use. Archivists can advise the donors on reasonable restrictions. Some sensitive items may be closed while others are simply returned to the donors. Prescreening works well in small, tightly focused, and well-funded collections where the staff members have the time to get to know the donors well and have a good intuitive grasp of what could potentially cause problems. It does not work well with voluminous holdings or in archives with a limited processing budget.

Institutional Review Boards

Reviews by respected peers have been very successful in preventing the release of damaging materials while permitting access. Researchers submit proposals and include safeguards for filtering out personal names and identifiers. A board of experts ensures that the best research continues without endangering vulnerable people. There are two difficulties with this approach. First, it is very time consuming and labor intensive. Second, it is an unequal process, but ultimately a very useful one. It may facilitate research more quickly than blanket restrictions and it may be more equitable to the greatest number of stakeholders. This approach is increasingly common in the European context.

Should the archives try to shift all responsibility for privacy protection to the donor and the researcher? Or should the archives try to screen collections and prevent embarrassing incidents on their own? Can the responsibility be shifted to a review board? Hodson counsels archives to consider which approach best suits their own collections and their own ability to take on different levels of risk. There are risks associated with any of these approaches. There is a fourth default response.

Responding to Complaints Case by Case

The sheer volume of most modern archives has resulted in a default approach in which privacy complaints are dealt with as they come up, basically on a case-by-case basis. This is the policy used by the University of California San Francisco for private data that is found in the cigarette papers, discussed previously. If someone objects to private data appearing in the vast database, an archivist will look at the offending information and make a determination whether or not to delete it. If it is a matter of obscuring a social security number, it is easily done. If satisfying the complaint requires censorship of the content, then the requested change is not made. Similarly, Google Street View responds to complaints on a case-by-case basis. By the time a determination is made, the information has been public for some time. That is just the nature of large databases, according to this view.

Traditionally, unprocessed materials were kept closed for the very reason that they could contain unknown sensitive items. The influential article by Mark Greene and Dennis Meissner has changed thinking about this on a national scale, and more and more unprocessed or partially processed collections are being served in reading rooms. The Greene-Meissner argument is that making large collections available to scholars with minimal description and processing fulfills the archivist's duty better than allowing inaccessible backlogs to build up. The authors persuasively argue that time-consuming but nonessential practices (such as removing staples and paperclips) slow down productivity to the point that research is obstructed.[36]

Greene and Meissner do not discuss the issue of screening for documents that involve invasion of privacy. What about removing sensitive items such as social security numbers, love letters written by living persons, evidence of malfeasance, alcoholism, or financial problems? This type of screening is just as time consuming, but could prevent an unpleasant situation with a donor or third party. If access trumps fine tuning, then this type of inspection would be superseded by the need to make the documents available. When large unscreened collections are opened or placed online, the default process is to respond to complaints on a case-by-case basis.

Greene and Meissner do make provisions for different levels of processing for different types of materials within the same collection. Certain series within a collection may require more intensive work than others. Under this policy, uniform processing of the entire collection is not required. In many situations one can judge whether there is a likelihood of private embarrassing documents. It is possible to spot check a series containing case files to determine whether social security numbers were entered in the forms, then make the determination about a closer inspection of those particular files, while allowing more innocuous materials to be bulk processed. This kind of calibrated approach helps with accelerating processing in general, but prevents harm to individuals when it is possible.

In choosing among these four models, it helps to consult with colleagues. The Society of American Archivists hosts a Privacy and Confidentiality Roundtable, a group that evolved informally out of a series of annual breakfast meetings to discuss this vexing issue, which resists easy answers. The group has actively proposed and sponsored well-attended and well-received conference sessions over the years. It maintains a useful and frequently updated bibliography on the SAA website. For archivists the best introduction comes by way of the much-cited SAA reader, *Privacy and Confidentiality Perspectives.*[37]

Archival work can provide a meliorating effect with intelligent policies that ensure people can see data collected on themselves, that they have the right to correct errors in the files, that they can request the deletion of private data such as social security numbers from the files. Archivists can play a critical role in the arena of privacy and access. They can preserve documents such as the Thomas Jefferson Farm Book and family accounts. They can restrict materials, such as the Thomas Mann diaries, and rescue history for future research. They can work with families on restricted materials such as the transcriptions of Anne Sexton's therapy tapes. These strategies can be mapped over into the online environment. All of these small, sensible steps add up to a more civilized approach to privacy.

On the larger stage, archivists need to use their special knowledge more actively to guide the drafting of privacy legislation. Educational privacy laws (FERPA) and medical privacy laws (HIPAA), for example, could have been drafted in a much more useful way with more input from the archival profession. With all of the contradictory trends sketched above, privacy is one of the areas that requires more professional study and discussion. Archivists have a definite contribution to make to the national discussion. While there may not be any blanket solution, archivists, as professionals on the front line, need to share their experiences mediating these issues in a way that helps with the formulation of more meaningful policies in a rapidly changing information environment.

One last case study shows how strong legislation and meticulous implementation can reconcile privacy and access.

A Hybrid Solution to Privacy and Access

When the Berlin Wall fell in 1989–1990, the communist German Democratic Republic and the Federal Republic of Germany united with great speed. One of the many quandaries was how to manage the extensive files of the communist-era secret political police, known colloquially as the "Stasi." These files contained the reports made by an army of spies and informants. They included plans for suppressing and punishing East German dissidents through a variety of legal measures and extralegal dirty tricks. West German privacy law at the time of reunification would have required that the files be closed for a minimum of thirty years, and that files with personal data be closed during the lifetime of the people involved. Many German professional archivists wanted to apply the standard rules to this enormous, unruly collection. Former dissidents opposed applying the normal data protection rules, and there was enormous pressure to know who did what to whom. Officials warned that the information in the Stasi files, if released, would result in widespread retaliation and chaos.

Rather than frame the issue in terms of either completely opening or completely restricting the files, the materials have been placed under special legislation that carefully regulates access. A former East German Lutheran pastor, Joachim Gauck, worked out the provisions with great care. The most important access principle is that an individual "data subject" may examine the information collected on him or her. Second, government agencies can examine the files of people applying for tax-supported, government jobs, to determine whether they had been engaged in unsavory spying activities. Random access to the files is strictly prohibited: no fishing expeditions are allowed. Provisions are made for well-crafted research projects and for responsible journalistic purposes. The Stasi Records Act of December 20, 1991 was initially greeted with skepticism by West German officials and resented by former East German officials. The predicted murder and mayhem did not occur. Instead of tearing apart the social fabric, the carefully modulated balance of access and privacy strengthened democracy and faith in the government.[38]

The Stasi file experience demonstrates the benefits of a detailed access policy over blanket data protection restrictions. The European Union Directive on the Protection of Personal Data has a similar philosophy. While European privacy laws are certainly complex, they are not as convoluted as the seven hundred American laws governing privacy. The Stasi Records Act can be seen as a version of the third approach to privacy: combining access with controls such as use of review boards. It requires a great deal of staff time to screen research requests, and that means adequate funding. It is a model that should be considered for large collections of sensitive files, especially case files. It works best as a model for legislation; problems may arise when an individual archives adapts it as justification to vet researchers and their projects. Just as Europeans have learned from Americans about more open access, Americans can learn from the European experience about drafting technical requirements for opening records within a data protection policy.

There are efforts underway by various organizations and government agencies to formulate generally accepted privacy principles. Can these principles be woven into archival privacy policies? What elements should be included? The first principle is simply to have a privacy policy that is posted and made public. Ideally it would include the often cited principle that people have a right to know if data is collected on them. Given the size of modern archival collections, it is physically impossible to inform every person whose name appears in every collection. A more practical principle is that data subjects have a right to access information about themselves. Once someone knows that his or her personal information is in an archives, access can be permitted to that specific data. There could be an opportunity provided to correct errors unless such access conflicts with the rights of other persons. Data integrity is another much-discussed area. Any organization that holds personal data has an ethical responsibility to ensure the integrity of the information and protect it from alteration and malicious tampering. Repurposing data is another area of concern. Here archives need to validate scholarly research as an exception from the prohibition against repurposing personal data. Other safeguards can apply, such as user agreements, redacted data, privacy waivers, privacy board review, and institutional review boards. Tactics such as these are being explored and tested for viability and sustainability. In the end, each repository will need to construct its own combination of privacy safeguards in keeping with its mission, the nature of the collections, and its budget.

There are powerful, competing forces at work in our society that are changing the way individuals define themselves. As custodians of privileged data about individuals, archivists are in the center of the storm. At present the direction of change is not clear—only that change is occurring rapidly.

Questions for Evaluating Privacy Policies

When formulating privacy policies or when facing a particularly vexing privacy question, it is good to review a few basic questions. This level of detail certainly is not required on a daily basis, which would no doubt obstruct the work flow. Some small archives may not have access to legal counsel, or the lawyers available to them may not have the requisite knowledge of the field. Nonetheless, cultivating a relationship with a capable attorney or knowledgeable colleague is a very wise and useful first step. Identifying the types of records in a repository that come under statutory regulation is also important. The one essential ethical imperative is to develop an awareness of these questions.

1. Do you have access to legal counsel to discuss privacy issues?

2. Do you have a privacy policy that has been approved by legal counsel and by your parent institution?

3. Are there records in your custody covered by federal, state, or local privacy law?

4. Are there internal records from your own institution, and do you have a well-planned policy for access to them?

5. Are there records generated by privileged relationships such as student grades, medical records?

6. Are there confidential documents such as grant applications, case studies, tenure decisions, and personnel decisions?

7. Are there potentially sensitive materials such as financial transactions?

8. Should your particular archives systematically screen all incoming materials for sensitive materials?

9. Should your particular archives try to identify just the major potential problem areas for closer scrutiny?

10. Should your particular archives rely solely on the judgment of donors for identifying sensitive materials?

11. Should researchers be required to sign a privacy statement regarding publication of privileged data?

12. Should the requests for use of privileged files be submitted to a board to determine appropriateness and value of research projects?

13. Is there a mechanism in place for responding to complaints about violation of privacy?

14. Does the private data relate to living persons?

15. Does the private data relate to celebrities?

16. Is there a danger that private papers will be destroyed?

17. Have the heirs been consulted?

18. Is there a trusted representative who can act in the donor's best interest?

19. Will there be data transfer across national borders that needs to conform to the EU Directive of 1995?

20. Is there potential for harm such as identity theft or public embarrassment?

CHAPTER 7

Authenticity and Forgery

For 2,500 years and more, forgery has amused its uninvolved observers, enraged its humiliated victims, flourished as a literary genre, and, most oddly of all, stimulated vital innovations in the technical method of scholars.

—Anthony Grafton[1]

IN 2008, BRITISH POLICE CONFIRMED THAT THEY FOUND TWENTY-NINE FORGER-IES IN THE PUBLIC RECORD OFFICE. The documents had been surreptitiously inserted into twelve legitimate historical files sometime around the year 2000. The fakes were intended to discredit major public figures. One showed the Duke of Windsor as a traitor, and others represented that Winston Churchill ordered the murder of Heinrich Himmler in 1945—even though it is well established that Himmler committed suicide after he was captured by the Allies. The forgeries were easy to detect: a document dated 1945 had been produced on a laser printer. Despite the obvious fakery, by 2008 at least three history books had already been published citing these documents as evidence. Major university libraries in the United States diligently bought the books and placed them on the shelves, while Amazon.com posted glowing reviews encouraging their purchase. Reputable British historians were horrified that the public record had been tainted. According to Sir Max Hastings: "It is hard to imagine actions more damaging to the cause of preserving the nation's heritage than willfully forging documents designed to alter our historical record."[2] The archives administration promised more diligent security and installed cameras. The historical record had already been distorted.

Could this happen in American archives? It can and it does. In 2008, biographer Lee Israel published a confessional memoir about her career forging hundreds of celebrity letters for the autograph market.[3] She was amused by the dealers' lack of concern for authenticity and quipped that they must have thought that "provenance" was the capital of Rhode Island. She apparently spent many hours in elite manuscript reading rooms. First, she would copy out letters of colorful silent screen stars, then she would go back to her room and use aged paper and an old typewriter to create replicas to insert in the files. Almost universally the reference staff gave the manuscript boxes a mere cursory look when she returned them. Security was so lax that she had little trouble absconding with the originals to sell on the autograph market along with her own creations. Without a doubt, her behavior was immoral and criminal. She got away with it for so long because of a lapse in due diligence by reading room staff. Once she was finally apprehended, the judge was unusually lenient. If the thief had broken into homes instead of reading rooms, taking real diamonds and replacing them with glass, perhaps the judge would have been more stringent. Even some commentators found her reprehensible memoir entertaining. The people who purchased her forgeries probably are not as amused. Everyone responsible for supervising an archives or manuscript reading room needs to be familiar with this cautionary tale, preferably without paying for a copy of her book.

Lee Israel was caught, but it is unlikely that all of her forged letters have been retrieved from private and public collections. It is probable that many similar cases have gone undetected. Forgeries are circulating widely and find their way into collections on a routine basis. There needs to be a higher awareness of this simple fact. Forgery is simply wrong—a moral and legal issue. Negligence in reading room supervision is unethical. Participating in the purchase or sale of a suspicious document is unethical. Contending with deception is where archival ethics come in.

The author is familiar with one repository that had a well-known forgery in its holdings since World War II, fully cataloged. All the experts agreed that it was bogus. The problem was what to do about it, as generations of scholars had already looked at it. Rather than just removing the well-known document and have it mysteriously disappear, the staff decided to leave it in place, but to revise the cataloging description to ensure that readers were warned of the scholarly consensus. While this approach was deemed reasonable, it did not avert controversy. One researcher had spent years analyzing the document on the assumption that it was genuine, and he proudly published his findings. He became personally outraged at the revised cataloging description and wrote a stream of lengthy diatribes denouncing the archives and the staff to the highest levels of the administration. Conscientiously correcting the record is not always a trouble-free exercise.[4]

Forgery is nearly as old as writing itself. Most archives contain some fabricated, counterfeit, misattributed, fraudulent, or fake materials. Here the term *forgery* is used as an umbrella concept for any text that is presented under false pretenses with the intent to deceive, whether it is deliberately misidentified or concocted from scratch. An authentic document actually *is* what it is represented to be, written by the ascribed author, at the ascribed place and time, unaltered, without any intention to deceive. Authenticity is thus different from accuracy. The truth of the content is not the main issue, although it can play a role. The fundamental point is to establish the truthfulness of the purported identity of the document, or the degree of truthfulness.

There are specialized terms for different kinds of forgeries. *Pseudepigrapha*, for example, is the technical term for texts that have been purposefully attributed to a more illustrious author, such as a saint. At some points in history that practice was considered an acceptable manner for hallowing writing that would languish unread under modern concepts of correctly identified authorship. Archaeologists have noted that in many cultures important pronouncements are frequently attributed to holy sources in time-honored formulae. In this discussion misattribution will also be covered as a type of forgery. Some experts do not include pseudepigrapha as forgeries, but most modern readers today would consider the practice deceptive, especially in weighty matters such as religious prescripts.

On a less lofty level, forgery has also been used in both ancient and modern times as a practical joke to entrap the gullible or poorly educated. False claims of authenticity and authorship, various kinds of forgeries, have been found in ancient Egyptian inscriptions, as well as ancient Greek and Latin writings. Today, such entrapments are endlessly circulating and recirculating in cyberspace.

Evaluating authenticity is a necessary archival skill that needs to be cultivated. At the very least, an archivist must know enough to determine when a professional forensic analysis is needed and when to alert researchers to discrepancies. Otherwise archivists inadvertently and passively collude in perpetrating frauds and malicious amusements.[5]

Forgeries are a form of lying, misrepresentation, and hence in themselves ethically wrong, often criminal. Dealing properly with impropriety, morally with immorality, is always a challenge. For archivists, dealing ethically with archival forgeries in their collections is no exception. While no working professional has the time to analyze each document individually in great detail, an understanding of the process of authentication should permeate all phases of archival work from acquisitions to description to reference.

Forgeries are also intellectually interesting, often in ways the forger did not intend. Frequently they unintentionally document important social and political trends. False and falsified items come in a wide range of types, various formats, and many levels of duplicity. Studying them is an art in itself.

Numerous well known examples follow a certain pattern, which Anthony Grafton calls the great topos of forgery. This pattern can be perceived in forgeries from many different centuries and cultures, including contemporary America. It goes something like this: An affinity group of some kind—political, religious, national, or ethnic group—has been granted the documents or archives. They were written by an impressive source such as a divine agency, an emperor, brilliant ancestors, or important eyewitnesses of some kind. Unfortunately the original version was somehow lost, disintegrated over time, broken, burned, returned. Miraculously there is an authentic copy, faithfully executed and preserved, that attests to the desired narrative. Those people who want to believe in forgeries for strong emotional reasons are rather more credulous than they would be in other aspects of life. Grafton describes it thus: "one of the great topoi of Western forgery, the motif of the object found in an inaccessible place, then copied, and now lost, as the authority for what would have lacked credibility as the work of an individual." According to Grafton, it is even better from the forger's point of view to "claim to have consulted far-off official documents, preferably in an obscure language."[6]

The art and science of diplomatics grew out of the need to authenticate official documents and to detect forgeries. *Forensic document analysis* is the more current term, but *diplomatics* is less cumbersome and more historic.[7] It is the area of fakes and forgeries that really demonstrates the importance of retaining time-tested methods of description and analysis. The scope of importance is actually expanding as we adapt authentication procedures to the online environment, where hoaxes, both playful and malevolent, have proliferated in great numbers since the mid-1990s. Archival text always needs to be reviewed with a critical and skeptical eye, beginning with the classic questions about provenance and the chain of ownership. Archives should provide the setting for a close reading of documents; a search for anachronisms may be called for, or the examination of ink and paper.

Most importantly, every archivist should learn to distinguish authentic signatures from various types of facsimiles that have been used by secretarial staff over time (such as the autopen) and from carefully drawn, deliberately faked copies. One expert worth noting is Kenneth W. Rendell, who helped unmask Konrad Kujau's clumsy concoction of the so-called Hitler diaries and Mark Hofmann's technically brilliant forgeries of Mormon historical documents. Rendell provides examples in an excellent basic text: *Forging History: The Detection of Fake Letters and Documents.*[8] Charles Hamilton's classic book, *Great Forgers and Famous Fakes,* focuses exclusively on the American tradition.[9] He cites many technically useful examples of common forgeries that widely penetrated into archival collections around the country. He usefully provides examples of forged certificates of authenticity, a very common genre. Of even greater interest are his biographical sketches of the perpetrators. He illustrates with great psychological insight the motivations behind the crimes, some purely monetary, but most driven by some kind of pleasure in the art of deception. The chapter on Clifford Irving, who audaciously produced a fake autobiography of Howard Hughes while his subject was still alive, is especially revealing—the lure of great profits combined with the lure of adventure for both the author and the publisher in a *folie à deux*. The author had a compulsion to fake, and the publisher had a need to believe. Together, Hamilton and Rendell's work forms a warning about the prevalence of forgeries, even in contemporary America, and how they find their way into archival collections.

The ethical archivist needs to develop a range of skills in assessing the genuineness of records, manuscripts, and archives: locating and preserving evidence of provenance and accurately describing authorship, clarifying what is known and what is not known about the materials in question. This requires curiosity and a healthy sense of skepticism. Two key areas are acquisitions and reference. When it comes to acquisition purchases, authentication may require both consulting with outside experts and tapping into the specialized knowledge of the archives staff. When it comes to the reading room—online or physical—working archivists, who do not have the time to scrutinize every item individually, should still have the skills to assist researchers with authentication in a collaborative process. There should not be an automatic presumption of authenticity. The presumption should be that each document needs to be assessed. Because there are levels of truth, the assessment is an ongoing process, not a simple *yes* or *no* determination. Researchers should not be left with the impression that every question about the documents has been answered.

Just the seemingly straightforward task of distinguishing between an original document and a copy opens up a range of questions. The "original" is not necessarily a single unique item. The Magna Carta, for example, exists on several nearly identical pieces of parchment, all of which are historical originals. A copy may be an authorized text checked for accuracy, intended to provide easier access to the content rather than the artifact, in which case it is not a forgery. Or the copy may be fabricated to pass as the original, perhaps to be sold for its supposed artifactual value, in which case it is meant to deceive. In the online environment the distinction between original and copy is further blurred. David Levy maintains that in the digital world there are really no originals, just templates, digital files of bits, and a multiplicity of copies and variants.[10] Grafton maintains that overly defensive "claims of faithfulness in copying suggest...the presence of the forger."[11] This may also be true in the digital realm. And frequently, legitimate copies created in normal office conditions are converted to forgeries when they are misrepresented in a different context.

For copies, context is everything. Consider a high quality, two-sided color photocopy of a hundred dollar bill. If it is found in the collection of an entrepreneur it may be a token of the first profits from a new enterprise. It is part of the history of the business: a souvenir, not a fake. If it is identified as a copy and used in a classroom to show students what such a bill looks like, it is an educational tool, not a fake. It may be used to verify the signature of the secretary of the treasury that appears on U.S. bills. If it is pasted into a collage, it becomes art. If given as a gift, it may be a practical joke. If the same two-sided color photocopy is stripped of its label, presented as "real" money, and repurposed to buy a camera, it is a counterfeit and illegal. Context and provenance not only provide authentication, they provide meaning.

Authorship is another area that is surprisingly complex. As described above, attributing a text to a more illustrious author is a time-honored tradition. Even seemingly straightforward attributions can deceive. Many authors dictate their writings. Secretaries and editors may smooth, edit, and modify the author's words. Often there are different variants of a text, and it is quite difficult to determine which is closest to authorial intent. Ghostwriting and plagiarism are extremely common, especially in government offices. A major service of archives and manuscript repositories is to preserve the different drafts as evidence of how a text was compiled, and by whom.

The author once examined a first-person account of the Russian Civil War. The manuscript exists both in a handwritten Russian version and a typed English translation, an account ostensibly written by a great political leader. The claimed authorship did not correspond to the characteristics of the manuscript. The small, even Cyrillic handwriting did not match the great man's other writing samples, which were noticeably larger and bolder. The paper was a poor quality, wood-pulp notebook, not the fine water-marked stationery he otherwise used. And the writing was in pencil, not the usual ink. The most plausible explanation was that the great man's assistant, who lived and dined with him, wrote down the text. Was it dictated and recorded faithfully? Was it the remembered dinner conversations reworked in a narrative form by the assistant? Was it ghost-written at the great man's request? Was it the assistant's own wartime impressions attributed to the great man? A modern version of pseudepigrapha that publishers identify with the phrase "as told to..."? The typed English translation was even more problematic as the translator inserted historical explanations that would be needed by the American reader to make sense of distant events. The explanations were seamlessly included as the words of the "original" author. How much of the great man's words were in the text? Probably very little. Is it forged? Pseudepigraphic, misattributed, ghost-written? Is it still interesting if the secretary actually wrote it?

Should authorship even be taken into consideration in judging the intrinsic value of a text? An entire school of literary criticism advocated the evaluation of writings on their own terms, without reference to the author at all. This mid-twentieth-century trend—the New Criticism—is no longer new, but its theories remain relevant in any discussion of authenticity in archives.

The range of pseudepigrapha, ambiguous writings, and deliberate forgery is quite broad. On the more innocent end of the spectrum are simple acts that occur in the course of creating records. A concerned government employee might simply add an unauthorized memorandum to the official record to clarify his interpretation of events. It may be added to the files in such a way that the author is assumed to be someone else. More maliciously, employees have been known to insert fabricated memos to incriminate or implicate a rival in some negative way. A former secretary of state once told the author that this was the easiest way to dispatch a bureaucratic enemy: insert a memo of conversation in the filing cabinet and wait for the freedom of information process to lead to its discovery.[12] Not all papers in the same folder date from the same time or the same author.

When the communist-era secret police files of Eastern Europe were seized, there were charges that the files were salted with bogus evidence against targeted personal enemies. Bureaucrats, who have access to filing cabinets and hard drives, may add documents for a variety of reasons: some may be inserted with the intent to deceive. The papers may be a legitimate part of the archival record; but, like all documents, they need to be scrutinized with care and skepticism.

A kind of collaboration develops between the archivists and the researchers. The archivists typically establish the known context of the materials, such as the office where they originated, date of transfer, history of ownership. The researchers bring their knowledge as subject specialists to bear. One uses a microscope, the other a telescope. Without the details shared by the archives staff, scholars can easily misunderstand what they are reading. No archivist can be a specialist on all the topics in the repository. Without reading the conclusions of researchers who have wide experience in their fields, the archivists may not know the significance of the holdings and can go wildly off track.

Some fakes are the innocent by-products of overly wishful thinking or a lack of critical analysis on the part of archivists past or present: Many archives contain copies that may have been erroneously identified as the "original" text. The text may still be usable for research. The copy itself may have an interesting history, but the identification may need to be corrected. Often the false impression of the document is only a matter of a deliberately or inadvertently mislabeled folder. This error can be easily corrected, as long as the correcting process is documented. Most archivists encounter this problem. A copy may be identified as the oldest, the first, the genuine holograph. Here we have misattribution, public relations puffery, an effort at aggrandizement for the archives by excessively devoted and insufficiently critical archives staff. Intentional or not, the result is a text that is presented in a way that deceives.

Forgeries range in motivation: many are simply an attempt to make money; some form venerable foundation narratives; some are created to support ethnic cultural pride; others attempt to validate conspiracy theories; and some are malicious attacks on perceived enemies. To these categories one needs to append a discussion of digital forgery on the Internet. The following examples provide a sense of the spectrum of deception, from the sublime and benign to the ridiculous and malevolent.

The Profit Motive in Forgery

There is a wide range of motivations behind the forgery industry. Some forgeries are created for sale, to cash in on the high auction value of certain collectibles. The ubiquitous Lincoln signatures fall into this category, as do Lee Israel's celebrity letters. The infamous Hitler diaries were apparently created to bag a handsome multimillion dollar fee from a German magazine. While very crudely made, the Hitler diaries concocted by Konrad Kujau fooled an eminent British historian, Hugh Trevor-Roper.[13] Ironically, Trevor-Roper had previously unmasked a famous forger of Chinese documents, Edmund Backhouse, known as the Hermit of Peking, who salted the Bodleian Library's Asian collection with fakes. Some experts insisted that the sheer quantity of the Hitler diaries, some sixty volumes, would be impossible to forge. But given the price paid per volume, the time required to copy out Hitler's published writing was well remunerated.

While bafflingly common, this type of fraud as a money-making scam is criminal, and certainly hazardous if scarce funding is wasted on its purchase. Such materials need to be identified and exposed. Perpetrators need to be brought to justice. In the process, an important distinction should be made between worthless forgeries and those with intrinsic interest, however unintentional. In some cases, they should be simply removed from reputable collections. As always, deaccessioning requires ample documentation of the approval process. In other cases, the forgeries embody social or historical forces that are worthy of study in themselves. In the later situation, great care is required in the way such manuscripts are identified for the researchers. The Hitler diaries, a strictly for-profit endeavor, have no redeeming value, containing only text copied from published sources. The Russian Civil War diary mentioned above does have research value as a first-hand account—but one that is probably not by the stated author.

Forgeries as Foundation Narratives

By far the most interesting forgeries are created to substantiate the found-ing of a political, religious, or ethnic institution. These false records have a long and venerable history and are important documents in their own right. They have often played a huge role on the stage of history to establish the foundation narrative of great religions and nations. Such documents are often beautifully written and worthy of critical study. The truthful-ness may reside on an allegorical or metaphorical level. If a community takes the document seriously, so should the archivist, but from a different perspective. This is an area that can require sensitivity to other cultures. One cannot expect the group with a vested interest in the authenticity of a document to be objective and dispassionate about the subject. Archivists need to identify such items systematically, have them placed in context by experts, preserved, studied, and carefully monitored. And sometimes enjoyed for what they are. One must always be prepared for the passionate and irrational defense of the authenticity of such forgeries—and the high level of gullibility involved—especially with documents that provide a desirable foundation narrative or myth.

The *Donation of Constantine* is one of the most influential foundation narratives. It is a complex document that emerged in a politically charged situation, rightly called Byzantine. One can provide a simplified but still fairly accurate outline of its history. It is a well-known historical fact that the Emperor Constantine changed the course of European history in the fourth century CE by providing the once-persecuted Christians with a privileged position, including access to land ownership and secular power. His con-version provided the foundation for the ascent of the Christian church with its base in Rome. This is a great narrative, a compelling foundation story. Unfortunately there was no document to prove the great gift of Constantine to the church, or to delineate the exact clauses and provisions of the gift. Political developments in the Middle Ages, when privileges were being documented by charters, required such a document in Carolingian Europe, one of the great document-producing eras of history. When a document is needed for political or religious reasons, it often mysteriously appears

on cue. Sometime in the eighth century such a document, purporting to
originate in the fourth century, surfaced and was widely cited as proof of
Emperor Constantine's great gift to the church, an inheritance happily
accepted by generations of popes and emperors. The source document
did not survive, but there were copies that appeared authoritative. It went
unquestioned for centuries. Only seven hundred years later, with the rise
of Renaissance textual criticism, did the anachronisms and infelicities in
the language register as problems. Gradually it was unmasked as a forgery,
and the Catholic Church today accepts it as such without question. It
served its purpose and is no longer needed to attest to the legitimacy of the
Christian church. Today, we know why it was created, but we still do not
know who created it, when, or where. It is one of the unsolved mysteries
of the Middle Ages.[14]

Few American archivists will have custody of a forgery of such gravitas
as the Carolingian era's *Donation of Constantine*. Americans, however,
are not immune to the compelling need for documents that confirm an
institution's role in history. Peter Hirtle provides an example from the
historical narrative for the modern city of Baltimore. There was a perceived
need in the immediate post–World War II era to boost municipal pride in
Baltimore's rich heritage, especially its role in the founding of the United
States during the time of the American Revolution. Inconveniently, few
substantial traces remained to embody the city's august history in a dramatic and visual way that would appeal to tourists. Some civic boosters
decided Baltimore deserved a revolutionary-era foundation icon on the
level of the Liberty Bell in Philadelphia. One was supplied in the form of the
Constellation, a proud ship with a proud history that was made even more
impressive. Over time it was discovered that this venerable vessel, on imposing display in the Inner Harbor as a revolutionary-era frigate, was actually
a nineteenth-century Civil War vessel restored to appear sixty years older,
to date it to the founding of the nation. Elaborately forged documentation
was salted in the archives as evidence. According to Hirtle: "In the 1950s,
however, documents began to appear that Federal Bureau of Investigation
(FBI) investigators later determined were forged. One document, allegedly
written in 1918, was found to have been written with a typewriter made

after 1946. Some of the forged documents in the possession of researchers bore forged stamps indicating that they were copies of records found in the National Archives. Other forged documents were inserted into historical files at the National Archives and at the Franklin Roosevelt Presidential Library, where they were subsequently 'found' by researchers. The need to alter the archival written record to conform to a particular historical interpretation speaks to the power of archives to authenticate."[15] Obviously a great deal of effort went into the deception. It was archival supply meeting political demand generated by false civic pride.

Some make the case that the biblical narrative tracing the foundation of the law falls into this category. In the Old Testament, Moses claims that God carved the Ten Commandments into the stone tablets with his finger, a divine holograph. Later Moses smashed the tablets but the text obviously survived in authenticated biblical copies. The story conforms to Grafton's great topos. For many it does not matter who physically chipped the text in the stone, or that that the "original" was destroyed. One need not believe the story on a literal level to revere the Ten Commandments. Many generations of skeptics and agnostics have concluded that the text can stand on its own merits.

There are two major lessons in these cases: First, never take documentation of foundation narratives at face value. The second lesson is an appreciation of the power of foundation mythology in history.

Forgeries as Ethnic Cultural Monuments

Cultural aggrandizement has been a powerful motivation for forgeries over the centuries. In 1634 two Tuscan teenagers purported to find ancient Etruscan inscriptions. Their fabricated trophies were highly prized in the region that prided itself on its ancient Etruscan cultural roots. People wanted to believe that they were the descendents of a prehistoric, pre–Latin, vividly imagined utopian society. When Melchior Inchofer, a Jesuit priest in Rome, examined the inscriptions, he pointed out the inconvenient truths: The texts were written on paper, and the Etruscans themselves wrote on linen. The texts were written from left to right, not in the reverse style used seventeen centuries earlier.[16] Oddly enough, this same sharp-eyed Jesuit had defended the authenticity of a forged letter, ostensibly written by the Virgin Mary to the city of Messina, a letter which was the source of civic pride. It was not the only case of a forensic expert who applied his skills selectively.

The forgery industry grew in the eighteenth century as ethnic groups began to rediscover their heritage. It was the beginning of the great age of Herder and a national awakening that would lead to a heightened sense of nationalism among the ethnic groups in Europe, for better or worse. German speakers took great pride in their ancient literary heritage. It was seen as evidence that the Germans had a national identity even though they were fragmented into dozens of small separate principalities prior to German unification in 1870. In 1755, an original Middle High German manuscript of the medieval epic the *Nibelungenlied* was found in an obscure castle library. While the discovery story partially matches Grafton's topos for the origins narrative of a typical forgery, in this case some thirty original medieval manuscripts survived in different locations. In addition, the *Nibelungenlied* is only one of many well-written tales, all preserved in numerous ancient manuscripts, as part of a flowering of Middle High German literature in ca. 1200 CE. The *Nibelungen* epic is indisputably authentic. The ancient originals can be consulted and tested. The original manuscripts vary in length, and some have slight variations in wording, but clearly all of them basically tell the same story. Verifiability is key. The narrative of the *Nibelungenlied* traces the clash of richly detailed characters, Siegfried, Brünhilde, even Attila the Hun, all involved in high drama. It is the archetype of the stirring national epic and appealed to the emotionalism of the romantic era. It provided a sense of a cultural Germany over a century before a political Germany existed.

Other ethnic enclaves wanted to claim such a rich ancestry, especially those in competition with the Germans. Ethnographers began scouring old libraries and manuscript collections for ancient epics that would demonstrate the age-old cultural genius of their particular ethnic group. There was a demand for old literary manuscripts. Where there is a demand, there will soon be a supply.[17]

One of the greatest practitioners of nationalist forgery was James Macpherson who in 1761 fabricated an ancient Scottish national epic in the absence of the real thing. Macpherson probably used some old Scottish tales and songs for color, but it was his work attributed to anonymous medieval bards. The tale of Ossian resonated with the *Zeitgeist*: Napoleon was a fan, as was the great German poet Goethe. Ossian was almost as dramatic as Siegfried. Samuel Johnson immediately recognized the text as a fake, based on internal stylistic evidence, but that factual difficulty did not dampen the general enthusiasm for a work whose time had come. The question arises as to the merit of *Ossian* as a literary work in its own right, regardless of authorship. It is important to remember that the discovery of a forgery only begins the process of assessment. Some forged or misattributed works of art still have artistic merit, sometimes known as "true fakes." In the case of historical documents, the artistic merit is not the main issue. The forgeries may have much to say about the forces at work in a particular era.

Certainly Macpherson's *Ossian* unleashed pent-up nationalist emotions, what would today be called *identity politics*. The Czechs, long under the heel of the Austrian empire and its high Germanic culture, were seeking affirmation of their own greatness, and found it in a set of manuscript fragments in 1817–1818.[18] The staged discovery was greeted with great joy, but immediately aroused suspicion of forgery, which in fact was vindicated. The manuscripts' authenticity was first championed and then questioned by the renowned Czech scholar Josef Dobrovský. Nationalists seized upon the fakes as priceless relics of Czech creativity and cultural superiority. Skeptics were reviled as traitors to the Czech people and literally spat upon. The "Battle for the Manuscripts" raged for an entire century until the creation of Czechoslovakia in 1918. Jan Masaryk, founding president of Czechoslovakia, risked his career in honestly confronting the falseness of the manuscripts and the false basis it gave to Czech cultural history. He is quoted as saying: "I considered the Manuscripts issue to be first and foremost a moral issue: if they were forgeries we had to confess it to the world; our pride, our culture could not be based on a lie."[19]

The forgery remained a source of embarrassment, even to the postcommunist president Václav Havel, who used it as a negative example in the search for truth and justice for Czechs. Havel's take is that the manuscripts are "superbly written, and obviously inspired by good intention"—that is, to improve Czech self-confidence as they struggled for emancipation from foreign domination. Havel presents Masaryk as the model of an ethical leader: "To him, the only valid and viable cornerstone for his nation's new existence was truth."[20.]

These controversies from the national revivals of the eighteenth-century Enlightenment and early nineteenth-century romantic period have not yet entirely played themselves out. They are alive and well in the twenty-first century. Russian patriots have long treasured the medieval *Igor Tale*, sometimes called the *Song of Igor's Campaign*, which also surfaced in the late eighteenth century. Vladimir Nabokov, the eminent Russian émigré writer, traced the provenance thus: The original manuscript from 1187 is said to have been lost, but a later copy (perhaps from the sixteenth century) survived, and was rediscovered and published from a transcription in 1800. In 1795–1796 a transcription was given to Catherine the Great. It survived. The *Igor Tale* is superbly written and inspired Slavic pride. The sixteenth-century copy is said to have been burned in the Napoleonic invasion of Moscow in 1812. The tale's antiquity is a large part of its charm, as proof that the Slavs were capable of great literature. In the face of Russian feelings of cultural inferiority, there was a need for such an inspiring manuscript.

Nabokov devoted considerable time and effort to translating the *Igor Tale* into English. He defends it against the charges of Ossianism and champions it as the one and only medieval Slavic literary masterpiece that "rivals the greatest European poems of its day."[21] He admits that all other surviving Russian medieval writings, primarily chronicles and sermons, pale in comparison. It does seem suspicious that the one precious vintage copy of the only world-class medieval Russian epic disappeared, and only the late eighteenth-century copy remains. Did the magisterial Nabokov, the great skeptic, the master of languages, fall for a hoax? It is within the realm of possibility. New linguistic evidence is emerging that the *Igor Tale* may well have been written by a Czech. One likely suspect—with the linguistic acumen, historical knowledge, and literary flair to fabricate such a long and convoluted text—was the same famous Czech scholar Josef Dobrovský, who spent over a year studying a trove of ancient Russian manuscripts that had been collected from various monasteries and libraries.[22] Ardent Russian patriots, who continue to defend the authenticity of the transcribed manuscript, are scouring ancient manuscripts for linguistic evidence to validate their reverence for the *Igor Tale*. As of 2009, the main Wikipedia entry for the *Igor Tale* maintains that most scholars accept the authenticity. The discussion page has lively exchanges about this controversy. The circumstantial evidence suggests the need for extreme caution. Only detailed linguistic analysis by both Russian and non-Russian experts will eventually confirm or deny authenticity. The story is not over.

Scottish, Czech, and Russian medieval manuscripts may seem far removed from American archival experience. There is another Russian nationalist forgery, and this one appeared in postwar America. Just as eighteenth-century German pride in the *Nibelungenlied* created a demand for medieval epics among other nationalities in the Romantic era, the resurgence of German interest in its early history during the Nazi period resonated with Russians, including Russians in the emigration following the Revolution of 1917. Exile often enhances patriotic impulses. A reputed ancient Slavic text, the *Book of Vles*, or *Vlesova Kniga*, was published in the Russian émigré press in San Francisco in the 1950s. The editor of the magazine was a Russian émigré chemist-turned-journalist named IUrii Petrovich Miroliubov. The medieval book itself, allegedly scratched onto wooden planks in the ninth century CE, was said to have disappeared in World War II, and only a transcription survived. In 2000, the papers of Miroliubov, the original promoter of the *Book of Vles* as a cultural treasure, came up for processing, microfilming, and preservation under a grant sponsored by the National Endowment for the Humanities. There was much discussion among the archives staff about whether the collection merited cataloging or whether it was just questionable material, best consigned to benign oblivion. The archivists spent considerable time researching the authenticity of the alleged antiquity, and discussing the best disposition of the papers. They concluded that the *Book of Vles*, the most interesting subject in the collection, was indeed a hoax. The collection obviously does not contain the purported manuscript. It contains a transcription of the text and blurry copies of one of the "planks" scratched with letters that look like a cross between Cyrillic and Nordic runes. The collection contains extensive writings that praise the *Book of Vles* as an example of a highly literate, pre-Christian Russian culture. The materials provided insight into a classic case of nationalistic forgery. They were authentic papers in defense of a forgery, which embodied a certain nationalistic and patriotic impulse, however misguided. The Miroliubov collection received full cataloging, microfilm preservation copies were made, and information placed on the Internet. In order to be clear, the description identifies the *Book of Vles* as a forgery, in accordance with the latest research.[23]

A number of émigrés were extremely offended that doubt was cast on an object of national pride. In current day Russia and Ukraine, the *Book of Vles*, which surfaced in San Francisco in about 1950, is defended by nationalists as authentic and makes an appearance in school textbooks. It is considered the bible of a neopagan movement in Russia and Ukraine. The archives staff was pressured to change the cataloging description and let the researchers decide for themselves. In the end the staff decided that the evidence of forgery was sufficiently strong to merit the description. They felt an obligation to alert the unwary reader to the deception, as good ethical practice requires.

Forgeries as Manufactured Evidence for Conspiracy Theories

The noble pursuit of knowledge and truth has an evil twin in the conspiracy industry, which seeks to explain disturbing events as the result of the secret collusion of diabolical forces. One would assume that with a higher level of general education in society, the wilder and more fantastic interpretations of events would be automatically corrected by cool reason, by examining facts and deploying logic. Strangely, in our modern world, such implausible explanations seem to proliferate and create entire communities of believers in conspiracy theories.

Why would this phenomenon need attention from ethical archivists? Whatever their motivation, conspiracy theories are attempts at finding hidden truths, usually about nefarious power grabs by insidious criminal geniuses. The "truth" is established first, then the evidence is sought to substantiate it. If evidence cannot be found for strongly held beliefs, it is created. In the marketplace of delusional conspiracy plots, demand creates its own supply of compelling forgeries.

The classic example of documentary evidence manufactured to support a conspiracy theory is the *Protocols of the Elders of Zion*. This colorfully fraudulent publication of forged documents would be an amusing story like Dan Brown's vivid novel *The Da Vinci Code,* if the consequences had not been so tragic. The average working archivist will probably not encounter such a flagrant example, but less obvious forgeries do surface on a regular basis, so this example is perhaps a useful exhibit to keep in mind. The less obvious examples can remain "under the radar" longer and do damage over the long term.

The motivation behind the *Protocols* forgery is classic antisemitism, which has flourished in various forms in nineteenth-century France, in Tsarist Russia, in the United States in the 1920s, in Nazi Germany, and among certain contemporary Middle East extremists. Whether motivated by racism, envy, or general bigotry, there was a growing perception over many decades that an international cabal of Jewish leaders was usurping global wealth and power. There was no proof, so evidence was manufactured in the form of the *Protocols of the Elders of Zion.* The original version was a compilation of lightly modified text lifted from an 1864 French novel (*Dialogue aux enfers entre Machiavel et Montesquieu* by Maurice Joly) and plot elements from an 1868 Prussian novel (*Biarritz* by Hermann Goedsche). The French novel provided text about a Machiavellian plan to take over the world, and the monologue could be manipulated to create the impression of Jews taking power over non-Jews. The Prussian novel created an atmospheric scene in which prominent rabbis, the elders of Zion, meet together in the ancient Jewish cemetery in Prague to plan for conquering the world. Somehow minutes of the discussions are made, the *protocols* of the title. Sometimes the venue of the meeting was displaced to Basle, where Zionists had been holding conferences at the time of the forgery. Later the venue was given as an undisclosed location in France. The setting has the right sense of mystery to evoke fear and loathing. The work is pure fiction, but the fear it induced was real. From nineteenth-century France and Prussia, the collage went to late nineteenth-century–early twentieth-century Russia, where the Tsarist secret police were developing evidence of an international Jewish conspiracy following the assassination of Tsar Alexander II in 1881. Legitimate national security concerns often unleash unreasonable responses. In Russia, the texts were reworked, deliberately repurposed, and presented as the actual minutes or protocols of a dark meeting and a plot to take over the world. This case exhibits another recurring feature of paranoid forgeries: heavy plagiarism, as though the authors were too lazy to do their own writing.

The *Protocols of the Elders of Zion* became an underground cult classic republished in an American version by Henry Ford in the United States. The Baltic German racist Alfred Rosenberg conveyed it among Russian antisemitic tracts to Hitler in interwar Germany. The *Protocols* continue to be circulated today in various languages, including Arabic. One cursory reading makes it clear that the "minutes" are really an incoherent diatribe. It is a rather boring monologue, not the transcripts of a discussion at a meeting. The presentation of the protocols as a secret Jewish plot makes them useful pseudo-evidence for antisemites, even though the text does not have substance or credibility. Such is the power of conspiracy theory forgeries.

A raft of books and websites provide detailed information on the *Protocols* and their origins and authorship. On closer examination, much of this background is speculation.[24] The first published version is in Russian translation in 1903, but even the language of the hypothetical original source document is unknown. There is no firm evidence regarding who was responsible for the *Protocols*, or when or where they originated. The one important point is that the text was used as evidence, however weird and sketchy, of a Jewish conspiracy that had to be stopped. Thus it fueled hatred and eventually genocide in the twentieth century, and it continues to fuel antisemitism in the Middle East, where it remains widely circulated in the twenty-first century.

True believers cling to forgeries of documents and archives in a misplaced effort to provide documentary evidence to support a delusional theory. For those interested in the *Protocols* case, the Holocaust Museum in Washington, D.C., has pulled together on its website extensive documentation and analysis of this forgery and its various iterations as hate literature.[25]

At one point the author was shown a handwritten Russian copy of the *Protocols of the Elders of Zion*, which was misidentified as the historically valuable original source document. As presented, it was the falsely identified copy of a well-known forgery, based on a plagiarized piece of malicious fiction about a meeting that never took place. The penciled document was in fact interesting as antisemitic samizdat, in the Russian tradition of privately copying and distributing underground literature. It demonstrated the way in which fanatics disseminated it in the early twentieth century, a foreshadowing of the transmission via the Internet.

The topos of "secret records" has also entered the American culture and is unlikely to go away soon. The Internet has only amplified an existing tendency in American political life to explain uncongenial events as the result of secretive collusion. In 1966 the eminent historian Richard Hofstadter published *The Paranoid Style in American Politics*, which remains one of the best analyses of this phenomenon.[26] In that same year a well-respected professor at Georgetown University, Carroll Quigley, published an extremely odd book called *Tragedy and Hope* that circles around the theory of a secret elite group that aims to concentrate money and power, much as the "elders of Zion" were accused of doing. "I know the operations of this network because I have studied it for twenty years and was permitted for two years in the early 1960s, to examine its papers and secret records."[27] He names the conspirators as the Round Table Groups, probably interpreted by his readers as the "New World Order." There are no specifics as to who let him see the documents, what the documents are, where they are kept—just the sense that they cannot be studied by others, or confirmed or verified. This pattern of mystery once again fits that great topos of forgery identified by Grafton. Readers must accept Quigley's interpretation of the archives on faith. For some the secretive mystery of hidden archives adds credibility. For archivists it should always raise a red flag. Quigley has gone on posthumously to become a revered figure in conspiracy circles in the United

States. If ever there was a strong argument for open access for verification, this has to be one of the best exhibits.

Another documentary artifact of conspiracy theories is the bizarre recontextualizing of a spoof entitled *Report from Iron Mountain*, written by Leonard C. Lewin and first published anonymously as a leaked government document by Dial Press in 1967.[28] Intended as an obvious leftist satire of government reports on the necessity of the Vietnam War, it was accepted as an actual government document by right-wing militia groups, who interpreted it as proof of some kind of New World Order. This left-wing joke fueled antigovernment hatred on the right. Stripped of its provenance, the document continues to circulate on the Internet and supports groups that Lewin had no intention of helping. The obvious truth is: this is not an official government document. Like the *Protocols of the Elders of Zion*, the *Report from Iron Mountain* began as a work of fiction, and was plagiarized and reworked as fact in service of a political agenda—a classic forgery. Lewin has since died, and his clever but dangerous spoof has taken on a cyber life of its own. Here is a very strong argument in favor of maintaining the ancient science of diplomatics and authentication of government documents. The story argues for insisting on standards of proof, verifying provenance, finding original sources—all the old virtues, as propounded by Leopold von Ranke.[29]

Forgeries as Malicious Attacks on a Perceived Enemy

Many forgeries are complex hoaxes, motivated by a malicious joy in fooling an adversary, especially entrapping gullible opponents. The Mark Hofmann forgeries—fabricated documents related to the history of the Mormon Church—were apparently motivated by a desire to undermine the church. The forgeries were devised to attack the credibility of the foundation narrative of the Church of Latter Day Saints. Hofmann seemed to enjoy a sense of power in fooling Mormons and manuscript dealers and in sowing doubt and confusion. It was the result of an unhealthy obsession that grew out of disillusionment with his church. Kenneth Rendell describes in detail the great skill Hofmann developed in imitating nineteenth-century ink, in using the right kind of paper and convincing text. Even for an expert like Rendell, it was difficult to detect the true date of his work.[30] Found guilty of the bombing deaths of two innocent people, Hofmann was sentenced in 1988 to life in prison.

The desire to believe in a forgery is proportional to the need for evidence. This may have been the case when Dan Rather was presented with photocopies of documents that purported to show that presidential candidate George W. Bush evaded his military obligations in the Vietnam era, a frequently made charge with little solid proof. Rather offered the so-called Killian documents as contemporaneous evidence and thus news during the presidential campaign of 2004. The documents were quickly unmasked as forgeries: the typewriter used had proportional spacing features that were not commonly available until long after the Vietnam War. The furor generated over the authenticity of the documents displaced news about the Iraq war on the CBS show *Sixty Minutes.* Several high-level CBS producers were fired in the wake of the scandal. Dan Rather's credibility was badly damaged.

CBS investigated the incident. The provenance of the Killian documents was not clear. A former U.S. Army National Guard officer claimed to have received them from an unidentified source that got them from the personal files of Bush's commanding officer, the late Jerry B. Killian. The former officer also claimed that he faxed copies to CBS and burned the originals. The forensic analysts complained about the poor quality copies. Without access to the originals, they could not determine the authenticity of the documents. The motivation for the Killian documents is a source of speculation. Were they designed to embarrass the president during an election campaign, or were they designed to embarrass the president's opponents? The source of the Killian documents remains a mystery as of 2009.[31]

A good case can be made that the actual papers delivered to CBS—the original copies of forgeries, so to speak—are worthy of archiving because of the role they played at a pivotal moment in a hard-fought presidential campaign. They are valuable as artifacts of a major political fight. They should also be preserved for future research. It is possible that emerging technological advances might at some point enable experts to analyze them and determine more about their source.

Authentication, even with an original document, is not always so clear. The so-called Vinland Map, now in the Yale Library—a map purportedly demonstrating the Viking discovery of Newfoundland—has been subjected to numerous scientific tests, and yet its authenticity is still in dispute. Likewise it is still not clear after many years of research whether the "Bamboo Annals" are invaluable documents of ancient Chinese culture or blatant forgeries, or perhaps something in between. The texts, originally written on bamboo strips, are said to have been discovered in the third century CE in the tomb of a ruler who had died six hundred years earlier. The discovery occurred after the famous book burning that destroyed most ancient Chinese manuscripts. The original bamboo strips no longer exist, but copies have survived. For anyone familiar with Grafton's description of archetypal forgery narratives, this discovery story must raise suspicions.

While not all forgeries are this interesting, there are many of them. Grafton estimates that "half the legal documents we possess from Merovingian times [ca. 450–751 CE], and perhaps two-thirds of all documents issued to ecclesiastics before A.D. 1100, are fakes."[32] Of course, any document, forged or not, created in the early Middle Ages is still an important historic document, an original fake of sorts. How prevalent are forgeries in the modern era? Very. Are they also important? Sometimes. One should never underestimate the potential for fraud perpetrated for religious or political reasons. Despite such cases, the primary motivation for forgeries in modern American culture appears to be financial gain. There is certainly cause for vigilance. Antique dealers issue regular warnings. The Antiquarian Booksellers Association of America has a Questioned Imprints Committee to alert potential buyers to the dangers. Texas dealer Tom Taylor reported at a conference that he identified sixty copies of fifteen different forged documents purporting to be from the Republic of Texas. [33]

Digital Forgery, Email, and the Internet

All of the issues discussed above are amplified in the online environment. Certainly the Internet has created the tools, the venue, and the market for a new flowering of forgery to compete with the Merovingians. Luciana Duranti cites a study that concludes "Digital records make up to 80% of fraud investigation cases."[34]

A major part of the problem is the absence of an "original" in the analog sense. A bit stream is the source of documents, the exact form of which is variably expressed according to the software and hardware used to see it on a screen. The screen version is inherently ephemeral and unstable. It may look quite different on different systems, and the printouts may vary in type font and formatting. Over time the text may be intentionally changed many times, or even maliciously altered. The print versions will vary with the alterations caused at four points: the input text, the edits, the software that reads it, and the printer that fixes it on a sheet of paper. As technology changes, documents need to be migrated to new platforms, a process that introduces more changes. The result is myriad copies with no original, and no way of determining the sequence in which the variants were produced. Government records, once fixed and verifiable, are now subject to manipulation, degradation, and loss. New tools are being devised to fix the first version of a digital document with a so-called digital signature. Even with the best safeguards and the best intentions, authenticity is very uncertain in such an unstable format.

Of course, intentions are not always noble. Authentic-looking messages appear in almost everyone's email with perfect logos from well-known banks asking for private information or the transfer of funds. The IP and MAC addresses are usually transient and not traceable to the perpetrator. It may be difficult to determine which country the message is coming from. The fraudulent practices go largely unprosecuted. There are simply too many of them, and they are too difficult to trace. It is a chaotic environment, much like a freeway without lane markings, road signs, speed limits, or highway patrol. Some theorists insist that the only solution is to create a new parallel Internet from scratch with controls built in, and let the honest organizations change over to a new trusted system.

The Internet was made possible by a creatively libertarian ethos that is resistant to controls and regulations. Web pages carry a huge amount of unverifiable and untraceable data. Just the basic facts of authorship, date, and place of origin are usually difficult to ascertain. When the page is called up again, it may be completely different. The ease with which digital documents can be cut and pasted removes whatever meager traces of authorship or provenance were there in the first place. Electronic watermarks and security e-signatures have helped to some extent, but they are easily circumvented.

When digital records come into the archives there are two levels of authenticity to worry about. First, is the incoming record authentic? The accuracy of the information it contains is not the basic issue. The question is whether the record is what it purports to be, from the agency that claims to have produced it, by the person cited as responsible, etc. The second concern is how to preserve and maintain the authenticity of the digital records once they are "frozen" in the archives.

Much work is being done to create a trusted system of authentic government documents. Clearly organizations such as the Department of Defense need secure methods of managing digital documents. And the archival profession is making international attempts to provide standards for authenticity, notably the InterPARES Project: International Research on Permanent Authentic Records in Electronic Systems. Luciana Duranti founded InterPARES in 1999 to develop methods for ensuring the authenticity and preservation of digital records. Heather MacNeil has served as chair of the Authenticity Task Force.

Given the decentralized nature of online authorship and the wild west nature of the Internet, the most carefully planned digital documentation strategies will not be uniformly implemented. It would require cooperation at the moment a document is created, using some kind of document creation module that verifies authorship, supplies a time and place stamp, etc. The current culture is not amenable to such regulations. Printouts from the Internet record URL and date printed, but that information is not recorded for PDF files. Even some reports posted online by InterPARES in PDF are difficult to trace by author and date once they are printed out.

Possibly government agencies, responsible for weighty pronouncements, can enforce such a policy to create trusted, authentic, fixed documents. Simply the speed with which documents can be created, distributed, copied, and posted mitigates against proper identification procedures. Even the highest level government agencies such as the White House have difficulty controlling email messages. Techniques such as using a "check sum" to detect alterations in an electronic text can be deployed as part of a digital signature mechanism. Even with digital signatures, authentication of digital records will remain an elusive goal for the foreseeable future. One can expect to encounter a burgeoning body of forged, altered, and untraceable documents.

What can we learn from these problems? How should the working archivist respond? The first is the importance of being able to analyze and evaluate documents, paper or online, as artifacts. While some archivists may feel that this is the job of forensic experts, every archivist should hone these skills. The archivist needs to know enough to suspect a problem before it is possible to seek expert advice. Some of this skill is intuition developed over years of working with materials from different sources. Malcom Gladwell tells the famous story of the prized ancient sculpture, authenticated by scientific analysis, in the Getty Museum in Los Angeles. An Italian connoisseur took one look and declared the multimillion dollar marble statue a fake based on the immediate visual impression it made. As it turned out, intuition based on years of impressions was simply more reliable than chemical analysis.[35]

The second lesson follows from this hard truth: always consult with several experts. Solely relying on one's own judgment is often inadequate. The most reliable method is to compare the impressionistic reactions of experienced curators with the results of cold scientific examination. If the two different approaches yield the same judgment, the results are very convincing. No one person can be an expert on all documents—German as well as Chinese, ancient as well as modern— as the cases of Hugh Trevor-Roper and Melchior Inchofer demonstrate.

Third, all steps in the authentication process need to be thoroughly documented. This may seem obvious enough in a neutral discussion, but in the charged atmosphere that sometimes arises, it can be difficult to stop and make careful notes. One also needs to refer to these notes frequently to determine if steps have been omitted: Did the signature get tested? Did the typeface get tested? It is essential to document each step and each person consulted, as the CBS case of the Killian documents demonstrates. Each time a document is authenticated carefully, and the stages in the process are communicated to professional groups, our collective knowledge of diplomatics increases.

The fourth lesson is the need to consult with legal counsel about reporting offers of forged documents. Does one have an obligation to report the offer of bogus documents for sale? To whom? Certainly there is a duty to report to one's superiors. What other actions need to be taken? Reporting to the attorney general, to the police, or to Interpol? Informing the Society of American Archivists, manuscript societies, or other professional organizations? Posting the availability of such items on the Internet? Such decisions cannot be made in isolation. It is imperative to have a thorough consultation with legal counsel, someone who is familiar with archival issues and the law.

For the risk averse among us, these experiences can be daunting. Yet it is all a natural part of what Grafton calls the role of forgery to stimulate "vital innovations in the technical method of scholars." Given both the range and frequency of the various types of forgery in a continuous stream from ancient times to modern, it is best not to think of forgeries as some rare aberration that crops up from time to time in our collections. Instead it is more useful to think of the integral role that authentication plays in archival work. Different repositories will find different ways to divide the work between archivists and historians, staff and researchers, but both sides of the equation count. Without the archives' commitment to excavating the layers of truth about its holdings, historians can go wildly off track. Diplomatics should inform the entire range of archival work. Each acquisition requires a careful assessment; each collection should have as honest a description as possible; the provenance needs detailed documentation; and the context of the materials must be carefully preserved.[36] The nature of archival work is such that authentication is an ongoing process. Fortunately, it is an interesting and rewarding one.

Questions for Evaluating the Authenticity of a Document

The following somewhat arbitrary list of questions is provided to suggest the types of tests that need to be done on questionable materials. It is far from exhaustive. Some questions are classical, others technical, some pragmatic and others more philosophical. If different approaches—technical examination of the paper, stylistic analysis, and review of provenance—all turn up doubts, then a serious professional assessment is clearly indicated, and perhaps legal advice as well.

1. What is known about the provenance or source of the materials?
2. What is known about the chain of ownership?
3. Are there first-hand witnesses familiar with the work and its purported author?
4. If handwritten, are there verified samples of handwriting for comparison?
5. If typed, does the typeface and style match the country and era in question?
6. If online, can the electronic address such as IP address or MAC be traced?
7. Do paper and ink match the purported period of authorship?
8. Are there known copies or variants? How do they compare?
9. Have text blocks been cut and pasted from other source documents? This can sometimes be determined quickly with a keyword search on Google.
10. Are there anachronisms in the text?
11. Does the internal evidence match the external description of the document?
12. Are there internal inconsistencies in style? Are the style and grammar consistent with the purported author?
13. Can one find paper or electronic watermarks?
14. If a photograph, do the components fit together in the right scale? Do shadows fall at the same angle?
15. Who are the best experts to consult about the document?
16. Who needs to know that there are doubts?

17. How do you manage any public relations in connection with the suspected document?

18. Should the item be removed from the holdings?

19. Should an explanation be included in the description of the collection?

20. What are the possible motives—political, religious, or financial— for creating a forgery in this case?

CHAPTER 8

Displaced Archives

Archivists should cooperate in the repatriation of displaced archives.

—Code of Ethics, section 2, International Council on Archives[1]

THE TERM *DISPLACED ARCHIVES* IS A NEUTRAL EUPHEMISM TO DESIGNATE ARCHI-
VAL MATERIALS THAT HAVE BEEN LOST, SEIZED, REQUISITIONED, CONFISCATED,
PURCHASED UNDER DURESS, OR OTHERWISE GONE ASTRAY. Usually in such
cases, at least one party believes the materials have been illegally or unethically removed from their appropriate home. To put it more directly, the
documents are considered stolen goods. As a general rule, archives should
cooperate in returning displaced documents to the rightful owner, if that
entity can be determined definitively. This principle is counterbalanced
by another general rule: Americans regard physical possession of property
to be strong evidence of ownership. There may be special circumstances
when returning displaced documents does more harm than good. An
archivist can expect an inherent conflict in any claims that archives have
been improperly displaced. This discussion of displaced archives is meant
to provide an ethical context for informed discussion; it does not replace
the essential specialized works by legal experts. When legal questions arise,
always consult a qualified lawyer.[2]

At one time or another, most archives will encounter claims to return documents they may or may not have received improperly. The reverse also frequently happens. The archives will need to assert ownership over records illegally removed from its holdings. Replevin actions, as they are known, can be contentious. As highly portable property, archives are frequently removed from their original locations or from their most appropriate custodians. When a government agency claims the return of displaced archives, the dispute may end up in court. One would normally assume that public records are the inalienable property of the state, and that title cannot be transferred. In Europe the government's claim to its own archives has a strong legal foundation. In the United States there is a greater sense of freedom for the market in private property. The court decisions are not always predictable as the two following cases, one from North Carolina and one from South Carolina, demonstrate.

The North Carolina Bill of Rights Returned

In 1865, during the destruction and confusion of the Civil War, a Union soldier stole a copy of the Bill of Rights that he found in a welter of papers in the statehouse in Raleigh, North Carolina. It was the state's original signed copy, one of the thirteen sent out by George Washington to the newly forming states for ratification in 1789. The soldier took it as a souvenir of war. This Bill of Rights resurfaced decades later in 1897, when a newspaper reported that it hung, nicely framed, in an office in Indianapolis. An official request for its return to state custody in North Carolina was rebuffed. In 1925, a representative of the then-owner offered to sell it to the North Carolina State Archives, which refused to pay a steep price for what it considered its own lawful property. The document changed hands a number of times. Seventy years later, in 1995, the Bill of Rights was again put up for sale as a collectible artifact worth millions of dollars on the manuscript market. The state again refused to pay the fee and worked on recovering it. Restitution involved a sting operation to physically remove it from private hands. An FBI agent posed as a curator wishing to purchase the document for four million dollars. The charter then stayed in federal custody for a decade during litigation between the state of North Carolina and the private investors, who had hoped to make a tidy fortune on the sale.[3]

The litigation over the Bill of Rights was convoluted. Both sides analyzed the conflicting orders by the Union on the confiscation of Confederate property. Both sides looked to the Lieber Code (discussed later in the chapter) for justification. There was a discussion of whether seceding from the Union in the Civil War meant relinquishing claims to archives from the founding fathers. Scholars investigated the history of looting during the Civil War. The amended motion for summary judgment is ninety-six pages long and incorporates a great deal of historical research, painstakingly assembled. The burden of proof was on North Carolina, as the party demanding the transfer and restitution of the document. In the end, there were four main elements of the legal arguments:

- The first issue was whether the document in question was authentic, and whether it was the actual copy from North Carolina, or one of the others that had also gone astray. The authenticity was established. The North Carolina version was positively identified because of a unique anomaly specific to the North Carolina copy: the use of the word *where* rather than the word *wherein* that appears in the other copies.

- The state of North Carolina had to prove that the law required permanent retention of the Bill of Rights.

- The performance of public officials was scrutinized to determine if they behaved properly with regard to the document.

- The state had to prove that the Bill of Rights had been stored in the official archives and illegally stolen.

The document was physically returned to the state archives in 2005 after two appeals to the U.S. Fourth Circuit Court of Appeals in Richmond, but the dispute was not definitively settled until summary judgment was issued on March 24, 2008 in Wake County Superior Court in Raleigh. In effect, it took over a century from the first location of the stolen document to its recovery, including thirteen years of litigation, to validate the state's claim.

South Carolina Civil Gubernatorial Papers

In many cases governmental bodies have been able to retrieve "privatized" state records, as North Carolina was able to do. However, the American protection of private property is strong enough to favor the private owner in ways that surprise records managers. In her manual on law and archives, Menzi Behrnd-Klodt provides a cautionary example, from just next door in South Carolina: "To archivists familiar with the principle of provenance, it seems self-evident that a government or one of its agencies or designated repositories is the owner of documents that it created. Yet such was not the outcome in *Willcox et al. v. Stroup et al.*, No. 06-1179 (4th Cir., Oct. 27, 2006), where the parties contested the ownership of approximately 444 documents dated December 1860 through August 1864 and created during the Civil War era administrations of South Carolina governors Francis Pickens and Milledge Bonham."[4] Although clearly created at state expense and for official purposes, the state was unable to recover them from ownership by a private citizen who was interested in selling them. Behrnd-Klodt quotes the court's decision not to return the government documents because gubernatorial papers were held in many nonstate repositories, such as Duke University. If the court returned these documents, it maintained, "The State could claim ownership of other papers of Governors Pickens and Bonham held by the Library of Congress and Duke University, as well as papers of other South Carolina governors currently at institutions other than the State Archives. The result would be immense litigation over papers held by private owners, universities, historical societies and federal depositories....Disregard of possession as presumptive evidence of ownership would throw the whole of this important area into turmoil." In other words, the court was unwilling to open the floodgates to a large-scale transfer of state records from private hands to government repositories. Possession as evidence of ownership has a very strong history in this country.

Possession was also a factor in the February 27, 2009, Virginia court decision to allow a 1776 broadside copy of the Declaration of Independence to remain in private hands despite well-documented claims from the state of Maine.[5] Americans have been reluctant to recognize the inalienability of state records. The author asked two attorneys, both familiar with archives and replevin but with no prior knowledge of the case, to look at this final ruling. One lawyer found the reasoning well grounded and free of bias. The other had a completely different opinion.

Some states have tried to clarify the prevailing ambiguity. Tennessee, for example, has a clear public records law and circulates a brochure in both print and online versions to make that law clear: "At no time can public records legally be owned, traded, sold or bought by members of the public."[6] This statement is as unequivocal as possible.

Regardless of the law, from a strictly ethical point of view, new purchase or new acquisition of public records by a private repository is highly questionable. For collections that are already established, there is an important distinction to be made between displaced archives that are held by individuals trying to monetize the documents for the highest price without regard to intellectual values, and displaced archives that are held in repositories dedicated to their preservation and responsible use. There is such a quantity of alienated government archives that universal return has not been considered practical. In fact, the number of replevin actions is rather small compared to the huge quantities of government archives in private ownership. Even the return of high profile trophy items such as the North Carolina Bill of Rights can be difficult. In terms of priorities, money and effort should first be used to secure archives that are endangered when commercial factors take precedence over intellectual and cultural values.

Even when reclaiming lost items is impractical, theft remains illegal and unethical, and should not be quietly condoned. A reasonable compromise or balance needs to be established. There may be instances when a grandfather clause for older cases is a good solution. Such waivers would function best under certain well-defined circumstances. Two prime considerations are that the records are well cared for and that they are made available for research. In any case, there is a strong principle that removing government files, while once common, is not legal and not acceptable. The National Archives has a useful brochure on this topic entitled "Does That Document Belong in the National Archives?" It clarifies for nonspecialists the difference between government documents that were meant to be distributed and those that are meant to be kept in government archives. The online version of the brochure ("Help the National Archives Recover Lost and Stolen Documents") includes a list of missing items and information on reporting the location of stolen government archives. A press release from 2005 announces the prosecution of one thief, Howard Harner, who was convicted of stealing more than one hundred Civil War era documents between 1996 and 2002. His sentence and fine send a clear signal, according to former U.S. archivist Allen Weinstein, "that theft of cultural property belonging to the American people will not be tolerated. We are very grateful that the Judge recognized the seriousness of the crime."[7]

When an individual has recently removed a document from a reading room and then sold it on the manuscript market, it is easy for the general public to understand that this act is theft. The concept is less clear to non-archivists when the documents have been in private hands for a long period of time, or when they are preserved carefully in another archival repository. One can theoretically make the claim that all archives, as materials transferred from the originating office to a different repository, are displaced in a sense. It is fairly common for two or more parties to claim the same collection. Fortunately, most such challenges are resolved informally, out of court. For those other cases, every working archivist should be familiar with the legal landscape, and have a good sense of when to seek professional legal advice. Often, when there is no legal case to be made, archivists still must be aware of the moral and ethical ramifications of displaced cultural property including manuscripts and archives.

Displacement has many causes, from the mundane to the historic: department mergers, job changes, departing employees, death, divorce, theft, financial turmoil, office renovation, evacuation, interpersonal conflict, revolutions, floods, storms, war, decolonization, changes in sovereignty, and changes in borders. A donor's relative may challenge the right to deposit family papers in a repository. A government agency may demand the return of documents illegally removed from an office and taken home by a retiring employee. Competing archives may claim the same collection. In the most dramatic cases, countries demand the return of archives as cultural property displaced by revolution or war. The complexities of ownership and property law are such that both sides, or even all sides, may have a good faith claim to title. A veteran's hard-won souvenir from a treacherous battlefield abroad may be another country's official government property. High-profile archival documents serve as coveted trophies. Knowingly receiving stolen property is against the law, but there are gray areas. At times, an acquisition may be technically legal but ethically dubious.

Since replevin demands can come without warning, the archives staff should be familiar, well in advance, with a set of principles and procedures for guidance to handle the case in a judicious manner once a claim arises.

Basic Principles and Procedures

Generally speaking, the guidelines for appropriate placement follow common sense. Official government papers belong in official government archives, and should not be removed and transferred to private ones. Local history archives belong in the geographical area that created them. Special interest archives belong with sympathetic organizations. Archives are best served in the linguistic community of the main language in which they are written. Cultural heritage generally belongs in the culture that produced it, or its closest successor. There are many worthy exceptions that can be justified. An earlier chapter explored why Martin Luther King Jr. initially wanted his papers in Boston, rather than in the South, home to both his greatest work and most fervent enemies. Papers from the diaspora of an ethnic group may be better off in the country of refuge than the country of origin.[8] Understanding these exceptions is as important as knowing the basic principles and procedures.

As an essential precondition for ethical decision making, the archivist should have the permission from higher administration to turn down collections, even prestigious ones, if the materials appear to have been improperly removed from their original context. In theory at least, if enough archivists respected the rights of the repository with the best fit, all would eventually benefit, and the untoward effects of fighting over collections would be ameliorated. Shifting archival collections always involves some exposure to damaging conditions, so it is best that they are placed correctly in the first instance, reducing the need for transfers from one owner to another.

When reclaiming lost or stolen materials, the archivists need to find legal counsel with direct archival experience. The archives staff needs to be prepared for time-consuming work. First there is the research into the details of the case. Then staff members need to learn how to interpret general archival procedures in court to nonspecialists. The success of the replevin action may depend on the quality of routine archival practices, such as the accuracy of cataloging descriptions. Cultural property lawyers emphasize the importance of maintaining highly accurate and detailed descriptions of the holdings for identification purposes. It is also important to report losses promptly and make an active effort to reclaim them. Laws and standards vary considerably from state to state, and the advice of knowledgeable local counsel is of paramount importance. High on the list of questions for the attorneys should be a request for details about the statute of limitations in the state and when the clock starts to tick on claims. It is also important to learn about the array of possible remedies from both criminal law and civil litigation. In addition it would be wise to learn the advantages and disadvantages of different venues for the proceedings.

What should ethical archivists do when claims are made against their own institution's archives? When a challenge to ownership does arise, a repository has a right and an obligation to defend its property. As an employee, the archivist needs to make the best possible case for his or her institution to retain its holdings. At the same time, the ethical archivist needs to be able to see both sides of the issue in order to help the administration decide when a claim is genuinely justified. The burden of proof usually rests with the challenger. The holding institution has the obligation to respond promptly and conscientiously. The institutional decision either to retain or deaccession a collection in response to a competing claim should be collaborative and well documented. As a safeguard, no one person should make the final determination in isolation. How the challenge is met is almost more consequential than the outcome. As employees on payroll, the archivists have an ethical duty to defend the holdings of the employing institution. Furthermore, an archivist must avoid conflicts of interest—even the appearance of a conflict—that would accompany, for example, the removal and transfer of a collection to benefit a friend, relative, or coreligionist. That is the ethical side of the equation.

At the same time, a professional needs to be aware of the laws regarding archives as property and have a good sense of when to consult legal counsel. As a citizen, the archivist must make a good faith effort to comply with both legal and ethical requirements, even though they are often unclear or self-contradictory. Replevin cases can trigger a conflict between ethical behavior and legal compliance. For example, a party may have a reasonable legal claim to the papers, but be incapable of properly caring for them, or may intend to remove them from public accessibility. What if complying with the formal legal property rights undermines the ethical mandates of preserving joint cultural heritage?

A third factor is the larger moral dimension. Beyond ethical precepts or legal provisions for the claim, the claimant may have larger real or felt moral concerns that need to be addressed. The clearest example is Native American cultural property. Items that have scholarly value for anthropologists may have sacred value for the culture that produced the objects. Sometimes the religious character of materials, documents, and images requires special treatment. The moral context may require copying, sharing, or repatriation. Whether or not sovereignty has been officially recognized for particular Native American groups, archivists need to appreciate the wider context of their ancient heritage. The "Protocols for Native American Archival Materials" offer a guide for thinking through the issues.[9]

Then there are pragmatic issues as well that need consideration beyond the letter of the law. Many repositories are willing to make concessions to avoid litigation, even if there is a substantial chance of winning the case, due to the adverse publicity, legal fees, general financial burden, and diversion of staff time typically associated with a trial.

The well-considered response to a replevin claim recognizes legal, ethical, moral, and pragmatic principles. The archives' basic response plan could take the following form. A more detailed checklist appears at the end of the chapter.

1.   The first step is for a senior professional to alert the upper administration and legal counsel that there may be a claim.

2.   Senior archivists, preferably with assistance from an attorney, should listen carefully to the claimant with an open mind and friendly demeanor to record the full story. This initial fact-finding process needs to be made promptly and thoroughly to convey a positive professional attitude.

3.   With the details of the claim in place, the institution's upper management needs to be briefed fully about the situation from the outset, and consulted for guidance.

4.   If legal counsel permits, the claimant should usually be introduced to the repository and its role in the preservation and use of documentation, a step that has often changed the dynamic from an adversarial one to a collaborative relationship.

5.   Detailed research into the history of the acquisition—its background, provenance, and significance—should be done. All contracts, deeds of gift, warranties of title, bills of sale, export licenses, and relevant correspondence need to be carefully reviewed. The legal documents should be interpreted by legal counsel, in consultation with archival professionals. A series of questions—including whether the collection was generated by a government office, private organization, or an individual—should be addressed.

6.   The original donor or his heirs should be consulted with tact and diplomacy.

7.   If the collection legally belongs to the archives, and the determination is made not to return it to the claimant,

there should always be some effort to address the claimant's concerns. This stage should involve negotiation since there may be various approaches to making a satisfactory settlement. Would good quality scans be an appropriate substitute for the return of the originals? Are there components of the collection that need to be restricted for a specific length of time to prevent invasion of privacy?

8. If the original collection is returned, the archives would be wise to negotiate for the retention of a digital copy with a clear access policy.

9. The final decision, to retain or return the collection, needs to be carefully documented with clear written explanation of the reasons and the approval process.

Challenges can come from the donor's family, from government agencies, from foreign countries, or from competing archives. The following set of hypothetical situations are worth considering. What are the issues at stake and what are the distinctions that need to be made? How can these nine steps be applied?

Eight Case Studies on Restitution of Displaced Archives

These case studies were formulated by Trudy Huskamp Peterson for the Society of American Archivists Conference Panel, "Returning Displaced Archives: Legal and Ethical Perspectives," held in San Francisco in August 2008. The questions posed by these case studies may not have definitive answers. There may be alternative solutions to these questions, and different ways of balancing the competing claims.

1. A politician takes his private papers home when he leaves government service. He donates them to a private institution in a neighboring country. They are not records of the state, so the government has no claim of inalienability,

but they are arguably part of the cultural patrimony of the country. Can the repository ethically accept them? If the government seeks their return, how does the repository navigate between the donor's wishes and the government's desire to hold its national patrimony?

2.   After a woman dies, her daughter gives her diaries to the state historical society. A couple of years later the woman's son contacts the society and says the donation is not valid because he, too, was an heir; he wasn't informed of the donation and he did not sign the deed. Assuming that he is right, how does the society stay out of a fight between brother and sister over the diaries?

3.   The director of the state Commission on Women takes a mix of state records and personal papers with her when she leaves office. Later she donates them to her alma mater, a private university. Several years later the state archivist discovers that parts of the records are missing and are with the private university. The archivist asks the university to segregate the personal papers from the offi-cial records and give the official records back to the state. Should the university agree? What if, in the original order, the official and personal papers were intermingled?

4.   In the USSR, many papers of important literary figures were brought to Moscow to be stored in the central archives for literature. Now that the Soviet Union has broken up, the former SSRs want the literary archives to return the papers of their national poets and writers. What leverage do they have for effecting returns?

5.   A manuscript collector in the U.S. talks with a political leader in an unstable country and persuades him that the records of his ministry will be safer in the U.S. The leader agrees and sends the records, along with a deed. The regime in the country changes, and the new government

demands the return of the records. Who has the authority to revoke the deed? Was the deed valid in the first place?

6.   Right after World War II, a G.I. found a photo album lying in the street in Germany. He brought it home with him. It has a name written inside the front cover. Now he has offered the album to the manuscript collection at his alma mater. Should the manuscript curator accept it? If not, what should she advise the aged G.I.?

7.   During a war, the U.S. Army seized some personal papers. These were sent to the U.S. along with government records. The U.S. is now ready to return the government records to the government from which they came. Should the U.S. give the personal papers to the government, which never had them in the first place? If not, what should the U.S. do?

8.   Books and records from an Iraqi Jewish community center were brought to the U.S. for preservation, with the agreement between U.S. and Iraqi officials that they be returned to Iraq after treatment. There is no viable Jewish community left in Iraq, but there is an Iraqi Jewish community and archives in Israel and there are Jewish archives in the United States. Is it ethical to return the records of a private organization to the state? What is the balance between the interests of the faith community, now outside the country, and the interests of cultural patrimony of the country where the records were created?

Challenges from a Donor's Family

It often happens, as in case two, that a stranger will walk into the archivist's office and ask for the return of family papers that the relative alleges were improperly taken and donated. This kind of random event can be seen as a test of the professional preparation of the archives. It can trigger a confrontation, or it can validate the work of the archives. The time spent on staff training and tedious hours updating acquisitions forms suddenly pay off in these situations by having an integrated response plan in place.

With the preservation of family or personal papers, the goal is to reach a consensus of the interested parties about the best disposition of the materials. Unlike a bank account, an archival collection is not best served by dividing it into equal parts. The importance of the integrity of the collection needs to be tactfully communicated to all parties. There may be sensitive components of the collection that should be restricted. Sometimes the claimant just wants to know more about family history. Others are won over by the promise of a public exhibition or a publication.

Family feuds can be treacherous for outsiders such as archivists, and prevention is the best cure. One useful custom that has informally evolved for many families with a historical legacy is to designate one person to represent their interests, something of an informal family historian and legally designated literary executor. Usually this is an older, retired person with an interest in history, strong bonds with other members, and the time to devote to promoting the shared heritage. It helps if the "keeper of the flame" has been granted legal status as executor or with power of attorney. In negotiations it may be useful to introduce this concept of family historian and work closely with the designated representative to ensure that the various family branches are in accord with the management of the papers, access policies, and accuracy of descriptions. The extra time given to creating a consensus at the beginning of negotiations can prevent time-consuming disputes down the road.

Most situations involve a family member wanting the donated collection returned. Occasionally a reverse replevin scenario plays out. Sometimes a donor's will designates that family papers be left to a repository, but that legal document is not honored by the heirs. In this delicate situation, the archives administration needs to think through the costs and benefits of pursuing legal remedies. The author knows of one case in which the congenial but eccentric custodian of the papers was at odds with other family members who wished to implement their father's wishes as expressed in his will. No one was willing to call the police or enter into messy intrafamily litigation. The archives staff stayed in touch with the family by sending annual reports, cards, and by hosting an occasional lunch or archives tour. After thirty years, the eccentric custodian passed away, and the family delivered the papers in keeping with their father's and now grandfather's express wishes. This case is extreme, but does demonstrate the value of patience and good communication.

Government Claims

It is well known that the various branches and levels of government generate a vast flood of paperwork, some of which is worth retaining as priceless national cultural heritage, and some of which deserves a short retention cycle. Over the years a surprising amount of paper migrates from government offices to personal possession and into private repositories. Government documents regularly show up for sale in auctions.

One explanation is that the U.S. was slow to define the boundary between private and official papers. The U.S. National Archives was not founded until 1934. Even presidential papers were considered the personal property of the president until new legislation went into effect in 1981, astonishingly late for an industrialized democratic country. Government officials have a habit of taking home working papers and duplicates that find their way into private donations to repositories. Better guidelines have been drawn up, but the habit persists.

There is a noticeable trend toward a more consistent view that records created at government expense and for official purposes belong to that agency and should be governed by its retention policies. This view has been standard in Europe for centuries. The legislation on presidential, gubernatorial, and congressional papers is gradually giving state and the U.S. National Archives sole responsibilities for preserving these official records. Over time, the European model may well be more uniformly adopted in the United States: official documents are formally government property, and the government has a right to demand their return and placement in state or national archives depending on their origin. Such legislation is not retroactive and does not disrupt previous deposit agreements.

Archivists need to be aware that many factors, such as prestige and political clout, influence the transfer of a collection. When Ronald Reagan left the California state governor's office, he took his papers legally as his own property and placed them in the Hoover Institution at Stanford University. Later, as out-going president, his presidential papers were in the hands of NARA and the Reagan Library, built in Simi Valley, California. While the Hoover Institution had legal title to retain the gubernatorial papers, important advisors decided the papers should be held together to document Reagan's entire career in one place, and the gubernatorial collection was transferred to the Reagan Presidential Library in 2000. The California State Archives could have made a case for the records as well, but the law had not been clarified at the time the collection was removed from Sacramento. The prestige of the Reagan Presidential Library proved to be persuasive. Public records in private repositories will be vulnerable to claims. It is possible that such claims may become more common.

The seemingly obvious distinction between private papers and government documents varies a great deal from country to country. The inviolability of state records also varies from country to country. Were the papers generated by an official government agency, a private institution, a private individual or group? Were they generated by a private organization that functioned as the official government? Examples of private organizations that assumed the powers of the state include a wide range of models from absolute monarchical families to the Communist Party of the Soviet Union and the KMT Party in Taiwan before 1988. Even some church archives have been accorded the status of government vital records.

As a practical matter, the U.S. government itself rarely exercises the right to reclaim its displaced archives, at least at present, if the papers are in responsible hands. In the current environment, official agencies seem to take action primarily when the materials are not being cared for in a professional manner.

Theft from government repositories is rather frequent and such items can show up for sale on eBay or similar auction sites. Provenance and warranty of title need to be thoroughly scrutinized in the case of new acquisitions. Court battles to recover materials lost to theft can be lengthy and absorb enormous amounts of staff time and resources. The proper behavior of the staff is subjected to intense examination; staff is put in the position of being on trial for recovering its own property. Government archivists have to be prepared to put up a lengthy and complex legal fight to recover property. Perhaps these confusions and the costly litigation would ease if archivists help clarify the principle that official archives are "inalienable." The International Council on Archives Code of Ethics is explicit on the issue of repatriation. By implication the principle would apply to domestic restitution.

The Trade in Trophy Archives

Archival trophies can command a huge amount of money at auction. An original Magna Carta from 1297 was sold in 2007 for $21.3 million.[10] In this case, businessman David Rubenstein purchased it—the only one in the United Sates and the only one of the seventeen known copies to be in private hands—from the Perot Foundation, which had allowed the document to be displayed by the National Archives since 1988. Ross Perot purchased it from the Brudenell family of Deene Park in Northamptonshire in 1984. Rubenstein will continue the tradition of placing the document in the custody of the U.S. National Archives. As private property, it could be removed at any time and resold. Unlike the Bill of Rights, its privatization from public ownership in Britain has not been challenged. The commodification of the Magna Carta is disturbing nonetheless. Each sale pumps up the price.

In the absence of any legal challenge to such a sale, there is a strong ethical or moral context that the owners operate within. Legally, Mr. Rubenstein could keep the Magna Carta in his living room and read it while drinking a cup of coffee. For both Perot and Rubenstein there has been a sense of "rightness" that the document be treated with a special reverence for its role in the evolution of democracy. There is a strong sense that it should be provided with the most stringent preservation measures. There is a sense that it should be on public display, as the patrimony of democratic peoples. It is a British document, but there are several other originals in the United Kingdom. As the historical basis for the democratic themes of the Declaration of Independence and the Bill of Rights, it seems right that it be on display in Washington, D.C. The cost of purchasing and preserving the document gives one pause. Certainly the government could not purchase the Magna Carta at the price commanded, and very few citizens have the resources to provide a suitable home for such a document.

Displaced Classified Documents

The most sensitive displaced government archives are the ones bearing *secret* or *top secret* markings. There are detailed regulations governing the management of security classified documents and their distribution. Only cleared and trained personnel are permitted to handle them. By law, their storage and retention cycles are covered by strict accountability, supervised by a facility security officer (FSO). For that reason, many people are astonished to find documents stamped *secret, confidential,* or *top secret* showing up in private collections. In fact, it frequently happens. The stamps have a rather ordinary, stationery-store look. It is not always easy to determine whether a document with *confidential* typed or stamped at the top is actually security classified in the official sense, or whether a typist just wanted to limit access. Such documents need to be immediately withdrawn and reviewed with the appropriate agency. The Information Security Oversight Office (ISOO) at the National Archives is very helpful in evaluating classified documents and in expediting declassification. The Defense Security Service (DSS) can also provide assistance.[11]

Often the classified documents found in private repositories are quite old, such as World War II–era materials, and there is a presumption that other copies of it have probably been declassified long ago. Such items still need to be withdrawn and restricted until the disposition is clear. Unmarked documents, if they contain classified information such as handwritten notes on classified meetings, are also considered classified. Traditionally such materials could not legally be allowed to circulate until they have been officially declassified and stamped and dated with an authorization code. Given the volume of secret documents generated each year by the government, individual declassification has proved to be impractical and methods of mass declassification have been discussed. A Clinton-era executive order mandated mass declassification categorized by age of documents. While repeatedly amended and extended, the goal of the executive order is to finish a mass declassification project and automatically declassify any materials that are over twenty-five years old unless they have been specifically designated as classified by the originating agency. Executive orders come and go, and are subject to complex changes. When there is a question, it is always prudent to consult with ISOO or the DSS.

Competing Archives

It is difficult enough to restore documents from ordinary thieves to the appropriate government archives, as the Bill of Rights case in North Carolina demonstrates. The really tough cases occur when two or more sovereign states both claim a set of archives. Their archival agencies are drawn into a battle. Codes of archival ethics mandate cooperation and repatriation, in rather simplistic and disingenuous formulations. The 2005 Society of American Archivists Code of Ethics makes an effort to minimize competition between archives. Section 2 of the code stipulates:

> Archivists cooperate, collaborate, and respect each institution and its mission and collecting policy.[12]

The 1996 International Council on Archives Code of Ethics has a more explicit injunction in sections 2 and 10:

> Archivists should acquire records in accordance with the purposes and resources of their institutions. They should not seek or accept acquisitions when this would endanger the integrity or security of records; they should cooperate to ensure the preservation of

these records in the most appropriate repository. Archivists should cooperate in the repatriation of displaced archives.

Archivists should promote the preservation and use of the world's documentary heritage, through working co-operatively with the members of their own and other professions.

Archivists should seek to enhance cooperation and avoid conflict with their professional colleagues and to resolve difficulties by encouraging adherence to archival standards and ethics. Archivists should cooperate with members of related professions on the basis of mutual respect and understanding.[13]

From these codes of ethics one gets the sense that archives are supposed to voluntarily shift around collections to return displaced archives to the right home. In practice, the process is rarely that simple. The most difficult cases occur when archives are displaced across national borders. International restitution cases can fester for decades, even centuries.

International Claims

During wartime, soldiers take souvenirs. It is very common to come across such trophies in the personal collections of military veterans. These souvenirs may range in value from trinkets to treasures. The discussion of international disputes over displaced archives begins with the story of a priceless stolen manuscript: the Samuhel Gospels from the German city of Quedlinburg.

The Quedlinburg Treasures

There were many stranded German "orphan" manuscripts as a result of World War II. At the end of the war and during the occupation, American personnel opportunistically stole numerous items including documents and manuscripts in Japan and Germany. Such souvenir hunting has been officially illegal, and widely denounced as pillage, since at least the 1907

Hague Convention, and most likely since the 1863 Lieber Code. Despite this disapprobation, trophy-collecting remains a common practice, especially in wartime. One of these World War II trophies was the priceless medieval Samuhel Gospels.[14] This gospel text is beautifully hand-calligraphed in gold ink on 191 parchment pages. The ninth-century parchments are enclosed in an exquisite jewel and enamel encrusted gold binding crafted in the year 1225 CE. It is one of the finest surviving medieval manuscripts, and part of the ancient Quedlinburg church treasure trove, which consists of priceless gold, silver, and ivory religious art objects such as reliquaries and bibles. Some of the items had been at the Quedlinburg Cathedral for one thousand years. These treasures are associated with Henry I, the first German king and the founder of the Holy Roman Empire, who is buried in Quedlinburg. These objects, beyond their religious, historic, and artistic value, are directly connected with the German national identity.

During the wartime bombing, the treasures were moved to a hiding place, sometimes described as a cave or mine shaft, for protection. The advancing American army set up a military guard at the site to protect the treasures. Still, twelve of the items vanished from the cave in the confusion at the end of the war. Nearly half a century later, precious items began to resurface. In October 1988, a London rare book dealer offered to sell the Samuhel Gospels to an agency of the West German government, the Foundation for Prussian Cultural Heritage (Stiftung Preussischer Kulturbesitz) for $9 million. It was a known item—known to have been stolen from Germany. The German government wanted it back. As the South Carolina and Maine cases have since demonstrated, U.S. court decisions do not always side with the original owners of displaced documents. Acting pragmatically, but setting a questionable precedent, the German government decided to ransom the Quedlinburg treasures for $2.75 million with an out-of-court settlement rather than trust the unpredictable vagaries of the American litigation system.

During the negotiations, the details of the original wartime theft emerged. The Department of Justice initiated a criminal prosecution against several family members of the deceased ex-serviceman Joe T. Meador, a former art teacher and U.S. soldier in World War II. Meador stole the

Quedlinburg treasures from the cave in Germany after the war and shipped them, wrapped in brown paper, to his home in rural Texas. At parties in his home, Meador was known to take out the treasures, one of the rarest and most beautiful collections of medieval religious art, to entertain and amaze his friends. After Meador died in 1980 his family began to market some of the invaluable items, which eventually attracted the attention of the German government. The German government reached the contro- versial $2.75 million settlement with the family to secure the return of the treasures as expeditiously as possible. As part of the settlement, the German government informed the Department of Justice that it did not wish for the family members to be prosecuted. The case was dropped, and the family members were never prosecuted for attempting to sell stolen goods.[15] Ten of the twelve treasures, including the Samuhel Gospels, have been restored to the cathedral Stiftskirche St. Servatius in the city of Quedlinburg. Two of the jeweled reliquaries stolen by Lieutenant Meador are still missing.

The Quedlinburg case can be seen as theft on two levels. First there was an individual soldier, Joe T. Meador, stealing treasures he was charged with protecting; then, decades later, his relatives tried to realize a large profit by selling the stolen property. Most reasonable people would consider these actions morally wrong. The issues are more muddied in situations where the archives or manuscripts are seized by a sovereign state, and where the materials are in a well-managed repository with preservation and refer- ence services. With the exception of the Native American experience and the Civil War, Americans fortunately have little historical experience with invading armies and occupation forces, and the displacement of cultural property that goes along with shifting governments. Few American cultural treasures have been spirited abroad. To get a sense of how the Germans felt about the loss of the Samuhel Gospels, an American would need to imagine the Declaration of Independence being taken out of the country and then passed around at parties for entertainment, or the original U.S. Constitution on display in a museum in North Korea. It would not be easily tolerated.

Understandably, the most contentious and most interesting cases involve national pride. These international disputes highlight the role that official documents and revered manuscripts play in the transmission of national identity, and the link between government archives and sovereignty. While most archivists will not have to contend with items on the level of the Samuhel Gospels, they may well find World War II trophies in the papers of American veterans. Archivists should be aware of the history of these issues and the implications for archivists as professionals in a position of trust.

As we have seen, the most common cause for international archival disputes is the displacement of archives through war. The historical background provides perspective on some current misconceptions about ownership of foreign archives.

Archives have long served as trophies of war. An Egyptian text from the second millennium BCE boasts of extensive plunder following victory: the inventory lists captured chariots, slaves, weapons, musical instruments. One prize was a messenger who was taken captive along with his message, which was inscribed on a clay tablet. This inscribed tablet is surely one of the earliest extant records of displaced archives used in the triumphal celebration of military victory.[16] Every era seems to have prominent examples. Cultural artifacts looted from the Temple of Jerusalem in the year 70 CE are jubilantly depicted on the Arch of Titus in Rome to commemorate the defeat of the Jews. The booty almost certainly contained scrolls from the temple. The arch can still be seen adjacent to the Colosseum, the construction of which may well have been financed at least in part by the looting of Jerusalem. Over a millennium later, in the Thirty Years' War, the Swedish army seized the rare Codex Argenteus in Prague, among other documents and archives. Now, some four centuries later, these items have not been returned to the Czechs.[17]

Since the early modern era, treaties and conventions have been developed to bring some order to the chaos of war. They address boundaries and define sovereignty. As artifacts of sovereignty, the disposition of state records have, then, been regulated by treaties. In some ways the core value of archives was better appreciated in the seventeenth century than in the twentieth.

The Treaty of Westphalia

The entrenched wartime custom of using archives as military trophies began to shift in the seventeenth century, at the end of the Thirty Years' War. There was at the time a growing awareness of the desirable stability created by a system of sovereign states. It was the hard-learned lesson of decades of warfare. The 1648 Treaty of Westphalia included clauses mandating the return of official government records and accommodating the necessary availability of such records for successor states to function. Official archives were an essential tool for maintaining sovereignty, even the sovereignty of a defeated nation-state. Article XCV of the Treaty of Westphalia specifically addresses the need to restore government documents displaced in the long years of war and shifting borders. In a pragmatic and extraordinarily insightful provision, Article XCVI of the Treaty of Westphalia mandates the creation of copies of documents when there is an overlapping interest by two different governments: "If those Documents be publick, and concern in common and jointly the Lands yielded to the King, the Archduke shall receive authentick Copys of them, at what time and as often as he shall demand them." Article XCVI anticipates the use of surrogate copies for sharing what today is considered the modern concept of joint heritage.[18] The Treaty of Westphalia did not result in the return of trophy items such as the manuscript bible known as the Codex Argenteus. It did result in the return of government records, a major step forward in the evolution of international law.

The Lieber Code

Two centuries later, another step forward occurred when President Lincoln promulgated General Orders No. 100, known as the Lieber Code, in 1863.[19] The American Civil War, as a national tragedy on many levels, forced the rethinking of many fundamental issues. Francis Lieber, a man who had seen the tragedy of war in Europe, drafted provisions to bring modern warfare under legal constraints in order to render it less barbaric. He viewed peace as the normal condition of states and war as an abnormal condition. The objective of modern war, in his view, was to achieve peace and stability as quickly as possible. Today most people share this perspective and see war as an aberration, despite all the evidence to the contrary.

The Lieber Code is realistic about the prerogatives of power. It concedes that the victorious army has a right to seize property. Section II of the Lieber Code discusses the public and private property of the enemy. Articles 35 and 36 of the code specifically include libraries and "collections" in the list of establishments of education that are protected in times of war. As enemy property, they may be seized, but safeguarded and not appropriated. The disposition of the cultural property is to be determined by treaty. This is in keeping with the traditions that came out of the Treaty of Westphalia. One interesting provision of the Lieber Code regarding libraries and collections reads as follows: "In no case shall they be sold or given away, if captured by the armies of the United States, nor shall they ever be privately appropriated, or wantonly destroyed or injured."

In the case of the North Carolina Bill of Rights, the "Amended State's Memorandum of Law in Support of its Motion for Summary Judgment" cites articles 44, 45, 46, and 47 of the Lieber Code, which outlaws pillage and prohibits individual soldiers from seizing property for private gain.[20] The Lieber Code did not prevent pillage in the Civil War or later, but it made pillage illegal. And it represents progress in the codification of the "customs of war."

The Brussels Declaration

In the mid-nineteenth century, while the U.S. was struggling with the devastation of the Civil War and the abolition of slavery, Russia was in a parallel struggle with the consequences of the Crimean War and the abolition of serfdom. Following the death of his father, Tsar Alexander II was forced to deal with humiliating peace negotiations, and confront the reality that the Russian serf army was not able to compete with European forces. Alexander II instituted many legal reforms, including the abolition of serfdom. In 1874 he convened an international conference in Brussels to draft a convention on the laws and customs of war. This was another effort to tame the barbaric aspects of international conflicts. Like the Lieber

Code, the provisions are realistic about the power of victors in combat to seize the property of a defeated government. But there are limits to that power. In article 8, the Brussels Declaration addresses the protection of historic monuments and works of art and science. This article is understood to include archives: "All seizure or destruction of, or willful damage to, institutions of this character, historic monuments, works of art and science should be made the subject of legal proceedings by the competent authorities."[21] The Brussels Declaration, while never ratified, had a lasting impact on the development of international law and thinking about the conduct of war.

The 1907 Hague Convention

The next serious effort to establish a basis in international law to protect cultural property in time of war dates back to the 1899 and 1907 Hague conventions, convened by another Russian emperor, Tsar Nicholas II. The purpose of the Hague Conventions was to meliorate the devastation of war. Archives are not specifically mentioned, but are understood as a component of national patrimony. A distinction is made between private and state property. There is an absolute ban on looting private papers: "private property cannot be confiscated." The treaties extend the ban on seizure to cultural property: "All seizure of, destruction or willful damage done to institutions of this character, historic monuments, works of art and science, is forbidden, and should be made the subject of legal proceedings."[22]

Educational institutions are explicitly protected in article 27 and pillage is explicitly prohibited in article 28 of the 1907 Hague Convention. Occupying powers could seize and use the documents needed for administration, but with limits. Police records could, under these rules, be taken and used by the occupation. At the end of the conflict, the records are to be returned to the original owners. The language echoes the Brussels Declaration. The difference is that the United States, along with a long list of other governments, ratified the 1907 Hague Convention.

Treaty Provisions

From 1648 through the negotiations to end World War I, European treaties routinely included archival clauses. The Treaty of Versailles, the Treaty of St. Germain, the Treaty of Trianon, and the Treaty of Riga all have provisions that address the repatriation of cultural property. They provided for the return of displaced records, restitution for destroyed manuscripts, and also for the creation of copies as needed.[23] There were five highly effective elements to this diplomatic practice of drafting treaties that included provisions for the disposition of displaced archives:

- Treaties governing changes in sovereignty also include clauses on the disposition of archives, which "follow the flag."

- The two parties list the archives to be transferred or copied to share as joint heritage.

- The successor states receive documents needed for administration, or copies of them.

- Displaced archives are returned to the country of origin after the attainment of peace.

- The archives created by an occupation army remain the property of the occupying power.

The Washington Pact (Roerich Pact)

Provisions for safeguarding archives, libraries, or works of art and science can be found woven into the Treaty of Westphalia, the Lieber Code, the 1907 Hague Convention, and the treaties that concluded World War I, but the protection of cultural property is not the main objective of these treaties. The Washington Pact of April 15, 1935, is devoted exclusively to the protection of cultural treasures in war and peace. Sometimes known as the Roerich Pact, the text and related materials can be found on the website of the Roerich Museum in New York.[24] This agreement protects "historic monuments, museums, scientific, artistic, educational and cultural institutions in time of peace as well as in war." It was signed by President Franklin Roosevelt and ratified by Congress.

The Washington Pact was inspired by Nicholas Roerich, an émigré Russian artist, mystic, and self-taught archeologist. The ratification of the pact can no doubt be traced to Roerich's friendship with Roosevelt's then-influential political ally, the Russophile Henry A. Wallace. The primary target is the preservation of Latin American cultural heritage, but the general principles are well articulated and have a universal scope. The pact was formally supplemented and superseded by the Hague Convention of 1954, which was not ratified by the U.S. Senate until much later, in 2008. Although the Roerich Pact is not on the official State Department website and has been consigned to benign neglect, probably because of the eccentric nature of its author, the brief text is still worth reading for its exceptional clarity of purpose and simplicity. It provides for a banner to protect cultural sites, much as the Red Cross flag is used to protect hospitals. This idea was later adapted, using a different symbol, by the 1954 Hague Convention. Despite the controversial nature of Roerich's philosophical ideas, his appreciation of the cultural value of archeological artifacts was advanced for his time. While archives are not directly mentioned, it is assumed that they are included under "historic monuments," as venerable ancient documents in Europe are frequently described in this manner. The entire archives facility with its contents would be considered a protected "cultural institution." Antiquities are the major focus, but archives are implied as well.

The London Declaration

The biggest theft of archives in human history occurred during World War II, not long after the ratification of the Roerich Pact. Several agencies of the Nazi regime were dedicated to seizing records, fine art, decorative arts, furniture, and moveable property of all kinds. These agencies followed the victorious German armies into huge swaths of Europe and the Soviet Union. Thousands of box cars were loaded with goods from the occupied countries and sent to Germany. The stolen goods included official archives from a large number of occupied countries, from France to the Netherlands to Poland. As the scale of the heist became apparent, alarms were sounded. The denunciation of Nazi plunder is known as the Declaration of London, formally titled "The Inter-Allied Declaration against Acts of Dispossession Committed in Territories under Enemy Occupation or Control," January 5, 1943.[25] Among the signatories are the United States and the Soviet Union. While the text is brief, it takes the form of a strongly worded warning nullifying the legality of any seizure of property from occupied territory: "This warning applies whether such transfers or dealings have taken the form of open looting or plunder, or of transactions apparently legal in form, even when they purport to be voluntarily effected." Like the Lieber Code, the London Declaration outlawed plunder, but did not prevent it.

Unlike the Thirty Years' War, World War II ended without a definitive treaty and without carefully written clauses. Although the most pressing concern was the fate of displaced persons, the authorities improvised ways to manage displaced archives. As the Allies reclaimed occupied territory from the Germans, there were two very different operations for managing German property and the property stolen by the Nazis. With the cold war beginning even before World War II was entirely over, the Red Army and the Anglo-American forces acted independently of each other, not only using different methods and different legal logic, but without realizing exactly what the other side was doing.

Trophies of World War II

In 1945, the victorious Red Army began a large scale reparations campaign to compensate the Soviet Union for its devastating losses at the hands of the Nazis. Trains began to roll from Germany to Russia with thousands of freight cars loaded with goods: bicycles, watches, delicate oil paintings, plumbing fixtures, dismantled factories, books, and manuscripts. While a small overall percentage of the goods consisted of library materials, they filled hundreds of train cars; millions of books and documents were shipped to the Soviet Union. The archives included not just German records, but also French, Polish, Dutch, Belgian, and Czechoslovak archives, often official political police files. The non-German records had been looted by the Nazis, and then acquired by the Russians—"twice plundered" or "twice saved," depending on one's point of view.

On August 21, 1945, as the trainloads of plunder were arriving in Moscow, the Soviet security police and archival administrators discussed the disposition of these vast archives. Professor Vladimir V. Maksakov, a historian-archivist in charge of the central archives, pointed out that the archives brought from places like Czechoslovakia should not be retained but quickly processed and returned within three to five years, once "international matters are regulated." Maksakov was following the conventions of war as they had evolved from the time of the Treaty of Westphalia to the 1907 Hague Convention and the Roerich Pact. Prominent Russians had been involved in the formulation of these "customs of war." The security police (NKVD) officer, A. A. IUr'ev, opposed Maksakov's view. IUr'ev was in favor of retaining the files indefinitely, in secret, exclusively for the use of intelligence information. He insisted: "No access whatsoever can be permitted for representatives of any scholarly institutions."[26] In the debate between applying international law and applying the prerogatives of sovereign national power, the latter won out. The Soviet Union had no intention of complying with international standards on restitution despite having signed both the 1907 Hague Convention and later the 1954 Hague Convention. Stalin and his right-hand man, Lavrenti Beria, were contemplating a monumental museum for the display of such plunder, as vivid proof of victory over Germany. The plans were abandoned when both Stalin and Beria died in 1953, but the archives remained.

In the Russian case, it took half a century before the existence of the files became known; it took over a decade of tough negotiations after the disintegration of the Soviet Union before even selected record groups were returned to France, Belgium, the Netherlands, Luxembourg, and the Rothschild family, owners of a venerable banking empire. Most of the German archives were retained under special legislation passed by the newly constituted Russian parliament in 1998 and 2000.[27] The Russian restitutions will be examined in greater detail later in this chapter.

The Monuments Men

In 1945, the Anglo-American forces also seized huge quantities of military, foreign ministry, intelligence, and Nazi party papers. As military units discovered the enormous caches of art and archives, the management of cultural property was assigned to the Monuments, Fine Arts, and Archives section of the Office of Military Government. The American "Monuments Men," as they were called, made a distinction between the archives of the defeated enemy and the records swept up from other European countries. Efforts were made to return non-German files to the country of origin, including much Russian material that went to the Soviet Union. Given the volume of materials, it was usually impractical to return them directly to the original owners. Often Ukrainian materials were sent to Moscow since the Soviet Union was the sovereign country of origin. A special distinction was made in the case of Jewish files. Rather than turning them over to the country of origin, typically Germany or Poland, the papers were given to Jewish organizations. The Americans, like the Russians, treated the German archives first of all as an immediate source of essential intelligence, then as evidence for the Nuremberg trials of war criminals. Unlike the Soviet forces, the Anglo-Americans immediately made provisions for a third use of the records, as historical documentation, and for the prompt repatriation of the originals. These files were microfilmed for access by historians, and most of the originals were returned to West Germany in the 1950s. While good faith efforts to return displaced archives were made, the Anglo-American solution was not perfect. The German archivists and officials felt that the distribution of microfilm documents, some recent enough to violate the German privacy laws, represented a loss of control over state records, an affront to state sovereignty.[28]

The cold war interceded during the restitution negotiations, so that the Americans returned German archives to the West German government rather than to Berlin in the East. The Soviets returned some materials to East Germany, but, as mentioned, they retained much in secret. In general, despite numerous irregularities, the Anglo-American solution—to copy the archives, retain copies, and return the originals to the successor government—worked well. This was the solution advocated unsuccessfully for the Soviet side by Professor Maksakov in Moscow in 1945.

The American policy was congruent with the 1907 Hague Convention, which recognizes the right of military victors to seize records for intelligence purposes, but also mandates the prompt return of the original archives to the successor government. The United States signed the convention in 1910 and the Russians signed it in 1955. Trudy Huskamp Peterson supplies a lucid account of the requirements of the 1907 Hague Convention as it applies to displaced archives.[29] Historically, as has been noted, wartime looting was considered legal, at least by the victors. War booty was a major means of financing armies. Loot was part of the soldier's pay package, in a sense. Over the centuries, however, government archives were increasingly not considered plunder like cash or food stores. The Lieber Code both protects libraries and prohibits plunder by individual soldiers. The Hague Conventions formalized the principles in the Lieber Code in the international arena. However noble in intention and language, the Hague Convention of 1907 was clearly inadequate for the challenges posed by World War II.

The 1954 Hague Convention

A new and stronger protection was needed for protecting and regularizing the management of cultural property in time of war. The 1954 Hague Convention more explicitly protects archives, narrowly defined as the noncurrent official records of government.[30] While the United States was involved in the drafting of the 1954 convention, it was not formally ratified by Congress for decades. The U.S. Senate finally ratified the 1954 Hague Convention on September 25, 2008. American participation became official on March 13, 2009, according to the U.S. State Department website. All along, the U.S. mandated compliance with the spirit of the convention despite the lack of formal confirmation until decades later. The basic principle is that victors in war and the occupation army have a right to use such records for intelligence and administration, but not to permanently acquire them.

It is worth quoting at some length from this 1954 document, a direct response to the devastation of World War II. Manuscripts and archives are specifically listed in article 1(a) as types of cultural property that deserve special protection in times of war. The prohibition of plunder is especially clear in article 4, section 3:

> The High Contracting Parties further undertake to prohibit, prevent and, if necessary, put a stop to any form of theft, pillage or misappropriation of, and any acts of vandalism directed against, cultural property. They shall refrain from requisitioning movable cultural property situated in the territory of another High Contracting Party.

The convention is amplified by a protocol which provides one of the earliest clear mandates for the return of archives that have been displaced in wartime.

1. Each High Contracting Party undertakes to prevent the exportation, from a territory occupied by it during an armed conflict, of cultural property as defined in Article 1 of the Convention for the Protection of Cultural Property in the Event of Armed Conflict, signed at The Hague on 14 May, 1954.

2. Each High Contracting Party undertakes to take into its custody cultural property imported into its territory either directly or indirectly from any occupied territory. This shall either be effected automatically upon the importation of the property or, failing this, at the request of the authorities of that territory.

3. Each High Contracting Party undertakes to return, at the close of hostilities, to the competent authorities of the territory previously occupied, cultural property which is in its territory, if such property has been exported in contravention of the principle laid down in the first

> paragraph. Such property shall never be retained as war
> reparations.
>
> 4.   The High Contracting Party whose obligation it was to
>   prevent the exportation of cultural property from the ter-
>   ritory occupied by it, shall pay an indemnity to the hold-
>   ers in good faith of any cultural property which has to be
>   returned in accordance with the preceding paragraph.

This protocol provides one of the most decisive statements on the need for restitution of cultural property displaced in wartime. The massive amounts of art and archives seized first by the Nazi army in World War II and then requisitioned a second time by the Soviet Red army was simply unprecedented in history. The management of the Russian war trophy archives should have been addressed by this document, which was rati-fied by the Russian Federation, long before the extent of the problem was known in the West. The text includes a bold and unambiguous statement that cultural property "shall never be retained as war reparations."

As the advent of the cold war froze the problems in place, the United States, which was instrumental in drafting the convention, was unwilling to engage in the discussions of how this agreement would be implemented, even though it embodied the very principles that the Anglo-American authorities had followed in returning captured German archives. Certain sectors of American society deeply resented the United Nations, UNESCO, and the Hague international conventions, which they saw as an affront to U.S. sovereignty. For its part, the Soviet Union, which had much more at stake, allowed the Russian Federation to ratify the convention but was unwilling to disclose its captured plunder and begin the process of restitu-tion it had agreed to. One scholar has identified scores of disputed archival claims between nations, many of which stem from World War II.[31]

While the displaced archives of World War II were frozen in limbo, another problem emerged. Cultural treasures that had survived war were being stolen in times of peace, not as symbolic trophies but as highly mar-ketable merchandise. These depredations led to another convention.

The 1970 UNESCO Convention

The text of the 1970 UNESCO Convention on the Means of Prohibiting and Preventing the Illicit Import, Export and Transfer of Ownership of Cultural Property is available on the State Department website. The website also indexes the 116 signatories including the United States, the Russian Federation, Great Britain, Italy, Iraq, and China.[32] The 1970 UNESCO Convention directly acknowledges that it is articulating something beyond mere legal technicalities, but rather "universally recognized moral principles" and "moral obligations." And yet, it is an easier document to implement than the 1907 Hague Convention, the 1935 Washington Pact, or the 1954 Hague Convention.

For working archivists, the 1970 UNESCO Convention provides a more reliable basis for making decisions about acquiring foreign documents for six reasons:

1. Unlike the 1907 Hague Convention and the Washington Pact, archives, rare manuscripts, and multimedia records are specifically covered.

2. Unlike the 1954 Hague Convention, the focus is not on exceptional wartime conditions, but on the transport of rare items across borders at any time.

3. Policing is up to the individual states that protect their borders. Enforcement does not depend on international courts.

4. Each nation is responsible for defining what cultural property is covered. A state can nationalize private property that is deemed a national treasure, but it must do so in a clear and documented fashion. Each nation is responsible for providing export licenses to clarify what items can be legally removed from the country. In article 11, export under compulsion during the foreign occupation of a country is regarded as illegal.

5. The United States both ratified the convention and pro-
    vided legislation to implement it. It covers the nearly four
    decades prior to the U.S. Senate's ratification of the 1954
    Hague Convention in 2008.

6. The UNESCO Convention has acquired acceptance in
    the museum community and contributed to more readily
    applicable ethical standards.

The year 1970 has become a benchmark in an informal statute of limitations that imposes stricter ethical standards for the post-1970 era.

During the 1970s, the International Council on Archives periodically
addressed the issue of repatriation of displaced archives, primarily in connection with decolonization and the need for sharing government archives
between newly independent former colonies and the previous parent state.
The ICA Round Table (known as CITRA from the French acronym) con-
solidated the principle of the inalienability of state archives, codified in
the 1970 UNESCO resolutions.[33] As a practical matter, little material was
actually returned.

Repatriation at the End of the Cold War

When the cold war thawed, the problems began to emerge. The real test
for international cooperation in restitution came with *perestroika* in the
Soviet Union in the late 1980s, and intensified after 1991 when the Soviet
Union collapsed. The U.S. National Archives and the Hoover Institution
each held components of the prerevolutionary Russian embassy files. The
records had been removed after the recognition of the Soviet Union in
1933 led to the transfer of the embassy building from the old Tsarist-era
custodians to the new Soviet embassy staff. In 1934 an American foreign
services officer named Angus Ward retrieved U.S. records from the former
American embassy in Leningrad; but, for reasons that are not entirely
clear, the Tsarist-era records remained in the U.S., divided between these
two repositories. Many Americans did not approve of the diplomatic recognition of what they considered a rogue regime that had not honored its

debts to foreign countries. With Gorbachev's reforms and signs of democratic life, the rationale for keeping official Russian diplomatic archives
abroad evaporated. The National Archives and Hoover Institution each
microfilmed the set of Russian diplomatic files in its custody. The National
Archives returned the originals to the Foreign Ministry in Moscow on
January 31, 1990, and retained the microfilms as a security copy. The
Hoover Institution kept the original diplomatic files it had acquired in
the 1930s and shipped the filmed copies to the Russian State Archives in
February 1993. Either way, with originals or surrogate copies, the Russians
began to recover their lost heritage.[34]

The restitution dynamics also began to work in the other direction.
Experienced researchers, notably Patricia Grimsted of Harvard's Ukrainian
Research Institute, began tracing certain threads through the Russian
labyrinth. Word came out of the displaced western European records in
Moscow. German, British, French, Belgian, and Dutch archivists converged
on Moscow and began to negotiate with the new archivist of Russia, a Boris
Yeltsin ally named Rudolf Pikhoia. Initially the negotiations revolved
around the return of displaced property in the normal legal sense. With a
change in regime, it seemed a logical way to proceed. Yeltsin could place
the blame for hiding these collections on his disgraced predecessors. And a
series of agreements with western European countries were signed in 1992.
Given the economic tailspin that Russia was experiencing, countries such as
France greased the wheels by providing generous grants for preparing the
documents for transfer, or for microfilming them. Apparently the French
felt that the archives needed an infusion of cash simply to function, and the
cover story was a face-saving device. It is widely believed that this infusion
of money was siphoned off for personal profit and disappeared without
helping the archival institution in any way. The funds may not have been
intended as a bribe, as such, but in the atmosphere of general corruption,
the end effect was the same.[35]

The newly democratic Russian parliament intervened in these negotiations and passed legislation in 1994–1995 to halt all restitution initiatives. Rudolf Pikhoia was dismissed as head of the archive service, and was
replaced by Vladimir Kozlov, who had long been skeptical of returning

documents without demonstrable benefit to Russia. The parliament and Yeltsin went through various political struggles and the upshot was strict legislation, signed by President Vladimir Putin in 2000, prohibiting the return of German documents seized in World War II, but permitting Nazi Germany's enemies to claim collections if they are willing to make an equal exchange of documents or funds. The legislation requires some benefit for the Russian side. These exchanges, not to be called restitution, were initially implemented by means of parliamentary orders; later a council was established to shepherd the process.[36]

This mechanism was a major pragmatic breakthrough that permitted the essential return of displaced French, British, Belgian, Dutch, Luxembourg, and Liechtenstein state records. The tiny country of Liechtenstein purchased at an auction in the West some original Russian documents on the murder of the Romanov family to make the exchange for their missing state archives. The loophole in the legislation also enabled the Rothschild family to regain its private family and banking papers by means of buying up Tsarist correspondence on the auction market and then exchanging it for immensely valuable documents going back to the founding of the house of Rothschild. Like the German government paying millions of dollars for the stolen Quedlinburg treasures, the Rothschilds decided it was most expedient just to purchase what was already legally their property, rather than to rely on principles of international law.

As Patricia Grimsted explains, "Given the international political milieu, matters of archival restitution continue to be negotiated bilaterally and usually linked to high-level political and diplomatic expediency and State visits."[37] The price for substituting bilateral treaties for international law is that archives are still being treated as trophies. And the Germans still have not recovered their national patrimony.

From International Law to Bilateral Agreements

The unintended consequence of these successful restitution efforts, however, is that retrieving property is now more expensive and less certain for other claimants, especially those without the deep pockets to pay substantial ransom. These developments will also have a chilling effect domestically, where the return of an official document even as important as the Bill of Rights is not considered axiomatic. The treaties and agreements used by the Russians to implement restitution hark back to the diplomatic practice of the Treaty of Westphalia, and they also implicitly acknowledge the international legal principles articulated by the ICA in 1992–1995. While international law is difficult to implement, it forms a benchmark for case-by-case agreements. Following nonbinding conventions is more in the realm of ethics than law. Much work still needs to be done. Until such time as legal principles are more widely understood, as a pragmatic matter, archivists are well advised to think through these issues in advance of accepting a problematic collection, and also work professionally to build a consensus on the best disposition of archival collections.

Three Models of Cultural Property Ownership

When you look at the history of replevin and repatriation in the United States, Europe, and Russia, it is possible to discern different models. There is what might be styled a *free market model*, a *nationalist model*, and— somewhere in between—what might be called a *regulated model*.

The Free Market Model

This is the prevailing concept of ownership in the United States. This view regards private property as inviolable. Title confers total control to buy, sell, transport, exchange, alter, and auction off the goods one owns. In this model, nationalization and eminent domain are restricted to very specific situations—such as the government claiming immoveable property in the path of new roadways, and providing compensation for the loss. Stolen goods are not normally seen as marketable items, but in fact the free market model is so strong that once government documents have been in private hands for an extended period—such as the Maine broadside copy of the Declaration of Independence or the South Carolina Civil War–era papers—the claim of private parties becomes very strong. Such a sense of entitlement to sell stolen government property would be very rare in other countries.

Auction houses and museums have long thrived using the mechanism of the art market. Many archival repositories have large acquisitions budgets to purchase manuscripts from private individuals and from dealers. James Cuno provides a well argued defense of this model in his book *Who Owns Antiquity?*[38] The Manuscript Society maintains a replevin fund to assist members whose acquisitions are challenged. Another advocate for the free market model is Stanford law professor John Henry Merriman, who promotes a three-pronged test as to the best owner: preservation, scholarship, and access. Cultural property, according to this analysis, belongs with the entity that can best care for it and provide safe access for scholarly purposes—all functions that require substantial financial means. The Solomonic defense of the free market rests on the assumption that those countries with the means to purchase cultural artifacts have means to care for them. It is not a justification for theft or pillage, all outlawed under the National Stolen Property Act.[39]

Serious issues begin to arise when archives acquire foreign documents, a category where questionable provenance has traditionally been easier to cover up. Foreign purchases also lead to confrontations with different models of cultural title. Modern communications and travel have both increased international trade in archival materials, and made it easier to trace that trade. Long an issue for major international "encyclopedic" collections, this now also affects smaller repositories in a way impossible just a few decades ago.

The other serious issue arises when archives receive personal, "private" collections that contain intermingled government-generated papers acquired by the donor when it was common practice for officials to take use copies with them from a government office. Even the U.S. president's papers were considered his property until the 1970s. The concept of inviolable government property rights is becoming stronger; it is compatible with the idea of private property rights if one thinks of the government as an "owner," with the rights of ownership. The U.S. government is establishing more systematic guidelines for what materials can properly be taken home by employees. As a consequence, archives need to be alert to the presence of government records in private papers.

The U.S. does not use eminent domain or export licensing procedures to claim private archives that are about to be sent out of the country, probably because loss of cultural treasure is not prevalent in the United States. As a "receiving country," anxiety over the export of cultural property is not a part of our American intellectual landscape. It is a big issue in "contributing countries." American archivists need to educate themselves about these sensitivities as an ethical issue even when it is not a legal one.

The Nationalist Model of Ownership

A different view has prevailed in what is loosely called the East: the former Soviet Union, Eastern Europe, and China. This could be termed a nationalist model. Both Russia's feudal past and its recent communist legal system vested property rights firmly in the state. Postcommunist Russia and entrepreneurial China are both developing a strong sense of national patrimony as property of the state, not just the archives and other cultural property *generated* by the state. The government can and does claim control of cultural heritage that in the U.S. would be considered private. In the post-Soviet era, many of these government prerogatives were reinstated in the new legal systems. In eastern Europe and Russia the government feels free to claim the private papers of public figures, at its discretion, something unheard of in most of the West. The control is typically asserted when there is an attempt to remove the private papers from the country. This model is asserted in the 1970 UNESCO language that has each state decide what it will claim as its cultural property. Again, the two clearest categories are antiquities and state archives—these have the highest level of government protection. The papers of public officials, including papers located in a private residence, are generally included in the concept of state archives in the East. Hungary and Poland have clear legislation on this issue. The papers of eminent cultural figures, such as composers and writers, start out as private family papers and later may, if sufficiently central to national pride, pass into government protection.

Several other countries have laws that permit the state to halt the export of cultural property that is considered a national treasure. The Portuguese government stepped in to prevent the loss of poet Fernando Pessoa's archives, considered Portuguese national heritage, to another country, even though the papers were in private hands.[40] It is fairly common, outside of the United States, for a nation to extend special protections to cultural property that relates to the life and work of national leaders, scientists and artists. A form of eminent domain, this protection is provided for in the 1970 UNESCO Convention, which was ratified by the U.S.

American archivists should expect an extra layer of documentation when acquiring the papers of foreign cultural figures, just as museums need to examine the provenance of foreign antiquities. Export licenses, warranties of title, and chain of ownership are all crucial, especially for acquisitions that left the source country after 1970. A more sweeping convention, the 1995 Unidroit Convention on Stolen or Illegally Exported Cultural Objects, does not appear to be attracting very many signatories from among the "collecting countries," such as the United States.

The Regulated Model

A hybrid regulated model prevails in western Europe, where the different countries have found ways to balance private and public claims to cultural property. Different European states have formulated different kinds of legislation to harmonize the demands of cultural politics and the market forces. In Britain the laws are very detailed about items that require an export license. If in the export licensing process the state decides the item constitutes British legacy, the government authorities have a specified period of time to raise the money, and exercise first claim to purchase the item at close to market value. This right of first refusal to purchase is sometimes called preemption. The British have a system that is more restrictive than the American one, but still acknowledges the claims of private ownership and of the marketplace. Instead of prohibiting sales of cultural property, the United Kingdom uses export licensing regulations to moderate the loss of national treasures. When a foreign buyer applies for an export license for a major cultural artifact, the law mandates a period of time to seek a British purchaser before permitting the property to be sent abroad. The British call the success of the Harry Ransom Center at the University of Texas in acquiring English literary papers the "Drang nach Austin" (playing on the Nazi policy of "Drang nach Osten")—something they try to prevent, but without seizing property. This process balances the state's claim to cultural property with market forces.

In Italy the system is different. Foreigners can purchase designated cultural property such as antiquities, but not remove them from the country. The European concept of a regulated market model has had influence in the East. The European Council applied pressure on Russia to restitute trophy archives taken after World War II, and partially succeeded. This case proves that moderating influences can be strengthened through international cooperation.

Globalization is bringing the three different models of property ownership into closer competition. Just how the issues will be resolved is not clear. Returning to the opening comments on replevin, the examples examined here demonstrate the inherent conflicts in competing claims. These conflicting interests may never be fully resolved. In each case, the different sides will need to present their best arguments. The primary goal is establishing enough equilibrium to build faith in the possibility of a fair disposition. There is much work to be done to establish an accepted and ethical environment for resolving disputes. For cases of common theft, there needs to be enhanced communication and cooperation between archival professionals and the legal establishment to resolve competing ownership claims without decades-long litigation and without extortive out-of-court settlements. For displaced state records, the five elements that evolved from the Treaty of Westphalia and the 1954 Hague Convention are still valid. Such international conventions require detailed supporting legislation in each country. Professional archivists need to consult on the provisions of such legislation. Regarding the sale of privately owned cultural property, the export licensing and certification provisions of the 1970 UNESCO convention would go a long way to alleviate disputes. It is not a case of solving problems as much as balancing competing interests.

Achieving that balance requires a good sense of history, a sense of the international context, a sense of priorities, and dedication to the preservation and care of archives. And a lot of work.

Questions for Evaluating the Restitution of an Archival Collection

These points expand on the procedure outlined at the beginning of the chapter:

1. What is the claimant's case?
2. What is the chain of ownership of the collection in question?
3. Is there evidence of illegal transfer or illicit export of the collection?
4. What laws were in effect at the time of each transfer?
5. What is the legal status of the collection? Is there an existing contract governing the records, such as a deed of gift, warranty of title, bill of sale, transfer record, or export license?
6. What is the legal status of the current repository? Does the current repository have a legal mandate governing the collection of such documents, i.e., a formal collecting policy?
7. What is the legal status of the claimant's repository?
8. Are the records private or governmental?
9. Are there special privacy considerations that require restricting parts of the collection, such as personal identification numbers or medical information?
10. Does the collection contain evidence that might be needed in a criminal trial, evidence that requires proof that the documents have not been tampered with?
11. Which repository or owner is best able to preserve the collection according to modern standards?
12. Which repository or owner is best able to provide access both in terms of physical accessibility in a monitored reading room, and intellectual access in terms of cataloging and placement of metadata and even scans on the Internet?

13. Which repository or owner will best promote scholarship using the collection?

14. Which repository or owner is most vested in the subject matter?

15. Has the collection been nationalized?

16. Was it removed from its source country during time of war, after 1907, or after 1954?

17. Was it exported after 1970?

18. Is there room for negotiations such as supplying surrogate copies with scans, microfilm, or photocopies?

19. Is there need for protective custody while the collection's disposition is settled?

20. Is there a need for transparency and communication with the public about the disposition of the collection?

Trusted Archives

The introduction made several assertions about the unique nature of archival ethics and how they are distinct from those of related fields such as history and library science. It also asserted that the ethical quandaries for archivists are not amenable to a simple set of guidelines because they are intrinsic in the nature of primary sources, whether paper or digital. The chapters on acquisition, deaccessioning, access, proprietary information, privacy, authentication, and displaced archives provide examples of the types of issues that archivists confront, sometimes in a dramatic confrontation, but more frequently in small issues that need to be finessed, balanced, and harmonized many times a day. Casebook-style examples provide a sense of the spectrum of problems that can and do occur. The first step in addressing these issues is to ask the right questions, and lots of them, just to start the process of sorting through the factors in play. Specific questions will sometimes have specific answers. More often, coping strategies and negotiating skills serve the archivist better.

The archivist's code of ethics is an essential element of professionalization. It confirms the fact that archivists belong to a larger professional group with obligations and responsibilities that extend beyond the range of any specific employer. There are responsibilities to one's employer, certainly, and also to donors and researchers. Beyond that small circle is the obligation to the community, the state, and the nation. By reading international conventions, one gets a feel for the wider implications of the daily work to preserve cultural heritage. While essential, codes—which work well for other professions—have limits in the archival world. The most useful aspect is the work that goes into formulating them and repeatedly revising them, often based on reactions to real cases.

What is the sum of all of these codes, cases, and questions? The goal is to establish a standard of integrity that inspires confidence in the documentary record. The technical gurus talk about the "trusted archive," as a database that is continuously maintained and not corrupted over time. It is a good metaphor for ethically managed paper and multimedia archives as well. The foundation is a well-selected, accurately cataloged, well-preserved, and open collection. It should serve as a trusted source for historians, journalists, and policy makers. It should have a baseline of truthfulness that will encourage a respect for factual evidence. It should serve as a corrective to the wild interpretations that periodically invade political and cultural discourse. The result is a community with a vivid but accurate shared memory, one that is periodically reconceptualized to enhance an awareness of social responsibility.

In terms of acquisitions, collecting the traces of memory has two sides: positive and negative. One aspect is the archives as a source of narratives that capture the imagination. We know that every country, every ethnic and religious community, needs such inspiring founding stories to create social bonds. To have a lasting and positive influence, the group pride needs to be built on a truthful foundation. That truthful foundation must be collected and maintained, vetted and corrected, in trusted archives that build confidence even in troubled times.

Then there is the other side. The collective memory requires the strength of character to record the injustices of the past: the treatment of slaves in the United States, the brutality of the Soviet forced labor camps, the genocide perpetrated against the Jewish population of Europe in World

War II, the injustices of apartheid in South Africa, human rights violations in totalitarian countries, war crimes that occur and recur in violent times. All these troubling episodes need to be carefully documented. The archives generated by the truth and reconciliation commissions of the past decades provide a magnificent tribute to the international effort to create a just society. It is no longer possible to deny the human rights violations that occurred where those archives were gathered and preserved.

In terms of open access to information as an ethical imperative, there are outstanding examples in recent history. These experiences vindicate opening sensitive files as long as it is accomplished in ways that protect personal privacy and security. The archivists who opened the cigarette papers had a great deal of courage, but also professional competence and a clear sense of ethical priorities. Likewise, opening the political police files of the former East German political police required technical knowledge and political will. Rescuing the archives of South Africa during the transition to democracy also required tenacity and courage. It is interesting to note how often the successful cases rely on the resolution of a key individual. The success stories also tend to involve a team of professionals who are willing to roll up their sleeves, draft policies, and implement plans to balance the complex of competing interests.

Access to information has always been an ethical imperative. Now it is becoming an expensive imperative, since online databases require constant maintenance. Unlike books, one cannot just buy them once and leave them on the shelf. With the need for continuous patches, updates, and migration to current platforms, online data has to be in effect repurchased annually. Because of their essential role in a well-run democracy, online tools, which require upkeep in both good times and bad, need to be buffered from the sharp economic fluctuations that impact budgets.

Authenticity has been a major issue since antiquity, and it is becoming even more important with the growth of technical tools to manipulate data. Outlandish stories proliferate on the Internet and disrupt logical political discourse. Archivists are already participating in the effort to create norms for authenticating digital documents and online sources.

Scholarly communication needs to be protected. The cigarette papers case demonstrated the way the scientific process was manipulated and corrupted. Valid scientific studies on the effects of smoking were squelched, and false findings were distributed by seemingly reputable experts. Only by violating proprietary protections and opening the internal files of cigarette companies to international scrutiny on the Internet could this falsification be exposed. It is likely that increased vigilance will be needed in future years.

The various archival codes of ethics contain dozens of different provisions that at first appear to be exceptionally diverse—sometimes contradictory—and covering many facets of archival work. The thirty or more precepts in the codes have a common thread. That common element is to cultivate trusted archives based on intellectual integrity and to prevent the corruption of historical resources.

The cultural property we call archives should be maintained as a "multivalent" resource in a metaphorical sense. The collectors and curators of these treasures cannot and should not control how researchers will use them and how researchers will critique each other's conclusions. The unprogrammed aspect of collaborative research opens up new knowledge with unpredictable, sometimes counterintuitive conclusions. Archivists facilitate this process without interfering in the end results. The real value of archives is created by the researchers' interpretation of the documents and their interaction with each other in a free, uncensored, unrestricted give and take. For such creative research to take place freely, archives, manuscripts and records have to be treated as ends in and of themselves, not as a source of personal or corporate financial gain, not as a source of status, vindication, retaliation, triumphalism, or political advantage.

Protecting cultural heritage from theft and destruction is another ethical challenge. Theft is far more prevalent than generally recognized. It flourishes in the genteel world of manuscripts and archives when there is tacit collusion between the perpetrators and confrontation-averse staff. During periods of political turbulence, theft and looting predictably become big business. The biggest heist of archives occurred during World War II, twice. First the agencies of Nazi Germany seized vast accumulations of archives from all over Europe, then the Soviet army seized trainloads of stolen archives as trophies. More than half a century later, some sets of archives have been returned to their governments and others have not. The wars of the late twentieth and twenty-first centuries have also resulted in displaced archives. One hopes that it will not require another half century to restore these official government records to the sovereign states that created them. Archivists should be advising on these issues as well.

When archives are viewed not as a means to an end but as an end in themselves, several issues emerge:

- While archives are valuable artifacts at auction, their monetary worth is not their main value. The displacement, dismemberment, or theft of archives is more serious than the theft of furniture, for instance, with the same auction price.

- Certainly archives are valuable as sources of information that can be digitized and marketed. To maintain the research value of archives, digitization programs need to be structured to facilitate open and equal access. In an ethical environment, such commercial ventures should not exploit the salability of restricted and controlled access.

- Archives express different points of view, but they should not be instrumentalized to support a particular religious agenda or political ideology. Suppressing vital documents or disseminating misleading information in the interest of ideology or corporate profit fundamentally corrupts the research process. This does not mean that archivists cannot have their own opinions. An important distinction can be made between objectivity and neutrality. In fact, archivists actively acquire and preserve records as evidence of injustice.

- State archives support a nation's sovereignty and cultural coherence, and should not be transformed into trophies of conquest. The international law that protects archives as cultural property is woven into classic human rights conventions. These are the same treaties that protect human life and dignity, even in times of chaos and war. The preservation of authentic archives and manuscripts, as expressions of history and culture, is directly related to the protection of human rights.

This volume includes a diverse array of examples, many lists of questions, case studies, numerous codes, treaties and conventions, all drawn from various cultures and various historical periods. While often contradictory, they nonetheless share a common theme, which is to preserve documents as witnesses to what actually happened and to provide open access to these documents in trusted archives.

Ten Codes of Ethics Relating to Archives and Cultural Property

THESE PROFESSIONAL CODES COVER A WIDE RANGE OF ETHICAL PRINCIPLES FOR THE MANAGEMENT OF CULTURAL PROPERTY INCLUDING ARCHIVES, MANUSCRIPTS, AND RECORDS. The texts are reproduced with written permission from each professional organization. As these standards are constantly updated and revised, please consult with the organizations' websites for the most current versions of the codes and guidelines.

American Historical Association
    Main web page: http://historians.org/
    Professional Standards: http://www.historians.org/pubs/free/
    professionalstandards.cfm
    Guiding Principles on Taking a Public Stance:
    http://www.historians.org/governance/pd/2007_01_08_
    PublicStance.cfm

American Library Association
    Main web page: http://www.ala.org/
    Code of Ethics: http://www.ala.org/ala/aboutala/offices/oif/
    ifgroups/cope/Code%20of%20Ethics%202008.pdf

Association of Art Museum Directors
    Main web page: http://www.aamd.org/
    Code of Ethics: http://www.aamd.org/about/#Code

Association of Canadian Archivists
    Main web page: http://archivists.ca/
    Archivist's Code of Ethics: http://archivists.ca/content/
    code-ethics

Association of College & Research Libraries, Rare Books and
    Manuscripts Section
    Main web page: http://www.rbms.info/
    Code of Ethics for Special Collections Librarians: http://www.rbms.
    info/standards/code_of_ethics.shtml

Institute of Certified Records Managers
    Main web page: http://www.icrm.org/
    Code of Ethics: http://db.icrm.org/crm/index.
    jsp?submit_menu=118

International Council on Archives
    Main web page: http://www.ica.org/
    Code of Ethics: http://www.ica.org/sites/default/files/Ethics-EN.pdf

Manuscript Society
    Main web page: http://www.manuscript.org/
    Code of Ethics: http://www.manuscript.org/2009ethics.html

National Archives and Records Administration
    Main web page: http://www.archives.gov/
    The Archivist's Code: http://www.archives.gov/
    preservation/professionals/archivist-code.html

Society of American Archivists
    Main web page: http://www2.archivists.org
    Code of Ethics: http://www.archivists.org/governance/
    handbook/app_ethics.asp

American Historical Association

Guiding Principles on Taking a Public Stance

The constitution of the American Historical Association (AHA) states that "Its object shall be the promotion of historical studies through the encouragement of research, teaching, and publication; the collection and preservation of historical documents and artifacts; the dissemination of historical records and information; the broadening of historical knowledge among the general public; and the pursuit of kindred activities in the interest of history." In a wide range of situations, most of which have to do with the rights and careers of individuals, considered as historians, the AHA has the right to take public stands in defense of these objectives:

When public or private authorities, in the United States or elsewhere, threaten the preservation of or free access to historical sources. At least since the time of Tacitus, historians have worried that states can and will poison the wells of historical research by suppressing vital documents or supporting the spread of misleading information. As the forms of historical research, scholarship and teaching become more varied, and as the forms of document that historians depend on become more and more varied, it seems certain that these concerns will continue to arise, and that the AHA will have to confront an increasing variety of problems in this realm. In particular, the AHA should stand ready if political or commercial concerns threaten the professional administration of an archive, historical society or other institution that has custody of sources.

When public or private authorities, in the United States or elsewhere, censor the writing, exhibition or teaching of history. The AHA should stand ready to defend all historians against efforts to limit their freedom of expression.

When public or private authorities, in the United States or elsewhere, limit or forbid freedom of movement to historians. The AHA should defend the rights of American historians to travel to all foreign countries in order to study, teach, pursue research, or simply carry on discussions with other historians, and the rights of historians from foreign countries to study, teach, pursue research or carry on discussions with historians in the United States.

When public authorities or private entities attempt to compromise the mission of historical assets. The AHA should insist that all students and researchers, whether or not they are affiliated with particular institutions, have equal access to sites, documents, films, recordings and other historical materials in the possession of federal, state and local archives. It should also contest efforts to give preference to private entities in using and profiting from the merchandising of sites or materials.

In addition, the AHA should stand ready to support its sister organizations in defending the rights of scholars from all fields to have access to information, freedom of expression and freedom to travel inside and outside the United States. From the standpoint of most members, this is probably a secondary area for AHA intervention, but joint and supporting statements by the President, the Director, and the Council can and should be made in these circumstances as well.

In all cases, the facts should be established, to the extent that is possible, before a public statement is drafted—much less circulated. Consultation with all members of Council has proved an effective way to gain information rapidly in the past and should continue to be the normal practice.

American Library Association

Code of Ethics

As members of the American Library Association, we recognize the importance of codifying and making known to the profession and to the general public the ethical principles that guide the work of librarians, other professionals providing information services, library trustees and library staffs.

Ethical dilemmas occur when values are in conflict. The American Library Association Code of Ethics states the values to which we are committed, and embodies the ethical responsibilities of the profession in this changing information environment.

We significantly influence or control the selection, organization, preservation, and dissemination of information. In a political system grounded in an informed citizenry, we are members of a profession explicitly committed to intellectual freedom and the freedom of access to information. We have a special obligation to ensure the free flow of information and ideas to present and future generations.

The principles of this Code are expressed in broad statements to guide ethical decision making. These statements provide a framework; they cannot and do not dictate conduct to cover particular situations.

I. We provide the highest level of service to all library users through appropriate and usefully organized resources; equitable service policies; equitable access; and accurate, unbiased, and courteous responses to all requests.

II. We uphold the principles of intellectual freedom and resist all efforts to censor library resources.

III. We protect each library user's right to privacy and confidentiality with respect to information sought or received and resources consulted, borrowed, acquired or transmitted.

IV.   We respect intellectual property rights and advocate balance between the interests of information users and rights holders.

V.   We treat co-workers and other colleagues with respect, fairness, and good faith, and advocate conditions of employment that safeguard the rights and welfare of all employees of our institutions.

VI.   We do not advance private interests at the expense of library users, colleagues, or our employing institutions.

VII.   We distinguish between our personal convictions and professional duties and do not allow our personal beliefs to interfere with fair representation of the aims of our institutions or the provision of access to their information resources.

VIII.   We strive for excellence in the profession by maintaining and enhancing our own knowledge and skills, by encouraging the professional development of co-workers, and by fostering the aspirations of potential members of the profession.

Adopted June 28, 1997, by the ALA Council; amended January 22, 2008.

Association of Art Museum Directors

Code of Ethics

The position of a museum director is one of trust. The director will act with integrity and in accordance with the highest ethical principles. The director will avoid any and all activities that could compromise his/her position or the institution. The professional integrity of the director should set a standard for the staff. A museum director is obligated to implement the policy of the governing board for the benefit of the institution and the public. The director is responsible for ensuring that the institution adopt and disseminate a code of ethics for the museum board, staff, and volunteers.

It is unprofessional for a museum director to use his or her influence or position for personal gain. A director shall not deal in works of art or be party to the recommendation for purchase by museums or collectors of works of art in which the director has any undisclosed financial interest. The director shall not accept any commission or compromising gift from any seller or buyer of works of art.

If the director collects art, extraordinary discretion is required to assure that no conflict of interest arises between the director's personal collecting activity and the concerns of the museum. If there is perception of a conflict, the museum's governing board should be granted first option in acquiring for the museum the work or works in question. Gifts of works of art to the director by artists whose work is or may be shown or acquired by the museum can compromise the position of the director and of the institution and should be accepted only in special circumstances and with full disclosure. In such cases where there is the possibility of a perception of conflict of interest, the museum's governing board must be granted first option to accept these gifts for the museum.

A museum director shall not provide—for a fee or on a retainer—any certificate or statement as to the authenticity or authorship of a work of art, or any statement of the monetary value of a work of art.

A museum director should not knowingly acquire or allow to be rec-ommended for acquisition any object that has been stolen, removed in contravention of treaties or international conventions to which the United States is a signatory, or illegally imported in the United States.

A museum director shall not dispose of accessioned works of art in order to provide funds for purposes other than acquisitions of works of art for the collection.

AAMD members who violate this code of ethics will be subject to discipline by reprimand, suspension, or expulsion from the Association. Infractions by any art museum may expose that institution to sanctions, such as suspension of loans and shared exhibitions by AAMD members.

Adopted by the membership of the AAMD, June 1966; amended 1971, 1973, 1974, 1991, and 2001.

Association of Canadian Archivists

Code of Ethics

This Code consists of two parts: "Principles" and "Application of Principles."

Principles

1. Archivists appraise, select, acquire, preserve, and make available for use archival records, ensuring their intellectual integrity and promoting responsible physical custodianship of these records, for the benefit of present users and future generations.

2. Archivists have a responsibility to ensure that they and their colleagues are able to perform these and other professional activities in an environment free of discrimination and sexual or personal harassment.

3. Archivists encourage and promote the greatest possible use of the records in their care, giving due attention to personal privacy and confidentiality, and the preservation of records.

4. Archivists carry out their duties according to accepted archival principles and practices, to the best of their abilities, making every effort to promote and maintain the highest possible standards of conduct.

5. Archivists contribute to the advancement of archival studies by developing personal knowledge and skills, and by sharing this information and experience with members of archival and related professions.

6. Archivists use their specialized knowledge and experience for the benefit of society as a whole.

Applications of Principles

A. Appraisal, Selection, and Acquisition

A1.   Archivists appraise, select, and acquire records in accordance with their institutions' mandates and resources. These activities should be guided by consideration for the integrity of the fonds. Archivists document the criteria which governed the appraisal, selection, and acquisition of records.

A2.   Archivists do not compete for acquisitions when competition would endanger the safety of the records; they cooperate to ensure the preservation of records in repositories where they can be effectively managed and used.

A3.   Archivists, in determining acquisition, take into full consideration such factors as authority to transfer, donate or sell; financial arrangements, implications, and benefits; plans for processing; copyright, and conditions of access. Archivists discourage unreasonable restrictions on access or use, but may accept as a condition of acquisition clearly stated restrictions of limited duration and should suggest such restrictions to protect personal privacy. Archivists observe all agreements made at the time of transfer or acquisition.

A4.   Archivists appraise the monetary value of records for purchase or tax benefit for donation based on fair market value of the records at the time of purchase or deposit and in keeping with the principles, guidelines, and regulations established by relevant appraisal bodies and the government.

B. Preservation

B1. Archivists endeavour to protect the intellectual and physical integrity of the records in their care. Archivists document all actions which may alter the record.

B2. Archivists who find it necessary to deaccession archival records should make every effort to contact the donors or their representatives, and inform them of the decision. Archivists endeavour to offer the records to other repositories in preference to destruction. Archivists document all decisions and actions taken with regard to deaccessioning.

C. Availability and Use

C1. Archivists arrange and describe all records in their custody in order to facilitate the fullest possible access to and use of their records.

C2. Archivists make every attempt possible to respect the privacy of the individuals who created or are the subjects of records, especially those who had no voice in the disposition of the records. Archivists should not reveal or profit from information gained through work with restricted records.

C3. Archivists inform users of any restrictions on access and use placed on records. Archivists should apply all restrictions equitably.

C4. Archivists should endeavour to inform users of copyright restrictions on records, and inform users that it is their own responsibility to obtain copyright clearance from the copyright owners.

C5. Archivists protect each user's right to privacy with respect to information sought or received, and records consulted. Archivists may inform users of parallel research by others only with the prior agreement of the individuals concerned.

D. Professional Conduct

D1.   Archivists who use their institutions' records for personal research and/or publication must make these activities known to both their employers and to others using the same records. Archivists, when undertaking personal research, must not use their knowledge of other researchers' findings without first notifying those researchers about the use intended by the Archivist.

D2.   Archivists who acquire records personally, should inform their employers of their acquisition activities, should not compete for acquisitions with their own repositories, should not use privileged information obtained as a consequence of their employment to further these personal acquisition interests, and should maintain appropriate records of their acquisitions.

E. Advancement of Knowledge

E1.   Archivists share their knowledge and experience with other archivists for their mutual professional development.

E2.   Archivists share their specialized knowledge and experience with legislators and other policy-makers to assist them in formulating policies and making decisions in matters affecting the record-keeping environment.

Association of College and Research Libraries

Code of Ethics for Special Collections Librarians

Preamble

Special collections librarians share fundamental values with the entire library profession. They should be thoroughly familiar with the ALA Code of Ethics and must adhere to the principles of fairness, freedom, professional excellence, and respect for individual rights expressed therein. Furthermore, special collections librarians have extraordinary responsibilities and opportunities associated with the care of cultural property, the preservation of original artifacts, and the support of scholarship based on primary research materials. At times their commitment to free access to information may conflict with their mission to protect and preserve the objects in their care. When values come into conflict, librarians must bring their experience and judgment to bear on each case in order to arrive at the best solution, always bearing in mind that the constituency for special collections includes future generations.

Other stresses arise naturally from the fact that special collections often have great monetary as well as documentary and aesthetic value. Special collections librarians must exercise extreme caution in situations that have the potential to allow them to profit personally from library-related activities. The highest standard of behavior must be maintained, as propriety is essential to the maintenance of public trust in the institution and in its staff.

Definitions

Special collections librarian: An employee of a special collections library or any library staff member whose duties involve work with special collections materials. The principles in this Code relate primarily to professional staff (typically librarians, curators, archivists, and conservators), but all library staff members must be aware of the need to avoid potential and even apparent conflicts of interest.

Special collections library: A library, or an administrative unit (such as department) of a larger library, devoted to collecting, organizing, preserving, and describing special collections materials and making them accessible. Also referred to as "the institution."

Special collections materials: The entire range of textual, graphic and artifact primary source materials in analog and digital formats, including printed books, manuscripts, photographs, maps, artworks, audio-visual materials, and realia.

Code of Ethics

I.   Special collections librarians must not compete with their library in collecting or in any other activity.

II.   All outside employment and professional activities must be undertaken within the fundamental premise that the special collections librarian's first responsibility is to the library, that the activity will not interfere with the librarian's ability to discharge this responsibility, and that it will not compromise the library's professional integrity or reputation.

III. Special collections librarians must not engage in any dealing or appraisal of special collections materials, and they must not recommend materials for purchase if they have any undisclosed financial interest in them.

IV.   Special collections librarians must decline all gifts, loans, or other dispensations, or things of value that are available to them in connection with their duties for the library.

V.   Special collections librarians may not withhold information about the library's holdings or sequester collection materials in order to further their own research and publication.

VI. Special collections librarians are responsible for protecting the confidentiality of researchers and materials as required by legal statutes, donor agreements, or policies of the library.

Commentary

[Note: Articles I–V are based on Article VI of the ALA Code of Ethics ("We do not advance private interests at the expense of library users, colleagues, or our employing institutions"), and Article VI is based on Article III of the ALA Code ("We protect each library user's right to privacy and confidentiality with respect to information sought or received and resources consulted, borrowed, acquired or transmitted").]

I. Special collections librarians sometimes collect personally, as well as on behalf of their library. Personal collecting can add to the librarian's understanding of a collecting area and the marketplace for special collections materials. Consequently, personal collecting should not be discouraged. However, special collections librarians should disclose their personal collecting activity to their employer, especially when their collecting area coincides with that of the institution. When such coincidence occurs, the special collections librarian must not compete with the library, must not build his or her personal collection at the expense of the institution's collection, and must be diligent in distinguishing items acquired for the institution's collection from items acquired for the personal collection. In all instances, special collections librarians should conduct their personal collecting in a manner that avoids impropriety and prevents any appearance thereof.

II. Some forms of outside employment by librarians, such as teaching, lecturing, writing, and consulting, are conducive to professional development and benefit the library as well. Librarians have a primary responsibility to their institutions, and such employment must not interfere in any way with their principal duties. Since librarians engaged in independent outside employment may still be regarded as institutional representatives, their conduct should not compromise the library's reputation. Special collections librarians are encouraged to divulge all outside employment to the administration of their library.

III. "Dealing" is here defined as the regular purchase, sale, or trade of special collections materials for profit or other personal gain. "Appraisal" is here defined as the formal determination of the monetary value of special collections materials. Informal assessment and the valuation of such materials for internal administrative purposes are not considered appraisal. This provision grows out of the previous one and recognizes that potential conflicts of interest may arise when special collections librarians profit from the same materials they curate.

IV. All acquisitions decisions must be based on the professional judgment of the librarian, with due consideration given to the objectives and policies of the institution. While close relationships between librarians, dealers, and collectors are desirable, it is imperative that conflicts of interest do not arise. Conflicts clearly result when special collections librarians accept *substantial* gifts, loans, entertainment, or personal discounts from dealers, vendors, or donors. The issue of whether *any* entertainment should be accepted from these sources is problematic, and so librarians must make a judgment in each case as to whether the appearance of improper influence might result. Institutional policies regarding the acceptance of gifts or entertainment must also be observed. Special collections librarians should consider salaries and benefits provided by their institution to be the sole and complete remuneration for the performance of their duties.

V.   Personal research by special collections librarians should be encouraged since it furthers professional development and institutional aims. However, a librarian should not withhold information about library holdings from the public at large in order to further personal research. The library's rules for access and use must be applied and enforced equally, according to the terms of the ALA/SAA *Joint Statement on Access to Original Research Materials*. Special collections librarians are encouraged to obtain approval for anything other than incidental use of institutional facilities, staff, or equipment for personal research.

VI.   The special collections professional must heed all laws and contractual agreements protecting the privacy and confidentiality of researchers and materials in the custody of the repository. Failure to do so can expose the custodial institution to significant legal penalties, as well as undermine confidence that donors and sellers place in the institution. The nature of the information protected and the duration of protection are specified in federal and state laws addressing privacy and confidentiality of information. Other restrictions are the result of negotiations between donors and sellers on the one hand and repositories on the other. The terms of these restrictions imposed by donor or institution are not dictated by statute but are legally binding. Special collections librarians must take care to honor those terms, but they should also refuse to impose or accept restrictions that severely diminish the research value of materials being acquired.

Application

One of the most important functions of a professional association is to define the shared values of its members by creating a written code of ethics. This code of ethics should not only be observed by special collections librarians but must also be reflected in the policies and procedures of their institutions. Educators should incorporate the code of ethics into the curriculum when appropriate, and the code should guide administrators in the recruitment and training of staff. Special collections librarians should also make donors, vendors, and allied professional associations aware of the code. To remain vital, these principles of conduct must be integrated into the life of the profession.

The *ACRL RBMS Code of Ethics for Special Collections Librarians* is reprinted with express permission of the Association of College and Research Libraries. *Standards for Ethical Conduct for Rare Book, Manuscript, and Special Collections Librarians* first appeared in 1987 and was designed to amplify and supplement the American Library Association Code of Ethics. A second edition of the Standards was approved by ACRL in 1993. This version, recast as a simplified *Code of Ethics for Special Collections Librarians* with commentary, was approved by ACRL in October 2003. It is officially published on the ACRL website at: http/www.rbms.info/standards/code_of_ethics.shtml.

Institute of Certified Records Managers

Code of Ethics

Certified Records Managers should maintain high professional standards of conduct in the performance of their duties. The Code of Ethics is provided as a guide to professional conduct.

1. Certified Records Managers have a professional responsibility to conduct themselves so that their good faith and integrity shall not be open to question. They will promote the highest possible records management standards.

2. Certified Records Managers shall conform to existing laws and regulations covering the creation, maintenance, and disposition of recorded information, and shall never knowingly be parties to any illegal or improper activities relative thereto.

3. Certified Records Managers shall be prudent in the use of information acquired in the course of their duties. They should protect confidential, proprietary and trade secret information obtained from others and use it only for the purposes approved by the party from whom it was obtained or for the benefit of that party, and not for the personal gain of anyone else.

4. Certified Records Managers shall not accept gifts or gratuities from clients, business associates, or suppliers as inducements to influence any procurements or decisions they may make.

5. Certified Records Managers shall use all reasonable care to obtain factual evidence to support their opinion.

6. Certified Records Managers shall strive for continuing proficiency and effectiveness in their profession and shall contribute to further research, development, and

education. It is their professional responsibility to encourage those interested in records management and offer assistance whenever possible to those who enter the profession and to those already in the profession.

Ethics Review Procedure

If it is felt that a Certified Records Manager (CRM) has violated the Code of Ethics of the Institute of Certified Records Managers (ICRM), a letter stating such must be sent to the President of the ICRM, 403 East Taft Road, North Syracuse, NY 13212, U.S.A. This letter must identify the CRM, state the nature of the ethics violation charge and request that the ICRM investigate the matter. The person(s) making the charge must identify themselves. The ICRM will keep the identification of the person(s) making the charge confidential.

Upon receipt of this letter, the President of the ICRM will establish an *ad hoc* Ethics Committee and identify three individuals to serve on it, subject to the approval of the Board of Regents. No current member of the Board may serve on this *ad hoc* committee.

This Committee will be provided the letter requesting the review. The Committee will contact the person(s) making the accusation and obtain from them all available information on the issue. The Committee will also contact all involved parties, including the accused CRM to obtain any additional facts.

The Committee will consider the information gathered and reach a ruling for the Board. The ruling must reflect a unanimous vote of the Ethics Committee, repudiating or substantiating the ethics violation charge(s).

If a CRM has been cleared of the charges, a letter stating such shall be sent to all people contacted during the investigation.

If the Committee is unable to reach a unanimous decision concerning the charges, a second committee consisting of three non-Board CRMs will be formed to consider the case. They will operate in the same manner as the first committee. If the second committee cannot reach a decision, then all charges will be dropped against the CRM. A letter stating such will be sent to all people contacted during the investigation.

If the CRM has been found to be in violation of the Code of Ethics of the ICRM, then that individual shall be notified by the Secretary of the ICRM that they can no longer use the CRM designation. The CRM will not be eligible to apply for membership in the ICRM for a minimum of 5 years, at which time they must submit an application, be accepted to sit for the exam based on the qualifications in force at that time, take and pass all parts of the examination prior to regaining the status of CRM.

All Ethics Committee proceedings are confidential. No information on the case, either factual or non-factual, will be presented to the Board. The ruling of the Ethics Committee will be final. The Committee will seal the file after all business has been completed. The sealed file will be placed in the archives of the ICRM and confidentially destroyed after 10 years.

International Council on Archives

Code of Ethics

Introduction

A.   A code of ethics for archivists should establish high standards of conduct for the archival profession.

> It should introduce new members of the profession to those standards, remind experienced archivists of their professional responsibilities and inspire public confidence in the profession.

B.   The term archivists as used in this code is intended to encompass all those concerned with the control, care, custody, preservation and administration of archives.

C.   Employing institutions and archive services should be encouraged to adopt policies and practices that facilitate the implementation of this code.

D.   This code is intended to provide an ethical framework for guidance of members of the profession, and not to provide specific solutions to particular problems.

E.   The principles are all accompanied by a commentary; principles and commentary taken together constitute the Code of Ethics.

F.   The code is dependent upon the willingness of archival institutions and professional associations to implement it. This may take the form of an educational effort and the establishment of machinery to provide guidance in cases of doubt, to investigate unethical conduct, and if considered appropriate, to apply sanctions.

Code

1. Archivists should protect the integrity of archival material and thus guarantee that it continues to be reliable evidence of the past.

    > The primary duty of archivists is to maintain the integrity of the records in their care and custody. In the accomplishment of this duty they must have regard to the legitimate, but sometimes conflicting, rights and interests of employers, owners, data subjects and users, past, present and future. The objectivity and impartiality of archivists is the measure of their professionalism. They should resist pressure from any source to manipulate evidence so as to conceal or distort facts.

2. Archivists should appraise, select and maintain archival material in its historical, legal and administrative context, thus retaining the principle of provenance, preserving and making evident the original relationships of documents.

    > Archivists must act in accordance with generally accepted principles and practice. Archivists must perform their duties and functions in accordance with archival principles, with regard to the creation, maintenance and disposition of current and semi-current records, including electronic and multimedia records, the selection and acquisition of records for archival custody, the safeguarding, preservation and conservation of archives in their care, and the arrangement, description, publication and making available for use of those documents. Archivists should appraise records impartially basing their judgment on a thorough knowledge of their institution's administrative requirements and acquisitions policies. They should arrange and describe records selected

for retention in accordance with archival principles (namely the principle of provenance and the principle of original order) and accepted standards, as rapidly as their resources permit. Archivists should acquire records in accordance with the purposes and resources of their institutions. They should not seek or accept acquisitions when this would endanger the integrity or security of records; they should cooperate to ensure the preservation of these records in the most appropriate repository. Archivists should cooperate in the repatriation of displaced archives.

3.   Archivists should protect the authenticity of documents during archival processing, preservation and use.

Archivists should ensure that the archival value of records, including electronic or multimedia records is not impaired in the archival work of appraisal, arrangement and description, and of conservation and use. Any sampling should be carried out according to carefully established methods and criteria. Replacement of originals with other formats should be done in the light of the legal, intrinsic and information value of the records. Where restricted documents have been temporarily removed from a file, this fact should be made known to the user.

4.   Archivists should ensure the continuing accessibility and intelligibility of archival materials.

Archivists should select documents to be kept or to be destroyed primarily to save essential testimony of the activity of the person or the institution which produced and accumulated the documents but also bearing in mind changing research needs. Archivists should be aware that acquiring documents of dubious origin, however interesting, could encourage an illegal commerce. They should cooperate with other archivists and law enforcement agencies engaged in apprehending and prosecuting persons suspected of theft of archival records.

5.   Archivists should record, and be able to justify, their actions on archival material.

> Archivists should advocate good recordkeeping practices throughout the life-cycle of documents and cooperate with record creators in addressing new formats and new information management practices. They should be concerned not only with acquiring existing records, but also ensure that current information and archival systems incorporate from the very beginning procedures appropriate to preserve valuable records. Archivists negotiating with transferring officials or owners of records should seek fair decisions based on full consideration—when applicable—of the following factors: authority to transfer, donate, or sell; financial arrangements and benefits; plans for processing; copyright and conditions of access. Archivists should keep a permanent record documenting accessions, conservation and all archival work done.

6.   Archivists should promote the widest possible access to archival material and provide an impartial service to all users.

> Archivists should produce both general and particular finding aids as appropriate, for all of the records in their custody. They should offer impartial advice to all, and employ available resources to provide a balanced range of services. Archivists should answer courteously and with a spirit of helpfulness all reasonable inquiries

about their holdings, and encourage the use of them to the greatest extent possible, consistent with institutional policies, the preservation of holdings, legal considerations, individual rights, and donor agreements. They should explain pertinent restrictions to potential users, and apply them equitably. Archivists should discourage unreasonable restrictions on access and use but may suggest or accept as a condition for acquisition clearly stated restrictions of limited duration. They should observe faithfully and apply impartially all agreements made at the time of acquisition, but, in the interest of liberalisation of access, should renegotiate conditions in accordance with changes of circumstance.

7.   Archivists should respect both access and privacy, and act within the boundaries of relevant legislation.

Archivists should take care that corporate and personal privacy as well as national security are protected without destroying information, especially in the case of electronic records where updating and erasure are common practice. They must respect the privacy of individuals who created or are the subjects of records, especially those who had no voice in the use or disposition of the materials.

8.   Archivists should use the special trust given to them in the general interest and avoid using their position to unfairly benefit themselves or others.

Archivists must refrain from activities which might prejudice their professional integrity, objectivity and impartiality. They should not benefit financially or otherwise personally to the detriment of institutions, users and colleagues. Archivists should not collect original documents or participate in any commerce of documents on their own behalf. They should avoid activities that could create in the public mind the appearance of a conflict of interest. Archivists may use their institutional holdings for personal research and publication, provided such work is done on the same terms as others using the same holdings. They should not reveal or use information gained through work with holdings to which access is restricted. They should not allow their private research and publication interests to interfere with the proper performance of the professional or administrative duties for which they are employed. When using the holdings of their institutions, archivists must not use their knowledge of the unpublished findings of researchers, without first notifying the researchers about the intended use by the archivist. They may review and comment on the work of others in their fields, including works based on documents of their own institutions. Archivists should not allow people outside the profession to interfere in their practice and obligations.

9.   Archivists should pursue professional excellence by systematically and continuously updating their archival knowledge, and sharing the results of their research and experience.

Archivists should endeavour to develop their professional understanding and expertise, to contribute to the body of professional knowledge, and to ensure that those whose training or activities they supervise are equipped to carry out their tasks in a competent manner.

10.   Archivists should promote the preservation and use of the world's documentary heritage, through working co-operatively with the members of their own and other professions.

Archivists should seek to enhance cooperation and avoid conflict with their professional colleagues and to resolve difficulties by encouraging adherence to archival standards and ethics. Archivists should cooperate with members of related professions on the basis of mutual respect and understanding.

Adopted by the General Assembly of the International Council on Archives in its XIIIth session in Beijing, China, September 6, 1996.

Reproduced with the permission of the International Council on Archives.

The Manuscript Society

Code of Ethics

Article 1

All members of The Manuscript Society, institutional or individual, upon receipt of their application for membership or annual dues payment notice, new or renewed, are required to accept and agree to this Society's Code of Ethics. Acceptance shall be indicated by payment of the annual membership dues. Payment evidences acceptance of the Code of Ethics, and is an agreement that the breach of any of the Code provisions could subject the member to expulsion.

Article 2

Society members are required to abide by all Federal, state, and local laws and regulations related to purchase, sale, or related transactions concerned with the securing of autographs or autograph-related items. Any member's criminal act or misdemeanor, including but not limited to, the use, conversion, alienation, destruction, purchase or sale of manuscripts for which a member has been convicted in a court of law may subject the member to expulsion.

Article 3

Members agree not to purchase or sell any known stolen autographs or related items. Sellers are to pass on to buyers clear title to all materials sold.

Article 4

No member of the Society shall knowingly breach the terms of his contract to buy, sell or exchange manuscripts, except as permitted or required by law. No manuscript which is not authentic shall be knowingly purchased, sold or exchanged by a member of the Society unless all elements relating to its lack of authenticity are described in writing, provided to other parties to any transaction as an essential element thereof, and accompany the manuscript in question at the time of its delivery to the new owner.

Article 5

No member of the Society shall knowingly advertise to sell or exchange any manuscripts any element of which is not authentic (including signatures produced by mechanical reproduction, printed facsimiles of manuscripts and alterations to any manuscript in question) unless such element is described with particularity, in writing, in such advertisement.

Article 6

Legal defenses notwithstanding, any member of the Society who has sold or exchanged a manuscript not subject to the exceptions set forth in Article 4, that has proven not to be authentic in any respect, shall immediately give the holder, in exchange for said manuscript, the full value such member realized at the time he sold or exchanged said manuscript. An invoice or receipt (or copy thereof) issued at the time of such transaction shall be deemed conclusive proof of the value realized by such member.

Article 7

The seller is required to state in writing the terms in which he or she sells autographs or related materials, and to include a reasonable right to return items with a guarantee of a full refund on returned material. The purchaser has the right to return items received which are not as described by the seller.

Article 8

Sellers may advertise for sale only those items which are available at the time of their advertisement, and will honor all prices for a reasonable time after their publication.

Article 9

Persons involved in consignments of autographs or related materials are to make a written agreement concerning all of the elements of the consigned property, as well as terms of payment to both the consignor and consignee. The seller must agree not to alter any of the material he is handling on a consignment basis without written approval from the consignor.

Article 10

Members are responsible for items sent to them to examine for possible purchase. The sender is to supply a complete listing of all items included in the shipment. Should an offer to purchase prove to be unacceptable, the merchandise must be returned to the owner in at least the same manner it was shipped.

Article 11

Individual members or applicants for membership are to provide the Society with their full names and mailing addresses, and should notify the Society of any changes of name or address within 30 days of such change. Corporate or institutional members must provide the names and mailing address of the principal officer or designated legal representative, and should also notify the Society of changes of corporate or institution name, principal officer or designated legal representative, or address within 30 days of such change.

Article 12

Members are expected to cooperate with law enforcement authorities and the Society's Ethics Board, as well as kindred Boards of Societies operated by collectors and dealers in manuscripts, in their investigations of allegations concerning thefts of autographs, manuscripts and the like and trafficking in stolen materials. Members will cooperate with such individuals in efforts to return such materials to their rightful owners. Members who are able are encouraged to assist law enforcement authorities in apprehending and prosecuting those persons accused of theft or of trafficking in stolen autograph materials.

Article 13

A member's alleged violation of any Manuscript Society Code Article may be grounds for suspension or expulsion by a 2/3 vote of the Board of Trustees. Such action shall be taken only after a 30-day written notice shall have been forwarded by receipted letter to such member, together with a copy of the charges, and a date set by which the said member should present his or her written defense by mail or otherwise. A sanctioned party shall have a right of Final Appeal to the Manuscript Society's Executive Officers.

Adopted by the Board of Trustees of the Manuscript Society on May 26, 1999.

National Archives and Records Administration

The Archivist's Code

Note: The Archivist's Code, presented below, was developed by the National Archives in 1955 to guide staff in making professional decisions. For many years, it was the only written guidance on this topic for the archival profession in the United States. Although the guidance remains sound even today, as archival issues increased in complexity the profession saw the need for a fuller code of ethics. Accordingly, in 1992, the Council of the Society of American Archivists adopted the Code of Ethics for Archivists (see page 335).

The Archivist has a moral obligation to society to take every possible measure to ensure the preservation of valuable records, not only those of the past but those of his own times, and with equal zeal.

The Archivist in appraising records for retention or disposal acts as the agent of future generations. The wisdom and impartiality he applies to this task measure his professionalism, for he must be as diligent in disposing of records that have no significant or lasting value as in retaining those that do.

The Archivist must protect the integrity of records in his custody. He must guard them against defacement, alteration, or theft; he must protect them against physical damage by fire or excessive exposure to light, dampness, and dryness; and he must ensure that their evidentiary value is not impaired in the normal course of rehabilitation, arrangement, and use.

The Archivist should endeavor to promote access to records to the fullest extent consistent with the public interest, but he should carefully observe any proper restrictions on the use of records. He should work unremittingly for the increase and diffusion of knowledge, making his documentary holdings freely known to prospective users through published finding aids and personal consultation.

The Archivist should respond courteously and with a spirit of helpfulness to reference requests. He should not place unnecessary obstacles in the way of researchers but should do whatever he can to save their time and ease their work. He should not idly discuss the work and findings of one researcher with another; but where duplication of research effort is apparent, he may properly inform another researcher.

The Archivist should not profit from any commercial exploitation of the records in his custody, nor should he withhold from others any information he has gained as a result of his official duties—either in order to carry out private professional research or to aid one researcher at the expense of another. He should, however, take every legitimate advantage of his situation to develop his professional interests in historical and archival research.

The Archivist should freely pass on to his professional colleagues the results of his own or his organization's research that add to the body of archival and historical knowledge. He should leave to his successors a true account of the records in his custody and of their organization and arrangement.

Wayne C. Grover
Archivist of the United States
1948–1965

The Society of American Archivists

Code of Ethics for Archivists

Preamble

The Code of Ethics for Archivists establishes standards for the archival profession. It introduces new members of the profession to those standards, reminds experienced archivists of their professional responsibilities, and serves as a model for institutional policies. It also is intended to inspire public confidence in the profession.

This code provides an ethical framework to guide members of the profession. It does not provide the solution to specific problems.

The term "archivist" as used in this code encompasses all those concerned with the selection, control, care, preservation, and administration of historical and documentary records of enduring value.

I. **Purpose**

The Society of American Archivists recognizes the importance of educating the profession and general public about archival ethics by codifying ethical principles to guide the work of archivists. This code provides a set of principles to which archivists aspire.

II. **Professional Relationships**

Archivists select, preserve, and make available historical and documentary records of enduring value. Archivists cooperate, collaborate, and respect each institution and its mission and collecting policy. Respect and cooperation form the basis of all professional relationships with colleagues and users.

III. **Judgment**

Archivists should exercise professional judgment in acquiring, appraising, and processing historical materials. They should not allow personal beliefs or perspectives to affect their decisions.

IV.   Trust

Archivists should not profit or otherwise benefit from their privileged access to and control of historical records and documentary materials.

V.   Authenticity and Integrity

Archivists strive to preserve and protect the authenticity of records in their holdings by documenting their creation and use in hard copy and electronic formats. They have a fundamental obligation to preserve the intellectual and physical integrity of those records.

Archivists may not alter, manipulate, or destroy data or records to conceal facts or distort evidence.

VI.   Access

Archivists strive to promote open and equitable access to their services and the records in their care without discrimination or preferential treatment, and in accordance with legal requirements, cultural sensitivities, and institutional policies. Archivists recognize their responsibility to promote the use of records as a fundamental purpose of the keeping of archives. Archivists may place restrictions on access for the protection of privacy or confidentiality of information in the records.

VII.   Privacy

Archivists protect the privacy rights of donors and individuals or groups who are the subject of records. They respect all users' right to privacy by maintaining the confidentiality of their research and protecting any personal information collected about them in accordance with the institution's security procedures.

VIII. Security/Protection

Archivists protect all documentary materials for which they are responsible and guard them against defacement, physical damage, deterioration, and theft. Archivists should cooperate with colleagues and law enforcement agencies to apprehend and prosecute thieves and vandals.

IX. Law

Archivists must uphold all federal, state, and local laws.

Approved by the Council of the Society of American Archivists, February 5, 2005.

APPENDIX B

Sample Text of Acquisitions Guidelines and Collections Management Policy

The following text is reproduced from the website of the American Heritage Center of the University of Wyoming as a sample of an especially detailed and thoughtfully crafted policy statement. It covers acquisitions, management, and deaccessioning policies. For the latest version please consult the website at http://ahc.uwyo.edu/about/policies.htm. These guidelines are reproduced with the permission of the American Heritage Center director, Mark A. Greene. Many other such samples are available in manuals and on websites.

American Heritage Center

Acquisitions Guidelines

The American Heritage Center, an archival research institution at the University of Wyoming, acquires specific material relating to its core collecting areas: Wyoming and the Rocky Mountain West (including but not limited to politics, settlement, and western trails) environment and conservation, the mining and petroleum industries, air and ground transportation, the performing arts (particularly radio, television, film, and popular music), journalism, U.S. military history. In addition, the AHC maintains one of the largest and finest collections of rare books between the Mississippi and the West Coast, and is glad to consider donations to that collection. The AHC is also the archives for the University of Wyoming. The AHC is a public research repository, and accepts donations of collections with the primary purpose of making those collections available to students, scholars, and the general public.

The following document provides guidelines regarding the responsibilities of the Center to its donors, the conditions under which a donation may be accepted, and the types of material collected by the Center for the use of its patrons.

When accepting material, the American Heritage Center is responsible for:

1.   Maintaining the materials, ensuring accepted practice for preservation and security, preparing the materials for research use through professional arrangement and description and making them available in our research area to interested researchers on an equal basis during regular business hours.

2.   Ensuring that the use of any material identified as sensitive by the donor is restricted from use in accordance with an agreement in writing accepted by both the donor and

the AHC. The AHC cannot accept collections that are restricted indefinitely or for which the restriction cannot be enforced or applied equally to all researchers.

3. Returning to the donor, offering to another institution, or discarding materials that the AHC wishes to remove from the collection, in accordance with the donor's instructions in a written agreement accepted by both the donor and the AHC.

4. Securing legal documentation for every gift that makes clear the terms of the transfer and any instructions of the donor. The AHC only accepts collections for which legal title to the physical items is transferred to the University of Wyoming by deed of gift.

5. Asking donors to donate not only the physical papers but also any copyright in them that the donor might own. (Ownership of copyright is separable from ownership of the physical item—the letter or photo.) This request is made to make it easier for researchers to use quotations from the papers in their work. However, the AHC will consider donation of the physical material without donation of copyright.

When accepting material the American Heritage Center cannot:

1. Accept donations without transfer of title.

2. Accept material for which the donor does not have clear title.

3. Provide appraisals of the monetary value of gifts. This is forbidden by IRS regulations.

4. Accept liability for loss or damage of materials due to deterioration, fire, or other disasters which befall the material or are inherent within it.

Types of Material Collected

Personal Papers from Individuals

While it is important that AHC staff be permitted to survey papers or records in order to determine which materials have enduring historical value, listed below are types of materials that are often valuable to a researcher. This list, which is suggestive and not definitive, illustrates the wide range of documentation sometimes useful for historical and administrative research. If you have any questions about this list, please ask a member of our staff.

AHC generally acquires:

- Personal and professional correspondence
- Diaries, memoirs, or journals
- Research files compiled or created by the donor
- Final drafts of unpublished works (television and movie scripts may be an exception, where certain early drafts may be of interest)
- Personal or professional scrapbooks and memorabilia created by or directly relating to the donor
- Clearly identified photographs taken by or directly relating to the donor
- Clearly identified sound recordings, video tape, or movie film created by or directly relating to the donor
- Artistic or other creative materials produced by the donor or which have a direct correlation to the donor's collection
- Books, articles, scripts, music, pamphlets, or other material written or published by the donor or about the donor

AHC generally does not acquire:

- Personal financial records including checks or income tax returns
- Medical records

- Duplicates of any items
- General readership books, periodicals, or other printed material not written by or about the donor
- Art and artifacts
- Galleys, proofs, and final drafts of published works

Organizations and Institutions

Many of the records produced by an organization have long-term value. The AHC is interested in the records that best illustrate the purpose, activities, and policies of an organization. Such documents usually represent an "end product"—a final report, for example, instead of a draft. We are more interested in related groups of materials rather than individual items. Records should be inactive—that is, no longer regularly used for routine business. Before records are transferred to the AHC, an archivist should survey the organization's papers or speak with knowledgeable staff to determine which materials have enduring historical value. Listed below are some of the types of documentation that the AHC often preserves for historical and administrative research:

AHC generally acquires:

- Minutes
- Correspondence
- Annual reports
- Articles of incorporation and bylaws
- Financial ledgers up to 1900
- Non-confidential personnel rosters, directories, and similar records
- Annual or semi-annual balance statements
- Subject files
- Printed material including pamphlets, brochures, catalogs, newsletters, periodicals, etc., produced by the organization

AHC generally does not acquire:

- Personnel time cards, payroll documents, or confidential files
- Day-to-day financial records such as bank statements, canceled checks, receipts, daily balances
- Invoices
- General readership books, periodicals, or other printed materials not created by the organization (exceptions may be made for books, periodicals, or pamphlets of unique historical interest)
- Art and artifacts

American Heritage Center

Collections Management Policy

Mission

The American Heritage Center (AHC) is the repository for the University of Wyoming's (UW) special collections and archives, including the university's rare books library and one of the largest manuscript collections in the U.S. The American Heritage Center aspires to be widely acknowledged—by the University community, by the people of Wyoming, by scholars world-wide, and by our professional peers—as one of the nation's finest special collections repositories, bringing international distinction to the University of Wyoming by advancing scholarly research and education at the university and beyond. Our mission is to preserve a clearly defined set of primary sources and rare books—reflecting the written, image, and audio history of Wyoming, the Rocky Mountain Region, and select aspects of the American past—and to make those sources accessible to all. Our diverse collections support casual inquiry and international scholarship; most importantly, we play an active and creative role in the teaching, research, and service missions of the University.

Introduction

The AHC acquires and manages its collections in accordance with pre-vailing professional standards, state statutes, university regulations, and all relevant federal law. Specifically, the AHC collections management looks to standards and best practices defined by the Society of American Archivists, the American Library Association (and in particular its Rare Books and Manuscripts Section and Association of College and Research Libraries), the Association of Research Libraries, the American Association of Museums (particularly regarding deaccessioning), the Oral History Association, and the National Association of Government Archivists and Records Administrators. Particularly relevant university regulations are Regulations of the Trustees, Chapter IV, University Regulations 1 and

490. University records are governed by Wyoming Statutes 9-2-410 and 16-4-201.

For the purposes of this policy, the AHC is composed of three distinct collections: Manuscripts, Rare Books, and University Archives. For purposes of this policy, the Manuscripts collections encompass not only manuscripts as such, but sound and visual materials, oral history, maps, art,[1] and artifacts. Rare Books signifies the material collected and curated by the Toppan Library, which includes some non-book material. University Archives consist of those official records of the university deemed to have long-term historical value, and certain collections of private papers—such as the records of student organizations—with inextricable significance to the university's history. These three collections have separate collecting policies, acquisition procedures, and use policies, but share loan policies, and deaccession policies.

In all its collecting and collection management, the AHC cooperates with other collecting units on campus (particularly the UW Libraries and UW Art Museum), in the state (particularly the Wyoming State Archives and the Buffalo Bill Historical Center), in the region (particularly the major manuscript repositories in Colorado), and in the nation. Such cooperation not only fosters economy and efficiency in resource allocation, it should ultimately best serve the needs of students, scholars, and other researchers.

Manuscript Collections

At approximately 75,000 cubic feet, the AHC's manuscript collection is one of the largest in the United States. The Society of American Archivists' *A Glossary of Archival and Records Terminology* (2005) defines "manuscripts collection": "Although manuscript literally means handwritten, 'manuscript collection' is often used to include collections of mixed media in which unpublished materials predominate. They may also include typescripts, photographs, diaries, scrapbooks, news clippings, and printed works." Manuscripts collections may contain some printed/published material, but generally speaking printed/published material is collected and cataloged by libraries. Manuscripts collections include those created by individual and families, and those created by organizations such as businesses, fraternal groups, and non-profits. Manuscripts collections are also often referred to as "papers" (when discussing material generated by individuals and families) and "records" (when discussing material generated by organizations).

Collecting Policy

The collecting goals for this collection have varied greatly between the time of the AHC's founding in 1945 and this current iteration. The American Heritage Center accepts personal papers, the records of organizations, photographs, audio-visual materials, and other materials with likely value for research or teaching, across a specific set of geographical and topical categories. The collecting categories pursued by the AHC are defined in the Center's Manuscripts Collecting Policy, found at http://ahc.uwyo.edu/documents/about/administration/AHC%20Collecting%20Policy%20(3)%20rev.doc.

Acquisition Policy

The AHC accepts donations of as little as a single item and as large as hundreds of boxes. Material need not be organized; it need not be "old"; and it need not relate to a famous individual, event, or organization in order for it to be historically significant. Generally, however, we are more interested in a coherent body of material rather than individual items; photos, tapes, and films should be identified.

Types of material collected. With the important exception of the university's own records (see University Archives, below), the AHC collects only material created or collected by private individuals and organizations and not from units of government. Listed below are types of materials that are (and are not) often accepted as part of personal papers or organizational records. These lists are suggestive and not definitive. Additional information about types of material accepted and not accepted will be found in the descriptions of specific topical areas, below.

Individual and Family Papers

- letters
- memoirs/reminiscences
- diaries
- scrapbooks/photo albums
- professional papers
- family histories
- speeches/lectures
- business records
- final drafts of unpublished works
- legal documents
- visual materials produced by the donor such as posters, designs, blue prints, etc.
- publications, scripts, music, or other materials written by the donor
- brochures and flyers
- photographs (labeled)—including digital
- films/videos/audio tapes (labeled)
- emails
- personal websites and podcasts

Files relating to the individual's civic, business, religious, political, and social activities may also be of interest.

Records from Organizations and Institutions

Many of the records produced by an organization have long-term value. The AHC is interested in the records that best illustrate the purpose, activities, and policies of an organization. Such documents usually represent an "end product"—a final report, for example, instead of a draft. Generally related groups of materials rather than individual items are of historical interest. Records should be inactive—that is, no longer regularly used for routine business.

- Annual financial records
- Architectural records
- Articles of incorporation, charters
- Audio recordings
- Budgets (annual)
- Bylaws and revisions
- Clippings (about the organization)
- Constitution and revisions
- Correspondence and email of officers
- Directories
- Handbooks
- Legal documents
- Memoranda
- Minutes of meetings
- Membership lists
- Motion picture film and videotape (labeled)
- Newsletters and other publications (generated by the organization)
- Organizational charts
- Pamphlets, brochures, fliers, etc.
- Photographs (labeled)—includes digital
- Planning documents
- Press releases
- Reports (annual, committee, etc.)

- Rosters
- Scrapbooks
- Speeches
- Topical files
- Websites and podcasts

The AHC, like most repositories, may not accept everything that is offered to it because of staff and space constraints. Even material in the categories above may be removed from collections at the time of accessioning or during processing, if AHC archivists judge the material not to have sufficient historical and research value to warrant retaining. In addition, there are several categories of material that will generally not be accepted (or will be separated from collections when found).

Types of Material Generally Not Collected by the AHC

While there may be exceptions, the following types of material are usually not accepted by the AHC as collections or parts of collections:

- Records of government entities (with the exception of the records of UW itself)
- Records of primarily genealogical value (including sacramental records from churches)
- Records of primarily scientific value (including mining and petroleum test records)
- Detailed engineering drawings
- Duplicates
- General readership books, periodicals, or other printed material not written by the donor. The AHC does not acquire secondary sources to support research in its collections; such acquisitions are recommended to UW Libraries for their decision. **NB: Rare books or special collections of books, periodicals, or pamphlets of unique historical interest may be collected by the AHC's rare book library.**

- Art and artifacts

- Personnel time cards, payroll documents, and confidential files

- Day-to-day financial records (particularly from the 20th century) such as bank statements, canceled checks, receipts, invoices, and daily balances

Topical and Geographic Collecting Areas. UW's 2003 pre-planning document, *Moving Forward III*, notes that "the principal collection and preservation endeavors of the Center" will focus on Wyoming and West. However, as MFII also acknowledges, "UW still faces curricular challenges in counterbalancing the distinctive culture of the Mountain West with the rich array of cultures that characterize both the global community of scholars and the broader world that our students will enter," and to that end the AHC will also pursue judiciously select areas of national collecting.

Because the current state of Wyoming was part of various federal territories, and because even today family, social, cultural, political, natural resource, and business boundaries do not precisely follow state boundaries, this geographic focus is not precise. Within the general goal of documenting the history and peoples of Wyoming, the AHC collects broadly both in terms of types of material and in terms of topics/creators. The AHC is interested in documenting such topics as business (including but not limited to agriculture and ranching, transportation, mining, and petroleum); charitable, benevolent, and fraternal organizations; conservation and environmentalism; education; journalism; labor; military; arts, culture, and entertainment; politics, law, and public affairs; religion; race and ethnicity. This list is suggestive, rather than all-inclusive.

The AHC's specific areas of national documentation, along with additional details concerning Wyoming-related collecting, will be found in the separate "Collection Development Plan." There is a long tradition of special collections—at both land grant and private universities—collecting nationally in well-defined areas.[2] "As one of the nation's premier research universities," UW should be part of this broad humanistic tradition.

Conditions governing material to be acquired by the AHC. There are professional standards governing the conditions under which repositories should and should not accept collections. The information immediately below is largely adapted from the Society of American Archivists' *A Guide to Donating Your Personal or Family Papers to a Repository* (http://www. archivists.org/catalog/donating-familyrecs.asp) and *A Guide to Donating Your Organizational Records to a Repository* (http://www.archivists.org/ catalog/donating-orgrecs.asp).

1. The material must fit the current Collection Development Plan of the Center.

2. The donor must be the owner of the collection or be authorized by the owner to transfer title to the collection to the Center. The donor must sign a deed of gift, transferring title to the physical property, within a reasonable period of time after receipt of the property by AHC. The AHC will also seek, but will not require, formal transfer of the owner's copyrights in the collection.[3] The AHC can only invest materials and labor in the preservation of items that it owns. Therefore, we accept donations of collections, but will not accept such material on deposit or on loan.

3. The AHC is not able to promise that donated materials will be placed on exhibit or used in some other specific fashion as a condition of accepting the gift.

4. Material must undergo archival appraisal and will be retained only if it has research value, documented authenticity, and exists in reasonable physical condition. The material must be in a format that allows the Center to preserve it and make it available for research. Material may be rejected if conservation costs to restore material are excessive. Likewise, material may be rejected if the resources necessary to process, store, and/or make it accessible to

researchers are beyond the AHC's capacity or outweigh the likely research value.

5. The collection must be free of legal encumbrances and not received with any undue restrictions. While the AHC desires to make all papers freely accessible to researchers, it will agree to reasonable and equitable restrictions for limited periods of time.

6. AHC staff cannot give tax advice, nor are they permitted to appraise the monetary value of a collection. In certain circumstances, it may be possible for a donor to take a tax deduction for the donation of a manuscript collection to a repository. Donors are encouraged to speak with their tax accountants or attorneys about this possibility. AHC staff may be able to provide a donor with a list of local manuscript appraisers who can (for a fee) make monetary appraisals for the donor. It is up to the donor to arrange for and bear the cost of any such appraisal.

7. The donor gives consent to the Center to digitally reformat the collection or migrate existing digital content to new technical environments as appropriate for preservation and/or access purposes. However, this is not a commitment to digitize the collection. The AHC does not have the resources to digitize collections, or significant portions of collections, for donors. Exceptions may be made in instances where the donor is able and willing to support additional resources for a digitization project, through donation of funds; such exceptions will be made on a case by case basis by the director.

Acquisitions Process

1. The AHC acquires manuscript collections in the following ways: (1) additions to already accepted collections; (2) donations; (3) purchases. Additions to existing collections

(referred to internally at AHC as "accretions") are accessioned based on the professional judgment of the Manager of Archives Services, guided by the "types of material accepted" guidelines. Recommendations about new collections for donation or purchase are welcome from anyone. All proposed collections will be sent to the Center's Acquisitions Committee.

2. The Center's Acquisitions Committee will meet weekly. Representatives from the Center's reference, arrangement and description, accessioning, university archives, and administrative areas will serve on the committee. A representative from the rare books library will attend on occasion to present significant new acquisitions, when requested by the committee chair, or to propose a deaccession. Either the director or associate director will chair the committee.

3. The committee will make recommendations to the Center's director to accept or reject proposed acquisitions.

4. If a collection is accepted, a deed of gift will be sent to the donor; upon signature of the donor, the director or associate director of the AHC will countersign. The original deed of gift will be filed in secure storage, with a copy placed in the working donor files.

5. Because deeds of gift are binding obligations on the university, any proposed deed of gift with language that departs significantly from language already approved by UW Counsel, will be sent to UW Counsel for review prior to signature by the AHC.

Access and Use Policy

The collections of the American Heritage Center are available under the general archival principle of "equal access." In addition, the AHC abides by the "Joint Statement on Access to Original Research Materials" of the Society of American Archivists (SAA) and the Rare Books and Manuscript Section (RBMS) of the Association of College and Research Libraries (ACRL) of the American Library Association (ALA). The collections are available to University of Wyoming students, staff, and faculty, visiting scholars, and the general public with the following stipulations:

1. Material does not circulate (with the exceptions outlined in "Loan Policy," below). Researchers may not take collection material outside the reading room, and must accept and follow all rules and procedures set forth in the "Reading Room Rules for Use of Materials."

2. Where donors have placed restrictions upon collections, those restrictions shall be observed for their duration.

3. Where collections are fragile and could be damaged by further use or examination, such material may be withdrawn, at the discretion of an appropriate AHC faculty member, until the material can be conserved or made available in another format. A copy or facsimile of the withdrawn material will be made available if the safety of the material will not be significantly jeopardized by the creation of such copy/facsimile. Appeals by researchers to review decisions to withdraw or deny access to fragile material may be made to the AHC Director.

4. The reference faculty has the authority and obligation to determine whether collection material is too fragile to be safely photocopied; in such instances, other means of reproduction may be safely available, but the additional cost of that reproduction must be borne by the researcher. Appeals by researchers of decisions to prohibit photocopying on grounds of fragility may be made to the AHC Director.

5.   Requests for duplication of an entire collection, unless made by the original donor or a first generation heir, may be denied if the reference faculty has reason to believe that such a copy is intended for deposit in another repository, is intended for public distribution on the web or otherwise, or may violate copyright law. Any such denial may be appealed to the AHC Director.

6.   The reference faculty has the authority to stagger or postpone fulfillment of very large reproduction orders so as not to unduly delay fulfillment of smaller orders by other patrons. "Very large" and "unduly" are in the judgment of the reference faculty, taking into consideration the current and expected quantity and size of other orders, and the work schedules of those who perform reproductions. Any such staggering or postponement of reproduction orders may be appealed to the AHC Director.

7.   Access to unprocessed collections must be approved by the director or associate director, but normally will be granted unless the collection is extremely disorganized, physically unstable, or is likely to have within it the types of rare material usually retired to the vault.

8.   Anyone violating these Access and Use policies or Reading Room Rules may be barred from further presence in the reading room and use of the collections.

Toppan Rare Books Library

Mission

The Toppan Rare Books Library was created in 1994 through the generosity of Clara Toppan, to honor her husband Fred. As a department of the American Heritage Center, the Toppan Rare Books Library supports the AHC's vision and mission. In addition, as the University of Wyoming's repository for rare and special books, many transferred from Coe Library, it also supports the missions of the University Libraries and the University in general. The Toppan Rare Books Library is a teaching collection that also supports research. Materials are acquired to support small-group instruction for students—UW graduate and undergraduate, community college, high school, and others—as well as to support research in the AHC's manuscript collections, research on the history of the book, and topical research in a number of subject areas. As a teaching collection, the Rare Books Library places great emphasis on making its holdings physically and intellectually accessible to students. The Toppan Rare Books Library also actively engages in service and outreach, bringing the content and the inspiring physical presence of its holdings to members of the public as well. In sum, the mission of the Toppan Rare Books Library is to preserve and provide welcoming access to old, rare, and historically important books.

Criteria

There is no universally accepted definition of a "rare book." Most broadly, rare books have intrinsic importance or research value, and would be difficult to replace. Some general, but not exclusive, criteria for material to be acquired for the Rare Books Library are: books that are very old or fragile and require the extra protection of a closed-stack, non-circulating collection (i.e., pre-1850 imprints from the University Libraries are transferred to the Rare Books Library because of their physical fragility); true rarity, in the sense of being scarce and possibly irreplaceable should they be lost or damaged; significant monetary or research value, perhaps because they are first editions, are inscribed by their authors, or have some other unique characteristic.

Rare Books often have special artifactual characteristics, such as fine bindings; valuable prints or original photographs; early publishers' bindings; extra-illustrated volumes; decorated endpapers; fine printing; parchment, vellum, or high quality linen rag pages; portfolios containing unbound plates; valuable maps or plates; material requiring security (e.g., books in unusual formats, erotica); miniature books (10 centimeters or smaller); 20th century literary works with intact dust jackets. Dust jackets frequently contain important information (e.g., text, illustrative design, and price), and their presence greatly affects both the market and research value of 20th century books.

Some books are not rare or particularly valuable as individual volumes, but are part of a special collection. A special collection is a collection of great depth in a narrowly focused subject area. Examples of special collections in the Rare Books Library are fly-fishing and early publications of the Church of Jesus Christ of Latter Day Saints. Finally, some books not particularly rare are acquired and cataloged by the Rare Books Library because they support the teaching function of the library and the rare books curator: for example, reference books about books, and facsimiles of unobtainable originals (e.g., ancient scrolls or early Medieval manuscripts).

Copies that are badly worn, much repaired or rebound, are not generally included in the Rare Books collection, unless the age of the material preempts condition as a criterion. Nor is all the material in the Rare Books Library encompassed by a definition of "book." The collection includes newspapers, magazines, broadsides, manuscripts, pamphlets, and other materials, though the printed codex predominates by far.

Ultimately, the determination of whether a book or other material belongs in the Rare Books Library is a matter of the professional judgment and expertise of the rare books curator. The curator will be informed by national guidelines developed by the Rare Books and Manuscripts Section of the Association of College and Research Libraries, a division of the American Library Association: *Guidelines on the Selection of General Collection Materials for Transfer to Special Collections*, 2nd Edition (Rev),

1999, and will consult when appropriate with academic faculty, faculty of the University Libraries, and the AHC Acquisition Committee.

Procedures

Acquisitions. The Rare Books Library acquires material in the following ways: (1) transfers from the University Libraries (based on written agreements or mutual consent); (2) donations; (3) purchases. The "Conditions that must be met for material to be acquired by the AHC," for the manuscript collections, above, apply. Decisions to accept transfer and donated material for Toppan are based on the professional judgment of the Rare Books Curator, guided by a collection development plan. Purchase recommendations are made by the Rare Books Curator to the Associate Director of the AHC; the Associate Director may consult with the Director and/or the Acquisitions Committee at his/her discretion, for single purchases of up to $1,000. Recommendations for purchases of more than $1,000 must be approved by the Director.

Deaccessions. Deaccession procedures are those of the AHC generally, below.

Access and Use Policies

Access and use policies are those of the manuscript collections, above, with reading room rules specific to the Rare Books Library.

University Archives

Mission

The University of Wyoming Archives serves as the official repository for the permanent records of the University of Wyoming. Its primary purpose is to serve the administrative, teaching, research, and public service needs of the university and other user communities. However, it is also responsible for assisting the University to fulfill its legal obligations under Title 9, Chapter 2, Article 4 (governing public records) of Wyoming Statutes. In order to fulfill its purpose and responsibility, the University Archives acquires official (public) records generated by the University, and also collects (through donation) private records and papers. Hence the University Archives is the repository for some records mandated by law and records and papers that have enduring value to documenting the history of the University of Wyoming, its administration, programs, services, and members of its community. The University Archives preserves these records and makes them available for researchers. Public records in the University Archives are accessible under applicable state statutes; the accessibility of private records and papers is governed by deed of gift, though the University Archives works with donors to make such material quickly and freely accessible.

Criteria

The University Archives seeks to document the University of Wyoming community, which includes the administration, faculty, students, alumni, and staff. In assessing records appropriate for permanent retention, the University Archives attempts to collect the documentation produced from the conduct of university business. There are seven functions common to the operations of most academic institutions: convey knowledge; advance knowledge; confer credentials; foster socialization; maintain and promote culture; sustain the institution; and provide public service.

Record Types and Formats

A. **Official Records of the University of Wyoming.**
    These records (which give evidence about the functions, policies, and decisions of the university), are governed by state statute, and include material (described below) created and received by administrators and staff in conducting University business. Records created or received by faculty in administrative and University committee capacities are also official University records. University records are the property of the University and not of the administrators, faculty members, or staff who create them

or to whom they are entrusted. University records are
not to be destroyed or otherwise disposed of except in
accordance with procedures and schedules established by
the University Archives through its records management
program.

University records include, among many different forms,
correspondence, reports, minutes, directives, announce-
ments, publications, architectural and building plans,
electronic files, and any other material produced by the
University in pursuance of its functions. The University
Archives also works with the University Libraries to manage the publications, newsletters, or booklets distributed
by University of Wyoming including dissertations and
theses. Audiovisual records documenting the development
of the university such as photographic prints and nega-
tives, slides, motion picture film, oral history interviews,
audio and video tape, discs, and recordings are solicited.
The University Archives will work with departments to
manage their electronic data files generated for conducting university business in cooperation with Information
Technology, including electronic mail and Web sites. The
University Archives will consider retaining selected artifacts relating to the history of University of Wyoming.

B.   **The Papers of University of Wyoming Faculty.**
As an important part of its mission of documenting the
life of the University of Wyoming community and placing it in a broader social context, the University Archives
actively seeks to acquire (through donation), organize,
and make available the personal and professional papers of
select University of Wyoming faculty. Faculty papers offer
insight into the history and operation of the University
that otherwise may be lost by relying only on official
administrative records. They reveal professional interests

and opinions that frequently clarify matters mentioned in the official records of the central administration. Faculty papers document the academic life of the University and relate one's academic career to his or her total interests, thereby constituting an important record and providing a full compliment of perspectives regarding the historical activities of University of Wyoming.

The following types of documentation reflect and illuminate the careers of the University of Wyoming faculty and are sought by the University Archives: official, professional, and personal correspondence; biographical material; photographs; class syllabi, including online classes; research files; departmental or committee minutes and records (which may be official University records); single copies of articles, books, and reports written; diaries; and scrapbooks. **NB: Papers relating to those aspects of a faculty member's life and career not related to the University of Wyoming may be considered for acquisition, but as part of the manuscripts collection rather than university archives.**

C.   **Records of Student and Affiliated Organizations.** Because the intellectual development of students does not occur in a vacuum, documenting student life means going beyond the limits of the classroom. The University Archives collects (through donation), preserves, and makes available materials documenting student involvement in fraternities, sororities, student government, religious associations, publications, social events, athletics, and other activities that contribute to the total student experience in higher education, including activities after graduation.

Procedures

A.   **Transfer of Official University Records.**

The University Archives will only accept University records that are scheduled for permanent retention and will not accept records that are scheduled for destruction. University records considered for transmittal to the University Archives for permanent retention must be reviewed and appraised by the University Archivist prior to transfer acceptance. All transfer of records must be placed in acid-free records cartons (available at the UW Bookstore) and accompanied by a listing of the contents in electronic form. The University Archives will only accept records based upon retention schedules approved by the Wyoming State Records Committee, and accompanied by an official transfer of records form signed by the Director of the American Heritage Center and the administrator from the transferring office.

B.   **Donation of Faculty or Student Papers.**

All material considered for donation to the University Archives for permanent retention must be reviewed and appraised by the University Archivist in consultation with the AHC Acquisitions Committee prior to donation acceptance. While content lists and acid free boxes are not required, as for University Records, they are greatly appreciated. The University Archives will not accept materials without a legal transfer of title through a deed of gift, which must be signed by the Director of the American Heritage Center and the donor.

C.   **Access and Return of Records.**

Once in AHC custody, university records are available for use during normal business hours, subject to the manuscript collections "Access and Use" policies (above) and any restrictions by federal or state statute, or as specified in the deed of gift. If however, the donating unit requires that the records be returned to them for a specified period of time or longer, the AHC will make arrangements for the records transfer. The unit requesting the transfer assumes responsibility for care of these records and assures their return to the University of Wyoming Archives within a reasonable period of time.

D.   **Closed Collections.**

University records may be open records, and are subject to state (and in some cases federal) freedom of information laws. Specific records that contain personally identifiable information will be closed to protect individual privacy. The closure of university records is subject to compliance with applicable federal and state laws. Faculty and student papers may be donated with explicit provisions to restrict access for a limited period of time; such restrictions must be specified in the deed of gift.

E.   **Deaccessioning.**

University records in AHC custody can be subject to a reevaluation of earlier appraisal decisions. Such periodic reappraisal of collections is a legitimate and necessary part of development in archives and manuscript repositories, and allows the identification of materials that would not be accepted today or are no longer appropriate to the institution's mission. An important part of a collections management policy is deaccessioning and any reappraisal of university records will follow the AHC's deaccessioning procedures.

Loan Policy

General

The AHC follows the RBMS/ACRL's "Guidelines for the Loan of
Rare and Unique Materials" and "Guidelines for Borrowing and
Lending Special Collections Materials for Exhibition." The AHC
may lend material from the collections to qualified institutions upon
receipt of a formal loan request and satisfactory completion of a
facility report (indicating that the facility is in all relevant respects
capable of safely storing and exhibiting the material). All loans are
subject to conditions specified by the AHC.

Organization and Business Donors

In recognition of the generosity of those organizations and businesses who donate historical material for research use, the special
needs of such donors to celebrate milestones and occasionally for
litigation, and the widespread though informal willingness of repositories across the country to accommodate such needs when possible,
the AHC will consider short-term loans (usually not exceeding 30
days) back to such donors. However, such loans will not be made
if the AHC has reason to believe that the physical integrity or historical authenticity of the material will be compromised by such
action. Such loans will occur only with the written consent of the
AHC Director, accompanied by an item list of material, and a written acknowledgment from an appropriate officer of the borrowing
organization or business that the material in question remains the
property of the AHC and will be returned by the date specified. An
absolute minimum of three weeks notice is required for such loan
requests.

University of Wyoming and UW Foundation

In certain circumstances, items may be allowed out of the AHC
for teaching purposes. This is only possible for UW classes, and an

AHC faculty member must transport the material and be present during all such uses to ensure the care and security of the materials for the period of the loan. In addition, there may be unusual circumstances where AHC collection material can be of such significant assistance to the university or to the UW Foundation that its use outside the AHC for a presentation or event may be warranted. Again, an AHC faculty member must transport the material and be present during all such uses to ensure the care and security for the period of the loan. All such loans, for teaching or other uses, will occur only with the written consent of the AHC Director, accompanied by an item list of material, so requests must be made at least three weeks in advance of need.

Deaccessioning

Cultural institutions' missions and collecting areas change with time, making it necessary to have in place a mechanism which allows for re-evaluating earlier appraisal decisions. Such periodic reappraisal of collections is a legitimate and necessary part of development in archives and manuscript repositories, and allows the identification of materials that would not be accepted today or are no longer appropriate to the institution's mission. An important part of a collections management policy is deaccessioning.[4]

The American Heritage Center may under certain circumstances and under carefully controlled conditions deaccession collections from its holdings. By adhering to the principles below, the Center will more efficiently fulfill its mission to preserve and make available its resources to UW students and faculty, visiting scholars, and the general public who wish to use the Center's collections.

Deaccessioning is considered only for material that meets one or more of the following conditions:

1.   it is no longer relevant and useful to the mission of the AHC

2. it cannot be properly stored, preserved, or used

3.   it no longer retains its physical integrity, identity, or authenticity

4. it is unnecessarily duplicated in the collections

5. it is part of a larger collection other portions of which are owned by another repository that makes its holdings accessible to the public

In addition, deaccessioning can occur only when the item is clearly owned by the AHC. This includes ownership by provision of Wyoming Statute 34-23-101 as it relates to undocumented material.

The AHC always considers the donor's intent in the deaccessioning process. Express or specific restrictions relating to AHC custody accompanying the original donation are followed unless adherence to such restrictions is no longer possible or would be detrimental to the collections or the repository. When the acquisition includes a restrictive statement regarding custody, the AHC will consult the donor or donor's heirs before proceeding to deaccession. If necessary, however, the AHC may seek relief from such restrictions through legal action.

Deaccessioning Procedures

When the conditions for deaccessioning have been met, any AHC faculty or staff may recommend deaccessioning to the Acquisitions Committee. The Acquisitions Committee will make a recommendation regarding deaccessioning to the director. In some special cases the director will ask the Board of Faculty Advisors for their advice, but the final decision will be made by the director.

The basis upon which the Acquisition Committee makes its recommendation will be recorded in the committee minutes, a copy of which will be placed in the relevant accession and donor files. A formal document, indicating that all necessary recordkeeping has been accomplished, and signed by the director, will further document the decision and process.

Documentation of the disposition of deaccessioned materials is also maintained as part of the AHC's permanent records.

Disposition of Deaccessioned Material

The decision about method of disposition is separate from the decision to deaccession. That is, material will not be deaccessioned for the purpose of a specific disposition.

As a first principle, the AHC endeavors to ensure continued scholarly and public access to the deaccessioned material, though this is only true regarding original material in sound condition. In practice, material to be deaccessioned may be transferred to other repositories, returned to the donor, offered for public sale, or destroyed. Destruction is entirely appropriate for deaccessioned collections that are duplicated in another repository, physically unstable, illegible, or simply too fragmentary or insignificant to be of use to another repository. Appropriate staff and the director will determine the method of disposition jointly. Disposition of material with substantial research value will be governed by the following considerations:

A.   Material will be offered to other University of Wyoming units, particularly the UW Libraries, if the material falls within the content and material types collected by that unit.

B.   Material will be returned to the donor (or heirs) only if the deed of gift requires this.

C.   With the possible exception of instances where the deaccessioned material has significant monetary value, a good faith attempt will be made by AHC faculty/staff to identify a repository to which the material can be donated. The repository must be accessible to scholars and the public, with an interest in the material and the resources necessary to catalog, store, and make the material accessible.

D. In instances where deaccessioned material has (or likely
    has) significant monetary value, good faith consideration
    will be given to offering it for sale at a discount to an
    appropriate repository, so that the material may remain
    accessible to researchers.

E. Unless offered at a discount to a repository, sales of deac-
    cessioned material will be by public auction or through a
    process of sealed bids.

F. All proceeds from the sale of deaccessioned material will
    be used solely for the acquisition or direct care of the
    AHC's collections.

G. Materials will not be given or sold to UW employees or
    trustees, or their immediate families.

Ethics Statement

A possibility for conflict of interest exists whenever an employee of the
AHC collects items of a type collected by the AHC. When collecting, those
individuals should always consider the interests of the AHC over their own
personal interests.

An employee considering the acquisition of historically significant
material that may be within the AHC's collecting goals (as identified in
the Collection Management Policy and the Collection Development Plan)
should bring the intended acquisition to the attention of the Acquisitions
Committee in a timely manner to determine whether or not the AHC is
interested in acquiring the material for the collections (and has funds
available for purchase, if relevant). If the AHC does not intend to acquire
the item, the individual may then proceed with his/her acquisition. If
it is not possible to consult the Acquisition Committee in advance, the
individual may acquire the item but should then inform the Acquisition
Committee—and be prepared to donate or sell (as applicable) the acquisition to the AHC, if the committee recommends such action.

AHC employees may not use their institutional affiliation to promote their own or their family members' personal collecting or business activities. No employee may participate in any dealing (buying or selling for profit as distinguished from occasional sale or exchange from a personal collection) in material similar or related to material collected by the AHC.

Information of a sensitive and/or confidential nature that an employee might acquire in the course of performing his/her duties must be treated as proprietary to the AHC and should not be used for personal advantage or for the purposes of damaging the AHC or UW. No person associated with the AHC may use confidential information outside the scope of his/her assigned duties without the prior permission of the AHC Director.

Adopted January 2003
Revised May 2007
Revised November 2008

Notes for Appendix B

[1] Within the next five years, the AHC and the UW Art Museum are committed to developing a unified collection management policy for art on the university campus. Listing art as one of the material types in the AHC manuscript collections is merely a reflection of current reality and not a commitment to the future.

[2] Just a few examples of national collecting areas at land grant universities: Minnesota (social welfare, history of computing, immigration, African American authors), Texas (media professionals, mathematics, literary figures, film makers, popular music, performing arts), Ohio State (polar exploration, cartoon art, theater), Illinois-Urbana (professional organizations, fraternities, marching bands, advertising, 3rd Armored Division), Wisconsin (mass communication, social action, film and theater, labor), Michigan (radicalism, transportation, Revolutionary War, U.S. cultural and political history to 1920).

[3] Assignment of copyright is often complex, and AHC staff will be glad to discuss this with donors. Generally, copyright belongs to the creator of writings and other original material (such as photos and music), but can be legally transferred to heirs or others. Moreover, ownership of copyright is separable from ownership of the physical item (the letter or photo). The AHC asks donors to donate

not only the physical papers but also any copyright in them that the donor might own. This request is made to make it easier for researchers to use quotations from the papers in their work. However, the AHC will consider donation of the physical material without donation of copyright.

[4] The U.S. archival profession has nothing official to say about deaccessioning—either as policy or procedure. The AHC instead follows the recommendations and ethical standards of the museum community. See the American Association of Museums, Code of Ethics for Museums (Washington, DC: American Association of Museums, 1994), 8-9. See also International Council of Museums (ICOM), ICOM Code of Professional Ethics, http://icom.museum/ ethics_rev_engl.html; American Association of Museums, Curators Committee, "Code of Ethics for Curators," *Museum News* 62, no. 3 (February 1983): 38–40; American Association of Museums, Registrars Committee, "A Code of Ethics for Registrars," *Museum News* 62, no. 3 (February 1985): 42–46; Association of Art Museum Directors, "A Code of Ethics for Registrars," *Professional Practices in Art Museums* (New York: Association of Art Museum Directors, 1992), 8, 17–22. The American Library Association does not mention deaccessioning in its code of ethics, but its Office for Intellectual Freedom created a Workbook for Selection Policy Writing, http://www.ala.org/alaorg/oif/workbook_selection. html, which notes that policies for "reevaluation (weeding)" are an essential part of a selection policy. The Rare Books and Manuscripts Section of ALA, however, has a full statement on deaccessioning as part of its ethics document: see www.rbms.nd.edu and click on "standards."

Selective List of Federal Legislation Affecting Access to Private Information

STATE LEGISLATURES AND CONGRESS HAVE PASSED HUNDREDS OF LAWS THAT AFFECT ACCESS TO PRIVATE INFORMATION. The following selective list of major federal legislation serves as an introduction to the acronyms of privacy and exposure. A more comprehensive analysis is provided in the privacy reader edited by Menzi L. Behrnd-Klodt and Peter Wosh. Some of these federal statutes are not primarily about privacy, but contain regulations for the release and processing of private data. They are arranged chronologically to suggest the trends and countertrends at work in American society.

1966	FOIA Freedom of Information Act
1968	Omnibus Crime Control and Safe Streets Act
1970	FCRA Fair Credit Reporting Act
1973	Crime Control Act
1974	Privacy Act
1974	FERPA Family Educational Rights and Privacy Act

1978   Right to Financial Privacy Act

1980   Electronic Fund Transfer Act

1980   Privacy Protection Act

1984   Cable Communications Privacy Act

1986   ECPA Electronic Communications Privacy Act

1988   Computer Matching and Privacy Protection Act

1988   Video Privacy Protection Act

1988   Employee Polygraph Protection Act

1991   Telephone Consumer Protection Act

1994   Driver's Privacy Protection Act

1994   CALEA Communications Assistance for Law
        Enforcement Act

1994   Telemarketing and Consumer Fraud and Abuse
        Prevention Act

1996   HIPAA Health Insurance Portability and
        Accountability Act

1996   EFOIA Electronic Freedom of Information
        Act Amendments

1996   Telecommunications Act

1997   Consumer Credit Reporting Reform Act

1998   CMA Computer Matching and Privacy Protection Act

1998   COPPA Children's Online Privacy Protection Act

1999   GLB Financial Services Modernization Act
        (Gramm-Leach-Bliley Act)

2000   ESIGN Electronic Signatures in Global and
        National Commerce Act

2001   No Child Left Behind Act

2001   USA PATRIOT Act

2002   Homeland Security Act

Bibliography and Works Cited

THIS BIBLIOGRAPHY IS DESIGNED TO BRING TOGETHER IN ONE PLACE ALL THE WORKS CITED IN THE ENDNOTES TO VARIOUS CHAPTERS. The bibliography includes citations for examples used to provide perspectives from different countries and different eras. Some of the entries refer to negative examples, such as forgeries. For this reason the bibliography should not be considered a guide to works on archival ethics, although many such guides are embedded in it. Instead it is provided as a convenience for those who wish to follow up on subjects broached in this volume. Increasingly, online texts are the most accessible—and sometimes the only—version available. Every effort has been made to provide an accurate URL together with the date when the link was used. Given the unstable nature of URLs, and also their susceptibility to typos in the long strings of characters, it is often better to access online articles using a keyword search in a utility such as Google Scholar. The goal of the bibliography is to facilitate a continuing dialog on the subject of archival ethics.

Afanas´ev, Iu. N., et al., ed. *Istoriia stalinskogo Gulaga: Konets 1920kh–pervaia polovina 1950kh godov. Sobranie dokumentov,* 7 vols. [History of the Stalinist Gulag: The End of the 1920s to the First Half of the 1950s. A Collection of Documents]. Moscow: Rosspen, 2004–5.

American Association of Museums. "Code of Ethics for Museums." http://www.aam-us.org/museumresources/ethics/coe.cfm (accessed September 10, 2009).

American Heritage Center, University of Wyoming. "Academic Plan," "Acquisitions Guidelines," "Collection Management Policy," and "Collecting Policy." http://ahc.uwyo.edu/about/policies.htm (accessed September 9, 2009).

American Historical Association. "Guiding Principles on Taking a Public Stance." Approved January 7, 2007. http://www.historians.org/governance/pd/2007_01_08_PublicStance.cfm (accessed November 25, 2009).

American Historical Association, Organization of American Historians. *Final Report of the Joint AHA-OAH Ad Hoc Committee to Investigate the Charges against the Franklin D. Roosevelt Library and Related Matters.* Washington: American Historical Association, 1970.

Andolsen, Alan. "Choosing Ethical Solutions to RIM Problem." *Information Management Journal* 40, no. 5 (Sept./Oct. 2006): 46–52.

Applebaum, Anne. *Gulag: A History.* New York: Doubleday, 2003.

Archives of the Soviet Communist Party and the Soviet State: Microfilm, 1993-2004. Chadwyck-Healey/ProQuest, distributors.

Aristotle. *Ethics.* http://www.gutenberg.org/etext/8438 (accessed October 11, 2009).

Association of Art Museum Directors. "A Code of Ethics." http://www.aamd.org/about/#Code (accessed November 25, 2009).

Auer, Leopold. *Disputed Archival Claims. Analysis of an International Survey: A RAMP Study.* Paris: UNESCO, 1998.

Austen, Ian. "National Gallery of Canada Looks Beyond Controversy and Court." *New York Times,* December 28, 2008.

Baker, Nicholson. "Annals of Scholarship: Discards." *New Yorker,* April 4, 1994.

Baker, Nicholson. "Deadline: The Author's Desperate Bid to Stop the Trashing of America's Historic Newspapers." *New Yorker,* July 24, 2000.

Baker, Nicholson. *Double Fold: Libraries and the Assault on Paper.* New York: Random House, 2001.

Baker, Nicholson. "Letter from San Francisco: The Author vs. the Library." *New Yorker,* October 14, 1996.

Barzun, Jacques, and Henry Franklin Graff. *The Modern Researcher.* Belmont, CA: Thomson/Wadsworth, 2004.

Bauer, G. Philip. "Recruitment, Training, and Promotion in the National Archives." *American Archivist* 18 (October 1955): 291–305.

Bearman, David. "Moments of Risk: Identifying Threats to Electronic Records." *Archivaria* 62 (Fall 2006): 15–46.

Becker, Ronald. "The Ethics of Providing Access." *Provenance* 11 (1993): 57–77.

Behrnd-Klodt, Menzi L. *Navigating Legal Issues in Archives.* Chicago: Society of American Archivists, 2008.

Behrnd-Klodt, Menzi L., and Peter J. Wosh, eds. *Privacy and Confidentiality Perspectives: Archives and Archival Records.* Chicago: Society of American Archivists, 2005.

Benedict, Karen M. *Ethics and the Archival Profession: Introduction and Case Studies.* Chicago: Society of American Archivists, 2003.

Benedict, Karen M. "An Evolution in a Code of Ethics: the Society of American Archivists." Paper delivered at the International Conference on Archives, Vienna, August 23–29, 2004.

Benedict, Karen M. "Invitation to a Bonfire: Reappraisal and Deaccessioning of Records as Collection Management Tools in an Archives—A Reply to Leonard Rapport." *American Archivist* 47 (Winter 1984): 43–49.

Ben-Itto, Hadassa. *The Lie That Wouldn't Die: The Protocols of the Elders of Zion.* London and Portland, OR: Vallentine Mitchell, 2005.

Binyon, T.J. *Pushkin.* New York: Knopf, 2003.

Blanton, Thomas S. *White House E-mail: The Top Secret Computer Messages the Reagan/Bush White House Tried to Destroy.* New York: New Press, 1995.

Blouin, Francis X., Jr., and William G. Rosenberg, eds. *Archives, Documentation, and Institutions of Social Memory.* Ann Arbor, MI: Bentley Historical Library, 2000.

Blumenthal, Michael. "Allen Ginsberg, Millionaire?" *New York Times*, October 29, 1994.

Bodleian Library. "Using the Library."http://www.ouls.ox.ac.uk/bodley/services/using (accessed September 25, 2009).

Boles, Frank. "Enforcing Ethics." Policy statement, March 20, 2009. Society of American Archivists. http://www.archivists.org/news/ethics09.asp (accessed November 19, 2009).

Boles, Frank. "Sampling in Archives." *American Archivist* 44 (Spring 1981): 125–30.

Boles, Frank. *Selecting and Appraising Archives and Manuscripts*. Chicago: Society of American Archivists, 2005.

Boston University, Howard Gotlieb Archival Research Center. http://www.bu.edu/dbin/archives/ (accessed September 3, 2009).

Boulware, Jack. "Snatching Saroyan: How Stanford University Aced Out UC Berkeley and Acquired the Million-Dollar Archives of San Francisco's Most Prolific Author, William Saroyan—Without Paying a Dime." http://www.sfweekly.com/1998-02-11/news/snatching-saroyan (accessed March 26, 2009).

Bozeman, Pat, ed. *Forged Documents: Proceedings of the 1989 Houston Conference*. Houston: University of Houston Libraries, 1990.

Brent, Jonathan. *Inside the Stalin Archives: Discovering the New Russia*. New York and London: Atlas, Turnaround, 2008.

The British Library, National Library of Russia, St. Catherine's Monastery, and the Leipzig University Library. *Codex Sinaiticus*. http://www.codexsinaiticus.org (accessed August 9, 2009).

Bundesarchiv. "Benutzung." http://www.bundesarchiv.de/bundesarchiv/rechtsgrundlagen/benutzungsverordnung/index.html.en (accessed September 25, 2009).

Bundesbeauftragte für die Unterlagen des Staatssicherheitsdienstes der ehemaligen Deutschen Demokratischen Republik [Commissioner for the files of the state security service of the former German Democratic Republic]. "Akteneinsicht." [Inspection of Files]. http://www.bstu.bund.de (accessed September 25, 2009).

Burant, Jim. "Ephemera, Archives, and another View of History." *Archivaria* 40 (1995): 189–98.

Burrow, J.W. *A History of Histories: Epics, Chronicles, Romances and Inquiries from Herodotus and Thucydides to the Twentieth Century.* New York: Knopf, 2008.

Business Ethics Quarterly, a publication of the Society of Business Ethics. http://www.businessethicsquarterly.org (accessed January 6, 2010).

Butter, Karen, Robin Chandler, and John Kunze. "The Cigarette Papers: Issues in Publishing Materials in Multiple Formats." *D-Lib Magazine*, November 1996. http://www.dlib.org.

California State Archives. "Appraisal Policy." http://www.sos.ca.gov/archives/state-records-appraisal/ (accessed February 20, 2009).

Center for the Study of Ethics in the Professions, Illinois Institute of Technology, Chicago. http://ethics.iit.edu/index1.php/Programs/Codes%20of%20Ethics (accessed August 2, 2009).

Chan, May. "Deaccessioning Archives: The Ongoing Controversy." Unpublished paper, School of Library and Information Studies, University of British Columbia, 2004.

Chandler, Robin L., and Susan Storch. "Lighting up the Internet: The Brown and Williamson Collection." In *Archives and the Public Good: Accountability and Records in Modern Society*, edited by Richard J. Cox and David A. Wallace, 135–62. Westport, CT: Quorum Books, 2002.

Confucius. *Analects.* http://www.gutenberg.org/etext/3330 (accessed October 11, 2009).

Conway, Paul. "Digitizing Preservation." *Library Journal*, February 1, 1994.

Cook, Michael. "Professional Ethics and Practice in Archives and Records Management in the Human Rights Context." *Journal of the Society of Archivists* 27, no. 1 (April 2006): 1–15.

Cook, Terry. "'A Monumental Blunder': The Destruction of Records of Nazi War Criminals in Canada." In *Archives and the Public Good: Accountability and Records in Modern Society*, edited by Richard J. Cox and David A. Wallace, 37–65. Westport, CT: Quorum Books, 2002.

Cox, Richard J. *Ethics, Accountability, and Recordkeeping in a Dangerous World.* London: Facet, 2006.

Cox, Richard J. *No Innocent Deposits: Forming Archives by Rethinking Appraisal.* Lanham, MD and Oxford: Scarecrow Press, 2004.

Cox, Richard J. *Vandals in the Stacks? A Response to Nicholson Baker's Assault on Libraries.* Westport, CT: Greenwood Press, 2002.

Cox, Richard J., and David A.Wallace, eds. *Archives and the Public Good: Accountability and Records in Modern Society.* Westport, CT: Quorum Books, 2002.

Cuno, James B. *Who Owns Antiquity? Museums and the Battle over Our Ancient Heritage.* Princeton, NJ: Princeton University Press, 2008.

Danielson, Elena S. "The Displaced Documents of Central Europe." *Comma* 3–4 (2004-5): 197–203.

Danielson, Elena S. "Ethics and Reference Services." In *Reference Services for Archives and Manuscripts,* edited by Laura B. Cohen, 107–24. Binghamton, NY: Haworth Press, 1997.

Danielson, Elena S. "The Ethics of Access." *American Archivist* 52 (Winter 1989): 52–62.

Danielson, Elena S. "Privacy Rights and the Rights of Political Victims: Implications of the German Experience." *American Archivist* 67 (Fall/Winter 2004): 176–93.

Danielson, Elena S. "A Revolution in the Russian Archives: A Retrospective." Cold War International History Project, Special Report, Woodrow Wilson International Center for Scholars. http://www.wilsoncenter.org/topics/docs/ CWIHP_Special_Report.pdf (accessed November 8, 2009).

Davis, Shelley L. *Unbridled Power: Inside the Secret Culture of the IRS.* New York: HarperBusiness, 1997.

De Michelis, Cesare G. *The Non-Existent Manuscript: A Study of the Protocols of the Sages of Zion.* Translated by Richard Newhouse. Jerusalem: Hebrew University, 2004.

Derrida, Jacques. *Archive Fever: A Freudian Impression.* Chicago: University of Chicago Press, 1996.

Deschênes, Jules. *Commission of Inquiry on War Criminals: Report. Part 1.* Ottawa: Minister of Supply and Services, Canada, 1986.

Dewan, Shaila. "King Archives Will Be Sold at Auction." *New York Times,* June 9, 2006.

Dingwall, Glenn. "Trusting Archivists: The Role of Archival Ethics Codes in Establishing Public Faith." *American Archivist* 67 (Spring/Summer 2004): 11–30.

Dowler, Lawrence. "Deaccessioning Collections: A New Perspective on a Continuing Controversy." In *Archival Choices: Managing the Historical Record in an Age of Abundance,* edited by Nancy E. Peace, 117–32. Lexington, MA: Lexington Books, 1984.

Doylen, Michael. "Experiments in Deaccessioning: Archives and On-line Auctions." *American Archivist* 64 (Fall/Winter 2001): 350–62.

Duranti, Luciana. *Diplomatics: New Uses for an Old Science.* Lanham, MD: Scarecrow Press, 1998.

Duranti, Luciana. "An Overview of InterPARES3." *Archives and Social Studies* 1, no. 1 (September 2007): 577–603.

Eakin, Hugh. "Treasure Hunt." *New Yorker,* December 17, 2007.

Eckert, Astrid M. "'And Grant German and Foreign Scholars Access at All Times': Archival Access in West Germany During the Cold War." In *Political Pressure and the Archival Record,* edited by Margaret Procter, Michael Cook, and Caroline Williams, 75–91. Chicago: Society of American Archivists, 2006.

Eckert, Astrid M. *Kampf um die Akten: die Westalliierten und die Rückgabe von deutschem Archivgut nach dem Zweiten Weltkrieg.* Stuttgart: Steiner, 2004.

Eco, Umberto. *Foucault's Pendulum.* San Diego: Houghton Mifflin Harcourt, 1989.

Ellis, Judith A. *Keeping Archives.* Port Melbourne: D.W. Thorpe/Australian Society of Archivists, 1996.

Falcone, Michael. "Court Orders Search of White House Computers." *New York Times,* January 15, 2009.

Fenster, Mark. *Conspiracy Theories: Secrecy and Power in American Culture.* Minneapolis: University of Minnesota Press, 1999.

First Archivists Circle. "Protocols for Native American Archival Materials." http://www2.nau.edu/libnap-p/protocols.html (accessed February 10, 2010).

Franklin, John Hope. *Mirror to America: The Autobiography of John Hope Franklin.* New York: Farrar, Straus, and Giroux, 2005.

Gladwell, Malcolm. *Blink.* New York: Little Brown, 2005.

Glantz, Stanton A., et al. *The Cigarette Papers.* Berkeley: University of California Press, 1996. Also available online at the University of California, San Francisco, Digital Library at http://www.library.ucsf.edu/tobacco.

Glantz, Stanton A., et al. "Looking Through a Keyhole at the Tobacco Industry: The Brown and Williamson Documents." *Journal of the American Medical Association* 274, no. 3 (July 1995): 219–24.

Glantz, Stanton A., and Edith D. Balbach. *Tobacco War: Inside the California Battles.* Berkeley: University of California Press, 2000.

Goldman, Alan. *The Moral Foundations of Professional Ethics.* Totowa, NJ: Rowman and Littlefield, 1980.

Gordon-Reed, Annette. *The Hemingses of Monticello.* New York: Norton, 2008.

Gorenberg, Gershom. "The War to Begin All Wars." *New York Review of Books* 56, no. 9 (May 28, 2009): 38–41.

Gracy, David B., II. "What You Get Is Not What You See: Forgery and the Corruption of Recordkeeping Systems." In *Archives and the Public Good: Accountability and Records in Modern Society,* edited by Richard J. Cox and David A. Wallace, 245–63.Westport, CT: Quorum Books, 2002.

Grafton, Anthony. *Forgers and Critics: Creativity and Duplicity in Western Scholarship.* Princeton, NJ: Princeton University Press, 1990.

Grafton, Anthony. *New Worlds, Ancient Texts: The Power of Tradition and the Shock of Discovery.* Cambridge, MA: Belknap Press, Harvard University Press, 1992.

Greene, Mark A. "I've Deaccessioned and Lived to Tell about It: Confessions of an Unrepentant Reappraiser." *Archival Issues* 3, no. 1 (2006): 7–22. http://www.pacsclsurvey.org/documents/greene/IveDeaccessioned.pdf (accessed September 9, 2009).

Greene, Mark A. "The Power of Archives: Archivists' Values and Value in the Post-Modern Age." Presidential address delivered at the annual meeting of the Society of American Archivists, San Francisco, August 2008. http://www.archivists.org/governance/presidential/GreeneAddressAug08.pdf (accessed November 25, 2009).

Greene, Mark A., and Christine Weideman. "The Buckley Stops Where? The Ambiguity and Archival Implications of the Family Educational Rights and Privacy Act." In *Privacy and Confidentiality Perspectives: Archivists and Archival Records,* edited by Menzi L. Behrnd-Klodt and Peter J. Wosh, 181–203. Chicago: Society of American Archivists, 2005.

Greene, Mark A., and Dennis Meissner. "More Product, Less Process: Pragmatically Revamping Traditional Archival Processing." *American Archivist* 68 (Fall/Winter 2005): 208–63.

Grimsted, Patricia Kennedy. *Returned from Russia: Nazi Archival Plunder in Western Europe and Recent Restitution Issues.* Builth Wells, Great Britain: Institute of Art and Law, 2007.

Grimsted, Patricia Kennedy. *Trophies of War: The Archival Heritage of Ukraine, World War II, and the International Politics of Restitution.* Cambridge, MA: Harvard Ukrainian Research Institute, 2001.

Gunther, Gerald. *Learned Hand: The Man and the Judge.* New York: Knopf, 1994.

Guthrie, Kevin M. *The New-York Historical Society: Lessons from One Nonprofit's Long Struggle for Survival.* San Francisco: Jossey-Bass, 1996.

Ham, F. Gerald. "Archival Choices: Managing the Historical Record in an Age of Abundance." *American Archivist* 47 (Winter 1984): 11–22.

Hamilton, Charles. *Great Forgers and Famous Fakes: The Manuscript Forgers of America and How they Duped the Experts.* New York: Crown, 1980.

Hane, Paula. "OCLC to Open World Cat Searching to the World." Post, July 17, 2006. http://newsbreaks.infotoday.com/nbreader.asp?ArticleID=16951 (accessed March 26, 2009).

Harris, Verne. *Archives and Justice: A South African Perspective.* Chicago: Society of American Archivists, 2007.

Harris, Verne. "'They Should Have Destroyed More': The Destruction of Public Records by the South African State in the Final Years of Apartheid, 1990–1994." In *Archives and the Public Good: Accountability and Records in Modern Society,* edited by Richard J. Cox and David A. Wallace, 205–28. Westport, CT: Quorum Books, 2002.

Havel, Václav. "Address by Vaclav Havel, President of the Czech Republic in Acceptance of an Honorary Degree from the University of Michigan, Ann Arbor, USA, 5 September 2000." http://www.ns.umich.edu/Releases/2000/Sep00/havlrmrk.html (accessed July 4, 2009).

Hedstrom, Margaret. "Digital Preservation: A Time Bomb for Digital Libraries." *Computers and the Humanities* 31, no. 3 (1997): 189–202.

Heilbut, Anthony. *Thomas Mann: Eros and Literature.* New York: Knopf, 1996.

Helfferich, Tryntje. *The Thirty Years War: A Documentary History.* Indianapolis: Hackett, 2009.

Hernandez, Raymond, and David Kocieniewski. "As New Lawyer, Senator Was Active in Tobacco's Defense." *New York Times*, March 26, 2009.

Hershberg, James G. "Soviet Archives: The Opening Door." Woodrow Wilson Center, *Bulletin of the Cold War International History Project* 1 (Spring 1992): 1, 12.

Herzstein, Robert Edwin. *Waldheim: the Missing Years.* New York: Arbor House, 1988.

Hess, Pamela. "Official Urges U.S. to Redefine Privacy." *New York Times,* November 12, 2007.

Hilts, Philip J. "Tobacco Company Was Silent on Hazards." *New York Times,* May 7, 1994.

Hirtle, Peter B. "Archival Authenticity in a Digital Age." In *Authenticity in a Digital Environment,* 8–23. Washington, DC: Council on Library and Information Resources, 2000.

Hodson, Sara Sue. "In Secret Kept, In Silence Sealed: Privacy in the Papers of Authors and Celebrities." *American Archivist* 67 (Fall/Winter 2004). Also in *Privacy and Confidentiality Perspectives: Archives and Archival Records,* edited by Menzi L. Behrnd-Klodt and Peter J. Wosh, 131–48. Chicago: Society of American Archivists, 2005.

Hofstadter, Richard. *The Paranoid Style in American Politics.* New York: Knopf, 1965.

Honan, William H. "Journalist on the Chase." In *The Spoils of War: World War II and its Aftermath: The Loss, Reappearance, and Recovery of Cultural Property,* edited by Elizabeth Simpson, 153–55. New York: Harry N. Abrams, 1997.

Honan, William H. *Treasure Hunt: A New York Times Reporter Tracks the Quedlinburg Hoard.* New York: Fromm International Publishing, 1997.

Honore, Carl. "Stuff: History in a Dustbin." *Toronto Globe and Mail,* March 14, 1992.

Howard, Ronald A., and Clinton D. Korver. *Ethics for the Real World: Creating a Personal Code to Guide Decisions in Work and Life.* Boston: Harvard Business Press, 2008.

Hunter, Gregory S. *Developing and Maintaining Practical Archives: A How-To-Do-It Manual.* New York: Neal-Schuman, 2003.

Iggers, Georg G., and James M. Powell. *Leopold von Ranke and the Shaping of the Historical Discipline.* Syracuse, NY: Syracuse University Press, 1990.

International Council on Archives. "Code of Ethics." http://www.ica.org/sites/default/files/Ethics-EN.pdf (accessed June 2, 2008).

International Council on Archives. "Reference Dossier on Archival Claims." http://www.ica.org/en/node/39083 (accessed November 29, 2009).

Institute of Certified Records Managers. "Code of Ethics." https://db.icrm.org/ crm/index.jsp?submit_menu=118 (accessed November 25, 2009).

Israel, Lee. *Can You Ever Forgive Me? Memoirs of a Literary Forger*. New York: Simon and Schuster, 2008.

Jaschik, Scott. "Digital Archives That Disappear." *Inside Higher Ed*, April 22, 2009.

Jenkinson, Hilary. *A Manual of Archive Administration Including the Problems of War Archives and Archive Making*. Oxford: Clarendon Press, 1965. First edition 1922. Available online at http://www.archive.org/stream/manualo-farchivea00jenkuoft (accessed August 8, 2009).

Jimerson, Randall C. *Archives Power: Memory, Accountability, and Social Justice*. Chicago: Society of American Archivists, 2009.

Jimerson, Randall C. "Deciding What to Save." *OCLC Systems and Services* 19, no. 4 (2003): 135–40.

Johnson, Deborah G., ed. *Ethical Issues in Engineering*. Englewood Cliffs, NJ: Prentice Hall, 1991.

Jonas, Klaus W. "The Thomas Mann Archive in Zurich." *German Quarterly* 35, no. 1 (January 1962): 10–16.

Jones, Ashby. "Virginia Man Beats Maine in Declaration of Independence Smackdown." WSJ Blogs, Law Blog, February 27, 2009. http://blogs.wsj. com/law/2009/02/27 (accessed November 2, 2009).

Jonsson, Patrik. "A Bill of Rights, Looted Long Ago, Is Stolen Back." *Christian Science Monitor*, April 22, 2003.

Joyce, William L. "The Scholarly Implications of Documentary Forgeries." In *Forged Documents: Proceedings of the 1989 Houston Conference*, edited by Pat Bozeman, 37–48. Houston: University of Houston Libraries, 1990.

Kahlenberg, Friedrich P. "Governmental Rule and Archivists: The Historical Experience of the 20th Century in Central Europe." In *Political Pressure and the Archival Record*, edited by Margaret Procter, Michael Cook, and Caroline Williams, 59–71. Chicago: Society of American Archivists, 2005.

Kant, Immanuel. *Critique of Practical Reason*. http://www.gutenberg.org/ etext/5683 (accessed October 11, 2009).

Kant, Immanuel. *Fundamental Principles of the Metaphysic of Morals*. http://www. gutenberg.org/etext/5682 (accessed January 7, 2010).

Kecskeméti, Charles, and Iván Székely. *Access to Archives*. Strasbourg: Council of Europe, 2005.

Keenan, Edward L. *Josef Dobrovský and the Origins of the Igor' Tale*. Cambridge, MA: Harvard Series in Ukrainian Studies, Harvard University Press, 2003.

Ketelaar, Eric. "The European Union and Its Archives." *American Archivist* 55, no.1 (Winter 1992): 40–45.

Ketelaar, Eric. "Professional Ethics: The Moral Defence of the Archivist." http:// www.ucd.ie/archives/html/conferences/cyber4.htm (accessed February 8, 2010).

Ketelaar, Eric. "The Right to Know, the Right to Forget? Personal Information in Public Archives." *Archives and Manuscripts* 23 (May 1995): 8–17.

King Center. http://www.thekingcenter.org/ProgServices/Default.aspx (accessed September 3, 2009).

King, Martin Luther, Jr. *The Papers of Martin Luther King, Jr.*, edited by Clayborne Carson. Berkeley: University of California Press, 1992 (vol. 1), 1994 (vol. 2), 1996 (vol. 3), 2000 (vol. 4), 2005 (vol. 5), 2007 (vol. 6).

Kirsch, J.P. "Donation of Constantine." In *The Catholic Encyclopedia*. New York: Robert Appleton Company, 1909. http://www.newadvent.org/cathen/05118a. htm (accessed July 1, 2009).

Klein, Thomas R. "Legal Issues Relating to the Recovery of the Quedlinburg Treasures." In *The Spoils of War: World War II and its Aftermath: The Loss, Reappearance, and Recovery of Cultural Property*, edited by Elizabeth Simpson, 156–58. New York: Harry N. Abrams, 1997.

Kreder, Jennifer Anglim. "The Choice between Civil and Criminal Remedies in Stolen Art Litigation." *Vanderbilt Journal of Transnational Law* (October 1, 2005): 1199.

Kuperminc, Jean-Claude. "The Return of Looted French Archives." In *Returned from Russia: Nazi Archival Plunder in Western Europe and Recent Restitution Issues,* edited by Patricia Kennedy Grimsted, 135–88. Builth Wells, Great Britain: Institute of Art and Law, 2007.

LaFollette, Hugh, ed. *The Oxford Handbook of Practical Ethics*. Oxford, New York: Oxford University Press, 2003.

Landis, William E., and Robin L. Chandler, eds. *Archives and the Digital Library*. Binghamton, NY: Haworth Press, 2006.

Landman, A., and Stanton A. Glantz. "Tobacco Industry Efforts to Undermine Policy-Relevant Research." *American Journal of Public Health* 99, no. 1 (January 2009): 45–58.

Langbart, David A. "'No Little Historic Value': The Records of Department of State Posts in Revolutionary Russia." *Prologue* 40, no. 1 (Spring 2008): 14–23.

Ledwell, Mary P. "The Theory of Reappraisal and Deaccessioning of Archival Material." Unpublished master's thesis, School of Library, Archival and Information Studies, University of British Columbia, 1995. http://hdl.handle.net/2429/3994 (accessed September 9, 2009).

Leppard, David. "Forgeries Revealed in National Archives." *Times*, May 4, 2008. http://www.timesonline.co.uk/tol/news/ (accessed July 15, 2009).

Levy, David M. "Where's Waldo? Reflections on Copies and Authenticity in a Digital Environment." In *Authenticity in a Digital Environment*, 24–31. Washington, DC: Council on Library and Information Resources, 2000.

Lewin, Leonard C. *Report from Iron Mountain on the Possibility and Desirability of Peace*. New York: Dial Press, 1967.

Lipinski, Tomas A., and Johannes J. Britz. "Rethinking Ownership of Information in the Twentieth Century: Ethical Implications." *Ethics and Information Technology* 2, no. 1 (March 2000): 49–71.

Luegenbiehl, Heinz C. "Codes of Ethics and the Moral Education of Engineers." In *Ethical Issues in Engineering*, edited by Deborah G. Johnson, 137–54. Englewood Cliffs, NJ: Prentice Hall, 1991.

Mabillon, Jean. *De re dipomatica*. 2nd ed. Palma: Luteciae-Parisiorum, 1709. Undated modern facsimile.

MacDonald, Marianne. "Amis Letters to Larkin Stir Up Censorship Row: The Bodleian Is Sitting Tight." *Independent*, April 17, 1994. www.independent.co.uk (accessed March 27, 2009).

MacNeil, Heather. "Information Privacy, Liberty, and Democracy." In *Privacy and Confidentiality Perspectives: Archivists and Archival Records*, edited by Menzi L. Behrnd-Klodt and Peter J. Wosh, 67–81. Chicago: Society of American Archivists, 2005.

MacNeil, Heather. *Without Consent: The Ethics of Disclosing Personal Information in Public Archives*. Metuchen, NJ: Scarecrow Press, 1992.

MacNeil, Heather, et al. *Authenticity Task Force Report*. InterPARES, 2002. http://
www.interpares.org/book/interpares_book_d_part1.pdf (accessed February
10, 2010).

Mann, Thomas. *Tagebücher, 1933-1934*. Edited by Peter de Mendelssohn.
Frankfurt: Fischer, 1977.

Mapes, Mary. *Truth and Duty*. 2nd ed. New York: St. Martin's Griffin, 2006.

Marquardt, Alexander. "Obama Says Palin's Family Off Limits." CNN, September
2, 2008. http://www.cnn.com/2008/POLITICS/09/01/obama.palin/index.
html (accessed July 4, 2009).

Martines, Lauro. "Shoeless Soldiers." *Times Literary Supplement*, September 25,
2009, 12–13.

Masaryk, T.G. *Talks with T.G. Masaryk*. North Haven, CT: Catbird Press, 1995.

Mendelssohn, Peter de, and Herbert Wiesner. *Thomas Mann 1875-1975*. Bonn:
Inter Nationes, 1975.

Menne-Haritz, Angelika. "Privacy and Access in German Archives." Unpublished
paper delivered at the annual meeting of the Society of American Archivists,
Chicago, August 30, 2007.

Merriam-Webster OnLine. http://www.merriam-webster.com.

Michaud, Christopher. "Magna Carta Fetches $21.3 Million at Sotheby's Auction."
Reuters, December 19, 2007. http://www.reuters.com/article/rbssIndus-
triesMaterialsUtilitiesNews/idUSN1854840520071219 (accessed October
23, 2009).

Middlebrook, Diane Wood. *Anne Sexton: A Biography*. Boston: Houghton Mifflin,
1991.

Morehouse College, Robert W. Woodruff Library of the Atlanta University Center.
http://www.auctr.edu/mlkcollection/phase-one.asp (accessed September 3,
2009).

Morris, Benny. "Politics by Other Means." *New Republic*, March 22, 2004. Quoted
in the *New York Review*, May 28, 2009.

Nabokov, Vladimir. *The Song of Igor's Campaign: An Epic of the Twelfth Century*.
Translated from Old Russian by Vladimir Nabokov. New York: Vintage
Books, 1960.

Nelson Mandela Foundation. http://www.nelsonmandela.org (accessed January
6, 2010).

Nicholas, Lynn. *The Rape of Europa: The Fate of Europe's Treasures in the Third Reich and the Second World War*. New York: Knopf, 1994.

O'Neill, James E. "Replevin: A Public Archivist's Perspective." *Prologue* 11 (Fall 1979).

Otáhal, Milan. "The Manuscript Controversy in the Czech National Revival." *Cross Currents: A Yearbook of Central European Culture* 5 (1986): 247–77.

O'Toole, James M. "Archive on Trial: The Strange Case of the Martin Luther King, Jr., Papers." In *Archives and the Public Good: Accountability and Records in Modern Society*, edited by Richard J. Cox and David A. Wallace, 21–35. Westport, CT: Quorum Books, 2002.

Peace, Nancy E. *Archival Choices: Managing the Historical Record in an Age of Abundance*. Lexington, MA: Lexington Books, 1984.

Pearce-Moses, Richard. *A Glossary of Archival and Records Terminology*. http://www.archivists.org/glossary/term_details.asp (accessed September 22, 2009).

Peckham, Howard. "Aiding the Scholar in Using Manuscript Collections." *American Archivist* 19 (July 1956): 221–28.

Peterson, Gary M., and Trudy Huskamp Peterson. *Archives and Manuscripts: Law*. Chicago: Society of American Archivists, 1985.

Peterson, Trudy Huskamp. "Archives in Service to the State." In *Political Pressure and the Archival Record*, edited by Margaret Procter, Michael Cook, and Caroline Williams, 259–76. Chicago: Society of American Archivists, 2006.

Peterson, Trudy Huskamp. "Privacy Is not a Rose." Unpublished paper delivered at the annual meeting of the Society of American Archivists, Chicago, August 30, 2007.

Pikhoia, Rudolf, interview with Grigorii Tsitriniak. "O chem molchat archivy" [What the archives are silent about]. *Novoe russkoe slovo* 84, no. 29 (May 7, 1993), unpaginated feuilleton.

Pitti, Daniel V. "The Berkeley Finding Aids Project: Standards in Navigation." Paper presented at the Association of Research Libraries Fourth Symposium on Electronic Publishing on the Network, November 1994. In *Filling the Pipeline and Paying the Piper: Proceedings of the Fourth Symposium, November 5–7, 1994*, edited by Ann Okerson. Washington, DC: Association of Research Libraries, 1995. http://sunsite.berkeley.edu/FindingAids/EAD/arlpap.html (accessed July 29, 2009).

Pitti, Daniel V. "Encoded Archival Description: An Introduction and Overview." *D-Lib Magazine* 5, no. 11 (November 1999). http://www.dlib.org.

Posner, Ernst. *Archives and the Public Interest: Selected Essays,* edited by Kenneth W. Munden. Introduction by Angelika Menne-Haritz. Chicago: Society of American Archivists, 2006. First edition 1967.

Posner, Ernst. *Archives in the Ancient World.* Chicago: Society of American Archivists, 2003. First edition 1972.

Posner, Richard A. "Review: The Learned Hand Biography and the Question of Judicial Greatness." *Yale Law Journal* 104, no. 2 (November 1994): 511–40. Available at http://www.jstor.org/stable/797010?seq=2 (accessed July 27, 2009).

Procter, Margaret, Michael Cook, and Caroline Williams, eds. *Political Pressure and the Archival Record.* Chicago: Society of American Archivists, 2006.

Prosser, William L. "Privacy." In *Privacy and Confidentiality Perspectives: Archivists and Archival Records,* edited by Menzi L. Behrnd-Klodt and Peter J. Wosh, 31–52. Chicago: Society of American Archivists, 2005.

Pugh, Mary Jo. *Providing Reference Services for Archives and Manuscripts.* Chicago: Society of American Archivists, 1992. Revised and expanded 2005.

Pushkin, Alexander. *Eugene Onegin.* Translated and edited by Vladimir Nabokov. Princeton: Bollingen and Princeton University Press, paperback edition, 1981.

Quigley, Carroll. *Tragedy and Hope: A History of the World in Our Time.* New York: Macmillan, 1966.

Quinn, William. "The Other End of the Abu Ghraib Camera." *New York Times,* July 25, 2009.

Ranke, Leopold von, and Wilhelm Humboldt. *The Theory and Practice of History.* Indianapolis: Bobbs-Merrill, 1973. First German edition 1824.

Rapport, Leonard. "No Grandfather Clause: Reappraising Accessioned Records." *American Archivist* 44 (Spring 1981): 143–50.

Rendell, Kenneth W. *Forging History: The Detection of Fake Letters and Documents.* Norman: University of Oklahoma Press, 1994.

Rich, Motoko. "Harry Belafonte Withdraws Dr. King's Documents from Auction." *New York Times,* December 11, 2008.

Ricœur, Paul. *History and Truth.* Translated by Charles A. Kelbley. Evanston: Northwestern University Press, 2007.

Ricœur, Paul. *Memory, History, Forgetting.* Translated by Kathleen Blamey and David Pellauer. Chicago: University of Chicago Press, 2004.

Rogers, David. *The Bodleian Library and its Treasures, 1320-1700.* Henley-on-Thames: Aidan Ellis, 1991.

Rosenberg, Karen. "Gemlike Paintings Set Free from Words." *New York Times,* June 19, 2009.

Rosenzweig, Roy. "Can History Be Open Source? Wikipedia and the Future of the Past." *Journal of American History* 117 (June 2006).

Routledge Encyclopedia of Philosophy. http://www.rep.routledge.com.

Rowland, Ingrid D. *The Scarith of Scornello: A Tale of Renaissance Forgery.* Chicago: University of Chicago Press, 2005.

Ryan, Judith, and Alfred Thomas, eds. *Cultures of Forgery: Making Nations, Making Selves.* New York and London: Routledge, 2003.

Schellenberg, T. R. *The Appraisal of Modern Public Records.* Washington, DC: U.S. Government Printing Office, 1956.

Schmid, Randolph E. "Privacy Questioned under New Law." *New York Times,* January 5, 2007, sec. 6A.

Segel, B.W., and Richard S. Levy. *A Lie and a Libel: The History of the Protocols of the Elders of Zion.* Lincoln: University of Nebraska Press, 1995.

Shmelev, Anatol. "Privacy in the Russian Archives." Paper delivered at the annual meeting of the Society of American Archivists, Chicago, August 30, 2007.

Simpson, Elizabeth, ed. *The Spoils of War: World War II and its Aftermath: The Loss, Reappearance, and Recovery of Cultural Property.* New York: Harry N. Abrams, 1997.

Smith, Nancy Kegan, and Gary M. Stern. "A Historical Review of Access to Records in Presidential Libraries." *Public Historian* 28, no. 3 (Summer 2006): 79–116. http://caliber.ucpress.net/doi/pdf/10.1525/tph.2006.28.3.79 (accessed September 24, 2009).

Smith, Robert Ellis. *Ben Franklin's Web Site: Privacy and Curiosity from Plymouth Rock to the Internet.* Providence, RI: Privacy Journal, 2000.

Smith, Robert Ellis. *Compilation of State and Federal Privacy Laws with Current 2009 Supplement.* Washington, DC: Privacy Journal, 2009.

Society of American Archivists. "Commentary on Code of Ethics." *American Archivist* 43 (Summer 1980): 415–18.

Society of American Archivists. "Publications, Brochures." http://www.saa.org (accessed February 12, 2009).

Solove, Daniel J. *The Future of Reputation: Gossip, Rumor, and Privacy on the Internet.* New Haven: Yale University Press, 2007.

Solove, Daniel J. "Privacy and Power: Computer Databases and Metaphors for Information Privacy." *Stanford Law Review* (2001): 1393.

Solove, Daniel J. *Understanding Privacy.* Cambridge, MA: Harvard University Press, 2008.

Solzhenitsyn, Alexander. *Arkhipelag GULag.* Paris: YMCA Press, 1973.

Stanford Encyclopedia of Philosophy. http://plato.stanford.edu (accessed August 2, 2009).

Stanford University, The Martin Luther King, Jr., Research and Education Institute. http://mlk-kpp01.stanford.edu (accessed September 23, 2009).

The State, South Carolina, "Exclusive: Read E-Mails between Sanford, Woman." June 25, 2009. http://www.thestate.com/sanford/story/879225.html (accessed July 24, 2009).

Sweden, Riksarkivet. "Brochure on Swedish National Archives." http://www.riksarkivet.se/ (accessed September 25, 2009).

Thomassen, Theo. "Archivists between Power and Knowledge." http://pagesperso-orange.fr/felina/doc/arch/thomarch.pdf (accessed February 10, 2010).

Turley, Richard E. *Victims: The LDS Church and the Mark Hofmann Case.* Urbana: University of Illinois Press, 1992.

Tvorogov, Oleg. "Vlesova kniga." *Trudy Otdela drevnerusskoi literatury* 43 (1990): 170–254.

Ungar, Sanford. *The Papers and the Papers: An Account of the Legal and Political Battle over the Pentagon Papers.* New York: E.P. Dutton, 1972.

University of California, San Francisco. Legacy Tobacco Documents Library. http://legacy.library.ucsf.edu/about/about_collections.jsp (accessed February 10, 2010).

U.S. Department of Health, Education, and Welfare. Secretary's Advisory Committee on Automated Personal Data Systems. *Records, Computers, and the Rights of Citizens.* Cambridge, MA: MIT Press, 1973.

U. S. Information Infrastructure Task Force. Privacy Working Group. *Privacy and the National Information Infrastructure: Principles for Providing and Using Personal Information* (June 6, 1995). http://aspe.hhs.gov/datacncl/niiprivp.htm (accessed February 10, 2010).

Valla, Lorenzo. *Treatise on the Donation of Constantine, 1440.* Translated by Christopher Bush Coleman. New Haven: Yale University Press, 1922. Text available at Google Books, http://books.google.com (accessed October 13, 2009).

Vincent, Nicholas. "Free and Forest-Born." Review of *The Magna Carta Manifesto* by Peter Linebaugh. *Times Literary Supplement,* July 4, 2008.

Wagner, Ralph D. *A History of the Farmington Plan.* Lanham, MD: Scarecrow Press, 2002.

Warren, Samuel D., and Louis D. Brandeis. "The Right to Privacy." In *Privacy and Confidentiality Perspectives: Archivists and Archival Records,* edited by Menzi L. Behrnd-Klodt and Peter J. Wosh, 15–30. Chicago: Society of American Archivists, 2005.

Whitaker, Reg. *The End of Privacy: How Total Surveillance Is Becoming a Reality.* New York: New Press, Norton, 1999.

White, Gayle. "King Papers Go Public Today with Online Access." *Atlanta Journal-Constitution,* January 13, 2009.

Whorley, Tywanna. "The Tuskegee Syphilis Study and the Politics of Memory." In *Archives and the Public Good: Accountability and Records in Modern Society,* edited by Richard J. Cox and David A. Wallace, 165–75. Westport, CT: Quorum Books, 2002.

Wiener, John. "The Cigarette Papers." *The Nation,* January 1, 1996.

Williams, Robert C. *The Historian's Toolbox.* Armonk, NY: M.E. Sharp, 2003.

Wood, Lamont. "The Lost NASA Tapes: Restoring Lunar Images after 40 Years in the Vault." *Computerworld,* June 29, 2009. www.computerworld.com (accessed July 27, 2009).

Wright, Elaine. *Muraqqá: Imperial Mughal Albums from the Chester Beatty Library, Dublin.* Alexandria, VA: Art Services International, 2008.

Wurl, Joel. "Ethnicity as Provenance: In Search of Values and Principles for Documenting the Immigrant Experience." *Archival Issues* 29, no. 1 (2005): 65–76.

Zinn, Howard. *A People's History of the United States 1492–Present,* 20th anniversary edition. New York: HarperCollins, 1999.

Zinn, Howard. *The Zinn Reader: Writings on Disobedience and Democracy.* New York: Seven Stories Press, 1997.

Notes

Introduction

[1] Nelson Mandela Foundation, "Memory for Justice: Report on a Colloquium," August 18, 2005, quoted in Randall C. Jimerson, *Archives Power: Memory, Accountability, and Social Justice* (Chicago: Society of American Archivists, 2009), 366. For background see Nelson Mandela Foundation website, http://www.nelsonmandela.org (accessed January 6, 2010).

[2] For those interested in exploring the work of the great ethical philosophers, a useful portal is the Stanford Encyclopedia of Philosophy (SEP), http://plato.stanford.edu (accessed August 2, 2009). The SEP is constantly updated and expanded, and it remains available free of charge. Of particular note for archivists is the entry for the French philosopher Paul Ricœur (1913–2005), author of *History and Truth* and *Memory, History and Forgetting*. Downloadable English text for the works of the great ethical philosophers can be found free of charge at Project Gutenberg. For Aristotle's *Ethics* see http://www.gutenberg.org/etext/8438. For the *Analects* of Confucius see http://www.gutenberg.org/etext/3330. For Immanuel Kant's *Fundamental Principles of the Metaphysic of Morals* see http://www.gutenberg.org/etext/5682, and for his *Critique of Practical Reason* see http://www.gutenberg.org/etext/5683 (accessed January 7, 2010). These fundamental texts are still thought-provoking centuries after they were

written, and they provide a foundation for understanding the long history of ethics as a field.

[3] http://www.merriam-webster.com/dictionary/ethic (accessed February 17, 2010).

[4] *Routledge Encyclopedia of Philosophy*, ed. E. Craig, s.v. "Professional Ethics" (by Ruth Chadwick), http://www.rep.routledge.com/article/L077 (accessed April 8, 2010).

[5] Heinz C. Luegenbiehl, "Codes of Ethics and the Moral Education of Engineers," in *Ethical Issues in Engineering*, ed. Deborah G. Johnson (Englewood Cliffs, NJ: Prentice-Hall, 1991), 138. For more on general professional ethics, primarily law, medicine and business, see Alan Goldman's widely available classic, *The Moral Foundations of Professional Ethics* (Totowa, NJ: Rowman and Littlefield, 1980). While published decades ago, Goldman's analysis continues to provide a sound basis for understanding the issues. Also useful for methodology is the *Oxford Handbook of Practical Ethics*, ed. Hugh LaFollette (Oxford, NY: Oxford University Press, 2003). For a brief online guide to applying formal ethics to information management problems see Alan Andolsen, "Choosing Ethical Solutions to RIM Problems," *Information Management Journal* 40, no. 5 (2006): 46–52, http://proquest.umi.com (accessed October 7, 2009). For the more current debates, see journals such as *Business Ethics Quarterly*, back issues available on JSTOR and Philosophy Online.

[6] Center for the Study of Ethics in the Professions, Illinois Institute of Technology, Chicago, http://ethics.iit.edu/codes (accessed August 2, 2009).

[7] Menzi Behrnd-Klodt and Peter J. Wosh, eds., *Privacy and Confidentiality Perspectives: Archivists and Archival Records* (Chicago: Society of American Archivists, 2005).

[8] The author consulted a facsimile edition of Jean Mabillon's 1681/1709 *De re diplomatica*. One does not need to know Latin to appreciate the examples. A good working definition of diplomatics: "The study of the creation, form, and transmission of records, and their relationship to the facts represented in them and to their creator, in order to identify, evaluate, and communicate their nature and authenticity" in Richard Pierce-Moses, *A Glossary of Archival and Records Terminology* (Chicago: Society of American Archivists, 2005), http://www.archivists.org/glossary (accessed August 31, 2009).

[9] Luciana Duranti, *Diplomatics: New Uses for an Old Science* (Lanham, MD: Scarecrow Press, 1998).

[10] For an English translation see Leopold von Ranke and Wilhelm Humboldt, *The Theory and Practice of History*, ed. Georg G. Iggers and Konrad von Moltke (Indianapolis: Bobbs-Merrill, 1973; first German edition 1824). For Humboldt and Ranke's famous injunction to "tell it like it actually was" see xix, xxiv, 5, 137.

[11] Georg G. Iggers and James M. Powell, *Leopold von Ranke and the Shaping of the Historical Discipline* (Syracuse, NY: Syracuse University Press, 1990).

[12] Ranke and Humboldt, *Theory and Practice of History*, 45.

[13] Ranke and Humboldt, *Theory and Practice of History*, xv.

[14] Jacques Derrida, *Archive Fever: A Freudian Impression* (Chicago: University of Chicago Press, 1996).

[15] Verne Harris, *Archives and Justice: A South African Perspective* (Chicago: Society of American Archivists, 2007).

[16] Benny Morris, "Politics by Other Means," *The New Republic*, March 22, 2004. Quoted by Gershom Gorenberg, "The War to Begin All Wars," *New York Review of Books* 56, no. 9 (May 28, 2009), 38.

[17] Gorenberg, "The War to Begin All Wars," 38–41.

[18] Richard J. Cox and David A. Wallace, *Archives and the Public Good: Accountability and Records in Modern Society* (Westport, CT: Quorum Books, 2002), 2.

[19] Anthony Grafton, *New Worlds, Ancient Texts: The Power of Tradition and the Shock of Discovery* (Cambridge, MA: Belknap Press, Harvard University Press, 1992), 134.

[20] Howard Zinn, *A People's History of the United States 1492-Present*, 20th anniversary edition (New York: Harper Collins, 1999). In the afterword he states: "From first grade to graduate school, I was given no inkling that the landing of Christopher Columbus in the New World initiated a genocide, in which the indigenous population of Hispaniola was annihilated." In a paper delivered at the Society of American Archivists annual meeting in 1970 in Washington, D.C., he expressed his dissatisfaction with the teaching of American history: "It is easy to detect the control of the German scholars or the Russian scholars, but much harder to recognize that the high school texts of our own country have fostered jingoism, war heroes, the Sambo approach to the black man, the vision of the Indian as savage, the notion that white Western Civilization is the cultural, humanistic summit of man's time on earth." In Howard Zinn, *The Zinn Reader: Writings on Disobedience and Democracy* (New York: Seven Stories Press, 1997), 520.

[21] Alexander Solzhenitsyn, *Arkhipelag GULag* (Paris: YMCA Press, 1973). Solzhenitsyn was working from sketchy documents and eyewitness accounts. After the fall of communism, the secret official government archives were opened and microfilmed by a consortium including the Hoover Institution, Chadwyck-Healey, and Rossarkhiv. The film set, which consists of 11,818 reels, is now marketed by ProQuest as *Archives of the Soviet Communist Party and Soviet State: Microfilm, 1993–2004*. In 2009, 192 researchers used the microfilm set in the Hoover Institution Archives at Stanford University. A seven-volume set of documents, drawn primarily from the microfilm, was edited by Russian archivists and published by Rosspen: Iu. N. Afanas´ev, et al., ed., *Istoriia stalinskogo Gulaga: Konets 1920kh–pervaia polovina 1950kh godov. Sobranie dokumentov*, 7 vols. [History of the Stalinist Gulag: The End of the 1920s to the First Half of the 1950s. A Collection of Documents] (Moscow: Rosspen, 2004–5), ISBN 5824306044 (set).

[22] Anne Applebaum, *Gulag: A History* (New York: Doubleday, 2003). This documentary history won the 2004 Pulitzer Prize for Nonfiction and Britain's 2004 Duff-Cooper Prize. For Rudolf Pikhoia's role in stopping destruction of archives see his interview with Grigorii Tsitriniak, "O chem molchat archivy" [What the archives are silent about], *Novoe russkoe slovo* 84, no. 29 (May 7, 1993), New York, unpaginated feuilleton.

[23] Robert Edwin Herzstein, *Waldheim: the Missing Years* (New York: Arbor House, 1988).

[24] Menzi L. Behrnd-Klodt, *Navigating Legal Issues in Archives* (Chicago: Society of American Archivists, 2008). With the understanding that some technical points are now out of date, it is also still worth consulting the older volume on archives and the law by Gary Peterson and Trudy Huskamp Peterson, *Archives and Manuscripts: Law* (Chicago: Society of American Archivists, 1985).

[25] Karen M. Benedict, *Ethics and the Archival Profession: Introduction and Case Studies* (Chicago: Society of American Archivists, 2003).

[26] Randall C. Jimerson, *Archives Power: Memory, Accountability, and Social Justice* (Chicago: Society of American Archivists, 2009). See also Cox and Wallace, *Archives and the Public Good*, and Harris, *Archives and Justice*. Another resource on accountability is *Archives, Documentation, and Institutions of Social Memory*, ed. Francis X. Blouin Jr. and William G. Rosenberg (Ann Arbor, MI: Bentley Historical Library, 2000).

Chapter 1

[1] Quote from an early version of the Archivist's Code is available on the U.S. National Archives and Records Administration website: http://www.archives. gov/preservation/professionals/archivist-code.html (accessed November 25, 2009). See appendix A.

[2] Eric Ketelaar, "Professional Ethics: The Moral Defence of the Archivist," October 1998, http://www.ucd.ir/archives/html/conferences/cyber4.htm (accessed February 8, 2010).

[3] Philip G. Bauer, "Recruitment, Training, and Promotion in the National Archives," *American Archivist* 18, no. 4 (October 1955): 291–305. The seven elements for GS-7 qualification are listed on page 296; the Archivist's Code is published on pages 307–8. This version is slightly different from the one posted on the NARA website. Grover's earlier version is referenced in "Minutes, Council Meeting 28 January 1980, Commentary on Code of Ethics," *American Archivist* 43, no. 3 (Summer 1980): 415–18. See also Karen Benedict, "An Evolution in a Code of Ethics: the Society of American Archivists," paper delivered at the International Conference on Archives, August 23-29, 2004, Vienna, http://www. Wien2004.ica.org (accessed January 2008). For several hundred professional codes consult the Center for the Study of Ethics in the Professions, Illinois Institute of Technology, http://ethics.iit.edu/index1.php/Programs/Codes%20 of%20Ethics. The need for constant code revisions is not new. One of the oldest and most respected professional codes, the Hippocratic Oath for medical doctors from ca. 300 BCE, forbids physicians from performing surgery to remove kidney stones. This provision is clearly out of date.

[4] Ernst Posner, *Archives and the Public Interest: Selected Essays by Ernst Posner*, edited by Ken Munden, with a new introduction by Angelika Menne-Haritz (Chicago: Society of American Archivists, 2006; 1st edition 1967), 21.

[5] Society of American Archivists, "Council Meeting 28 January 1980," *American Archivist* 43, no. 3 (Summer 1980).

[6] David E. Horn, "The Development of Ethics in Archival Practice," *American Archivist* 52, no. 1 (Winter 1989): 64–71. Quote from page 65; recommendation for a manual on ethics is on page 69.

[7] The Manuscript Society, "The Manuscript Society Code of Ethics," adopted by the Board of Trustees May 26, 1999, http://www.manuscript.org/2009ethics. html (accessed November 1, 2009). See appendix A for the basic text.

[8] Institute of Certified Records Managers (ICRM), Code of Ethics and Ethics Review Procedures, https://db.icrm.org/crm/index.jsp?submit_menu-118 (accessed November 25, 2009).

[9] International Council on Archives, Code of Ethics, http://www.ica.org/sites/default/fiels/Ethics-En.pdf (accessed November 19, 2009).

[10] U.S. Government Ethics Standards, http://rf-web.tamu.edu/security/security%20guide/Ethics?Intro.htm (accessed September 3, 2009).

[11] Association of Art Museum Directors, Code of Ethics, http://www.aamd.org/about/ (accessed November 25, 2009).

[12] Karen Benedict, "An Evolution in a Code of Ethics: The Society of American Archivists" (paper delivered at the International Conference on Archives, Vienna, August 23–29, 2004), 4, http://www.Wien2004.ica.org (accessed January 2008).

[13] American Library Association Code of Ethics website, http://www.ala.org/ala/aboutala/offices/oif/statementspols/codeofethics/codeethics.cfm (accessed November 19, 2009).

[14] Frank Boles, "Enforcing Ethics," March 20, 2009, Society of American Archivists website, http://www.archivists.org/news/ethics09.asp (accessed November 19, 2009).

[15] American Historical Association, "Guiding Principles on Taking a Public Stance," approved January 7, 2007, http://www.historians.org/governance/pd/2007_01_08_PublicStance.cfm (accessed November 25, 2009).

[16] Glenn Dingwall, "Trusting Archivists: The Role of Archival Ethics Codes in Establishing Public Faith," *American Archivist* 67 (Spring/Summer, 2004): 11–30.

[17] International Council on Archives, Code of Ethics, http://www.ica.org/sites/default/files/Ethics-EN.pdf (accessed June 2, 2008).

[18] Elena Danielson, "The Displaced Archives of Central Europe," *Comma* 3-4 (2004): 197–203.

[19] Randall C. Jimerson, "Rethinking Archival Ethics," in *Archives Power: Memory, Accountability, and Social Justice* (Chicago: Society of American Archivists, 2009): 342–63.

[20] Mark A. Greene, "The Power of Archives: Archivists' Values and Value in the Post-Modern Age" (SAA presidential address, San Francisco, August 2008), www.archivists.org/governance/presidential/GreeneAddressAug08.pdf (accesssed November 25, 2009).

Chapter 2

[1] Verne Harris, *Archives and Justice: A South African Perspective* (Chicago: Society of American Archivists, 2006), 104.

[2] Jack Boulware, "Snatching Saroyan: How Stanford University Aced Out UC Berkeley and Acquired the Million-Dollar Archives of San Francisco's Most Prolific Author, William Saroyan—Without Paying a Dime," February 11, 1998, http://www.sfweekly.com/1998-02-11/news/snatching-saroyan (accessed March 26, 2009).

[3] Judith A. Ellis, *Keeping Archives* (Port Melbourne: D.W. Thorpe/Australian Society of Archivists, 1996), 460. The working definition is "Materials received by a repository as a unit; an accession" according to Richard Pierce-Moses, *A Glossary of Archival and Records Terminology* (Chicago: Society of American Archivists, 2005), http://www.archivists.org/glossary.

[4] Ernst Posner, *Archives in the Ancient World* (Chicago: Society of American Archivists, 2003; 1st edition 1972), 64.

[5] Gary M. Peterson and Trudy Huskamp Peterson, *Archives and Manuscripts: Law* (Chicago: Society of American Archivists, 1985).

[6] Menzi L. Behrnd-Klodt, *Navigating Legal Issues in Archives* (Chicago: Society of American Archivists, 2008).

[7] Karen M. Benedict, *Ethics and the Archival Profession: Introduction and Case Studies* (Chicago: Society of American Archivists, 2003), 50.

[8] Harris, *Archives and Justice*, 104.

[9] Thomas S. Blanton, *White House E-mail: The Top Secret Computer Messages the Reagan/Bush White House Tried to Destroy* (New York: New Press, 1995).

[10] T.R. Schellenberg, *The Appraisal of Modern Public Records* (Washington, DC: U.S. Govt. Print. Off., 1956).

[11] Frank Boles, *Selecting and Appraising Archives and Manuscripts* (Chicago: Society of American Archivists, 2005). The literature on acquisitions is vast; the bibliography in Boles's manual is a good starting point. Also useful is the bibliography in Randall C. Jimerson, "Deciding What to Save," *OCLC Systems and Services* 19, no. 4 (2003).

[12] Kevin M. Guthrie, quoted in Richard J. Cox, *No Innocent Deposits: Forming Archives by Rethinking Appraisal* (Lanham, MD and Oxford: Scarecrow Press, 2004), 63. See also Kevin M. Guthrie, *The New-York Historical Society: Lessons from One Nonprofit's Long Struggle for Survival* (San Francisco: Jossey-Bass, 1996).

[13] For a sample of a simple mission statement see Boles, *Selecting and Appraising Archives and Manuscripts*, 71–72. A model suite of collecting policies is posted on the website of the American Heritage Center of the University of Wyoming, http://ahc.uwyo.edu/about/policies.htm (accessed September 9, 2009). See appendix B.

[14] Ralph D. Wagner, *A History of the Farmington Plan* (Lanham, MD: Scarecrow Press, 2002).

[15] James M. O'Toole, "Archives on Trial: The Strange Case of the Martin Luther King, Jr., Papers," in *Archives and the Public Good: Accountability and Records in Modern Society,* ed. Richard J. Cox and David A. Wallace (Westport, CT: Quorum Books, 2002), 21–35. An update on the King papers was kindly provided by Tywanna Whorley, telephone discussion, January 21, 2009.

[16] See http://www.codexsinaiticus.net (accessed February 19, 2009).

[17] See review of exhibition, Karen Rosenberg, "Pages of Gold" in "Gemlike Paintings Set Free from Words," *New York Times*, June 19, 2009.

[18] Elaine Wright, *Muraqqáʿ: Imperial Mughal Albums from the Chester Beatty Library, Dublin* (Alexandria, VA: Art Services International, 2008).

[19] Wright, *Muraqqáʿ,* xviii.

[20] Verne Harris, "'They Should Have Destroyed More': The Destruction of Public Records by the South African State in the Final Years of Apartheid, 1990–1994," in Cox and Wallace, *Archives and the Public Good,* 205–28.

[21] Hilary Jenkinson, *A Manual of Archive Administration Including the Problems of War Archives and Archive Making* (London: P. Lund, Humphries, 1965; 1st edition 1922), http://www.archive.org/stream/manualofarchivea00jenkuoft (accessed August 8, 2009).

[22] Boles, *Selecting and Appraising Archives and Manuscripts*, 14–15.

[23] The traditional archivist "must not be talkative, but must have his tongue in his heart and not his heart upon his tongue. He should have adequate fundaments and should in general talk very little lest he blab out the secrets of his registry." Quote from Ernst Posner, *Archives and the Public Interest: Selected Essays by Ernst Posner,* ed. Kenneth W. Munden (Chicago: Society of American Archivists, 2006; 1st edition 1967), 95. These remarks should be understood as ironic, as Posner himself was famous for his gregarious nature.

[24] Benedict, *Ethics and the Archival Profession,* 22–23.

[25] See Society of American Archivists website, "Publications, Brochures," http://www.saa.org (accessed February 12, 2009).

[26] Benedict, *Ethics and the Archival Profession,* 66–68.

[27] Boles, *Selecting and Appraising Archives and Manuscripts,* 95.

[28] Boles, *Selecting and Appraising Archives and Manuscripts,* 139.

[29] See *New York Times,* March 21, 2009. For a profile of the Marion True case, see Hugh Eakin, A Reporter at Large: "Treasure Hunt," *New Yorker,* December 17, 2007, 62.

[30] The author had several conversations in 1994–1995 with potential sellers who were quite certain that their papers were just as valuable as Ginsberg's and felt entitled to a similar price. See also Michael Blumenthal, "Allen Ginsberg, Millionaire?" *New York Times,* October 29, 1994, http://www.nytimes.com books/01/04/08/specials /ginsberg-millionaire (accessed March 26, 2009).

[31] The Society of American Archivists Code of Ethics for Archivists, 2005, http://www.archivists.org/governance/handbook/app_ethics.asp (accessed September 3, 2009). See appendix A. These codes are continuously under review and frequently revised, but the basic content is fairly stable. See website for the most current version.

[32] The International Council on Archives, Code of Ethics, 1996, http://www.ica.org/en/node/30046 (accessed July 5, 2008). See appendix A. These codes are continuously under review and frequently revised, but the basic content is fairly stable.

[33] O'Toole, "Archives on Trial," 21–35. O'Toole sums up his impressions as of 1993 on page 29: "The 'punch line' to my testimony…was to ask whether I thought the collection at Boston University had been handled in accord with sound professional practice. I answered that I thought it had not." On page 32 O'Toole concedes that, as of 2002, neither location was providing the King papers with the treatment they deserved. An update on the King papers was kindly provided by Tywanna Whorley, telephone discussion, January 21, 2009. All three major repositories and Stanford have helpful websites: the Robert W. Woodruff Library of the Atlanta University Center, http://www.auctr.edu/mlkcollection/phase-one.asp; the Howard Gotlieb Archival Research Center at Boston University, http://www2.bu.edu/dbin/archives/; the King Center of Atlanta, http://www.thekingcenter.org/ProgServices/Default.aspx; and the Martin Luther King, Jr., Research and Education Institute, http://mlk-kpp01.stanford.edu (accessed September 3, 2009).

[34] Shaila Dewan, "King Archives Will Be Sold at Auction," *New York Times,* June 9, 2006, http://query.nytimes.com (accessed January 19, 2009).

[35] Motoko Rich, "Harry Belafonte Withdraws Dr. King's Documents from Auction," *New York Times,* December 11, 2008.

[36] Martin Luther King, Jr., *The Papers of Martin Luther King, Jr.,* ed. Clayborne Carson (Berkeley: University of California Press, 1992, 1994, 1996, 2000, 2005, 2007).

[37] The Martin Luther King, Jr., Research and Education Institute, "Online King Records Access (OKRA) Launched," press release, May 18, 2009. For further information see http://www.kingpapers.org (accessed September 3, 2009). See also Gayle White, "King Papers Go Public Today With Online Access," *Atlanta Journal-Constitution,* January 13, 2009, http://ajc.printthis.clickability.com (accessed January 20, 2009).

[38] The memo can be found on the website, http://mlk-kpp01.stanford.edu by searching "FBI" (accessed September 8, 2009).

Chapter 3

[1] Frank Boles, *Selecting and Appraising Archives and Manuscripts* (Chicago: Society of American Archivists, 2005), xv.

[2] Richard Pearce-Moses, *A Glossary of Archival and Records Terminology,* http://www.archivists.org/glossary (accessed September 14, 2009). The definitions for *deaccessioning* and *weeding* are accompanied by helpful notes on the process: Materials may be deaccessioned because the repository has changed its collections policy and the material is no longer within its scope. Materials may be deaccessioned because they have been reappraised and found to be no longer suitable for continuing preservation. Materials that are badly decomposed and beyond repair may be deaccessioned. Deaccessioned material may be offered back to its donor, offered to another institution, or destroyed. Also called permanent withdrawal. Weeding and culling connote item-level separation, where purging, stripping, and screening connote removal of materials at the folder level or higher.

[3] A useful statement of deaccessioning policy can be found on the website of the American Heritage Center at the University of Wyoming in its "Collection Management Policy," available at http://ahc.uwyo.edu/about/policies.htm (accessed September 9, 2009). See appendix B.

[4] Leonard Rapport, "No Grandfather Clause: Reappraising Accessioned Records," *American Archivist* 44, no. 2 (Spring 1981): 143–50.

[5] Frank Boles, "Sampling in Archives," *American Archivist* 44, no. 2 (Spring 1981): 125–30. Quote on page 125.

[6] Karen M. Benedict, "Invitation to a Bonfire: Reappraisal and Deaccessioning of Records as Collection Management Tools in an Archives—A Reply to Leonard Rapport," *American Archivist* 47, no. 1 (Winter 1984): 43–49.

[7] Mary P. Ledwell, "The Theory of Reappraisal and Deaccessioning of Archival Material" (unpublished master's thesis, School of Library, Archival and Information Studies, University of British Columbia, 1995), http://hdl.handle.net/2429/3994 (accessed September 9, 2009).

[8] American Association of Museums, Code of Ethics for Museums, available at http://www.aam-us.org/museumresources/ethics/coe.cfm (accessed September 10, 2009). See appendix A.

[9] Kevin M. Guthrie, *The New-York Historical Society: Lessons from One Nonprofit's Long Struggle for Survival* (San Francisco: Jossey-Bass, 1996), 154–56. An online public domain version is available at Connexions, http://cnx.org/content/col10518/1.1/.

[10] May Chan, "Deaccessioning Archives: The Ongoing Controversy" (unpublished paper, School of Library and Information Studies, University of British Columbia, 2004).

[11] Mark A. Greene, "I've Deaccessioned and Lived to Tell about It: Confessions of an Unrepentant Reappraiser," *Archival Issues* 3, no.1 (2006): 7–22, http://www.pacsclsurvey.org/documents/greene/IveDeaccessioned.pdf (accessed September 9, 2009). I am grateful to Mark Greene for updating me on his reappraisal program in an email, September 14, 2009.

[12] Terry Cook, "'A Monumental Blunder': The Destruction of Records of Nazi War Criminals in Canada," in *Archives and the Public Good: Accountability and Records in Modern Society,* ed. Richard J. Cox and David A. Wallace (Westport, CT: Quorum Books, 2002), 55.

[13] Jim Burant, "Ephemera, Archives, and Another View of History," *Archivaria* 40 (1995): 189–98. See also Carl Honore, "Stuff: History in a Dustbin," *Toronto Globe and Mail,* March 14, 1992.

[14] American Association of Museums, Code of Ethics for Museums, http://www.aam-us.org/museumresources/ethics/coe.cfm (accessed September 10, 2009).

[15] Michael Doylen, "Experiments in Deaccessioning: Archives and On-line Auctions," *American Archivist* 64, no. 2 (Fall/Winter 2001): 350–62.

[16] See report in the *New York Times*, March, 18, 2009, available at www.nytimes.com/2009/03/18/arts (accessed March 23, 2009).

[17] Frederick Stratton, trustee, Frank Lloyd Wright Foundation, email communications to author, March 21, 2009 and March 27, 2009.

[18] See report in the *New York Times*, June 23, 2009.

[19] Richard J. Cox and David A. Wallace, *Archives and the Public Good: Accountability and Records in Modern Society* (Westport, CT: Quorum Books, 2002).

[20] Cook, "'A Monumental Blunder': The Destruction of Records of Nazi War Criminals in Canada," 37–65. Quote on page 37.

[21] Jules Deschênes, *Commission of Inquiry on War Criminals: Report. Part 1* (Ottawa: Minister of Supply and Services Canada, 1986).

[22] Verne Harris, "'They Should Have Destroyed More': The Destruction of Public Records by the South African State in the Final Years of Apartheid, 1990–1994," in Cox and Wallace, *Archives and the Public Good*, 205–28. Quotes from pages 205–6.

[23] Shelley L. Davis, *Unbridled Power: Inside the Secret Culture of the IRS* (New York: HarperBusiness, 1997). See also Shelley Davis, "The Failure of Federal Records Management: The IRS versus a Democratic Society," in Cox and Wallace, *Archives and the Public Good*, 115–33.

[24] Ian Austen, "National Gallery of Canada Looks Beyond Controversy and Court," *New York Times*, December 28, 2008.

[25] California State Archives appraisal policy, http://www.sos.ca.gov/archives/state-records-appraisal/ (accessed February 20, 2009).

[26] Michael Falcone, "Court Orders Search of White House Computers," *New York Times*, January 15, 2009. This is just one of many disputes over high-level email.

[27] Several anecdotes are drawn from the author's observations at different repositories. Names have been omitted since the intention is simply to provide general background.

[28] Nicholson Baker, "Annals of Scholarship: Discards," *New Yorker*, April 4, 1994, 64–86; "Letter from San Francisco: The Author vs. the Library," *New Yorker*, October 14, 1996, 50–62; "Deadline: The Author's Desperate Bid to Stop the Trashing of America's Historic Newspapers," *New Yorker*, July 24, 2000, 42–61; *Double Fold: Libraries and the Assault on Paper* (New York: Random House, 2001).

[29] Baker, "Letter from San Francisco: The Author vs. the Library," quotes from pages 50 and 57.

[30] Baker, "Deadline: The Author's Desperate Bid to Stop the Trashing of America's Historic Newspapers," 51.

[31] Richard J. Cox, *Vandals in the Stacks? A Response to Nicholson Baker's Assault on Libraries* (Westport, CT: Greenwood Press, 2002).

[32] Stanton A. Glantz, *The Cigarette Papers* (Berkeley: University of California Press, 1996).

[33] Guthrie, *The New-York Historical Society: Lessons from One Nonprofit's Long Struggle for Survival*, 4–5.

[34] Guthrie, *The New-York Historical Society: Lessons from One Nonprofit's Long Struggle for Survival*, 31.

[35] Guthrie, *The New-York Historical Society: Lessons from One Nonprofit's Long Struggle for Survival*. The discussion of acquisitions and deaccessioning is found on pages 154–57; the quotation is from page 157.

[36] Richard J. Cox, *No Innocent Deposits: Forming Archives by Rethinking Appraisal* (Lanham, MD: Scarecrow Press, 2004), deaccessioning checklist on page 108. See also the deaccessioning checklist in Menzi L. Behrnd-Klodt, *Navigating Legal Issues in Archives* (Chicago: Society of American Archivists, 2008), 64–67.

Chapter 4

[1] The freedom to "receive and impart information" is enshrined in article 19 of the Universal Declaration of Human Rights, http://www.un.org/Overview/rights.html (accessed March 6, 2009).

[2] John Hope Franklin, *Mirror to America: The Autobiography of John Hope Franklin* (New York: Farrar, Straus, and Giroux, 2005), 83–88, 119. Thanks are due to Prof. Tywanna Whorley for bringing this and other instructive examples to my attention.

[3] Sara S. Hodson, "In Secret Kept, in Silence Sealed: Privacy in the Papers of Authors and Celebrities," *American Archivist* 67, no. 2 (Fall/Winter 2004): 197. Also in *Privacy and Confidentiality Perspectives: Archivists and Archival Records*, ed. Menzi L. Behrnd-Klodt and Peter J. Wosh (Chicago: Society of American Archivists, 2005), 131–48. For specific examples of discriminatory access policies in previous eras, see page 134.

[4] Code of Ethics for Archivists, approved by the Society of American Archivists Council, February 5, 2005, http://www.archivists.org/governmance/handbook/

app_ethics.asp (accessed September 3, 2009). While frequently revised, archival codes normally have similar provisions for open and equitable access. *Access* is defined as "n. ~ 1. The ability to locate relevant information through the use of catalogs, indexes, finding aids, or other tools. – 2. The permission to locate and retrieve information for use (consultation or reference) within legally established restrictions of privacy, confidentiality, and security clearance. – 3. COMPUTING The physical processes of retrieving information from storage media." Quote from Richard Pearce-Moses, *A Glossary of Archival and Records Terminology*, http://www.archivists.org/glossary/term_details.asp (accessed September 22, 2009).

[5] Mary Jo Pugh, *Providing Reference Services for Archives and Manuscripts* (Chicago: Society of American Archivists, 1992; updated and greatly expanded 2005).

[6] Howard Peckham, "Aiding the Scholar in Using Manuscript Collections," *American Archivist* 19 (July 1956): 221–28. This quotation is cited in the first edition of Pugh, *Providing Reference Services for Archives and Manuscripts*, 5.

[7] T. J. Binyon, *Pushkin: A Biography* (New York: Knopf, 2003), 355. "Archival youths" show up in Pushkin's epic poem *Eugene Onegin*, book seven, stanza XLIX, as self-indulgent young aristocrats interested only in occupying undemanding sinecures. Vladimir Nabokov explains the topos of the soft jobs in the records office in a commentary. *Eugene Onegin*, translated and edited by Vladimir Nabokov (Princeton: Bollingen and Princeton University Press, paperback edition, 1981), 119–20. These literary references provide a sense of the archival profession of that earlier era as an elite, privileged club.

[8] "Using archive information from public administration is, in Sweden, the right of everyone since the ratification of the Press Act in 1766." Quote from "Brochure on Swedish National Archives," http://www.riksarkivet.se/ (accessed September 25, 2009).

[9] Ernst Posner, *Archives and the Public Interest* (Chicago: Society of American Archivists, 2006), 26.

[10] Charles Kecskeméti and Iván Székely, *Access to Archives* (Council of Europe, 2005), 12–14. See also Eric Ketelaar, "The European Union and Its Archives," *American Archivist* 55, no.1 (Winter 1992): 40–45.

[11] Examples are taken from the author's diaries, 1998–2005.

[12] For the access policies of the Bodleian Library see http://www.ouls.ox.ac.uk/bodley/services/using (accessed September 25, 2009). For the origins of the reader's oath see David Rogers, *The Bodleian Library and its Treasures, 1320–1700* (Henley-on-Thames: Aidan Ellis, 1991), 9, 56, 122.

[13] Marianne MacDonald, "Amis Letters to Larkin Stir up Censorship Row: The Bodleian Is Sitting Tight," *Independent*, April 17, 1994, www.independent.co.uk (accessed March 27, 2009).

[14] See http://www.huntington.org (accessed September 25, 2009). Click on "Research" for access policies which include special provisions for independent scholars. For a model access policy from the pragmatic tradition see the homepage for the Bentley Historical Library at the University of Michigan, http://bentley.umich.edu/refhome/guide.php (accessed September 28, 2009).

[15] Access policy is available at http://www.bundesarchiv.de/bundesarchiv/ rechtsgrundlagen/benutzungsverordnung/index.html.en (accessed September 25, 2009). Note paragraph 3 (5): "Sollen aus dem Archivgut gewonnene Erkenntniss für anders als im Benutzungsantrag genannte Themen oder Zwecke verwendet worden, ist ein neuer Antrag erforderlich." [A new research application is required if the information acquired from the archival material is used for other purposes than the themes or purposes named in the original application.]

[16] The access policy for the East German secret police files, the so-called Stasi archives, is available online in both German and English. See www.bstu.bund. de; click on "Inspection of Files" (accessed September 25, 2009).

[17] Friedrich P. Kahlenberg, "Governmental Rule and Archivists: The Historical Experience of the 20th Century in Central Europe," in *Political Pressure and the Archival Record*, ed. Margaret Procter, Michael Cook, and Caroline Williams (Chicago: Society of American Archivists, 2005), 59–71. See reference to opening Stasi files on page 69. See also Elena Danielson, "Privacy Rights and the Rights of Political Victims: Implications of the German Experience," *American Archivist* 67, no. 2 (Fall/Winter 2004): 176–93.

[18] Orlando Figes, "Putin vs. the Truth," *New York Review of Books* 56, no. 7 (April 30, 2009), http://www.nybooks.com/articles/22642 (accessed April 21, 2009).

[19] Jonathan Brent, *Inside the Stalin Archives: Discovering the New Russia* (New York, London: Atlas, Turnaround, 2008).

[20] In the very first *Cold War International History Project Bulletin*, Spring 1992, James G. Hershberg reported from Moscow in an article entitled "Soviet Archives: The Opening Door." He realized that "As in Eastern Europe, political, academic, and archival figures must balance imperatives to study and ventilate past abuses and at the same time to safeguard the privacy rights of individuals; this dilemma is particularly acute in the case of the KGB. Pikhoia said that [then] current plans called for a seventy-five year restriction on materials that impinge on personal privacy, except for official documents and those documenting state persecution or criminal activity." Quote on page 14.

[21] Access policies for the Russian archives as of 1998 have long been available in English on the website of the International Institute of Social History in Amsterdam, in a section called Archeobibliobase: http://www.iisg.nl/abb/abb_rules.php (accessed March 5, 2009). For the most current rules, in Russian, see the homepage of the Russian Archives Service: http://rusarchives.ru (accessed September 25, 2009).

[22] See Library of Congress Special Collections policies, http://www.loc.gov/rr/rarebook/policies.html (accessed September 25, 2009). NARA has a clear, step-by-step website for planning a research visit: http://www.archives.gov/research/start/plan-visit.html (accessed September 28, 2009).

[23] See American Library Association Code of Ethics, http://www.ala.org/ala/aboutala/offices/oif/statementspols/codeofethics/codeethics.cfm (accessed September 25, 2009).

[24] Posner, *Archives and the Public Interest*, 95.

[25] For the current version of the ALA-SAA Joint Statement on Access, see Society of American Archivist website, http://www.archivists.org/statements/alasaa.asp.

[26] Pugh, *Providing Reference Services for Archives and Manuscripts*; for quotes see pages 21 and 150–51, for checklist see 318–22.

[27] Elena S. Danielson, "The Ethics of Access," *American Archivist* 52 (Winter 1989): 52–62; Ronald Becker, "The Ethics of Providing Access," *Provenance* 11 (1993) 57–77; Elena S. Danielson, "Ethics and Reference Services," in *Reference Services for Archives and Manuscripts*, ed. Laura B. Cohen (Binghamton, NY: Haworth Press, 1997), 107–24.

[28] For a more detailed discussion of these constraints on access see Menzi L. Behrnd-Klodt, *Navigating Legal Issues in Archives* (Chicago: Society of American Archivists, 2008), chapter 10; and Pugh, *Providing Reference Services for Archives and Manuscripts*, chapter 6.

[29] See http://www.archives.gov/isoo/contact/general.html (accessed July 27, 2009).

[30] Mark A. Greene and Dennis Meissner, "More Product, Less Process: Pragmatically Revamping Traditional Archival Processing," *American Archivist* 68, no. 1 (Fall/Winter 2005).

[31] Pugh, *Providing Reference Services for Archives and Manuscripts*, 225–39. For a sample online copyright reminder see http://library.stanford.edu/libraries_collections/copyright_reminders/ (accessed November 17, 2009).

[32] Gerald Gunther, *Learned Hand: The Man and the Judge* (New York: Knopf, 1994). See also Richard A. Posner, "Review: The Learned Hand Biography and the Question of Judicial Greatness," *Yale Law Journal* 104, no. 2 (1994): 511–40, available at JSTOR: http://www.jstor.org/stable/797010?seq=2 (accessed July 27, 2009).

[33] American Historical Association, Organization of American Historians, *Final Report of the Joint AHA-OAH Ad Hoc Committee to Investigate the Charges Against the Franklin D. Roosevelt Library and Related Matters* (Washington, DC: American Historical Association, 1970). Francis L. Loewenheim, an academic historian, accused archivists at the Franklin D. Roosevelt Library of withholding documents from him so that they could publish the materials first. The American Historical Association and the Organization of American Historians investigated the charges and in a 448-page report vindicated the archivists, who in fact had not withheld any documentation to further their own careers. Despite that fact, the report lists six recommendations for archivists to improve their communication with historians, such as expediting processing and publicizing the opening of collections. An unfortunate unintended consequence of the report is a chilling effect on the scholarly work of archivists, who probably should be publishing more of their findings when historians have not done so.

[34] Sanford Ungar, *The Papers and the Papers: An Account of the Legal and Political Battle over the Pentagon Papers* (New York: E.P. Dutton, 1972).

[35] Roy Rosenzweig, "Can History Be Open Source? Wikipedia and the Future of the Past," *Journal of American History* 93, no. 1 (June 2006).

[36] Abby Smith, "New-Model Scholarship: How Will It Survive?" (Washington, DC: Council on Library and Information Resources, 2003), 10.

[37] Tomas A. Lipinski and Johannes J. Britz, "Rethinking Ownership of Information in the Twentieth Century: Ethical Implications," *Ethics and Information Technology* 2, no. 1 (March 2000): 49–71. Quote from page 61.

[38] Scott Jaschik, "Digital Archives That Disappear," *Inside Higher Ed*, April 22, 2009, http://www.insidehihered.com/layout/et/print/news/2009/04/22/record (accessed April 22, 2009).

[39] Lamont Wood, "The Lost NASA tapes: Restoring Lunar Images after 40 years in the Vault," *Computerworld*, June 29, 2009.

[40] David Bearman, "Moments of Risk: Identifying Threats to Electronic Records," *Archivaria* 62 (Fall 2006). For more on Bearman's publications see http://www.archimuse.com (accessed July 27, 2009). See also Paul Conway, "Digitizing Preservation," *Library Journal* (February 1, 1994): 42–45. See also Margaret

Hedstrom, "Digital Preservation: A Time Bomb for Digital Libraries," *Computers and the Humanities* 31, no. 3 (1997): 189–202.

[41] Daniel V. Pitti, "The Berkeley Finding Aid Project: Standards in Navigation" (paper presented at the Association of Research Libraries Fourth Symposium on Electronic Publishing on the Network, November 1994), in *Filling the Pipeline and Paying the Piper: Proceedings of the Fourth Symposium, November 5–7, 1994*, ed. Ann Okerson (Washington, DC: Association of Research Libraries, 1995), http://sunsite.berkeley.edu/FindingAids/EAD/arlpap.html (accessed July 29, 2009).

[42] See the American Forest and Paper Association website, www.afandpa.org/Content NavigationMenu/Pulp-and_Paper/Fun-Facts (accessed March 26, 2009).

[43] Adrian Turner (Data Consultant, California Digital Library), email communication to author, May, 12, 2009.

[44] Daniel V. Pitti, "The Berkeley Finding Aid Project."

[45] For the Library of Congress American Memory database see http://www.memory.loc.gov/ammem/index.html. NARA has finding aids for fifty million unique records at "Access to Archival Databases" and 126,500 scanned digital documents at the "Archival Research Catalog," both available at http://www.archives.gov/research/tools/checklist.html. For the Librarians Internet Index see http:www.lii.org; and for another perspective see Research Buzz, http://www.researchbuzz.org (accessed April 2, 2009).

[46] Robin L. Chandler and Susan Storch, "Lighting Up the Internet: The Brown and Williamson Collection," in *Archives and the Public Good: Accountability and Records in Modern Society*, ed. Richard J. Cox and David A. Wallace (Westport, CT: Quorum Books, 2002), 149.

[47] Paula Hane, "OCLC to Open World Cat Searching to the World," posted July 17, 2006, http://newsbreaks.infotoday.com/nbreader.asp?ArticleID=16951 (accessed March 26, 2009).

[48] William E. Landis and Robin L. Chandler, eds., *Archives and the Digital Library* (Binghamton, NY: Hayworth Press, 2006), 57–58.

[49] Ronald Jantz and Michael Giarlo, "Digital Archiving and Preservation: Technologies and Processes for a Trusted Repository," in *Archives and the Digital Library*, 197.

Chapter 5

[1] Karen Butter, personal communication with the author, May 29, 2009.

[2] From its inception, the Legacy Tobacco Documents Library at the University of California medical school in San Francisco has collected documents that "were made available through litigation brought by the National Association of Attorneys General (NAAG) that resulted in the Master Settlement Agreement (1998)"; see http://legacy.library.ucsf.edu/about/about_collections.jsp. The UCSF website has a brief history of the collection: "The MSA settlement mandated that the tobacco companies release their internal company documents to the public by depositing them into a repository in Minnesota as well as creating and maintaining websites containing searchable electronic versions of the documents. The Legacy Tobacco Documents Library preserves and maintains electronic versions of these released documents, making them widely available to researchers and the general public"; see http://legacy.library.ucsf.edu/help/faq.jsp. Other online sources, such as the depository in Minnesota and industry websites, may eventually be closed. The LTDL website is considered the most permanent location for the "tobacco papers"; see http://legacy.library.ucsf.edu/about/about_data.jsp. While the initial box from an anonymous source had a puzzling history, all documents and multimedia items that are added to LTDL now have clearly traceable provenance. (All websites accessed June 7, 2009.) The author is grateful to Polina Ilieva for assistance in navigating these websites.

[3] Philip J. Hilts, "Tobacco Company Was Silent on Hazards," *New York Times*, May 7, 1994; Stanton A. Glantz, et al., "Looking Through a Keyhole at the Tobacco Industry: The Brown and Williamson Documents," *Journal of the American Medical Association* 274, no. 3 (July 1995): 219–24, also related articles in the same issue; Stanton A. Glantz, et al., *The Cigarette Papers* (Berkeley: University of California Press, 1996), also available online at UCSF library website; John Wiener, "The Cigarette Papers," *Nation,* January 1, 1996, also available at http://www.pbs.org/wgbh/pages/frontline/smoke/readings/wienerarticle.html (accessed April 9, 2009); Karen Butter, Robin Chandler, and John Kunze, "The Cigarette Papers: Issues in Publishing Materials in Multiple Formats," *D-Lib Magazine*, November 1996; Stanton A. Glantz and Edith D. Balbach, *Tobacco War: Inside the California Battles* (Berkeley: University of California Press, 2000); Robin L. Chandler and Susan Storch, "Lighting Up the Internet: The Brown and Williamson Collection," in Cox and Wallace, *Archives and the Public Good;* A. Landman and Stanton A. Glantz, "Tobacco Industry Efforts to Undermine Policy-Relevant Research," *American Journal of Public Health* 99, no. 1 (January 2009): 45–58.

[4] Personal communication. Unless otherwise noted, all quotes from Stanley A. Glantz in author's notes from an hour-long telephone interview conducted May 27, 2009.

[5] Personal communication. All quotes from Karen Butter are taken from an email to the author dated May 29, 2009.

[6] For examples of efforts to damage the careers of Glantz and his co-workers see Chandler and Storch, "Lighting Up the Internet," 138. For more on retaliation by the tobacco companies see Landman and Glantz, "Tobacco Industry Efforts to Undermine Policy-Relevant Research."

[7] "Walk the plank" quote in Glantz interview with author, May 27, 2009. See also discussion of university legal department support in Glantz, *Cigarette Papers*, xix.

[8] Chandler and Storch, "Lighting Up the Internet," 147. See also Wiener, "The Cigarette Papers," 5.

[9] Glantz, *Cigarette Papers,* 15–21.

[10] Glantz, *Cigarette Papers*, 328–37.

[11] Glantz, *Cigarette Papers*, 397, 415, 432.

[12] Glantz, *Cigarette Papers*, 242.

[13] Glantz, *Cigarette Papers*, 230.

[14] Glantz, *Cigarette Papers*, 246.

[15] Glantz, *Cigarette Papers*, xiv.

[16] Raymond Hernandez and David Kocieniewski, "As New Lawyer, Senator Was Active in Tobacco's Defense," *New York Times*, March 26, 2009, http://www.nytimes.com/2009/03/27/nyregion/27gillibrand.html (accessed October 5, 2009).

[17] Glantz, *Cigarette Papers,* 6–14.

[18] Glantz, *Cigarette Papers*, 14.

[19] Butter, Chandler, and Kunze, "The Cigarette Papers: Issues in Publishing Materials in Multiple Formats," 2.

[20] Karen Butter, personal communication with the author, May 29, 2009.

Chapter 6

[1] The Universal Declaration of Human Rights is available at the United Nations website, http://www.un.org/en/documents/udhr (accessed October 7, 2009). The quote from Scott McNealy is from Daniel J. Solove, *The Future of Reputation: Gossip, Rumor, and Privacy on the Internet* (New Haven: Yale University Press, 2007), 105. The quote from Vinton Cerf was published by Chelsea Anne Young,

"Digital Revolutionaries Discuss Past, Future of Technology," *Stanford Report*, March 5, 2009, http://news.stanford.edu/news/2009/march11/technology-google-microsoft-hennessy-03110 (accessed March 9, 2009).

[2] Trudy Huskamp Peterson, "Privacy Is not a Rose" (paper delivered at the annual meeting of the Society of American Archivists, Chicago, August 30, 2007), available at http://www.trudypeterson.com/documents/Privacyisnotaroserev.doc (accessed October 9, 2009).

[3] For the Swedish government listing of tax payments see http://www.taxeringskalendern.se (accessed July 20, 2009). Prof. Astrid Hedin of Uppsala University verified the access to tax data collected by the Swedish government, email communication, July 14, 2009.

[4] U.S. Department of Health, Education, and Welfare, Secretary's Advisory Committee on Automated Personal Data Systems, *Records, Computers, and the Rights of Citizens* (Cambridge, MA: MIT Press, 1973), quoted in Robert Ellis Smith, *Ben Franklin's Web Site: Privacy and Curiosity from Plymouth Rock to the Internet* (Providence, RI: Privacy Journal, 2000), 329.

[5] U.S. Information Infrastructure Task Force, Privacy Working Group, *Privacy and the National Information Infrastructure: Principles for Providing and Using Personal Information (June 6, 1995)*, quoted in Daniel J. Solove, "Privacy and Power: Computer Databases and Metaphors for Information Privacy," *Stanford Law Review* 53, no. 6 (2001): 1393, footnote 284.

[6] Annette Gordon-Reed, *The Hemingses of Monticello* (New York: Norton, 2008).

[7] http://www.masshist.org/thomasjeffersonpapers/farm/farmhemings.html (accessed July 18, 2009).

[8] Gordon-Reed, *The Hemingses of Monticello*, 16.

[9] Thomas Mann, *Tagebücher, 1933-1934*, ed. Peter de Mendelssohn, vol. 1 (Frankfurt: Fischer, 1977), 66, author's translation.

[10] Klaus W. Jonas, "The Thomas Mann Archive in Zurich," *German Quarterly* 35, no. 1 (January 1962): 10–16, http://www.jstor.org/stable/402301.

[11] Peter de Mendelssohn and Herbert Wiesner, *Thomas Mann 1875-1975* (Bonn: Inter Nationes, 1975).

[12] Mann, *Tagebücher*.

[13] Anthony Heilbut, *Thomas Mann: Eros and Literature* (New York: Knopf, Random House, 1996).

[14] Diane Wood Middlebrook, *Anne Sexton: A Biography* (Boston: Houghton Mifflin, 1991).

[15] Diane Middlebrook's website once contained a bibliography for articles on both sides of the debate: http://www.dianemiddlebrook.com (accessed July 10, 2009). The website encourages a discussion: "To explore ethical issue raised by the biography click on *Controversy.*"

[16] Hillary Clinton, interview with Matt Lauer, "The Today Show," NBC, January 27, 1998. Mrs. Clinton's restraint did not prevent bloggers from creating fictitious diaries attributed to her as an amusement.

[17] Robert Ellis Smith, *Compilation of State and Federal Privacy Laws with Current 2009 Supplement* (Washington, DC: Privacy Journal, 2009).

[18] Menzi L. Behrnd-Klodt and Peter J. Wosh, eds., *Privacy and Confidentiality Perspectives: Archivists and Archival Records* (Chicago: Society of American Archivists, 2005); and Menzi L. Behrnd-Klodt, *Navigating Legal Issues in Archives* (Chicago: Society of American Archivists, 2008).

[19] See Library of Congress, "Primary Documents in American History," http://www.loc.gov/rr/program/bib/ourdocs/bilofrights.html (accessed October 9, 2009).

[20] The author is grateful to two colleagues for copies of their conference papers on German and Russian archival privacy laws: Angelika Menne-Haritz, "Privacy and Access in German Archives, " and Anatol Shmelev, "Privacy in the Russian Archives." Both papers were delivered at the annual meeting of the Society of American Archivists, Chicago, August 30, 2007.

[21] Trudy Huskamp Peterson, "Privacy Is not a Rose," 2.

[22] The Universal Declaration of Human Rights is available at the United Nations website, http://www.un.org/en/documents/udhr (accessed October 7, 2009). The European Convention and privacy directives are available at http://conventions.coe.int/treaty/en/Treaties/Html/005.htm (accessed October 9, 2009) and http://ec.europa.eu/justice_home/fsj/privacy/ (accessed October 9, 2009).

[23] Behrnd-Klodt wrote a very accessible overview for the appendices of *Privacy and Confidentiality Perspectives*, 269–93.

[24] Mark A. Greene and Christine Weideman, "The Buckley Stops Where? The Ambiguity and Archival Implications of the Family Educational Rights and Privacy Act," in *Privacy and Confidentiality Perspectives*, 181–203.

[25] Behrnd-Klodt and Wosh, *Privacy and Confidentiality Perspectives*, 58.

[26] Smith, *Ben Franklin's Web Site*, 234–36.

[27] Reginald Whitaker, *The End of Privacy: How Total Surveillance is Becoming a Reality* (New York: New Press, Norton, 1999).

[28] Solove, "Privacy and Power: Computer Databases and Metaphors for Information Privacy," 1393. For Census Bureau marketing and comment on watching every click, see pages 1408 and 1412.

[29] See "FBI Wins Rosemary Award, March 13, 2009," National Security Archives, document available at http://www.gwu.edu/~nsarchiv/news/20090313/FBI_Background_Memo-Rosemary.pdf. The report documents the demand for unreasonable privacy waivers from Middle East suspects on page 4.

[30] Heather MacNeil, *Without Consent: The Ethics of Disclosing Personal Information in Public Archives* (Metuchen, NJ: Scarecrow Press, 1992).

[31] Heather MacNeil, "Information Privacy, Liberty, and Democracy," in *Privacy and Confidentiality Perspectives*, 67–81. Quote on page 70.

[32] Alexander Marquardt, "Obama Says Palin's Family Off Limits," CNN, September 2, 2008, http://www.cnn.com/2008/POLITICS/09/01/ obama.palin/index.html (accessed July 4, 2009).

[33] Smith, *Ben Franklin's Web Site,* 93.

[34] Smith, *Ben Franklin's Web Site,* 284–308.

[35] Sara S. Hodson, "In Secret Kept, In Silence Sealed: Privacy in the Papers of Authors and Celebrities," in *Privacy and Confidentiality Perspectives,* 131–48. Case on page 142.

[36] Mark A. Greene and Dennis Meissner, "More Product, Less Process: Pragmatically Revamping Traditional Archival Processing," *American Archivist* 68, no. 2 (Fall/Winter 2005): 208–63.

[37] Behrnd-Klodt and Wosh, *Privacy and Confidentiality Perspectives.*

[38] Elena S. Danielson, "Privacy Rights and the Rights of Political Victims: Implications of the German Experience," *American Archivist* 67, no. 2 (Fall/Winter 2004): 176–93.

Chapter 7

[1] Anthony Grafton, *Forgers and Critics: Creativity and Duplicity in Western Scholarship* (Princeton: Princeton University Press, 1990), 5.

[2] David Leppard, "Forgeries Revealed in National Archives," *Times,* May 4, 2008, http://www.timesonline.co.uk/tol/news/uk/article3867853.ece (accessed July 15, 2009).

3 Lee Israel, *Can You Ever Forgive Me? Memoirs of a Literary Forger* (New York: Simon and Schuster, 2008).

4 This example comes from the author's professional experience.

5 For more examples see David B. Gracy II, "What You Get Is Not What You See: Forgery and the Corruption of Recordkeeping Systems," in *Archives and the Public Good: Accountability and Records in Modern Society*, ed. Richard J. Cox and David A. Wallace (Westport, CT: Quorum Books, 2002), 245–63. See also William L. Joyce, "The Scholarly Implications of Documentary Forgeries," in *Forged Documents: Proceedings of the 1989 Houston Conference*, ed. Pat Bozeman (Houston: University of Houston Libraries, 1990), 37–48.

6 Grafton, *Forgers and Critics*, 9.

7 Two classic texts on classical diplomatics and on authentication in the online environment are Luciana Duranti, *Diplomatics: New Uses for an Old Science* (Lanham, MD: Scarecrow Press, 1998) and Peter B. Hirtle, "Archival Authenticity in a Digital Age," in *Authenticity in a Digital Environment* (Washington, DC: Council on Library and Information Resources, 2000), 8–23.

8 Kenneth W. Rendell, *Forging History: The Detection of Fake Letters and Documents* (Norman: University of Oklahoma Press, 1994).

9 Charles Hamilton, *Great Forgers and Famous Fakes: The Manuscript Forgers of America and How they Duped the Experts* (New York: Crown, 1980).

10 David M. Levy, "Where's Waldo? Reflections on Copies and Authenticity in a Digital Environment," in *Authenticity in a Digital Environment*, 24–31.

11 Grafton, *Forgers and Critics*, 8.

12 Author's diary, entry for July 10, 1985.

13 Rendell, *Forging History*, 106–23.

14 A 1922 English translation of the unmasking of the forgery is available on Google books: Christopher Bush Coleman, *The Treatise of Lorenzo Valla on the Donation of Constantine*, 1440. For the Catholic Church's acceptance of the fact that it is a forgery, see J. P. Kirsch, "Donation of Constantine," in *The Catholic Encyclopedia* (New York: Robert Appleton Company, 1909), http://www.newadvent.org/cathen/05118a.htm (accessed July 1, 2009).

15 Hirtle, "Archival Authenticity in a Digital Age," 9.

16 Ingrid D. Rowland, *The Scarith of Scornello: A Tale of Renaissance Forgery* (Chicago: University of Chicago Press, 2005).

[17] Judith Ryan and Alfred Thomas, *Cultures of Forgery: Making Nations, Making Selves* (London: Routledge, 2003).

[18] Called the Královédvorský and Zelenohorský manuscripts. See Milan Otáhal, "The Manuscript Controversy in the Czech National Revival," *Cross Currents: A Yearbook of Central European Culture* 5 (1986): 247–77. See also Václav Havel, "Address by Vaclav Havel, President of the Czech Republic in Acceptance of an Honorary Degree from the University of Michigan, Ann Arbor, USA, 5 September 2000," http://www.ns.umich.edu/Releases/2000/Sep00/havlrmrk. html (accessed July 4, 2009).

[19] T.G. Masaryk, *Talks with T.G. Masaryk* (North Haven, CT: Catbird Press, 1995).

[20] Havel, "Address by Vaclav Havel."

[21] Vladimir Nabokov, *The Song of Igor's Campaign: An Epic of the Twelfth Century*, translated from Old Russian by Vladimir Nabokov (New York: Vintage Books, 1960), 1–20. Quote from page 13.

[22] Edward L. Keenan, *Josef Dobrovský and the Origins of the Igor' Tale* (Cambridge, MA: Harvard Series in Ukrainian Studies, Harvard University Press, 2003).

[23] See description in Online Archive of California; see also Oleg Tvorogov, "Vlesova kniga," *Trudy Otdela drevnerusskoi literatury* 43 (Leningrad, 1990): 170–254. Anatol Shmelev, an expert on the *Vles Kniga*, provided this reference.

[24] Cesare G. De Michelis, *The Non-Existent Manuscript: A Study of the Protocols of the Sages of Zion*, trans. Richard Newhouse (Jerusalem: Hebrew University and University of Nebraska, 2004). See also B. W. Segel and Richard S. Levy, *A Lie and a Libel: The History of the Protocols of the Elders of Zion* (Lincoln: University of Nebraska Press, 1995). As archetypal conspirators, the fictional Elders of Zion make an appearance in the quintessential novel on conspiracy: Umberto Eco, *Foucault's Pendulum* (San Diego: Houghton Mifflin Harcourt, 1989).

[25] Various articles can be found by searching the keyword *protocols* on the website of the U.S. Holocaust Memorial Museum, http://www.ushmm.org. (accessed October 19, 2009). See also Hadassa Ben-Itto, *The Lie That Wouldn't Die: The Protocols of the Elders of Zion* (London/Portland, OR: Vallentine Mitchell, 2005).

[26] Richard Hofstadter, *The Paranoid Style in American Politics* (New York: Knopf, 1965).

[27] Mark Fenster, *Conspiracy Theories: Secrecy and Power in American Culture* (Minneapolis: University of Minnesota Press, 1999), 98. See also Carroll Quigley,

Tragedy and Hope: A History of the World In Our Time (New York: Macmillan, 1966). Quigley claims to have worked with original manuscripts from secret societies. He claims to have studied the papers and secret records of an organization he calls the Round Table Groups (page 950). No one can identify what group he means or locate the papers he cites.

[28] Leonard C. Lewin, *Report from Iron Mountain on the Possibility and Desirability of Peace* (New York: Dial Press, 1967).

[29] Fenster, *Conspiracy Theories,* 115–16.

[30] Rendell, *Forging History,* 124–40. See also Joyce, "The Scholarly Implications of Documentary Forgeries," 37–48, especially 39. See also Richard E. Turley, *Victims: The LDS Church and the Mark Hofmann Case* (Urbana: University of Illinois Press, 1992).

[31] Mary Mapes, *Truth and Duty,* 2nd ed. (New York: St. Martin's Press, 2006).

[32] Grafton, *Forgers and Critics,* 24.

[33] Gracy, "What You Get Is Not What You See: Forgery," 245–63. See also Joyce, "The Scholarly Implications of Documentary Forgeries," 37–48.

[34] Luciana Duranti, "An Overview of InterPARES 3," *Archives and Social Studies* 1, no. 1 (September 2007): 577–603.

[35] Malcolm Gladwell, *Blink* (New York: Little Brown, 2005; Back Bay Paperback 2007), 3–17.

[36] For a savvy historian's approach to authenticity see Robert C. Williams, *The Historian's Toolbox* (Armonk, NY: M.E. Sharp, 2003).

Chapter 8

[1] International Council on Archives, Code of Ethics, http://www.ica.org/sites/default/fiels/Ethics-EN.pdf (accessed October 9, 2009).

[2] An excellent guide to replevin is chapter 16 of *Navigating Legal Issues in Archives,* edited by Menzi L. Behrnd-Klodt (Chicago: Society of American Archivists, 2008). See also Gary M. Peterson and Trudy Huskamp Peterson, *Archives and Manuscripts: Law* (Chicago: Society of American Archivists, 1985), 92–93. See also James E. O'Neill, "Replevin: A Public Archivist's Perspective," *Prologue* 11 (Fall 1979).

[3] See "One of 14 Original Copies of the Bill of Rights Has Resurfaced, but who Owns it?" *New York Times,* August 11, 2003; and "National Briefing, South: North Carolina: Bill of Rights Is Returned," *New York Times,* August 5, 2005. See also Patrik Jonsson, "A Bill of Rights, Looted Long Ago, Is Stolen Back,"

Christian Science Monitor, April 22, 2003, http://www.csmonitor.com (accessed July 5, 2008). See also *State of North Carolina, Plaintiff v. North Carolina's Original Copy of the Bill of Rights, in rem, In the General Court of Justice Superior Court Division 03-CVS-16816, Amended January 2008.*

⁴ For the South Carolina case see Behrnd-Klodt, *Navigating Legal Issues in Archives*, quotes on pages 175–77. For opinion on the Maine broadside copy of the Declaration of Independence see *State of Maine v. Record No. 080987 Richard L. Adams, Jr.*, Opinion by Justice Barbara Milano Keenan, February 27, 2009, Circuit Court of Fairfax County. For the formulation that government records are "inalienable and imprescriptible," see pages 27 and 45 in the International Council on Archives, *Reference Dossier on Archival Claims*, http://www.ica.org/en/node/39083 (accessed January 31, 2009).

⁵ Ashby Jones, "Virginia Man Beats Maine in Declaration of Independence Smackdown," WSJ Blogs, Law Blog, February 27, 2009, http://blogs.wsj.com/law/2009/02/27, contains link to opinion (accessed November 2, 2009).

⁶ For the Tennessee brochure see http://state.tn.us/tsla/aps/replevin.htm (accessed March 2, 2010).

⁷ National Archives Administration, "Does That Document Belong in the National Archives?" General Information Leaflet No. 74, Washington, DC, 2005. "Help the National Archives Recover Lost and Stolen Documents" is available at http://www.archives.gov/research/recover/#q3. The list of missing items is available at http://www.archives.gov/research/recover/missing-documents.html. The press release on the sentencing of Howard Harner is available at http://www.archives.gov/press/press-releases/2005/nr05-71.html (accessed October 23, 2009). These websites encourage citizens to report the location of missing documents by contacting the email address MissingDocuments@nara.gov or phoning the number on the NARA website.

⁸ Joel Wurl, "Ethnicity as Provenance: In Search of Values and Principles for Documenting the Immigrant Experience," *Archival Issues* 29, no. 1 (2005): 65–76.

⁹ "Protocols for Native American Archival Materials," available at http://www2.nau.edu/libnap-p/protocols.htm (accessed November 2, 2009).

¹⁰ Christopher Michaud, "Magna Carta fetches $21.3 million at Sotheby's Auction," Reuters, December 19, 2007, http://www.reuters.com/article/rbssIndustriesMaterialsUtilitiesNews/idUSN1854840520071219 (accessed October 23, 2009). See also Nicholas Vincent, "Free and Forest-Born," *Times Literary Supplement*, July 4, 2008, a review of Peter Linebaugh, *The Magna Carta Manifesto* (Berkeley: University of California Press, 2008).

[11] Information Security Oversight Office (ISOO) is based in the National Archives and has a website at http://www.archives.gove/isoo. The email address is isoo@nara.gov.

[12] Society of American Archivists, Code of Ethics, http://www.archivists.org/governance/handbook/app_ethics.asp (accessed October 27, 2009).

[13] International Council on Archives, Code of Ethics, http://www.ica.org/sites/default/fiels/Ethics-EN.pdf (accessed October 9, 2009).

[14] Constance Lowenthal, Willi Korte, William H. Honan, and Thomas R. Kline, "Case Study: The Quedlinburg Church Treasures," in *The Spoils of War: World War II and its Aftermath: The Loss, Reappearance, and Recovery of Cultural Property*, ed. Elizabeth Simpson (New York: Harry N. Abrams, 1997), 148–58. For essential background see Lynn Nicholas, *The Rape of Europa: The Fate of Europe's Treasures in the Third Reich and the Second World War* (New York: Knopf, 1994).

[15] Jennifer Anglim Kreder, "The Choice between Civil and Criminal Remedies in Stolen Art Litigation," *Vanderbilt Journal of Transnational Law*, October 1, 2005, page 1199.

[16] J.W. Burrow, *A History of Histories: Epics, Chronicles, Romances and Inquiries from Herodotus and Thucydides to the Twentieth Century* (New York: Knopf, 2008), 6.

[17] On the Codex Argenteus see Elena S. Danielson, "Displaced documents of Central Europe," *Comma* 3–4 (2004–5): 197–203. Regarding looting as normal method for financing armies see Lauro Martines, "Shoeless Soldiers," *Times Literary Supplement*, no. 5556, September 25, 2009, 12-13. Martines cites Tryntje Helfferich, *The Thirty Years War: A Documentary History* (Indianapolis: Hackett, 2009).

[18] The relevant text of the Treaty of Westphalia is available from the Avalon Project: Documents in Law, History and Diplomacy at the Yale Law School, http://avalon.law.yale.edu/17th_century/wetphal.asp (accessed October 31, 2009).

[19] The text of the Lieber Code is available from the Avalon Project, http://avalon.law.yale.edu/19th_century/lieber.asp (accessed October 31, 2009).

[20] *State of North Carolina, Plaintiff v. North Carolina's Original Copy of the Bill of Rights, in rem, In the General Court of Justice Superior Court Division 03-CVS-16816, Amended January 2008.* For citations from the Lieber Code, see pages 90–93.

[21] The Brussels Declaration is available at the website of the International Committee of the Red Cross under the official title "Project of an International

Declaration concerning the Laws and Customs of War. Brussels, 27 August, 1874": http://www.icrc.org/IHL.NSF/INTRO/135?OpenDocument (accessed October 31, 2009).

[22] The formal title is "Laws and Customs of War on Land (Hague IV): October 18, 1907." For the text see http://www.yale.edu/lawweb/avalon/lawofwar/hague04.htm (accessed August 16, 2008). For a discussion of the implications see Trudy Huskamp Peterson, "Archives in Service to the State," in Margaret Procter, Michael Cook, and Caroline Williams, eds., *Political Pressure and the Archival Record* (Chicago: Society of American Archivists, 2006): 259–76.

[23] The International Council on Archives has compiled a dossier of the provisions relating to archives found in international conventions, laws, and best professional practice entitled *Reference Dossier on Archival Claims*; it is available at http://www.ica.org/en/node/39083 (accessed January 31, 2009). The relevant sections of the World War I treaties are reprinted in *The Spoils of War: World War II and its Aftermath: The Loss, Reappearance, and Recovery of Cultural Property*, ed. Elizabeth Simpson (New York: Harry N. Abrams, 1997), 280–85.

[24] For the text of the Washington Pact of April 15, 1935, known as the Roerich Pact, see http://www.roerich.org/nr_RPact.html (accessed August 16, 2008).

[25] The text of the London Declaration of 1943 is available on page 7 of the *Reference Dossier on Archival Claims,* at http://www.ica.org/en/node/39083 (accessed January 31, 2009).

[26] Patricia Kennedy Grimsted, *Trophies of War: The Archival Heritage of Ukraine, World War II, and the International Politics of Restitution* (Cambridge, MA: Harvard Ukrainian Research Institute, 2001), 300.

[27] Patricia Kennedy Grimsted, *Returned from Russia: Nazi Archival Plunder in Western Europe and Recent Restitution Issues* (Builth Wells, Great Britain: Institute of Art and Law, 2007).

[28] Astrid M. Eckert, *Kampf um die Akten: die Westalliierten und die Rückgabe von deutschem Archivgut nach dem Zweiten Weltkrieg* (Stuttgart: Steiner, 2004). Also Astrid M. Eckert, "'And Grant German and Foreign Scholars Access at All Times': Archival Access in West Germany During the Cold War," in Margaret Procter, Michael Cook, and Caroline Williams, eds., *Political Pressure and the Archival Record*, 75–91. Reference to German attitudes to microfilm of their records on page 79, "For archivists, then, the access clause coupled with the microfilming meant a loss of control over 'their' records....The loss of control was a loss of power, and both were a sting for the professional pride."

[29] Trudy Huskamp Peterson, "Archives in Service to the State," in *Political Pressure and the Archival Record,* 259–76.

[30] The formal title is "Convention for the Protection of Cultural Property in the Event of Armed Conflict with Regulations for the Execution of the Convention 1954," The Hague, May 14, 1954. The text is available on the UNESCO website: http://portal.unesco.org (accessed November 1, 2009). Official participation by the United States as of March 13, 2009 is reported on the U.S. State Department website, http://exchanges.state.gov/heritage/culprop/laws.html (accessed November 1, 2009).

[31] Leopold Auer, "Disputed Archival Claims. Analysis of an International Survey: A RAMP study" (Paris: UNESCO, 1998), 20-21.

[32] The text of the UNESCO 1970 convention is available on the U.S. State Department website, http://exchanges.state.gov/heritage/culprop.html (accessed November 2, 2009). Also available at the website of Yale's Avalon Project, http://www.yale.edu/lawweb/avalon.

[33] For the formulation that government records are "inalienable and imprescriptible," see pages 27 and 45 in the International Council on Archives, *Reference Dossier on Archival Claims,* http://www.ica.org/en/node/39083 (accessed January 31, 2009).

[34] See NARA publication M-1486 "Records of Imperial Russian Consulates in the United States, 1862-1922" (1992). Available on the NARA website, http://www.archives.gov/microfilm/m1486.pdf (accessed August 21, 2009). For the return of U.S. consular records from the Soviet Union see David A. Langbart, "'No Little Historic Value': The Records of Department of State Posts in Revolutionary Russia," *Prologue* 40, no. 1 (Spring 2008).

[35] See Patricia Kennedy Grimsted, *Returned from Russia,* especially chapter by Jean-Claude Kuperminc, "The Return of Looted French Archives," 145.

[36] Elena S. Danielson, "A Revolution in the Russian Archives: A Retrospective," CWIHP Special Report, Woodrow Wilson International Center for Scholars, posted November 5, 2009, available at http://www.wilsoncenter.org/topics/docs/CWIHP_Special_Reprot.pdf (accessed November 8, 2009).

[37] Patricia Kennedy Grimsted, *Returned from Russia,* 119.

[38] James B. Cuno, *Who Owns Antiquity? Museums and the Battle over Our Ancient Heritage* (Princeton, NJ: Princeton University Press, 2008).

[39] United States National Stolen Property Act, U.S. Code Title 18; see http://exchanges.state.gov/culprop/18-2314.html (accessed August 16, 2008).

[40] "Portugal Holds On to Words Few Can Grasp," *New York Times,* July 15, 2008.

Index